The Babe in Red Stockings

*An In-depth Chronicle of Babe Ruth
with the Boston Red Sox, 1914-1919*

Kerry Keene
Raymond Sinibaldi
David Hickey

SAGAMORE PUBLISHING
Champaign, IL 61820

Book design, editor: Susan McKinney
Dustjacket design: Michelle R. Dressen

ISBN:1-57164-112-9
Library of Congress Catalog Card Number: 97-65486

Printed in the United States.

For Elizabeth, Margeau, Joshua and Rachael—you are the beacons that light my way.

—Ray

For Corey, Shawn and Sam—you fulfill my life completely.

—David

To Pam, Zachary, and Molly; and to Mom, who instilled the love of the game.

—Kerry

DON'T MISS
THE BATTLEMAGE

BOOK THREE

**IN THE SUMMONER TRILOGY, THE *NEW YORK TIMES*–
AND *USA TODAY*–BESTSELLING SERIES**

Contents

Acknowledgments

The authors must give a tip of the cap to baseball historian Dick Thompson of Bridgewater, Massachusetts for providing access to his personal library of research material. A special thanks also goes to Dorothy Ruth's daughter Linda Tosetti for her extreme graciousness. A sincere debt of gratitude is owed to Mike Pearson of Sagamore Publishing Company for being a close ally and sharing a vision.

A nod should also go to Dick Johnson of the Sports Museum of New England; Rudy Van Veghten and William Pond of Meredith, New Hampshire; Robert Olmstead and Elsa Turmelle of the Plymouth, New Hampshire Historical Society; Kathy Hiller of the Pease Public Library in Plymouth, New Hampshire; Curt Garfield of the Sudbury, Massachusetts Historical Society; John Dorsey and Aaron Schmidt of the Boston Public Library; Janet T. Dever of the Middlesex County (MA) Registry of Deeds; Fran Barba of the Manatee County Florida Central Library; Pat Kelly and staff at the National Baseball Library Photo Dept.; Dick Bresciani, Matt Roebuck, and Larry Cancro of the Boston Red Sox; Robert Howard of Dallas, Texas; Pam, Microtext Dept. of Lebanon Valley College in Pennsylvania; Michelle Dressen and Susan McKinney of Sagamore Publishing Company; and John Butman of the Sports Information Dept. at Holy Cross University.

In addition: Mike Keough; Phil Bergen; Len Levin; George Lally; William Reid; David Pietrusza; Jack Kavanagh; Bill Ryczek; John Hooper, Robert MacCormack, the staff in the Microtext Dept. of the Boston Public Library; the staff at the Massachusetts Registry of Vital Records; the staff at the Venice, Florida Public Library; and the Lebanon, Pennsylvania Historical Society.

Not to be forgotten are Paul Shannon and Arthur Duffy of *The Boston Post;* Burt Whitman and Bob Dunbar of *The Boston Herald;* and James O'Leary of *The Boston Globe.* It is through their eyes and with their eloquent language that Babe's story was preserved to be re-told.

In addition:

I would like to thank my wife, Corey, who during a very busy time in our lives allowed me to live a dream, I love you very much. My children, Shawn and Sam, for their love, patience, and understanding, for without it this would not have been possible.

Ray and Kerry—I recall a story told on March 14th, 1991, " . . . we'll meet back here in Cooperstown on the third Thursday . . . ", well guys I was wrong, Cooperstown came to us. Thanks for uncovering a drive and desire in me, I couldn't ask for two better friends.

To everyone else in my family, thanks for all your interest, support and well wishes.

—DH

The man who is able to engage in an endeavor for which he has a deep passion is truly blessed. The opportunity to share in the creative process with two very special friends makes him doubly so. To my partners David and Ray, we have completed a long occasionally arduous journey. I cannot think of two characters with whom I'd rather taken the trip.

Dick Thompson has been a great source of both reference material and inspiration, leading by example in the field of baseball research.

Large amounts of inspiration were provided by my great friend David Flebotte, who quietly demonstrates that a dream plus perseverance equals achievements of which to be proud.

And my terrific wife Pam, who must have felt as though she was playing second fiddle to an endless stream of microfilm and reference books for the past two years. Her support, patience and tolerance helped make it all possible.

—KK

The old African tribal notion that it takes a village to raise a child was never more true than in my case. I would therefore be remiss if I did not acknowledge my village.

All villages have a chief and we call our chief Papa. There are no words to express the respect, admiration, and love that I feel so I must simply say thank you for all that you are. To my mother whose sweet gentility has always been and forever will be with me. Marie whose warmth and kindness brings out the best that we can offer. Despite her best efforts to escape, she will always be one of us.

My sister Nancy, who I always said was the best of us, her husband Steve and their gang of Cara, Kristi, Steven and Scotty; for helping me to hold it together when all I had left was scotch tape and glue. Bill and Paula, you are a constant source of support and encouragement, not to mention financial advice, and I love you. To Marc, Eric and the newest members of the tribe Jill and Jaimie; your youthful enthusiasm is an inspiration and I'm glad you are in my life. Ruthann, thank you for your prayers. In those times when God simply takes care, I am convinced that it is at your urging. Mary, my third sister, though time, space and circumstance keep us apart we are always together, you will always be Christmas to me. Jackie O'Brien, you taught me of life, death and the eternity of love and "Pistol" Pete Hunton, thirty years later you remain my role model as a coach.

Throughout the years the village has grown and some leave an indelible mark. Paul and Dennise thanks for always letting me know where I could find the key and Leah I kept the room warm waiting for you. Bob and Kris you stood with me and faced the devil and with love we conquered him. "Mick" I never would have made it without those many hours of chasing that ball. I carry you with me always. To the Colasantis, thanks for opening your hearts and home to the Sinibaldis. "The captain", Lizzy and crew stood with me when the days were darkest and Lynda you gave me the light to find my way home. Mary Erickson it was you who made me believe it could be done and Lynne, "Sully", Briana, Jason, Karen, Grandma and Marie I can't imagine not being on the Cape for our week.

Annie and the rest of the Goggans I am forever indebted to you for your efforts on behalf of my children. Dem and the neighborhood that goes for you as well. Paul and "Tiny" thanks for being Grandma and Grandpa to three little tikes who just moved in. To my colleagues and friends at the Venice Little League for allowing me the opportunity to teach the game that I love and to all the kids for just being them. To Joe, Kathy, Pammy and Joey thanks for Sunday dinners and making us feel at home and Joe for all your input solicited or otherwise. Mrs. Welch for your countenance and your ear I thank you. You are the consummate professional. Stanford, I do not spend a day in the classroom that you are not with me.

To Hick and "Way Cool" thanks for helping to build a dream.

Finally I want to thank Rory for sharing his space and his Mom, it is not easy being invaded by our motley crew. Julie you will always have a place to lay your head. Beth, Boom, Mookie and Rach; you have put up with a lot and I'm glad you're my kids. Last and certainly not least, Colleen your never ending capacity to give has enriched my life and that of my children in ways that can never be measured. You are and will always be in my heart.

—RS

Foreword

By Linda Ruth Tosetti

It is truly a pleasure for me to write about a subject of which I am extremely proud, my grandfather, George Herman "Babe" Ruth.

Babe epitomized the very best of baseball, our national pastime. By the sheer strength of his personality and the power of his bat, he saved America's game after the 1919 "Black Sox" scandal. He dominated the game and still holds records for his accomplishments on the playing field. He helped lift the salaries of athletes from a modest level to respectability. He changed the game from "bunt and run" to the home run. Babe Ruth became one the greatest idols of America's youth, instilling leadership and good sportsmanship. Today he is still vivid in the hearts and minds of the American people, as well as people from other nations.

My mother Dorothy, Babe's daughter, would sit and tell us stories of her father. She told of the wonderful years on the farm in Sudbury, Massachusetts, where they continued to live even though professionally he had moved on to New York. She recalled that Babe had raised all sorts of animals, from bull terriers to turkeys! In 1988, a year before she passed away, my Mom got to visit the farm. The house and barn are still there, but the land around it has since been developed. It was a great reunion. She got to "go home", and I got to go along. Dorothy remembered the Sudbury years with Babe and Helen as some of the happiest in her life.

Babe loved to bring children from Boston-area orphanages as well as inner-city children to "Home Plate Farm" to let them run and play. Of course, he was playing right beside them. He'd always have plenty of hot dogs for them to eat, and he always had gifts. He would come out of the barn with a wheelbarrow full of bats, balls, and gloves for them to take home. My mother told me that Babe had a personal and special relationship with his fans. He considered his fans family, he displayed affection for them, and the magic between Babe and his fans still exists today.

In 1981, Babe was honored in Washington by being part of the "Champions of American Sports", an exhibition of outstanding American sports heroes and heroines of the past century or more, mounted by the National Portrait Gallery of the Smithsonian Institution.

Boston too, has never forgotten his big-league beginnings there, and has honored him in several ways for his contributions as a Red Sox player. In 1983 he was elected by the fans as the best left-handed pitcher on the Gillette All-Time Red Sox Dream Team, along with such greats as Ted Williams, Jimmie Foxx, and Carl Yastrzemski. In 1968, the South Boston section of the city, where Babe had spent a great deal of time, re-named a boulevard and park area, "Babe Ruth Park Drive".

In 1995, I had the honor of attending my grandfather's induction into the newly formed Boston Red Sox Hall of Fame. It was one of the proudest moments of my life.

There isn't a day that goes by that I don't have a fan come up to me and tell me how much they love my grandfather. This year will be his 102nd birthday, and his grandchildren, my five brothers and sisters and I, are proud and fascinated by the special, even magical relationship he has with his fans. Now, with what follows on these pages, we finally have a well-documented, detailed account of his time in Boston.

—December, 1996

Authors' Note

Upon learning that another book has been published about Babe Ruth, there are no doubt those who will wonder, "What more can be written that hasn't appeared in the numerous existing biographies"?

Virtually without exception, each of these efforts represent the daunting task of covering a life that lasted 53 years, and included a remarkable professional baseball career that spanned 22 years. In light of his truly phenomenal achievements as a member of the New York Yankees for 15 seasons, it is only natural that this period tends to be the primary focus. *The Life that Ruth Built* by Mathew Smelser and *Babe: The Legend Comes to Life* by Robert Creamer are among the more comprehensive, and it is understandable that a limited amount of space could be devoted to the Boston years.

Although certainly not ignored, his beginnings in major league baseball—five plus seasons with the Boston Red Sox—tend to be somewhat glossed over. The extent of Ruth's accomplishments on the field with Boston, as well as his enormous popularity of that period have never been fully appreciated. In addition, there are dozens of interesting incidents and anecdotes still left to be told.

The aim here was to create an extremely in-depth, accurate account of the formative years of baseball's most fabulous career. When discussing a figure as historically important as Babe Ruth, the approach was taken that no detail was too small, and what some may term minutiae hopefully serves only to make the study more complete. An attempt has also been made to not repeat anecdotes that have appeared in other biographies, though in some cases this was unavoidable.

The vast majority of biographies of Ruth were written either in the late 1940s prompted by his illness and subsequent death, or in the mid-1970s, with interest rekindled by Hank Aaron's pursuit of his home-run record. At both of those times, there were many individuals still alive who personally knew Ruth well, and had many stories to tell. In the mid-1990s, there were precious few left who had close personal contact with him in his Red Sox years. This left a nearly complete dependence upon printed material and microfilm of various publications of the day. The upside, however, is that reports filed at that time by competent and talented sportswriters are often more accurate than individuals attempting to recall details of several decades before with sometimes vague memories.

Readers will note that passages and quotes from publications of the 1914-1919 period are utilized liberally to assist in the telling of the story. It is also interesting to get a glimpse of the writing styles of the various writers represented, and to compare how different they are from the writers of today. Another by-product of the chronicling of Babe's Red Sox years is the virtual day-to-day reporting of three ultimately successful pennant races in 1915, '16, and '18. The four-season span was clearly the most successful in the history of the star-crossed franchise.

Much of the microfilm research for this book was conducted at Boston's venerable Public Library, located in historic Copley Square, coincidentally where Babe spent his first days in the city in 1914. Today, standing on the steps of the library, scanning the landscape from right to left, one will see the Back Bay Railway Station, where Babe caught many a train; the classic Copley Plaza Hotel; the Trinity Church, an architectural marvel built in the 1880s (the Brunswick Hotel, where Babe was a guest countless times formerly stood just behind); and to the extreme left, the Old South Church, which dates back to the mid-1800s. The library itself was constructed in 1895, the year of Ruth's birth.

It is remarkable to realize that all of these classic buildings which make up a large part of Copley Square were standing when a 19-year-old Babe emerged from Back Bay Station in July of 1914. If somehow magically Ruth could be transported to the present and placed in the middle of the square, aside from being awed by a few nearby skyscrapers, he would clearly recognize where he was. It is our fervent hope that if he were to also peruse a copy of *The Babe in Red Stockings*, it would bring back many fond memories.

Introduction

I t had been 13 years since he had belted his last home run, 10 years since his brief stint as a coach with the Brooklyn Dodgers had ended, and 16 years since his last season of dominance culminated with his legendary "called shot" in the 1932 World Series. Yet in August of 1948, kids, many too young to remember these events, had gathered in the lobby of Memorial Hospital as "the Babe" lay dying upstairs.

He died in the wee hours of the morning of August 16, never publicly acknowledging the cancer that was ravaging his body. His death came as somewhat of a surprise to the American public, who had grown accustomed to Babe slipping in and out of the hospital for a variety of ailments throughout the 1940s.

Two months earlier, in his last public appearance at Yankee Stadium, he told the huge crowd how happy and proud he was to have hit the first home run in the history of this great ballpark. Following the ceremonies, he sat in the clubhouse with old team-mate and friend Joe Duggan. Through tears of resignation and in a barely audible voice, he looked at Duggan and muttered, "Joe, I'm gone, I'm gone, Joe." His last poignant moments spent in the house that he had built.

The August 17 edition of the *New York Times* dedicated five pages to the life and times of this American legend. One story chronicled his 54 major league records, 10 American League records, and 24 World Series records (all batting).

More than 60 years have passed since his last at-bat, and his slugging prowess remains unequaled. Of course, Roger Maris hit the extraordinary total of 61 home runs in 1961. Hank Aaron reached the unreachable star when he hit home run number 715 in April of 1974. But no one has come close to Babe's average of a home run for every 11.76 times he officially stepped up to the plate. His lifetime slugging percentage of .690 heads a list of only five men to have topped .600. Every 3.79 times at bat he drove in a run. In games spent as an outfielder, he astonishingly drove in virtually an RBI per game. No other player can lay claim to an RBI in less than every fourth at bat.

One hundred plus years after his birth, 60 plus years after his retirement, and 45 plus years after his death, he remains unquestionably the greatest slugger the game has ever known. He is the quintessential American hero whose legendary status preceded his death. If there were such a thing as American mythology, he would reign as America's Zeus. The mere mention of his name evokes a myriad of images to teenagers and octogenarians alike; from the ardent fan to the most casual observer. The vast majority of those images recall a hulking, pot-bellied, moon-faced character sporting the classic pin-striped New York Yankee uniform. The indelibly etched newsreel footage shows the distinct swing, eyes following the skyward flight of the ball, and the pigeon-toed trot around the bases.

Yet through it all, his baseball beginnings remain obscured by his insatiable and legendary appetite for life. Obscured by his aforementioned slugging prowess and 54-ounce bat. Obscured by the birth of the Yankee tradition and the house he built. And seemingly forever obscured by his own success as baseball's most feared, most dominant hitter of all time.

Joseph Lannin, owner of the Boston Red Sox purchased him in July of 1914 along with two other players from the Baltimore Orioles of the International League. He was strictly a pitcher at that time with less than three months of professional experience, but was sought after by many teams. At 19 years old, the six-foot two-inch George Ruth was among the best pitching prospects of his day, and Lannin scored a coup in landing him.

Immediately inserted into Manager Bill Carrigan's rotation, Ruth's major league debut was a success. His season, however, would be spent split between the Red Sox minor league affiliate in Providence, Rhode Island and the parent club. Appearing in only four games in his inaugural season, Ruth went home to Baltimore poised and ready to become a stalwart on the '15 staff.

And a stalwart he was, his 18 victories falling one shy of a tie for the team lead. This on a team so rich in pitching that it boasted two members, Ernie Shore and Smoky Joe Wood with ERA's under 2.00; so laden in talent that Ruth was not even needed in the World Series. Shore, "Rube" Foster, and "Dutch" Leonard overpowered the

Phillies in five games, leading the Sox to their second world championship in four years.

In 1916, Ruth would leave no doubt as to who was the premier left-handed pitcher in the American League. He started 41 games, setting the standard that Red Sox lefties since have tried unsuccessfully to achieve. His 1.75 ERA led the league, and nine of his 23 wins were shutouts, including a 1-0 13-inning complete-game masterpiece over Walter Johnson. That classic confrontation remains to this day the longest complete game shutout by any southpaw in Red Sox history. No other American League left-hander has thrown more shutouts in a single season, though Ron Guidry equaled the mark with his Koufaxian season of 1978. Having gone from stalwart to the ace of the staff, he would be called upon in this World Series and he would not disappoint! On the hill to open game two, he surrendered a run in the first inning. From there he proceeded to hold the Brooklyn Robins scoreless for the next THIRTEEN innings, notching his first World Series victory, 2-1. This began what was to become a streak of 29 2/3 consecutive scoreless World Series innings, setting a record that would be held until broken by Whitey Ford in the Fall Classic of 1961.

1917 brought more of the same. His 24 wins made him the winningest left-hander in all of baseball. He threw six more shutouts while posting an ERA of 2.01. He completed 35 of his 38 starts, earning a tie for the major league lead in that category. His 326 1/3 innings pitched led the staff while establishing a record for Red Sox left-handers which he still holds. And with the way today's pitchers are used (or not used), it is likely it will never be broken. By the conclusion of the 1917 season, there was little doubt that this big strapping 22-year-old kid from Baltimore was the premier left-handed pitcher in all of baseball.

By 1918, his value as a batsman was ever increasing. The result was more time spent at other positions (first base and the outfield) and less time on the mound. However, he still won 13 of 20 decisions while posting a 2.22 ERA. He completed 18 of his 19 starts, threw the last shut out of his career, and when the World Series opened at Comiskey Park on September 5, Babe was on the mound. He was nothing short of brilliant, firing a six-hit shutout in a 1-0 Red Sox victory. He was on the hill again for game four at Fenway Park. His dominance continued as he held the Cubs scoreless until there were two outs in the eighth when they pushed across two runs, giving them the lead and ending Ruth's scoreless inning streak. The Red Sox scored in the bottom of the inning and went on to win 3-2, earning for Ruth his second win of the series and for the Red Sox an insurmountable three games to one lead. This would turn out to be Ruth's last World Series appearance with the Boston Red Sox. It would also be the last time a Red Sox starting left-handed pitcher would win a World Series game for 68 years until Bruce Hurst shut out the New York Mets 1-0 in Game One of the 1986 series. The Red Sox went on to win the '18 World Series, four games to two, claiming their third world championship in four years.

In those Red Sox glory years of 1915 through '18, Ruth topped his circuit many times. In 1916 he led the league in ERA, shutouts, games started, and fewest hits per nine innings. In 1917 he led in complete games, finishing second in the American League in wins. By the 1918 season, his league leads were coming in other categories, such as home runs and slugging percentage. Yet he remained a formidable enough force on the mound as his performance in the 1918 World Series would indicate.

With the 1919 season, his conversion to the outfield was nearly complete. Used in only 17 games as a pitcher, he went 8-5 while completing 12 of his 15 starts. Also, his only two relief appearances resulted in saves. More significantly, however, were his 29 home runs, breaking the long-standing major league record and sealing his fate on the mound.

From 1914 to 1919, Babe Ruth appeared in 391 games for the Boston Red Sox. 170 of them were played in the outfield, 17 at first base and 158 as a pitcher. Of those 158 games, he started 143 of them and completed 105. He won 89 while losing 46 for a winning percentage of .659, a figure that stands as the best of any Red Sox left-hander in team history. He led the team twice in wins, twice in innings pitched, twice in complete games, twice in shutouts, and once each in appearances, strikeouts, ERA, and saves. His 24 wins in 1917 have been topped by only five pitchers in Red Sox history. His 40 starts in 1916, 35 complete games, and the aforementioned 326 1/3 innings pitched in 1917 still stand as a record for Red Sox southpaws.

The August 17, 1948 edition of the *New York Times* listed a total of 88 records that Babe owned or shared. Nowhere did it mention that at the time of his death, he had won more games in one season than any other left-handed Red Sox pitcher. Ignored were his Red Sox records for lefties including: starts in a season, complete games in a season, and innings pitched in a season. Completely overlooked was his American League record for shutouts in a season by a left-handed pitcher.

His performances in the Fall Classic were equally impressive. A composite look at his World Series statistics reveal a pitching exhibition that is nothing short of phenomenal! He started only three games and won them all. One of those wins was the 14-inning complete-game victory in '16. It remains to this day the longest complete game win in the near 100-year history of the World Series. In 31 innings pitched, he surrendered but three runs for an infinitesimal ERA of 0.87. And as was mentioned, 29 2/3 of those 31 innings were consecutively scoreless. It bears repeating that this record was held for 43 years before being broken. In five seasons as a pitcher (three full ones), he led the Red Sox to three world championships. It is worth noting that it would take him nine years as a Yankee to duplicate that effort.

George Herman "Babe" Ruth, "The Bambino," "The Sultan of Swat," legend, myth, real life American hero, all of the above. It is the spring of 1995 in the rural community of Raynham, Massachusetts, some 35 miles southwest of Fenway Park. Seven-year-old Zachary Keene is playing in his first season of Farm League baseball. Sitting in the dugout, two players are choosing their bats as they prepare to take their swings. They lift one and check the number on the bottom of the bat. "It's a 28," one is heard to say. "Yeah, this is a 29, it's a lot heavier. Did you know that Babe Ruth used a size 75?" the youngster replied. "A 75!!! Awesome!"

It is the fall of 1995 in the city of Bradenton, Florida, some 1,200 miles southwest of Yankee Stadium. A classroom filled with predominantly black middle school students is asked by the teacher, "Who is Babe Ruth?" Every single student answers correctly, one going so far to say, "He was the greatest baseball player of all time." Another asked, "Didn't he hit a baseball a mile once?"

The stories surrounding his hitting prowess have bridged a century while reaching mythical proportions. The tales become "Bunyonesque" as they are passed from generation to generation. He stands non-paralleled as a hitter, as a slugger, as the most widely recognized name in the history of American sports. All of this achieved as a result of his adeptness with the bat. Yet the reality is that if he had never taken to the outfield and instead toiled his entire career on the mound, the pitchers of today might be competing for the "Babe Ruth Award" as the best pitcher in each league.

Everyone knows that Babe was a Yankee. Nearly everyone knows he began his career with the Red Sox, and most know that he began his career as a pitcher. In Boston, people knew enough to name him to their all-time Red Sox team as the left-handed pitcher in 1983. The fall of 1995 saw the creation of a Red Sox Hall of Fame, and Ruth was among the initial inductees.

All in all, relatively few seem to realize the magnitude of his pitching prowess in his three years as a full-time pitcher, as he was much in the same class as Grover Cleveland Alexander and Walter Johnson. As a left-hander, he took a back seat to no one. Herein lies the story of the Babe in red stockings.

▬ One ▬

1914: Lannin Goes Shopping in Baltimore

It was a vastly different place and time—a time when a brand new automobile could be purchased for $600, a men's three-piece suit for $17.50. Newspapers—as many as a dozen in major cities—were the primary source of information, and when it came to long distance travel, the train was king.

The year 1914 was far and away the most remarkable—up to that point—in the young life of George Ruth. In five months' time he went from virtual incarceration in St. Mary's Industrial School for Boys, where he had spent the majority of the previous 12 years, to his debut as a major league ballplayer. Located at Wilkens and Caton Avenues in Baltimore, the institution was part trade school, part orphanage, and part reformatory. It was operated by Xaverian priests, who were Ruth's legal guardians until he was to turn 21.

Jack Dunn, owner and manager of the minor league Baltimore Orioles of the International League, was always in search of young talent that could be developed into major league caliber. There was much money to be made by selling these young stars to the highest bidder when they were deemed ready. Well-known to the Brothers of St. Mary's, Dunn had seen young Ruth pitch in the late summer of 1913 against a rival school. Before this particular game, the St. Mary's band had come marching across the field with Ruth banging on a big bass drum.

Dunn knew a thing or two about pitching himself, having played in the major leagues between 1897 and 1904. His high point came in 1899, having won 23 games for the National League champion Brooklyn Superbas (later known as the Dodgers). He also played for the American League's Baltimore Orioles in that circuit's inaugural season of 1901. After the 1902 season, that edition of Orioles transferred to New York City, becoming the Highlanders, which was changed a decade later to "Yankees."

As a player, Dunn displayed remarkable versatility throughout his career, for while he pitched in 142 big-league games, he also played many others at second base, shortstop, third base, and the outfield.

On February 14, 1914, eight days after his 19th birthday, Ruth was signed by Dunn to pitch for the Orioles. The contract called for Ruth to be paid the princely sum of $100 per month during the season. As minuscule as this seems by today's standards, young George surely must have thought that he had struck gold. He reportedly collected his first paycheck and promptly purchased a spanking new bicycle to tool around the city.

On March 3 he arrived in Fayetteville, North Carolina to begin his first professional training camp. Part of the agreement with St. Mary's was that Dunn was to assume legal guardianship of Ruth. Sam Steinman, a coach at the Orioles camp immediately began referring to the gangling teenager as "Dunn's Baby." The veterans followed suit, and quickly shortened it to "Babe", the name that was to become the most widely recognized in the history of American sports.

In the following seven weeks, he pitched six times against major league teams, beating the world champion Athletics, the Phillies, and the Dodgers. The appearance against the Athletics served as a showcase for manager Connie Mack, whom Dunn felt might pay a handsome sum for such talent at some future point. His performance received national acclaim as *The Sporting Life*, a national publication based in Philadelphia that specialized in baseball coverage noted:

> "The Baltimore club seems to have unearthed a coming pitcher in Ruth. The lad is only 19 years old, and last winter attended St. Mary's Industrial School of Baltimore. He evidently took up a course in curves...."

On April 21, the International League season of 1914 opened ominously for the Orioles club. The newly-formed independent Federal League, which had declared itself a major league, had placed a franchise in Baltimore. Known as the Terrapins, the Feds played their home games in a park directly across the street from the Orioles. The consequence of the new renegade league was felt immediately by Dunn and his Orioles.

With International League President Ed Barrow in attendance, the Orioles drew an embarrassing total of less than 200 spectators, while the Federal League team entertained nearly 20,000 on that same afternoon. By luring players from established teams and placing franchises in cities already occupied by Organized Baseball, the new outlaw league touched off a war within the game that dominated the sports pages. The city of Baltimore itself was excited by the prospect of having a team that was regarded as "major league," and the minor league Orioles were seemingly cast aside.

As the season progressed, Dunn became increasingly desperate as the situation did not improve. He had assembled one of the strongest minor-league teams Organized Baseball had ever seen, and many felt that they could have competed well against second-division major league teams. Unfortunately for Dunn, his payroll was almost at major league level as well, and averaging a few hundred paying customers per game, he was losing up to $2,000 per week.

Though the Orioles were experiencing colossal problems at the gate, they were clearly the class of the league on the field. Their success was due in no small part to the rookie Ruth. In the May 16, 1914 issue of *The Sporting Life,* Emanuel Daniels wrote:

> "Babe Ruth, the sensational youngster added another game to his string of victories and certainly this back lot left-hander looks like the find of the season."

Ruth's performances were beginning to draw attention, and his potential was not lost on the lecherous Federal League. In early June there was a report out of Baltimore that the Feds had approached Ruth and made a substantial offer for him to jump to the new league. In fact, representatives from the Brooklyn Tip Tops team were chased away from Oriole Park by a gun-toting Dunn. Ruth always said that not signing with the Feds cost him $30,000, as they had offered him a $10,000 signing bonus and a salary of $10,000 for two seasons. What prevented him from signing was the threat by Organized Baseball to bar any player for life from returning after jumping to the outlaw league. What he seemed to overlook was the fact that Dunn, now his legal guardian, would obviously never have permitted such a signing.

Major league teams were beginning to show interest in Ruth as well. The *Baltimore Sun* of July 7, 1914 reported rumors that the New York Yankees offered Dunn $25,000 for Ruth, Cree, Midkiff, and Gleichmann. It is interesting to learn that Ruth could have become a Yankee five and a half years sooner than he did. Dunn turned the offer down, saying he wanted more money for the quartet. Ruth had just made an impressive appearance in relief against Providence, getting credit for the victory, which would turn out to be the last time he wore the black cap of his hometown Orioles.

The Yankees had been turned down, the Giants, Reds, and Braves expressed interest, and the White Sox actively pursued.

"Mgr. Dunn of Baltimore last week announced that he had turned down an offer from Charles Comiskey of the White Sox for the purchase of six Baltimore players." *The Sporting Life*, 6/27/14

The six players coveted by Comiskey were Birdie Cree, Bert Daniels, Ezra Midkiff, Claude Derrick, George Twombly, and Ruth. Dunn, not yet out of options, turned this offer down as well. Now, if the deal had been completed, and Ruth was still a member of the White Sox in 1919 …

ə.

In mid-June, Organized Baseball's ruling body, the National Commission, met with International League officials to map out strategy to deal with the Federal League. At that meeting there was talk of organizing a new major league, made up of the strongest cities in the International League and the American Association, two of the top level minor leagues. With Baltimore included in the plan, Dunn had some reason to feel optimistic about his fight against the Federal League. If the Orioles were elevated to major league status, he felt they would be able to compete against the neighboring Terrapins on a level playing field. Unfortunately for Dunn, talk of the new major league died before it ever got off the ground.

The city of Richmond, Virginia offered to bring the Orioles there for the remainder of the season. However, due to the presence of a Virginia League team in that city, the deal fell through, and Dunn decided to stick it out in Baltimore for the season's duration. Having lost an estimated $20,000, he appealed to the National Commission to abolish the draft of minor league players by major league teams so that he might retain his star players longer, but was denied. Rebuffed at every turn, Dunn felt he had little choice but to start selling his star players to major league teams in order to recoup his losses. League President Barrow, who would play a big part in Ruth's career years later, gave Dunn his blessing.

To some, it seemed a foregone conclusion that Ruth would become a member of Connie Mack's World Champion Philadelphia Athletics.

"Jack Dunn has found two wonderful pitchers in Ruth and [Ernie] Shore—two more for Connie Mack. Ben Egan says Shore is the best twirler that he ever caught, and the Athletics think pretty well of Ruth." *The Sporting Life,* 7/11/14

As expected, Dunn offered Ruth to Mack and his Athletics, as Mack and Boston Red Sox owner Joseph Lannin had aided him in meeting his payroll in spring training. Though the A's were running away with first place in the American League, Mack claimed he was experiencing financial difficulties, and simply wasn't in a position to buy.

During the week of July 4, the Red Sox were in Washington for a series against the Senators. Sox owner Lannin, also in town, held discussions with Dunn about a possible deal. Boston manager Bill Carrigan contacted Orioles shortstop/coach Freddy Parent and asked Parent to meet him and Sox coach Heinie Wagner to discuss Ruth and Shore. Parent had been the shortstop on Boston's inaugural edition of the American League franchise in 1901, and played in the first modern World Series against Pittsburgh in 1903. He actually out-performed his counterpart Honus Wagner as the Boston Pilgrims, as they were known then, prevailed in eight games.

Several decades later, Parent recalled his meeting with Red Sox representatives: "Bill Carrigan wanted to know about Ruth. I traveled from Baltimore to Washington to have dinner with him and Heinie Wagner. I told him they should buy Ruth and Shore. If you can get those two, you'll win the pennant."

Parent also related one humorous story involving Ruth from his Oriole days. "I coached Babe more than anybody else at that time," he recalled. "I remember he was pitching in the late innings of a close game and there were two outs and the bases loaded and a dangerous left-handed hitter was up. He got two strikes on him, and I ran out and told him to waste a pitch. The next pitch he threw right down the middle. Oh, gee, a triple. Babe comes in and I said, 'What happened?' He said, 'I threw one waist high, didn't I?'"

Another ex-major leaguer, Patsy Donovan, was acting as a scout for the Red Sox at that time. He had visited Baltimore weeks before and had recommended to Sox officials that negotiations begin.

On the afternoon of July 7, Dunn's fire sale commenced as he sold outfielder Birdie Cree to the Yankees for $8,000. He stated at that time that he had to make up for his overwhelming losses at the gate. Dunn admitted that Lannin wanted to purchase Ruth, Shore, and first baseman Gleichmann, but said he intended to hold on to these players. The following day, Wednesday the 8th, shortstop Claude Derrick and outfielder George Twombly were sold to the Cincinnati Reds for $15,000. The dismantling of one of the finest minor league teams ever assembled was well underway.

Twombly, a native of the Boston area, went on to play in a total of 150 games for three major league teams between 1914 and '19. In the mid 1960s, in a self-published book about his life experiences, Twombly stated that he had shown Ruth how to hit outside pitches to leftfield. He also noted that Ruth could "hit a left-hander's curve like nobody can today."

It was on Thursday afternoon, July 9, that the historic deal was struck via long distance telephone from Boston to Baltimore. The Red Sox were to receive Babe Ruth, right-handed pitcher Ernie Shore, and catcher Ben Egan for a sum of cash. Exactly how much cash was involved varies greatly depending on which source is consulted. The morning edition of the *Boston Globe* of July 10 trumpeted the news with the front page headline:

"Three new men for Sox"
Players to report tomorrow —
More than $25,000 paid

The article stated, "Lannin was particularly anxious to get Ruth," and also stated that the three players "caused owners to separate themselves from $30,000 for their services."

A headline in the *Boston Herald* of July 10 read:

"Red Sox pay $30,000 for Three Minor Stars"

The *Boston Post* of July 10 reported the price to be in excess of $25,000 and on July 15th, the day after Shore pitched in his Red Sox debut, the *Boston Traveler* wrote:

"5100 fans who came to see the game were unanimous in the belief that $27,000 wasn't any too high a price for baseball goods of the Ruth and Shore variety."

The Sporting Life, in its subsequent issues following the transaction made several references to the purchase price. Among them:

"President Lannin paid more than $25,000 for pitchers Ruth and Shore and catcher Ben Egan."

" ...the three players represented an outlay of more than $25,000 by the Boston club."

Ruth's hometown newspaper, the *Baltimore Sun,* questioned the reported price in their morning edition of July 10:

"Reports from Boston said Dunn received $25,000, however it is believed that he got no more than $20,000."

The paper also predicted great things for the local boy, stating:

"After Ruth has pitched in his first contest he will be a favorite, for there is no doubt he has the ability to twirl in any league. Moreover, his coolness under fire, his ability to hit, and his careless, almost indifferent manner are bound to win the fans."

In the many decades that followed, the Ruth sale to the Red Sox was recalled in detail in numerous books, however many referred to a drastically lower price. In his book, *The Boston Red Sox* published in 1947, esteemed sportswriter Frederick Lieb listed the purchase price at $8,000, with Ruth representing $2,900 of the total. Donald Honig in his book, *The Boston Red Sox—An Illustrated History* echoed the $8,000 price, and Tom Meany, whose biography *Babe Ruth,* published shortly after Ruth's death in 1948 listed the price at $8,500 for the three players.

Perhaps an item from the *Boston Daily Record* of January 19, 1943 comes closest to the real truth. Joe Cashman, a veteran Boston sportswriter, sat down with Ruth's first Sox manager Bill Carrigan and discussed the circumstances surrounding his purchase. The following passage from that interview is Carrigan's version:

"'On a trip to Washington early in July' he related, 'I got in touch with Freddy Parent, who had been the Red Sox shortstop when I broke in. He was acting as one of the Orioles master-minds at the time and I figured he could give me the dope.'"

"'Shore's ready to win in the majors right now,' Fred opined. 'Ruth is still very crude. He's been playing in the minors only a couple of months. But he can't miss with a little more experience.' That was good enough for me. I needed pitchers. I wired Lannin to get the two if he could reach a satisfactory agreement with Dunn on the price. Lannin offered $15,000 for the pair and said he would give no more.'"

"Dunn apparently couldn't get a better offer from anybody else, so he finally came up with a counter proposal. He offered Ruth, Shore, and catcher Ben Egan for $18,000. We didn't need a catcher, but Lannin fortunately agreed to this proposition."

"I've read that Egan was the fellow we wanted. He wasn't. We sold him soon after getting him, to Cleveland. We wanted Shore and Ruth. If we had to make a choice, I imagine we'd have taken Shore".

Nearly five years after the sale, *The Sporting News* of February 6, 1919 (Ruth's 24th birthday) ran an item in which Dunn told his version. Although he didn't mention the entire price Boston paid for all three Orioles, he was specific regarding the Ruth portion of the transaction:

"The offer of the Boston Red Sox—$12,500—was the best. I accepted it, not because I wanted to sell Ruth, but because I knew that if I didn't sell him then that the major leagues would draft him for about $1,500, a month or six weeks later. In other words, I had to choose between selling Ruth in July for $12,500 or disposing of him in September for $1,500."

It is entirely feasible that Ruth may have accounted for $12,500 worth of the overall purchase price of $18,000 for all three players.

Shore was not regarded as nearly the prospect Ruth was, and Egan was essentially a throw-in. Thus, the Dunn version seems to corroborate Carrigan's recollection so many years later.

Consider how the history of the game of baseball may have been drastically altered had Mack decided at that time that he simply could not have passed up on a diamond in the rough such as Ruth. How might Ruth's pitching performances from 1915 through 1917 have changed the fortunes of Philadelphia, who floundered badly after their loss to the Miracle Braves in the 1914 World Series? Would a colorful young and rising pitching phenom like Ruth have captured the imagination of A's fans, improving the team's financial picture in the process? Would an improved situation have prevented Mack from selling at least some of the parade of stars that he shuttled off in the mid-to-late teens? It only stands to reason that a fairly dramatic shift in the balance of power in the American League may have occurred.

Lastly, would a conservative old manager like Mack have been so quick to convert the best left-handed pitcher in the American League to an outfielder? If by chance he hadn't, Ruth never would have set a new home run record with 29 in 1919. It was that impressive achievement, and the public's reaction to it that prompted American League President Ban Johnson to secretly order the ball to be juiced up. The incredible offensive explosion that followed might be indirectly attributable to Connie Mack uttering, "No, thank you." Otherwise, the sluggers of today might be winning home run titles with thirteen round-trippers.

ð

Ruth's future was undoubtedly bright, but his promotion to the major leagues so soon was almost directly due to the presence of the Federal League team in Baltimore. Dunn had a habit of hanging on to his stars as long as possible in order to maximize his gate potential, and to increase the amount he might receive when he did decide to sell. His handling of budding superstar Lefty Grove in the 1920s serves as the best example. Dunn held Grove down in the International League for five years, and from 1920 through 1924, he recorded win totals of 12, 25, 18, 27, and 27.

He finally sold Grove to Connie Mack for $100,000 after the 1924 season, and he debuted in majors the following spring at the age of 25. Without the financial hardship created by the Baltimore

Terrapins, Dunn would have likely attempted to keep Ruth for several more seasons and reap thousands off him as a great drawing card. He admitted as much in the aforementioned 1919 article that if the draft situation hadn't existed at the time, such would have been the case.

ᢞ

The Ruth sale caused a considerable amount of discord among other organizations, not the least of which was the New York Giants and their legendary manager John McGraw. Dunn had been managed by McGraw on the '01 Orioles, and again on the Giants from '02 through '04. McGraw had seen Ruth's potential that spring, and asked Dunn to let him know when he was ready to sell. When he didn't, McGraw reportedly never spoke to him again. Also, in *The Sporting Life*'s July 18 issue, New York columnist Harry Dix Cole questioned why Ruth and Shore were permitted to be purchased by Boston without the Yankees making a serious offer. At the time of the sale, the Yankees were mired in seventh place and were desperate for pitching.

With the deal now finalized, it was agreed upon that the three new Sox would report to Boston on Saturday morning, July 11. Dunn then figured that in Ruth's final two days as an Oriole, he could take advantage of his potent bat, and inserted him in leftfield on Thursday and Friday against Newark. He didn't provide much offense however, stroking one double in four at-bats on Thursday, then going 0 for 3 in his Oriole finale. In both games, Dunn's son, Jack Jr., played centerfield next to Ruth. The Orioles were still in first place by four games at this time, but with the continued loss of their star players, their fortunes would surely change.

Rolling the clock ahead 81 years, the city of Baltimore would unveil a statue of Ruth on the centennial of his birth, depicting him wearing his Orioles uniform.

ᢞ

Ruth said good-bye to Dunn on Friday night, July 10, and boarded a train bound for Boston. With him was Shore, Egan, and Oriole Secretary Billy Wicks, whom Dunn sent along to ensure that the trio reached their destination. Many of the Ruth biographies have attempted to retrace his footsteps that first morning in Boston, however an item from the *Boston Traveler* two days later presents a reasonably clear picture. It stated that the three players arrived at the Back Bay Station at 10 a.m. via the Federal Express, and were met there by Lannin. The men then took the trolley to the Red Sox downtown offices located on 70 Devonshire Street in the city's financial district.

Later on when the new Boston players arrived at Fenway Park, Ruth was promptly informed by Manager Carrigan that he needed him to start against Cleveland that afternoon. The Red Sox pitching staff was in need of reinforcements, with Smoky Joe Wood having elbow problems, and starter George Foster having suffered a knee injury in late June.

Bill Carrigan, a native of Lewiston, Maine, was a no-nonsense leader who commanded the respect of all in his charge. Nicknamed "Rough," he attended Holy Cross University in the early 1900s and debuted as a catcher with the Red Sox in 1906. He became their regular backstop in '09, and midway through the '13 season, just a few months before turning thirty, he was appointed player-manager. Years later, both Ruth and Shore identified Carrigan as the best manager for whom they had ever played..

Neither Shore nor Egan were complete strangers to major league baseball. The six-foot-four inch Shore, a giant in those times, actually pitched one game for the Giants in 1912. Egan had two brief trials catching for the Philadelphia Athletics in 1908 and 1912.

Ruth would be making his major league debut that Saturday afternoon, July 11, against the Cleveland Naps, soon to be known as the Indians. At the time, the Sox were languishing in sixth place in the eight team American League with a 40-38 record. Among those who took the field for Boston at the 3 o'clock starting time were legendary Hall of Fame centerfielder Tris Speaker, and shortstop Everett Scott, whose 1,307 consecutive game streak was the record until Lou Gehrig came along. Harry Hooper, another future Hall of Famer, was not in his usual rightfield spot that day, but was instead given the day off by Carrigan.

The last place Naps featured all-time great second baseman Nap Lajoie, whom the team was named after, and the fabled "Shoeless" Joe Jackson. Ruth would later credit Jackson's left-handed swing as the model for his own.

With Carrigan behind the plate, Cleveland's lead-off hitter Jack Graney singled in the top of the first, and Ruth's major league career was underway. It would have been impossible for the 11,087 patrons in attendance to have any clue as to the significance of the event. Ruth would cruise along for seven quality innings, giving up three runs on eight hits, all of them singles. Shoeless Joe accounted for two of the singles, and Lajoie went hitless in his three at-bats against Ruth, who struck out one and walked none.

With the score tied 3-3, Carrigan sent Duffy Lewis up to pinch hit for Ruth in the bottom of the seventh inning. Lewis, the regular leftfielder, singled and was subsequently driven in by a Tris Speaker single. Holding a slim 4-3 lead, Carrigan brought in left-hander Hubert "Dutch" Leonard to start off the eighth inning. Normally a starter, Leonard was on his way that season to setting the all-time single-season record for lowest earned-run average among starters at 1.01, which still stands over 80 years later.

Leonard came in and struck out four of the six batters he faced, and Ruth had recorded his first major league victory. The *Boston Sunday Globe* ran the following headline on its July 12 sports page:

"Ruth leads Red Sox to victory"

"Southpaw displays high class in game against Cleveland"

Respected Boston sportswriter, Tim Murnane, wrote:

"The Red Sox introduced Mr. Ruth, one of the Baltimore recruits, yesterday to the crowd at Fenway Park. . . . All eyes were turned on Ruth, the giant left-hander, who proved a natural ballplayer, and went through his act like a veteran of many wars. He has a natural delivery, fine control, and a curve ball that bothers the batsman, but has room for improvement, and will undoubtedly become a fine pitcher under the care of manager Carrigan."

In Joe Cashman's 1943 *Boston Daily Record* interview with Carrigan, that debut was recalled. Said Bill:

"If I remember, Babe was crude in spots. Every so often he served up a fat pitch or a bad pitch when he shouldn't have. But he showed plenty of baseball savvy. He picked a runner off third base. He also cut off a throw from the outfield and threw a runner out at second. Anybody could see he'd quickly develop into a standout with a little more experience. He had a barrel of stuff, his speed was blinding and his ball was alive."

As for the future slugger's performance in his two at-bats that day, he was struck out by left-hander Willie Mitchell in his first appearance, and later flied out to Jackson in right. Interestingly enough, the *Globe*, in its game account reported:

> "Ruth received a perfect ovation when he went to the bat, and shaped up like a good batsman."

By pitching on that Saturday, Ruth had performed in his third professional game in three days. He had played a full nine innings in leftfield on both Thursday and Friday with the Orioles, then traveled 600 miles via train all Friday night and started for the Red Sox on Saturday. It is difficult to envision a professional athlete of today enduring such a hardship.

Meanwhile in Baltimore, Dunn's dismantled Orioles would draw a grand total of twenty-six fans to their game on the same day that Babe debuted with the Red Sox.

꒰ꔛ

Virtually every biography of Ruth has told variations of the story of how he met his first wife Helen on his first day in Boston. Helen, not quite seventeen years old, worked as a waitress in Landers' Coffee Shop while living with her family in the South Boston section of the city. Interestingly, the location of Landers' restaurant seems to move around, depending on the source.

Certainly some of the confusion is created by the fact that there were six different Landers' restaurants in Boston in 1914, three owned by Alvin F. Landers, and three owned by his brother John N. Landers.

When Helen passed away in 1929, the *Boston Post* offered a slightly different version of their meeting, which may lead to a discovery of the truth:

> "Ruth met his wife shortly after he came to Boston to play for the Red Sox. He soon became a steady customer at Billy Pink's restaurant on Columbus Ave. in the south end, where Helen Woodford was a waitress."

Billy Pink's restaurant, known as Pink's Sea Grill, was actually located at 208 Dartmouth Street, near the corner of Columbus Avenue, but did not exist in 1914.

On the occasion of Helen's death 15 years after she met Babe, it was apparently recalled that she had worked at that location, though under different ownership. In reality, the Landers' at 196 Dartmouth was just a few doors down from where Pink's would later be, at number 208. Thus, the Dartmouth Street Landers, which incidentally was directly across the street from the Back Bay Station, appears to make the most sense. Of course there is also the possibility that working for Alvin Landers, Helen may have waitressed at all three of his restaurants at various times.

ॐ

One aspect of Ruth's personality that is well chronicled was his difficulty in remembering names. One story goes that when pitcher Waite Hoyt, a teammate of Ruth for a decade, was traded, he was bidding his farewells and Babe approached and said, "Goodbye Walter." In the autobiography, Ruth referred to Helen, to whom he was married for over a decade as Helen "Woodring" rather than Woodford. The "Woodring" example serves as the prime example of Ruth's inability to recall names.

It has also been written several times that Ruth's first start against Cleveland was the first major league game that he ever witnessed. Though this cannot be disproved unequivocally, there is evidence to suggest otherwise. On Monday, May 25, 1914, Ruth's Orioles had an off day during a series in Newark. Some of the Baltimore players went over to the Polo Grounds that afternoon to watch the Yankees play the Chicago White Sox. If Ruth had never seen a major league game up to this point, would he have passed up the opportunity to tag along with his mostly older teammates to see the game? If in fact he was in attendance, he witnessed Yankee pitcher Jack Warhop get defeated by the Sox 1-0. One year later, Ruth would slug his first major league home run off Warhop at these same Polo Grounds.

On May 29, 1914, four days after the Orioles attended the Yankees-White Sox game, they found themselves with another day off in Providence, Rhode Island. Many of the players reportedly took the train up to Boston to take in a double-header between the Red Sox and the Washington Senators. In the first game, Senators ace Walter Johnson hurled a three hit 1-0 shutout against the Sox.

Having grown up in Baltimore, Ruth may well have considered the nearby Senators the "home" team as a youth. Again, if Ruth hadn't yet seen a major league game, could he have passed on the chance to observe the great Johnson perform on the mound?

The notion that Ruth's debut against Cleveland was the first big league contest he ever witnessed is rejected here.

❦

In his first days in Boston, he was staying at the Brunswick Hotel at the corner of Boylston and Clarendon Streets. Lannin had agreed to pay him at a rate of $2,500 per year, or roughly $416 per month. Ruth was no doubt visiting Helen at Landers on nearly a daily basis, traveling his new urban playground via trolley. Without a legal guardian to monitor his activities for the first time in his young adult life, Ruth was fast becoming a man about town. It is unlikely though, that he was exposing himself to Boston's cultural institutions such as museums, the symphony, or the Boston Public Library.

On Tuesday, the 14th, Ruth sat on the bench and watched Shore, his former Oriole teammate, make his exceedingly impressive Red Sox debut. Facing Cleveland at Fenway Park, the 6'4" righthander did not allow a hit until the sixth inning. He would complete the game, giving up only two hits as the Red Sox would win 2-1, giving Shore his first major league victory. *The Globe* boasted, "Still another $10,000 beauty has made good for the Red Sox."

The following day, in the last game of the series against the Naps, Dutch Leonard hurled a seven-hit 4-0 shutout. One noteworthy incident occurred late in the game with Cleveland at bat. Home plate umpire Tommy Connolly, a future Hall of Famer, ejected eight Red Sox players from the Boston dugout for taunting remarks aimed at the visitors. Luckily, Ruth escaped banishment by being one of a small group of Sox pitchers out in the bullpen area.

Thursday, July 16, Carrigan gave Ruth his second starting assignment, facing a formidable Detroit Tiger lineup at Fenway. Although Ty Cobb was out of the lineup nursing an injured thumb, Ruth had to face the great Sam Crawford, highly productive Bobby Veach, and future superstar Harry Heilmann. According to Tim Murnane of the *Boston Globe*: "Ruth started the game and was doing nicely until [rightfielder Wally] Rehg lost Crawford's long drive..." He was pulled by Carrigan with none out in the fourth inning, the Tigers went on to win 5-2, and Ruth was tagged with his first big-league loss.

It is interesting to note that an umpiring crew for a major league game at that time consisted of only two men. One of the men in blue on this particular day was Bill Dineen, who had a distinguished pitching career himself. In 1903, hurling on the same Boston staff as Cy Young, it was Dineen who was the pitching hero in the first modern World Series. In the early part of this century, it was far more common for a player to make the transition to umpire after the conclusion of his career.

In a transaction that took place on the day of Ruth's loss to Detroit, the Red Sox acquired dependable first baseman Dick Hoblitzell from Cincinnati. He would find himself rooming with Ruth for part of that 1914 season. At some point during this time, Ruth reportedly took up residence in a rooming house run by Mrs. A. Josephine Lindbergh at 3 Batavia Street.

After his first two major league appearances, something happened to Ruth to which he hadn't been accustomed. He sat on the bench, not called upon, and simply observed for many weeks. At that time, Carrigan was using a rotation that consisted of Ray Collins, Leonard, Fritz Coumbe, George "Rube" Foster, and Shore, who was establishing himself quickly as a quality starter and top notch prospect.

Being a rookie and the youngest player on the team, Ruth had to endure his share of goodnatured abuse by many older teammates. In his autobiography, *The Babe Ruth Story,* as told to Bob Considine, he said that Ben Egan was his special friend, and if other players' practical jokes went too far, Egan would take his side. Ruth also credited him with giving him many good pointers as his first catcher. Decades later, Egan graciously stated that Ruth knew how to pitch the first day he saw him, and that he really didn't have to teach him anything.

Two-and-a-half weeks after arriving in Boston, Egan was promptly traded to Cleveland without ever entering a game. His official record therefore, as listed in the various baseball registers, does not reflect his time in a Red Sox uniform. Though his major league career ultimately consisted of 121 games and 352 at-bats, he would forever be linked with Ruth. When Egan passed away in 1968 in Sherrill, New York, the headline of his obituary in the *Utica Daily Press* read:

"Ben Egan, 84, Dies; Babe Ruth's Catcher"

❧

The Boston Braves, the Red Sox National League counterparts who played just a couple of miles away at the South End Grounds, were about to write the sports story of the year. On July 19, the team that would earn the nickname the "Miracle Braves" climbed out of last place on their way to the National League pennant. Their subsequent sweep of the heavily favored Athletics in that year's World Series would dominate the sports pages of the day.

July 24 saw Ruth embark on his first road trip with the Red Sox, riding the rails to Cleveland, Chicago, St. Louis, and Detroit. In his time with Baltimore, his travels through the International League took him to several northeastern cities, including Jersey City, Newark, Providence, Rochester, Buffalo, and across the border to Toronto and Montreal. He was now beginning to experience some of the major league cities in what was then the American League's "western swing."

On July 26 in Cleveland, Ruth watched as Shore pitched a complete game 4-1 victory, striking out four and walking only one. The following day, he witnessed all-star performances from both Dutch Leonard and Tris Speaker against the Naps. Leonard contributed to his record setting ERA by hurling a 3-0 complete game shutout; Speaker went three for three, including two singles and a triple, and recorded a remarkable eight putouts in centerfield. That season, Speaker, certainly one of the game's greatest defensive outfielders of all time, established a new single season record for putouts with 423.

It was announced on July 28 that the Red Sox had struck a deal with the Naps while in Cleveland, acquiring left-handed starter Vean Gregg for pitchers Adam Johnson, Fritz Coumbe, and catcher Egan. Gregg had won twenty or more games per year from 1911 through 1913, his first three major league seasons, and had a record of nine and three at the time of the deal. Philadelphia Athletics great second baseman Eddie Collins referred to Gregg around that time as the "left-handed Walter Johnson." In order for the Red Sox (who climbed into second place on July 22) to make a run of the league leading Athletics, Gregg would have to continue his performance.

The Red Sox new lefty would join the team in Chicago on July 29 for a series against the White Sox. Carrigan immediately gave Gregg the starting assignment and he pitched seven innings, was not involved in the decision, and the Red Sox went on to win 8-4 in ten innings.

On July 31, Sox owner Lannin opened his wallet again and made a purchase that would have an effect on Ruth's immediate future. Boston's millionaire owner acquired the Providence team of the International League along with their home grounds Melrose Park from the owners of the Detroit Tigers for $75,000. Lannin, who amassed much of his fortune in the hotel business in the Long Island, New York area, said at the time "The first ballgames that I ever saw were the hair-raising contests between Boston and Providence [National League] in the early 1880s."

The Detroit group, headed by Frank Navin, in turn purchased Buffalo's International League team. As a result, both the Sox and Tigers would now have a minor league affiliate far closer geographically. One stipulation of the deal allowed Detroit to select one player off of the Providence roster, which turned out to be left-handed pitcher Red Oldham. Luckily for the Red Sox, Detroit overlooked righthanded submarine pitcher Carl Mays, who became a key member of the Boston staff for several years. Oldham's career at the major-league level never amounted to much, winning 39 and losing 48 over the next seven seasons.

By early August, the Red Sox pitching rotation featured three lefties with Gregg, Ray Collins, and Leonard. With Ruth buried on the bench, Lannin attempted to put him on waivers for the purpose of sending him down to Providence. A number of teams, including the Cincinnati Reds tried to claim him, so Lannin was forced to pull him back. Lannin appealed the issue to the league, and the matter took nearly two weeks to resolve.

During late July and early August, Ruth saw his young teammate Shore turn in several fine performances on the mound. The North Carolina native's complete game 6-2 victory over the St. Louis Browns in the second game of a double-header at Boston on July 22nd helped move the Red Sox into second place. There was the complete game 4-1 victory at Cleveland on the 26th, and a 4-0 six hitter at Chicago's Comiskey Park on the 30th putting his record at four wins, no losses.

Shore experienced a heartbreaking loss against the Browns in St. Louis on August 4. He allowed only six hits, however the

Browns scored the winning run in the ninth inning and prevailed 2-1.

On that same day, there were two items regarding the relationship between the Red Sox and the neighboring Braves. Arrangements were made between Lannin and Braves owner James Gaffney to have the teams meet in a postseason series to determine the champs of the city. Such series were common at that time between American and National League teams that occupied the same city. It was a major league policy however, that teams who participated in that season's World Series were precluded from engaging in such a series. Such was the case with the Braves in 1914, and the city series ultimately did not take place.

The other item involved Lannin offering Gaffney's Braves the use of Fenway Park for the duration of the season when playing dates did not conflict. The Braves were climbing steadily in the standings, and Fenway's higher seating capacity would accommodate the increased fan interest. Gaffney would take Lannin up on the offer many times late that season.

Though Ruth's waiver situation was still a week and a half away from being cleared up, his transfer to Providence seemed a foregone conclusion. *The Sporting Life* of August 8th contained the following item in its International League notes column:

> "Oldham will be going to Detroit on Aug. 15, but Ruth who replaces him can be depended on to win lots of games for the Grays."

In the meantime, Ruth was in the midst of going 28 days without making an appearance in a game. On August 12, the Red Sox traveled approximately 40 minutes to nearby Lawrence, Massachusetts for an exhibition game versus the local New England League team. 3,500 locals attended the game at Riverside Park and watched Ruth defeat the Class "B" minor league team by a score of 6-4.

Five days later, the Red Sox journeyed to New Hampshire to engage in another exhibition, this time against Manchester, also of the New England League. The 2,500 in attendance at Textile Field witnessed Ruth pitch a complete game 4-2 victory, in what would be his last game in a Boston uniform for more than six weeks.

As for Ruth's first five weeks as a major leaguer, Duffy Lewis would recall three-and-a-half decades later:

"He was a happy-go-lucky kid with a giggle that would get everybody laughing. He was a youngster and he was full of life, but he wasn't fresh. He didn't pop off to anybody."

Lewis was, in all probability, the only person to witness Ruth's first and last major league home runs. In 1935, he was acting as the Boston Braves' traveling secretary while Ruth was wrapping up his playing career. In an interview with the Associated Press in 1979, he recalled that May afternoon at Forbes Field in Pittsburgh when Babe hit numbers 712, 713, and 714. Interestingly enough, he was still working in the same capacity for the Braves in Milwaukee in 1954, and was on hand when a young Henry Aaron hit home run number one of 755.

≈

Lannin was finally able to convince teams attempting to claim Ruth on waivers that he wasn't about to let him go, having paid such a high price only a month before. The Red Sox were in second place, ten games behind Philadelphia, and any hope of catching them was fading by the week. With Lannin's other team, Providence, only two games out of first place, he hoped that the addition of Ruth to the pitching staff could put them over the top. On August 18, Carrigan gave Ruth train fare and instructions to report to Providence and manager "Wild" Bill Donovan at Melrose Park.

As he was earlier in the season in Baltimore, Ruth was again in the hands of a manager who had considerable experience as a major league pitcher. Donovan, a righthander, had pitched from 1898 through 1912, compiling a 185-139 record with Washington, Brooklyn, and Detroit. He was actually a member of the same pitching staff as Jack Dunn in Brooklyn in 1899 and 1900.

≈

When Ruth arrived in Rhode Island on the 18th, the Providence Grays, informally known as the "Clamdiggers," trailed only league-leading Rochester, with a record of 65-45. When he reported to Melrose Park that Tuesday, Ruth no doubt recalled his first appearance there many months earlier. Visiting with the Orioles on May 28th, he came in to relieve against the Grays and pitched 6 2/3 innings, getting credit for the victory. He also slugged a triple in four at-bats in Baltimore's 7-4 win.

Melrose Park was a very spacious ballpark, with advertising signs painted neatly all along the outfield fence. The facilities were among the finer found in minor league baseball, with the home team's clubhouse located down the leftfield line, and the visitors in right.

The *Providence Journal* of August 19, 1914 contained the following item in its "Baseball Gossip" column:

> "Pitcher Ruth reported to Manager Donovan yesterday morning, the Red Sox having secured waivers on the big left-hander, who was bought from Baltimore about a month ago when Dunn began unloading his star players. The addition of Ruth makes the Grays' pitching staff look considerably better, the going of Bailey and Oldham leaving the club without a left-hander. Ruth was carded to come here last week, but Brooklyn and Cincinnati of the National League, and Washington of the American League refused to waive it at the time. President Lannin of the Red Sox secured the necessary waivers yesterday and at once sent the pitcher down to Donovan."

On Thursday, August 20, Rochester, holding a slim half-game lead over the Grays, arrived in Providence for a crucial four-game series. Lannin was in attendance for Thursday's game, along with league president Ed Barrow as guest. Grays ace Carl Mays dispatched Rochester with an 8-1 complete game effort, leapfrogging Providence into first place. The *Providence Journal* of that day also reported:

> "Both Ruth and [Guy] Cooper, the recruits from the Boston Americans, are reported to be in fine trim, and are spoiling for a chance to get at the Rochester outfit."

Rain postponed Friday's scheduled game, setting the stage for a banner day in the smallest state's largest city on Saturday. The double-header on August 22 featured Ruth's first appearance in a Grays' uniform in game one, which was greatly anticipated by local fans. In what was thought to be the largest crowd to ever attend a ball game in Providence up to that time, an estimated 12,000 fans were jammed into every corner of the park. They even stood behind a rope deep in the outfield, stretching from the leftfield corner to the rightfield corner.

In the *Providence Journal* of the following day:

"It was Ruth's debut in a Providence uniform, and barring one inning, the former Baltimore luminary gave a masterly exhibition. The crowd warmed up to him from the start, and even when he was being whacked soundly in the seventh, the fans cheered him on."

Though the partisan crowd was squarely in his corner, Ruth truly did not possess his best stuff that day. He walked five batters, struck out only three, and gave up nine hits in his nine innings pitched as the Grays came to bat in the ninth inning trailing 4-2. With one out, catcher Jack Onslow drilled a triple to centerfield, and was standing on third when Ruth came to the plate.

The *Providence Journal* reported:

"The din was terrific when Ruth, who had already smashed out a triple in a previous trip, lumbered to the plate, but it was not a marker to the tumult that would follow. The big stick tore through the air and met an Upham [Rochester pitcher] shoot with a crack that sounded above the roar of the fans. Higher and higher mounted the ball and then it descended in a beautiful spiral to land many feet over the heads of the fans in centre and in close proximity to the flag pole. A thousand straw hats were lost in the wild demonstration of joy that signalized the longest hit ever made at the ball park."

Ruth's second triple of the game made the score 4-3, and rightfielder Topsy Platte slugged yet another triple to send Babe across with the tying run. A couple of batters later, second baseman Dave Shean, later a Red Sox teammate of Ruth's, drove in Platte for an utterly crowd-pleasing victory. Carl Mays, who had dominated Rochester just two days before, completed the sweep of the double-header, also by a 5-4 margin.

Back in Boston the following day, the Braves moved into a first place tie with the New York Giants. In thirty-six days they had miraculously climbed from eighth place all the way to the top spot.

On Monday, August 24, the Grays embarked on a brief road trip that took them to Buffalo, Rochester, and across the border to Toronto. In the first game of the trip, Mays continued his excellent hurling, shutting out the Buffalo Bisons 4-0. The following day, the 26th, Ruth got his second start, albeit with rather disappointing results. Though he went the distance, he walked six, struck out two, and went down to an 8-2 defeat. Joe McCarthy, who would manage Ruth in New York in the early thirties, played second base for Buffalo and stroked a triple and a single in four at-bats. The August 29 issue of *The Sporting Life* said:

"Gilhooley, Vaughn, Channell, Lehr, and McCarthy drove in the runs for Buffalo with their timely smashes of Ruth's curves."

On the 29th, the Grays moved on to Rochester, and the Hustlers were to face both Ruth and Mays again in a Saturday double-header. In the first game, Mays twirled yet another shutout, winning by a score of 2-0. Ruth was sharp in game two, allowing only one run in the eighth inning for a 2-1 victory. The *Providence Sunday Journal* of the following day published a large photo of Ruth warming up on the sidelines. It was in all likelihood the first photo of him published wearing the Providence uniform.

There was also an item in that day's *Journal* in a column entitled, "On the Road with the Grays," that indicated that manager Donovan was considering a return to active duty as a pitcher. He had been keeping himself in good shape all season and had also developed a new, somewhat tricky breaking pitch.

Ruth would not take the mound again until one week later in Toronto on September 5, but it would turn out to be his greatest day as a minor leaguer. In the first game of a double-header, Ruth made his mark both on the rubber and at the plate.

The September 6 *Providence Journal* reported:

"Ruth pitched a magnificent game in the opener, allowing but one hit, a Texas Leaguer by Kelly in the fifth. The big fellow had barrels of speed and some great curves that had the Leafs completely buffaloed."

It was his trip to the plate in the sixth inning that would make the most lasting impression. With two Grays aboard, Ruth smashed a tremendous home run off Ellis Johnson that would be his first official professional homer, and the only one he would ever hit in a regular season minor league game.

On that same day back in Boston, the Red Sox completed a four-game sweep of the league-leading Athletics. Though they would temporarily narrow the margin, Boston's pursuit of Mack's A's fell short, and the Fenway faithful would wait 'til next year.

On September 7, Providence was back home to face Newark, and including his one-hitter on the 5th, Ruth was embarking on a personal streak of four victories in eight days. On the 7th he notched a complete game 9-2 victory with Newark scoring their only two runs in the eighth inning. *The Sporting Life* reported that "Babe Ruth was at his best and Newark never had a chance to tally until he eased up." At bat he went 2 for 4 with a triple and a run scored. Two days later, he beat the same Newark team 9-5, holding the Indians to seven hits.

On the 12th, Jersey City played a double-header at Melrose Park, and Ruth, taking a shutout into the eighth, went the distance for a 4-3 win in the opener. *The Sporting Life* stated "Ruth's effective pitching in the first game was the chief factor in Providence's victory" as he now sported a record of five victories against only one defeat.

The next day, Mays performed an ironman feat that seems remarkable today. The Grays traveled to Newark for a series that began with a double-header on September 13.

Mays pitched a complete game in the opener, suffering a heartbreaking 3-2 loss due to crucial errors. Undaunted, he came right back in the second game and scored a complete game 7-3 victory. Amazingly, Mays would go on to pitch all of both games of a double-header at least twice during his major league career.

Providence and Newark played yet another double-header the following day, as it was Ruth's turn to see action in both games, though not to such an impressive degree. He came up on the short end, 2-0 in game one, and pitched two ineffective innings in relief in game two, taking the loss.

Ruth may have been better off staying home, as two of the three losses he incurred in a Providence uniform came on this day.

As for where Babe called home during this period, it was recalled quite clearly eight decades later by 90-year-old Bill Considine. Only nine years old in 1914, Considine remembered that Ruth roomed with teammate Guy Tutwiler at 515 Elmwood Ave., at the corner of Earle St., now a vacant lot. "I lived right near him on Earle St., and sometimes I'd walk to the park with him. He helped me get a job taking tickets for the first few innings, then they let me in for free."

On September 17, Ruth's old team, the Orioles, came to Providence for a series against the Grays and presumably he had his first face-to-face meeting with Jack Dunn since the sale.

Dunn had continued to sell players after the Ruth deal, and his Orioles, once a sure pennant winner, had dropped out of first place for good by mid-August.

The next day, the 18th, Ruth got the start against Baltimore. Though he was relieved late in the game by Peter Bentley, Ruth was sharp, striking out five and walking only one in an 11-3 win. He also slugged a triple and scored a run. Three days later, he was particularly dominating against visiting Jersey City, striking out eleven in a complete game 8-3 victory.

On the 24th, Baltimore was back in town for a series that closed out the season. That day, Ruth tortured Dunn a little bit more, striking out eight Orioles and winning 4-2. On Friday, the 25th, Mays won his 24th game of the season, capturing the league pennant for Providence. In a game that took 68 minutes to complete, the Grays ace gave up only seven hits in a 2-0 shutout, ironically over the team that was the overwhelming favorite earlier in the season. It was the first pennant Providence had won since 1905, when the International League was known as the Eastern League. It is interesting to note that the manager of that squad was one Mr. Jack Dunn.

On the 26th, Providence closed out its season, playing a most unusual game against Baltimore. With nothing left at stake, the teams apparently decided to throw batting practice-style pitching, and an offensive explosion resulted. Ruth played the entire game in rightfield, as the Grays prevailed in the slug fest 23-19. In four official at-bats, Ruth hit two singles and a triple, scored three runs, and stole two bases. Manager Donovan even got into the act by relieving the final few innings. His team finished with a record of 95-59, while Baltimore dropped all the way to sixth place at 72-77.

A review of the box scores shows Ruth's pitching record to be nine wins and three losses, though this tends to vary slightly depending on the source. As a hitter he went 12 for 40 for an even .300 average, one home run, and ten runs scored.

That evening after the final game, the city of Providence paid tribute to the champion Grays in a rousing affair at the new Y.M.C.A. gymnasium. Before a packed house, manager Donovan was presented with a silver loving cup, and gave a heartfelt speech thanking his players and the fans. Each of the Grays' players was then given a gold watch fob, and was asked to say a few words.

The following afternoon, the Grays traveled to nearby Warwick, Rhode Island, to play an exhibition game against the Chicago Cubs at Rocky Point Park. The Cubs had been in Boston for a series against the Braves, and had an off day due to Boston's Sunday baseball ban. Ruth pitched the entire game, winning 8-7 and hitting a home run in his last appearance in a minor league uniform. After the game, the team returned to Melrose Park, and Donovan called the players into his office and thanked them for their efforts.

In his autobiography, Ruth said of Donovan, "He taught me a lot about pitching that came in handy later in my Red Sox experience." Wild Bill had helped to convince him that there was more to pitching than just striking batters out.

In the summer of 1995, the centennial year of Ruth's birth, the city of Providence erected a plaque on the site of the park, which was torn down in 1920. The marker commemorates the time that Ruth spent in Providence, and his contribution to the championship season of 1914.

*

On Monday morning, September 28, both Ruth and Mays took the train from Providence to Boston to join the Red Sox for the final week of the major league season. The 40-mile train trip was one that Ruth had made several times in the previous six weeks to visit Helen. The *Providence Journal* of the 28th wrote that "Ruth will pass the winter in Boston," however, Babe and Helen found more pressing matters of which they would tend to.

When the two rookies arrived in Boston, the Red Sox were still out on a road trip, and wouldn't be back for two more days. When they returned, the Sox began a series against the visiting New York Yankees. On Friday, October 2, Ruth was given the starting assignment for the third time in his young major league career. The Yankees committed five errors, and Ruth went all the way for an 11-5 win.

He recorded his first major league hit, a double off Leonard "King" Cole, and also scored his first run. Three days later with the Senators at Fenway, Carrigan sent him in to pinch hit for pitcher Ray Collins. He struck out against Walter Johnson, who won his league-leading 28th game by a score of 9-3.

On October 7, the Red Sox closed out the 1914 season against Washington. Ruth relieved starter Hugh Bedient in the fourth, pitched three innings, and was not involved in the decision. He did, however, stroke a single in his only at-bat. Washington Manager Clark Griffith, a Hall of Famer who eventually owned the team for more than four decades, made his final appearance as an active player, pitching the last inning of the game.

Boston finished in second place with a 91-62 record, behind pennant-winning Philadelphia, who was about to be stunned by the Braves. The Red Sox loaned the Braves the use of Fenway Park during that series due to its larger seating capacity. Games number three and championship-clinching game four took place there.

Ruth not only would not pass the winter in Boston, he would not stick around to attend any series games. He apparently had more pressing personal matters to attend to. He asked Helen, who was just turning 17, to come home to Baltimore with him and get married. Helen accepted the proposal, and they were off to Maryland, where they were wed in Ellicott City, a suburb of Baltimore on October 17. They would spend the winter living with Ruth's father in an apartment above his saloon located on Conway Street, which is just a fly ball from Oriole Park at Camden Yards. Babe kept busy by tending bar and helping to run a backroom gymnasium.

Babe's old friend Jack Dunn was making news in Baltimore that off-season. In early December it was announced that he was transferring his Orioles to Richmond, Virginia, rather than compete against the Federal League another season. The disbanding of the Feds after the 1915 season however, paved the way for Dunn's return in 1916. Dunn sold his interests in the Richmond team to local Virginia investors, and purchased the floundering Jersey City franchise, immediately moving them to Baltimore for yet another incarnation of Orioles.

When Frank Chance (of Tinker-to-Evers-to-Chance fame) stepped down as manager of the Yankees after the '14 season, he recommended Dunn as his replacement. Chance had been impressed by the manner in which Dunn had handled his less than desirable circumstances that season.

Dunn was not hired for the New York job, although it is interesting to note that "Wild" Bill Donovan was, leading the Yankees from 1915 through 1917. Dunn would go on to lead his Orioles to seven straight International League championships from 1919 through 1925.

Over the winter of 1914-'15, young George Ruth had championships of his own to look forward to.

▪ Two ▪

1915: A Spot
in the Rotation

With his big league debut now behind him, Ruth's first Boston Red Sox spring training camp lay just ahead. On Thursday, March 4th, Helen saw Babe off from Baltimore on a train bound for St. Louis, where he would hook up with a large Red Sox contingent. The group arriving from Boston, which had made its first stop in Albany, included Lannin, Carrigan, several Sox players, newspaper men, and many Boston followers known as the Royal Rooters. Ruth met them at Union Station in St. Louis as the final leg of the journey took them to the Red Sox training site in Hot Springs, Arkansas.

Shortly after boarding, Ruth surprised many members of the group by announcing that he had been married in the off-season to a Boston girl named "Woodward" (Woodford, Babe, Woodford!). The *Boston Post* of March 15, 1915 ran a photo of Ruth seated, looking rather dapper in a suit and tie with his young bride standing beside him. Under the title "Ruth put one over on his mates", it stated that he had sent a letter to the Red Sox headquarters in January informing them of his marriage. Additionally, two pieces of information contained within the item are curiously different from the generally accepted versions.

Regarding Babe and Helen's first meeting, it said that her brother, a big Red Sox fan, had met Ruth after his first game in Boston and subsequently introduced the two. It also indicated that the couple was married in October in Providence, though no record of that wedding appears to exist.

Hot Springs, a resort spa in the Ozark Mountains famous for its hot mineral baths was the gambling center of the lower Mississippi River and attracted tourists from all over. When the team pulled in on Saturday, March 6, and checked into the Hotel Majestic, they found it unseasonably cold. With the temperature in the mid-30s, it was the coldest March natives could recall. Workouts were put off temporarily, and Ruth found the time to attend church on Sunday morning with Lannin, Carrigan, and other members of the party.

Informal workouts began Monday, March 8 and Carrigan sent Ruth, who seemed slightly overweight, to the outfield to shag fly balls. He was regarded as somewhat of an extra pitcher at the time, as Carrigan was counting more on Shore, Foster, and lefties Ray Collins and Dutch Leonard. He was also hopeful that Smoky Joe Wood might rebound from a lame arm.

Wednesday the 10th was the best day to that point with sunny skies and temperatures reaching 50 degrees.

"For 1/2 hour, Collins, Ruth, and Leonard, three lefties, warmed up with smoke, showing great form." *Boston Post* 3/11/15

On Sunday the 14th, two excursions were planned for Ruth and his fellow rookies. One, a trip to the Mountain Valley Springs and the other a fishing trip. That morning, the remainder of the team arrived in town, headed by Tris Speaker. Only Harry Hooper remained absent. Monday's workout was postponed due to driving chilly winds and the following day saw the first full day of practice. Ruth was included in a group of pitchers who took a turn throwing batting practice. On Thursday the 18th, the Red Sox divided into two teams, The "Regulars" vs. the "Yannigans" for a six-inning scrimmage. Babe hurled the final three innings for the Regulars.

The 20-year-old Ruth was showing his youthful enthusiasm as an item from the *Boston Sunday Post* would indicate:

"Babe Ruth proved a regular glutton for work today (3/20). He was the first to get away from the hotel this morning and was serving up slow benders to the grounds-keeper when the rest of the squad arrived. He was the first pitcher to take his turn in the box and when relieved went at once to knocking out fungoes to the outfielders."

Imagine the memory of that groundskeeper being pitched to by a young Babe Ruth, and how it must have become more cherished as the years went by.

Red Sox owner Joe Lannin seemed to enjoy getting into the act with the players also, as *The Sporting Life* of March 27 noted:

> "Not finding golf strenuous enough, President Lannin of the Red Sox has joined his men in baseball practice at Hot Springs. He particularly likes to catch Babe Ruth when the youngster warms up."

The final week of March was spent by the Red Sox primarily scrimmaging amongst themselves when the weather allowed. Ruth's participation in a "Sox vs. Yannigans" matchup on Tuesday, March 23 proved noteworthy. Hurling for the Yannigans, he was very effective in the first three innings, and even hit a home run in the third that was the longest seen at Majestic Park that spring. In the fifth inning, he completely went to pieces allowing seven runs, and was subsequently relieved in that inning. Showing his competitive fire, Ruth was reportedly anxious to get revenge, and did so, pitching well four days later in a Yannigans-Sox rematch.

At the time it was reported that Ruth would likely be sticking with the Sox come the regular season, and indeed, his minor league days were behind him. He was developing nicely under the watchful eye of Carrigan, whom Babe looked upon as somewhat of a father figure. In his repertoire of pitches, Ruth had a good fastball and curve; the ability to change speeds; and he also displayed good control. Also important was that he seemed to have the instincts to know what to use and when.

Camp at Hot Springs was scheduled to break up on April 2 with the Red Sox traveling north to engage in a series of exhibitions. The final few days saw several noteworthy incidents, including star rightfielder Hooper's belated arrival on March 28. The 30th saw a thin blanket of snow covering the ground at Hot Springs as the area continued to experience a harsh, wet spring. The team's final full practice occurred April 1 with one last Regulars-Yannigans contest. This time, Ruth pitched for the Regulars, working the final four innings, allowing but one run.

Ruth's first big league camp was, one could surmise, a positive and enjoyable experience. Aside from winning a spot on a major league pitching staff, he had the opportunity to engage in activities he rarely, if ever, did before. Among those were mountain hikes, horseback riding, golf and fishing. One can imagine the comical sight of city boy Babe on horseback, showing far less aptitude with the reins than with a bat, ball, and glove.

&

The team departed Hot Springs on Friday, April 2, arriving in Memphis six hours later. They began a three-game series the following day against the Memphis Turtles of the Southern Association. Ruth did not appear in the first two exhibition games against the minor league team, which Boston won easily 7-2 and 10-2. In the final game on April 5, Ruth relieved Rube Foster and worked the final five innings as they again topped the Turtles, 10-5. Ruth's performance prompted the *Boston Post* to comment, "Babe showed that he is rapidly improving under Bill's coaching".

From Memphis the Red Sox journeyed to Louisville, Kentucky for a three-game set versus the local American Association team, however Babe was not used in any of those games. It was on the trek through Memphis and Louisville that Carrigan discovered Ruth's fondness for nightlife and good times. Babe had been teaming up with fellow lefty Dutch Leonard in nocturnal hijinks, and Bill had seen just about enough. Several Boston papers of 4/7/15 reported that Carrigan bawled out a "young pitcher with great promise" about transgressing training regulations. In Joe Cashman's 1943 *Boston Daily Record* series with the manager, Carrigan recalled:

> "He (Ruth) had to be taught right away that I was the boss and that he must obey orders. Otherwise he might ruin himself in a hurry and he certainly ruin the morals of my ballclub".

Carrigan's solution to curb the activities of his wayward lefties was to rent an adjoining suite when the team was on the road. He and coach Heinie Wagner would occupy one room, with Ruth and Leonard in the other. This enabled the pair to be monitored much more closely, and ensured that curfew would not be broken. Carrigan recalled the experience of living with the two for Cashman:

> "It was a pretty hectic experience. Leonard, much more worldly-wise than the Babe at the time, delighted in arguing. He couldn't draw Wagner or me into his discussion, but Babe would often fall

into the trap. Then the fun would begin. Many a time Heinie and I had to hold them apart to keep them from springing at each other's throat. And Babe was forever trying to think up schemes to get away from us . . . it was hard to get mad at him, no matter what he did, he was such a goodnatured guy. But I never let him get away with a thing".

Carrigan employed another tactic that greatly inhibited Babe's ability to run around. He arranged for Ruth to be paid only a portion of his salary, handing over the balance at the end of the 1915 season. Said Bill "Babe's conduct, under the restrictions we imposed on him, improved steadily".

$\approx$

The team traveled on to Cincinnati for three games against the Reds, their first major league competition of the spring. In the second game on April 10, Ruth started and pitched all seven innings, with the game called after the Red Sox batted in the eighth. Though the Reds prevailed 3-1, Babe pitched reasonably well, striking out three and walking three. In a *Boston Post* article dated April 10th entitled "Red Sox Rule as Favorites", Paul H. Shannon wrote:

"(Ruth) possesses a wonderful arm and a world of stuff, strength galore, and an overwhelming eagerness to be in the game. The Red Sox have a splendid prospect, but one who lacks a knowledge of real "inside baseball". Manager Carrigan is confident that he can teach him, and if so he will be a great acquisition to the corps".

After beating the Reds 2-0 in their final meeting on April 11, the Red Sox went on to Richmond, Virginia to play Jack Dunn's newly relocated ex-Orioles. They arrived at 6 p.m. on the 12th, exhausted from a road trip that inexplicably lasted 24 hours. Ruth had the opportunity to meet with his old mentor Dunn, but he did not see action in Boston's final exhibition of the spring, which they won 5-0.

The Red Sox were set to open their 1915 season on Wednesday, April 14 in Philadelphia, the city in which it would reach its ultimate conclusion almost exactly six months later. The starting pitching rotation appeared to be set with Shore, Foster, Ruth, Collins, and Mays. Shore, Babe's former Oriole teammate had roomed with him during the spring of '15, but apparently requested out of the pairing. The reasons have never been determined conclusively, but some sources suggest that Shore objected to Ruth using his toothbrush. Others point to Babe's crude habit of failing to flush the toilet. Regardless of his exact reasoning, Shore clearly lived in a different world than Ruth. He had taken post-graduate courses at Guilford College in North Carolina over the winter, and also taught at a local school. Such a lifestyle was likely somewhat foreign to the 20-year-old Babe. Still, the two will be forever linked, having come to the Red Sox together, and also for Ruth's role in Shore's most unusual perfect game in 1917.

Shore started the '15 opener against the defending A.L. champion Athletics at Shibe Park, as Philadelphia countered with young lefty Herb Pennock. The future Hall-of-Famer pitched like one, not giving up a hit until Hooper singled with two out in the ninth inning. He settled for the one-hitter and Shore took the complete game loss. Less than six weeks later, Pennock would be a member of the Red Sox.

The following day, Boston notched their first victory of the '15 campaign as they beat the A's 5-3. Ray Collins started and was relieved by Carl Mays, who earned the win when two runs scored in the ninth. Though Ruth was considered to be one with great promise, veteran Boston sportswriter Tim Murnane expressed the opinion that Mays was the young pitcher to watch. It is worth remembering that he was the ace of the staff of Providence's championship team of 1914 with an impressive 25 victories.

Ruth's chance to start came on Friday, April 16, in the last game of the Philadelphia series. He was cruising along until the fifth inning, having struck out six and allowing only one run, but suddenly couldn't find the plate. After giving up a leadoff single he walked four straight batters that inning. Carrigan failed to start warming up another pitcher until a run was walked in, prompting the Boston press to engage in the time-honored tradition of second-guessing the manager. Ruth was finally relieved by Ralph Comstock with no outs in the fifth, and Mays came on in the ninth. The game, however, was called at the end of the ninth with the score tied 6-6. In his four official innings pitched, Ruth flashed a little leather, recording three fielding assists; at bat he came up twice, his only hit a leadoff double in the fifth, and scored a run.

From Philadelphia it was on to Washington for a four-game series against the Senators. Ruth did not appear in the series, of which games one and three were won by Boston. The Washington baseball press noted that the Red Sox were picked by most critics as the likeliest team to win the pennant.

The 1915 home opener occurred at Fenway Park on Thursday, April 22, against the Athletics as the Ninth Regiment brass band played to celebrate the occasion. With Massachusetts Governor Walsh on hand, Boston Mayor James Michael Curley, one of the city's true political characters, threw out the first ball. Shore was the starting pitcher and was relieved by Comstock, who got the win in the ninth inning of a 7-6 thriller.

Two days later, Ruth saw his first action at home, this time in relief against the A's. In his first of four relief appearances in 1915, he came on for starter Leonard with two out in the fourth and proceeded to throw two wild pitches, letting one run score. He then settled down, and allowed no hits in his three and one-third innings pitched. Babe was pinch hit for by catcher Hick Cady in the bottom of the seventh, relieved by Foster, and the Sox went on to lose 6-3.

Being pinch hit for was something that happened only three times in 1915, and no doubt provided part-time player Cady something of which to boast in years to come. Ruth would more than make up for it however, pinch hitting for Cady three times in '15.

Ruth was being paid at a rate of $3,500 in 1915, which was slightly lower than the major league average. Now back in the city together, Babe and his young bride rented an apartment in nearby Cambridge, home of Harvard University. It was the first time the two were living alone together, without a close family member under the same roof. Less than 14 months removed from St. Mary's, Babe must have thought the old "home" seemed very far away.

Ꝫ

On April 26, Ruth got his first start of the season at Fenway Park, pitching against Philadelphia yet again. He looked sharp, pitching all seven innings of a 9-2 victory that was stopped due to rain. The *Boston Post* reported "Ruth had very good control and as a general rule he worried the batters to the limit" . . . "in the one session where things threatened to break very badly for him, he kept his head about him and got out of the hole with very little damage." In the third inning Ruth lead off at bat with a walk, and then scored on Wagner's single.

	IP	H	SO	BB	R
4/26/15 vs.					
Philadelphia	7	5	3	2	2

At bat: 0 for 1, 1 run scored

The following day, the 27th, the Yankees arrived in town for a series against the Red Sox, led by Babe's old pal, new manager Bill Donovan. On the 29th, in the second game of the series, Ruth pinch hit for Wagner with two out in the seventh inning. He smacked a double, scoring Hooper from first, and was then pinch run for by Mike McNally. Interestingly enough, Ruth would be called on to pinch hit a total of ten times in the 1915 regular season, yet the first time, for Wagner, would be the only successful attempt.

On Friday evening, April 30, the entire Red Sox team took a caravan of automobiles out to the neighboring town of Rockland, 20 miles southeast of Boston. They attended a minstrel show at the Rockland Opera House sponsored by the local council of the Knights of Columbus. Ruth, accompanied by Helen, and his teammates also watched moving pictures of the Sox taken during spring training by official team photographer George Murray.

After a brief two-game stint against the Senators at Fenway, the Sox trekked to New York for four games at the Polo Grounds. Game one on May 6 would be a bittersweet day for the young Baltimorean, but one that would take its place in Ruthian history. He would hurl 13 innings, allowing only two runs, yet watch four Boston errors contribute to a heartbreaking complete game 4-3 loss. It was his performance with the bat, however, that made the contest particularly noteworthy. It was leading off the third inning against Yankee pitcher Jack Warhop that Babe connected for home run number one of 714, ironically in a park he would later call home, and add many more to that total. The blast, the *Post* reported "went so far into the stands that the ushers never made any attempt to recover it".

	IP	H	SO	BB	R	ER
5/6/15 at						
New York	13	10	3	3	4	2

At bat: 3 for 5, 1 home run, 2 singles, 1 run scored

The final game of the series saw New York pummel the Red Sox 10-3, with the Yankees sending 16 batters to the plate in the fourth, scoring all ten of their runs. For a team that was thought to be the A.L. favorite, Boston was very slow out of the gate with a record of eight wins and eight losses. After the series in New York, it was on to Detroit for a tour of the A.L.'s "western" cities that would also include stops in Cleveland, Chicago, and St. Louis.

Ruth drew the starting assignment in a game against the Tigers on May 11, and had an abysmal outing. In just 5 2/3 innings, he surrendered nine hits, issued eight walks, and racked up only one strikeout. He was in some degree of trouble each inning, and when he walked three straight in the sixth, Carrigan had seen enough. Ruth was relieved by Mays, but was the pitcher of record in the 5-1 defeat. Boston fared better in the final three games of the series as complete game wins were recorded by Shore, Leonard, and Foster, boosting the team's record to 12-9.

Ruth at bat 5/11/15 at Detroit: 1 for 2, 1 double

At this time, it was reported in the Boston papers that certain Red Sox players were not putting forth their best effort. Speaker and Wood were criticized, and Carrigan, feuding with unnamed star players also suspended Leonard for failure to stay in top shape. The team seemed to feature two distinct off-the-field cliques around this period. One was headed by the Speaker-Wood duo; the other included Carrigan, Wagner, and Hooper. Wisely, Ruth tended to associate more with the latter.

In Cleveland on May 16, the Red Sox came to bat in the fourteenth inning of a 0-0 tie. Ruth was sent to pinch hit for Cady, and though he didn't reach base, Mays, Hooper, and Wagner would, all scoring for a 3-0 Boston win. In the final game of the series with the Indians on Wednesday the 19th, Ruth was sent in to relieve Foster with two out in the bottom of the fifth. He remained in the game until Carrigan had Del Gainer pinch hit for him in the top of the ninth. Cleveland prevailed 5-2 as the starter Foster took the loss, and the Red Sox began a five-game losing streak.

	IP	H	SO	BB
5/19/15 at Cleveland	3 1/3	1	3	1

At bat: 0 for 1

In an interesting side note, "Shoeless" Joe Jackson, playing in his eighth major league season, made his first-ever appearance as a first baseman this game.

In the next series in Chicago, Ruth saw action in two of the three games. The first, on May 21, was a 17-inning contest won by Chicago 3-2, as future Hall of Famer Red Faber won his seventh straight game. Ruth pinch hit for starter Shore in the eighth, striking out, and Mays relieved the rest of the game and took the loss.

The following day, Ruth started and had his worst, and shortest start to that point. In the first inning, he gave up three hits, three walks, four earned runs, tossed a wild pitch, and even chipped in with an error. Paul H. Shannon of the *Post* was scathing in his account of the game:

> "…the boneheadedness of Babe alone added to his fearful wildness practically threw the game away. He started badly by walking the first man up, then Roth hit an easy grounder to him; the Red Sox had a double play made to order in front of them, but Ruth threw the ball to center field and instead of having two down with the bases cleared, there were runners on first and third with no one down."

He came to bat in the top of the second and was struck out by Joe Benz on three pitches. Back on the mound in the bottom of the second, Babe gave up two quick singles, and was yanked in favor of Collins, who pitched the rest of the game as Boston lost 11-3. In the coming days, the Sox were read the riot act by both Lannin and Carrigan, furious over the team's poor play. While the Red Sox were suffering on the road, the Braves were celebrating back in Boston, as they raised their World Championship banner at Fenway Park on May 28.

As the seemingly endless road trip moved on to Philadelphia, Ruth had the chance to redeem himself in the first game of the doubleheader at Shibe Park on May 29. Redeem himself he did, however, the result was a heartbreaking 2-1 complete game loss. Ruth allowed one lone hit in the first eight innings, but suffered a letdown. With two runners in scoring position and two outs in the bottom of the ninth, pinch hitter Harry Davis singled, driving in both runs. Boston continued to flounder, and though their fortunes were about to turn, the team's record stood at 14-15.

	IP	H	SO	BB	ER
5/29/15 at Philadelphia	8 2/3	3	6	4	2

At bat: 0 for 3

While in Philadelphia, the Red Sox made an acquisition that would turn out to be quite a coup. The Athletics had placed young lefty Herb Pennock on waivers, and the Sox, who had been shut out by him on opening day, picked him up for $1,500. A's manager Connie Mack stated at the time that although Pennock may still be a great pitcher, he didn't think he would ever be of any use to the team again, as several men will be reporting to him soon that will more than make up for his departure. The former A.L. champs in four of the five previous seasons were, at the time of the transaction, nestled in last place with a record of 13-24. Philadelphia would go on to finish last in the league every year from 1915 through 1922, leading one to conclude that replacements for Pennock, who went on to win 240 games, were never forthcoming.

Connie Mack deserves credit for numerous shrewd personnel moves in his illustrious managerial career. Placing Herb Pennock on waivers was not among them.

The last stop on Boston's marathon 29-day road trip brought them back to where it began, New York's Polo Grounds. Ruth started the second game of the series, Wednesday, June 2, and looked as sharp as he had all season. In the complete game 7-1 victory, he allowed only five hits, and one walk while striking out four. He also connected for career homer number two, interestingly enough, off Jack Warhop, the same pitcher who surrendered his first, nearly a month earlier. The long drive came in the second inning with two men out and a runner on first while the score was knotted at 1-1.

"The home run hit he crashed today was a record breaker for distance, as it carried away the top of a chair in the Section One of the pavilions, and when the ball was last seen, it was headed for the North River." *Boston Post* 6-3-15

Yankee manager Donovan was well aware of the young pitcher's slugging capabilities and subsequently ordered him intentionally walked twice that day. An unfortunate incident occurred late in the game however, that caused Ruth to miss at least two starts, when in a fit of anger he kicked the bench, breaking a toe.

6/2/15 at NY, Ruth at bat: 1 for 3, home run,
2 intentional walks

While Babe was out of action for two weeks nursing the broken toe, the Red Sox were continuing their improved play, going 7-3 in that span. His next appearance occurred on "Bunker Hill Day", June 17 at home against the Browns. The *Post* reported the next day; "For six innings yesterday the Browns were literally forced to eat out of the generous-sized hand of Big Babe Ruth". Ruth had held St. Louis to four scattered hits, one run, and had struck out ten, when in the eighth he experienced a meltdown. After giving up four hits, two walks, and retiring just one batter he was pulled and Mays was brought in. Boston came out on top of the 11-10 slugfest and Ruth got credit for the win as the Red Sox were now tied with the Tigers for second place.

	IP	H	SO	BB
6/17/15 vs.				
St. Louis	7 1/3	8	7	4

At bat: 1 for 4, double off scoreboard, 1 run scored

In the series finale on June 19, Ruth was called on to pinch hit for catcher Chet Thomas, and the contest was halted after nine innings with the score tied 5-5.

The Red Sox arrived in the nation's capital on June 21 for a quick road trip, a five-game series with the Senators, and would head directly back to Boston. Ruth got the nod in game one of the series, the first of a twin bill, and scored a complete game 8-3 win. It was the only action he would see on the field that series. As for off the field, one can only speculate.

	IP	H	SO	BB	R	ER
6/21/15 at						
Washington	9	6	7	4	3	2

At bat: 1 for 4, double, run scored

Back in Boston on Friday, June 25, the Yankees were in for a rare six-game series, and game one would be eventful for Ruth both as a pitcher and hitter. He hurled yet another complete game as the

Sox prevailed by a margin of 9-5. When Ruth came to face Yankee pitcher Ray Caldwell, he smacked a tremendous home run, his third of the year, all of which had come against New York. As it was leaving the yard, the blast sailed over the head of Babe's ex-Oriole teammate Birdie Cree, now a Yankee outfielder. Later in the game he singled off his former manager Bill Donovan, who would insert himself into nine games during the 1915 season.

	IP	H	SO	BB	R
6/25/15 vs.					
NY	9	11	8	4	5

At bat: 2 for 3, home run, single, 2 runs

In a column dated June 26 in *The Sporting Life*, Boston writer A.H.C. Mitchell wrote:

"The feature of this particular game [6/25] was a home run drive into the rightfield seats by pitcher George Ruth. With the exception of Frank Shulte, who put the ball in the same place about a month ago, Ruth is the only player to accomplish the feat since Fenway was opened in 1912 ... he is one of the hardest wallopers in the big leagues. He takes a regular haymaker swing at the ball using a heavy bat which he grasps close to the handle as he can possibly can. Ruth is improving in his pitching, but there is a feeling of anxiety toward the last of the games he pitches. He is apt to lose the plate as the games wear on, and in order to find it he loses his stuff, the result being that the opponents pickle the ball. However he is improving all the time. He is a big strong youth, and being able to wallop the ball the way he does makes him a valuable man to have on the Red Sox roster".

In a feature in the *Boston Post* entitled "Talking it over in the dugout at Fenway Park", Ruth's knack for hitting homers versus the Yankees was discussed:

"Donovan had warned his pitchers to 'keep the ball wide' and therefore play it safe, but the desire to 'sneak one across' and then 'curve ball him to death' led the New York pitcher to take daring and fatal chances. When in doubt hereafter, our Babe will always be walked."

The Red Sox closed the series against New York on June 29 the way they began it—with a complete game win from Ruth. The ten-inning affair, which saw Babe pinch hit for by Gainer in the bottom of the tenth featured five singles by Tris Speaker in five at-bats. Red Sox 4, New York 3.

	IP	H	SO	BB	R
6/29/15 vs. NY	10	8	4	4	3

At bat: 0 for 3

Connie Mack brought his woeful Athletics into town for a series beginning June 30, and before it was over, the Red Sox would acquire another valuable member of his team. On July 2, Boston purchased long-time A's shortstop Jack Barry, a vital cog Mack's so-called $100,000 infield. As Mack continued to dismantle his once mighty team, Joe Lannin reportedly paid him $8,000 for Barry, and was to assume his salary of $5,000 per year. Nearly a decade before, the Holy Cross alum had been a teammate of Carrigan, who planned on using Barry at second base. The *Post* of July 3 wrote that, "A warm personal friendship between Carrigan and Barry dating back to their college days insures the new Red Stocking a welcome reception . . ." In the coming years, Ruth would also form a close friendship with the new infielder that would extend well beyond the playing field.

On the 3rd of July the two teams engaged in a Saturday double-header, and Ruth fruitlessly pinch hit for Leonard in the ninth inning of a 7-3 loss. In the second game the Sox trounced the A's 11-0 as Barry made his first appearance in a Boston uniform, playing the final two innings at second base. Sunday, the fourth of July found the Red Sox with a day off due to the ban on Sunday baseball that still existed in many major league cities. Sox third baseman Larry Gardner would say years later that he and his teammates from this period would often go to nearby Revere Beach on their Sundays off at home.

The following day, Washington was in town for a grueling three doubleheaders in three days. The only playing time Ruth saw was in the second game of the first day, but he would certainly do his part against the Senators. Babe extended his personal winning streak to six games, pitching a five-hit, 6-0 shutout and scoring two of the runs himself. With his lone hit in his two official at-bats he reached another milestone—his first major league triple. Ruth also made a great defensive play in the third inning on a rain soaked field when speedy Clyde Milan hit a hard grounder back to the box. Babe stabbed it, and after slipping in the mud, threw out Eddie Foster at the plate. Boston went on to sweep all three doubleheaders, and thus found themselves on July 7 just two percentage points behind first-place Chicago.

On that same day, an incident occurred in Cleveland involving "Shoeless" Joe Jackson that bears re-telling. Ruth was said to have modeled his swing after Jackson's, and given Babe's reputation as a careless, even reckless driver, one might wonder if his vehicular prowess was inspired by Jackson as well.

While driving along with his wife, Joe thought something was wrong with the car's engine. He then allowed Mrs. Jackson to take over the driving while he climbed out on the running board, and with the car still in motion he lifted the hood to investigate. At this time a truck belonging to the Glenville Lumber Company came along from the other direction, knocking him off. He was taken to a local hospital and treated for his injuries, and would miss three weeks' worth of action. The Glenville Lumber Company filed suit in Common Pleas Court in Cleveland weeks later to recover $27.15 in damages.

Jackson's level of intelligence has long been in question, and incidents such as this certainly do not help his case.

ða

On the eve of the one-year anniversary of Ruth's purchase from Baltimore, July 8, the team left from Back Bay Station for a two-and-a-half week road trip. Amid a large crowd of fans on hand to give them a royal sendoff, the Sox set out for a tour of the A.L.'s four western cities. Ruth started the first game of the trip in Detroit on July 9 and it proved to be his shortest outing of the season. The *Post* reported "Ruth was bad enough but his support was even worse". His two hits allowed and two walks issued, along with shoddy defense led to four runs, and Ruth was yanked by Carrigan after just one third of an inning. The Tigers went on to embarrass Boston 15-4.

His next start came in Cleveland on the 13th in the first game of a Tuesday doubleheader. This was more like the Ruth who went

5-0 in June as he scored a complete game 7-3 win over the Indians. He pitched a beautiful game, and was deprived of a shutout due to an infield error and questionable umpiring in the third inning. The win propelled the Red Sox into first place temporarily, and Ruth reportedly asked Carrigan if he could pitch the second game of the twin bill as well. Carrigan nixed the idea, but may have wished he hadn't as Boston dropped the contest 6-5.

	IP	H	BB	R
7/13/15 at				
Cleveland	9	8	0	3

At bat: 0 for 3, 1 run

Babe had one more crack at the Indians, starting the final game of the series on July 16, but inclement weather may have robbed him of a potential victory. The *Post* reported:

> "Ruth, who was pitching for Boston, had the Indians at his mercy. He was so effective that the Cleveland team was glad when the weatherman intervened ... the locals failed to get anything that remotely resembled a hit".

Boston had the bases loaded with none out in the top of the fourth inning when the rain came, negating Ruth's dominating performance. The Red Sox then moved on to Chicago on July 17 for an all-important five-game series against the first-place White Sox. The teams split a doubleheader the first day, but the next day, July 18, Boston's 6-2 victory would leapfrog them into first place. The Red Sox also took the final two games of the series, a series in which Ruth would not make an appearance. He may well have been conserving his energy, because getting the start in the first game of the St. Louis series on July 21 he let loose with a tremendous display. The fact he hurled 8 1/3 innings and capped a 4-2 win is only part of the story. His four hits on the day included a monumental home run that the locals hailed as the longest ever seen at Sportsman's Park. The blast carried over the rightfield roof, across a street and through a car dealer's window. After the game, Babe proudly posed for pictures in front of the shattered window.

The two runs that he allowed the Browns were primarily due to two Heinie Wagner errors, and when Carrigan lifted Ruth with one out in the ninth, St. Louis fans gave him an ovation rarely given to a visiting player. He was only 20 years old, but the Ruthian legend was already taking seed.

	IP	H	SO	BB	R
7/21/15 at					
St. Louis	8 1/3	5	3	2	2

At bat: 4 for 4, 1 hr, 2 doubles, 1 single, 3 RBI

The final day of this western swing was July 25, and Ruth was to start the first game of the Sunday doubleheader against the Browns. It was a short outing though, with him being pulled by Carrigan with one out in the third inning. The *Post* reported:

> "Ruth started and looked like another Walter Johnson for two innings, and when placed in a hole through his own wildness, his end was hastened through a bad slip-up by Scott, which handed the Browns four unearned runs".

Ruth retired the first batter in the bottom of the third, then walked the next two. Shortstop Scott then committed the crucial error on a double play ball which loaded the bases. This was followed by a double that scored two, and a single that scored two more, and Mays, who then came on in relief was the eventual loser of the 9-8 game.

	IP	H	SO	BB
7/25/15 at				
St. Louis	2 1/3	4	1	2

At bat: 1 for 1, single run scored

It was reported in the July 31 issue of *The Sporting Life* that the outlaw Federal League was planning an aggressive attempt to lure major league stars such as Speaker, Ty Cobb, Grover Cleveland Alexander, and Eddie Collins among the more prominent names. Ruth was also mentioned as a possible target, and Federal League team owners reportedly set aside a million dollar fund to carry out the raids. League President James Gilmore stated "We are ready to grab all the stars in sight". In an ominous sign for the Feds however, it was revealed that the Kansas City franchise was the only one not losing money. The owners met again a week later in Atlantic City and reiterated their intentions to sign the big stars. They also let it be known that the Federal League champions would be challenging Organized Baseball's World Series winner to a playoff.

Back home in early August, the Red Sox suffered rainouts three consecutive days against Cleveland on the 4th, 5th and 6th. It was on the 4th that Chicago had dumped a doubleheader to Washington, dropping the White Sox into third place, now behind Boston and Detroit. Ruth had last appeared in a game on July 25 in St. Louis, and was not to be used again as either a pitcher or pinch hitter until August 10 against the Browns.

The Red Sox were in the midst of another span of three doubleheaders in three days, and Ruth started the second game of the second day, Saturday the 10th. He was very effective in the 10-3 win, allowing only seven hits, striking out seven, and walking none in his tenth victory of the year. With the bat he went 2 for 4, stroking a double and scoring a run. The *Post* wrote:

> " . . . Babe Ruth, the hardest hitting pitcher in captivity made monkeys out of the Browns aggregation . . . Babe himself had been a big factor in the scoring with one of his lengthy drives to right for extra bases and a timely hit later on".

In his *Boston Post* article entitled "Arthur Duffey's Comments n Sports", Duffey wrote that "although Boston fans are happy to have him as a pitcher, it is his 'willow wielding' that endears him to fans".

Ruth was clearly attracting attention throughout the league for his offensive capabilities. In a *Sporting Life* column dated August 7, Senators beat writer Paul W. Eaton wrote:

> "Ruth appears to be one of the best natural sluggers ever in the game, and might even be more valuable in some regular position than he is on the slab—a free suggestion for Manager Carrigan".

A week later, Eaton repeated this sentiment adding:

> " . . . Ruth would be a valuable asset if he could be fitted in somewhere as a regular. This pitcher is the most natural batsman who has broken into the game since Ty Cobb."

These items may well have been the first occasions of such suggestions regarding Ruth's transformation to a position player appearing in a national publication. As unique as this situation seems, there were actually two other American League rookies that season of whom this same question was being raised. George Sisler of the Browns and Sam Rice of the Senators both began their major league careers as pitchers in 1915. In both cases, their transition to position players due to their offensive prowess—Sisler to first base and Rice to rightfield would be complete the following year. Like Ruth, both would make it to the Cooperstown based primarily on their batting achievements.

Ruth's next start found him matched up against Washington's fireballing righthander Walter Johnson at Fenway on Saturday, August 14. The headline on the *Post*'s sportspage the next day boasted:

"Johnson fails to stop Hustling Red Sox"
"Washington star outpitched by Babe Ruth in 4-3 contest".

Brimming with confidence, Babe pleaded with Carrigan to allow him to take the hill. He then went out and proceeded to back up his bravado, and the *Post* reported that "nearly 16,000 witnessed the triumph of Babe Ruth over his mighty adversary". It was a great day for Ruth, who fully deserved a shutout, but highly questionable decisions by Umpire Bobby Wallace practically handed the Senators their three runs. Ruth was involved in the Sox rally in the eighth that put them over, singling to right and advancing Henricksen to third. He also had an impressive at bat in the fifth with the Sox trailing 3-1. With two outs and two strikes on him, Ruth sent a screaming single to center scoring Gardner from second. With a lofty .370 batting average, Babe was now ranked second in the A.L. behind only Cobb.

	IP	H	SO	BB	R
8/14/15 vs. Washington	9	5	5	2	3

At bat: 2 for 3, 2 singles, 1 run

The feature in the *Boston Post* entitled "Talking it over in the dugout at Fenway Park" on August 15 touched on Babe's batting prowess and philosophy:

> "Babe Ruth has the laudable ambition to be one of the leading southpaws, but he likewise cherishes the hope that he may some-day be the leading slugger of the country. He has put the ball in the rightfield bleachers at Fenway park and now his aim is to bust one into the centerfield seats. He has done this three times in morning batting practice. Babe has not much regard for single base hits, and oftentimes after driving out a two-base clout he comes back to the bench with a downhearted admission that he 'didn't get a good hold on it'. Yet he has made a national reputa-tion as a slugger all right, and it is really laughable to see the backward parade of the three rival outfielders whenever the Babe steps up to bat".

ð

Two days after Ruth bested Johnson, Smoky Joe Woods' 1-0 complete game win over the Senators insured the Red Sox sweep of Washington in it's eleven games at Boston in 1915.

August 18 brought a significant event in Boston baseball his-tory as the newly completed Braves Field opened for business. Hosting the St. Louis Cardinals, the Braves had already abandoned the South End Grounds and now would no longer need to borrow Fenway Park. Their new state-of-the-art ballpark billed as the world's largest had an unprecedented seating capacity of 42,000 plus. Lo-cated approximately one mile from Fenway, Braves Field would be significant in the career of Babe Ruth for several reasons. The park would be the home site of his first World Series, and it was also the last park he would call home 20 years later during his 1935 swansong with the Braves. The stadium, though drastically modi-fied, still exists to this day as Boston University's Nickerson Field.

ð

In the Red Sox 2-1 loss to host Chicago on August 19, Ruth came in to pinch hit for starter Foster in the top of the seventh, popping up to first baseman Jimmy Collins. He then pitched the game's final two innings, allowing just one hit, one walk, and no runs, and Foster was tagged with the defeat. In his only other at-bat

Ruth ended the game by grounding out to pitcher Red Faber. The Tigers, having beat the hapless Athletics that day were now just two one-thousandths of a point behind the first place Red Sox.

In a major transaction in the American League on August 20, the third-place White Sox purchased Joe Jackson from the Indians in exchange for Bobby "Braggo" Roth, Ed Klepfer, a player to be named later, and $31,500. Roth would end up the A.L.'s leading home run hitter for '15 with a truly "dead ball era" total of seven. New York beat writer Harry Dix Cole questioned why the Yankees did not make a serious bid to purchase Jackson, who was now in place to meet his date with destiny four years later.

On to St. Louis, Ruth was given the starting assignment against the Browns on August 21. He again dominated St. Louis as he had a week and a half earlier, completing a 4-1 win.

	IP	H	SO	BB	R
8/21/15 at					
St. Louis	9	9	6	1	1

At bat: 0 for 3, 1 sacrifice

The first game of the Tiger series in Detroit on Tuesday August 24 featured an interesting incident involving the irascible, high-strung Ty Cobb. *The Sporting Life* reported:

> "After Cobb was thrown out in the 8th he attempted to explore the Boston dugout. A dozen players quickly surrounded him and he was forced to return to his own bench".

Ruth started the second game of the series the following day, and though he pitched well enough to win, he came away with no decision. He was relieved by Leonard with two outs in the ninth as the score was tied 1-1. In the top of the thirteenth inning, Sox shortstop Everett Scott drove in the go ahead run with a double. The Tigers threatened in the bottom of the inning, but defensive wizard Speaker helped save the day in centerfield;

> "with two out in the bottom half of the 13th, Cobb doubled to left, but Speaker raced nearly into the next county to haul down [Sam] Crawford's drive". *The Sporting Life* 9/4/15

Boston had just won its seventh straight game, and were now a remarkable 19 and 2 in their previous 21 games.

	IP	H	SO	BB	R
8/25/15 at Detroit	8 2/3	5	5	0	1

At bat: 0 for 2

The final game of the series on the 26th also went extra innings, this time with Detroit winning 7-6 in twelve. Boston pulled out of Detroit with a 4 1/2 game lead over the Tigers.

Just three days later, now having moved on to Cleveland, Ruth took the hill in the first game of a doubleheader. He was driven from the mound with one out in the seventh, relieved by Mays, but was credited with the 5-3 victory.

	IP	H	SO	BB
8/28/15 at Cleveland	6 1/3	6	5	4

At bat: 1 for 3, single, run scored

At the conclusion of the Cleveland series, Boston traveled to Toledo to engage in an exhibition against the city's American Association squad. The minor league team did not offer much competition, falling to the Sox 6-1. Ruth was not called upon in the contest.

The final step on the nearly three-week road trip brought the Red Sox into Philadelphia. When they arrived in the city, Ruth, along with teammates Hoblitzell, Foster, Thomas, and Shore went directly to the Baker Bowl to watch their potential World Series opponents, the Phillies, in action. The Phils were engaged in a doubleheader, and though Ruth and company arrived in time to see only part of the second game, they were reportedly none too impressed.

The next day before the Sox- A's opener, Jack Barry, playing his first game in the city against his former team was presented a silver service by the fans in a pre-game ceremony. Having smoothly made the transition from shortstop to second, there were many at this time that thought he was now the best defensive second baseman in the league.

Ruth's turn to start came on September 2 in game two of the four-game set, and he went the distance for an 8-3 win. The *Post* reported that "Babe Ruth wasn't quite himself this afternoon and his speed slants not quite as pronounced as when he last went against the Detroits". Five Athletics were strikeout victims, while he issued only one free pass. Ruth went hitless in three official at-bats, but was credited with a sacrifice.

Boston's sixth consecutive win came the next day in Shore's 10-2 win over Philadelphia. Though again unsuccessful, Ruth was sent in to pinch hit for Cady in the fourth inning, striking out. Boston completed the four-game sweep over Connie Mack's fallen champions on September 4 behind the fine pitching of Dutch Leonard. *The Sporting Life*'s "Pointed Paragraphs" observed that the 1915 World Series could be like 1914, a Boston—Philadelphia matchup—only with the leagues reversed. The Phillies, behind the phenomenal pitching of Grover Cleveland Alexander were now the odds-on favorite to capture the N.L. flag.

The Red Sox returned from their road trip to begin a homestand that would take them through the duration of September. The Yankees came into Fenway to begin a three-game series, and the first day, September 6, drew up to that point a season-high 27,000 fans. That day, Ruth started the second game of the doubleheader and took a no-hitter into the seventh inning. He was then touched for three hits and was relieved by Leonard, and New York went on to win 5-2, sweeping the doubleheader. Detroit had swept a doubleheader from St. Louis the day before and were right on the Red Sox heels, just percentage points behind in second place.

9/6/15 vs. New York
At bat: 2 for 3, 1 double and 1 single

The Athletics came into town, seemingly not a moment too soon, and although they did beat Shore in a 1-0 heartbreaker the first day, Boston took the remaining three games. In that first game, September 8, skipper Carrigan sent Ruth in to pinch hit for him in the ninth inning but watched him strikeout to end the game. At this time, Babe was ranked third in the American League in batting. Rightfielder Hooper was also making big offensive contributions to the Red Sox cause, as A. H. C. Mitchell wrote "... Hooper has been batting in sensational style for several weeks".

Ruth got the start in the final game of the Athletics series, Friday the 10th, and while Ernie Shore's one hitter the day before was a tough act to follow, Babe performed admirably. He went the distance, allowing Mack's men just five hits as the 7-2 victory was his fifteenth of the year. Defense was a standout feature as the *Post* wrote "Scott, Barry, Hoblitzell, and Gardner formed a stonewall defense in the infield, while Babe Ruth covered his own position like an extra infielder" . . . "Speaker had a grand day in the outfield, making a series of startling catches [7 putouts]".

	IP	H	SO	BB
9/10/15 vs.				
Philadelphia	9	5	6	2

At bat: 0 for 4, 1 run scored

The *Post's* "Arthur Duffey's Comments on Sports" of Sunday, September 12 contained the following item that provides a glimpse into the Ruth persona as well as his legendary ravenous appetite:

"There is one player on the Red Sox team who doesn't need to acquire any 'pep'. This is Babe Ruth, whose eccentricities in the past have kept the manager and half the team stirred up. According to Mrs. Ruth, and she ought to know, the Babe will eat two-and-a-half pounds of rare beefsteak for dinner any day excepting Friday. And at every such meal he consumes, unaided, an entire bottle of chili sauce. This is pepper with a vengeance".

The Chicago White Sox and their new outfielder Joe Jackson were next up for a five-game series beginning September 11. A story published in Chicago a few weeks earlier indicated that the White Sox would have purchased Jack Barry from Philadelphia back in July except that owner Charles Comiskey's mail was delayed due to the fourth of July holiday, and he didn't receive Mack's notice that he was for sale. Comiskey stated that had he known, he would have outbid Lannin. Barry of course, became a key member of the Red Sox not only in 1915, but in the coming years as well.

In any event, Boston dominated Chicago, winning four of the five games, with Ruth's start occurring on September 14. He had what was likely his best game of the season, hurling a two-hitter and extending the team winning streak to seven. The Red Sox themselves only managed three hits, and Ruth accounted for two of them, a double and a single in his three at-bats. In its re-cap, the *Post* wrote:" . . . this home run clouter improves in effectiveness every time that he goes into the box . . . In turning the White Sox back yesterday, Big Babe pulled off the greatest pitching stunt of this hot series.

	IP	H	SO	BB
9/14/15 vs. Chicago	9	2	5	3

In the series finale, in which Boston was one-hit by Chicago's Red Faber, Ruth was called on to pinch hit for Cady in the sixth inning, again going down on strikes.

A crucial four-game series with the second-place Tigers was set to begin at Fenway Park on September 16. Both teams entered the series with 90 wins, but Detroit with 48 losses had four more than Boston. A Tiger sweep would put the two teams dead even in the all-important loss column.

That week, Baltimore beat writer Emanuel Daniel wrote:

"The fans here are evenly divided about the American League race. Many hope to see [Tiger manager and ex-Oriole Hughie] Jennings come out the victor, while a host of fans are pulling for Carrigan's crew, due to the fact Babe Ruth and Ernie Shore, former Orioles, have done such good work for the crimson-hosed crew".

The Red Sox were handled easily by Detroit in game one, falling 6-1, but the contest did feature another noteworthy incident involving Ty Cobb. Carl Mays who had a peculiar submarine style delivery, came on in relief in the sixth inning. In the eighth inning with Cobb at bat, Mays threw two pitches near his head, and the next pitch clipped him on the wrist. Cobb then whirled and threw his bat out to the mound, though it went wide of Mays, and while the benches emptied, nothing came of it. In the next inning, immediately after Cobb caught the final out in centerfield to end the game, fans spilled out of the stands and began to surround him. Boston police came out on the field to his aid and proceeded to escort him off without further incident.

It was not uncommon at that time for loyal Red Sox fans to become actively involved with their beloved team. In a *Sporting Life* column dated September 18, A.H.C. Mitchell commented on how Boston fans were becoming extremely loud in an attempt to rattle opposing teams:

"Royal Rooters are marching 300 strong, toting instruments, often singing 'Tessie' as they did years before, including the 1903 World Series. Clark Griffith had recently remarked 'you can't play ball in Boston with that infernal Tessie ringing in your ears. I was 'Tessieized' out of a pennant in 1905. That song certainly gets the goats of opposing teams".

The following two days the Red Sox were the beneficiaries of superb pitching—a 7-2, three-hitter by Leonard, and a 1-0, 12-inning win by Shore, said at that time to be the greatest game ever seen in the Hub. After a day off on Sunday, Ruth started the final game of the series on Monday, September 20, which was attended by U.S. Vice-President Thomas Marshall. Until he was relieved by Foster with two out in the eighth, he had only surrendered six hits, sent down five on strikes, and came away with a 3-2 win. Babe also hit safely once, a single in three at-bats. The Sox now had a measure of breathing room over Detroit, and the pennant was seemingly theirs to lose.

After the first game of the Cleveland series was rained out on the 21st, the Red Sox swept back to back doubleheaders from the Indians the next two days. The second game of the second doubleheader saw Shore spin a five-hitter, holding old friend Ben Egan hitless in two at-bats. Ruth did little more than observe this series, but started the first game of the St. Louis series at home on Friday, September 24. He did a fair amount of observing this game as well, as he was lifted with no outs in the third inning after giving up six Brown hits. The *Post* reported that ". . . he was banished to the dugout in the third after the Brown's had made it very plain that the Red Sox could not win with the Babe in charge of their destinies". The Sox fell 8-4 and Ruth was tagged with the loss, his final one of the year.

That week, Sox president Lannin announced that he had accepted the offer of Braves owner James Gaffney to use the spanking new Braves Field in the upcoming World Series should the Red Sox capture the pennant. Allowing his friendly rival to take advantage of the higher seating capacity, Gaffney was returning the favor of a year before when his "miracle Braves" borrowed Fenway. With a couple of days off after the Browns series, the A.L. leaders held practices at the Braves new stadium in order to get used to the new field. The players, who found the footing softer and more uneven than Fenway, divided up into two teams and engaged in a five-

-inning game. Ruth was among a group of pitchers who took their turn on the mound.

As the Red Sox were boarding a train for Washington on Thursday, September 30, they heard the news that Detroit had just lost to St. Louis, which officially clinched the pennant for Boston. The Phillies had captured the N.L. flag the day before against the Braves in Boston with several Red Sox players on hand to observe their upcoming foes.

The Red Sox had two series remaining before closing out their regular season, and in a doubleheader against the Senators on October 2, Ruth saw action in both games. In game one with Walter Johnson beating Boston 3-1 on a six-hitter, Ruth pitched the final two innings. Of the nine batters he faced, he struck out two, walked two, and allowed one hit, while he went 0 for 1 in his lone at-bat. The second game saw Ruth make his final pinch hitting appearance of the regular season, batting for starter Shore in the seventh inning. Hitless again, his pinch hitting average for '15 would now stand at .100.

The next day, Detroit beat Cleveland to close out its season, finishing with a record of 100-54, becoming the first team to win 100 games and not win the pennant. That game, Cobb stole his 96th base of the year, a record that would stand for 47 years until Maury Wills surpassed it in 1962.

The Red Sox traveled back up the east coast for a final meaningless five-game series versus the Yankees. On October 6, the next to last day of the season, they engaged in yet another doubleheader, Boston's 28th of the year! In the second game of the afternoon, Ruth dominated the New Yorkers as he seemingly did in each of his games against them that season. He went the entire way for a 4-2 victory, allowing only five hits while striking out six. His own three at-bats yielded one double and one run scored.

Boston dropped its final game of the season to New York 4-3 on October 7, finishing with an impressive 101-50 record. Though the Tigers had threatened to overtake them, the Red Sox never relinquished their hold on first place after capturing the top spot on July 18. It was Boston's remarkable record of 41-13 in August and September that helped them overcome their mediocre beginning.

A review of team statistics for 1915 shows that other than wins, Boston did not lead the league in any significant category, while second-place Detroit led in team batting average, slugging average, runs, doubles and stolen bases.

≈

Ticket prices for the series were to range from a top price of $5 for box seats, down to $1 for bleacher seats, though games at Braves Field would feature a 50 cent bleacher seat. At the Baker Bowl, 400 additional seats were temporarily installed in deep right-centerfield for the series, and the reduced dimensions would be a factor later on.

The Red Sox reigned as favorites by the experts, and *The Sporting Life* wrote "The Boston pitching staff is not to be sneezed at . . . Shore, Ruth, Leonard, and Foster are a mighty quartet of pitchers". Smoky Joe Wood, who had rebounded from early season arm woes to lead the A.L. in ERA, was again experiencing difficulties and would not be available. The Phillies staff was led by the fabulous Grover Cleveland Alexander, who topped N.L. hurlers with an incredible 31 wins, as well as leading in strikeouts, ERA, winning percentage and complete games. Their offense was powered by rightfielder Gavvy Cravath, who led his circuit in home runs, RBI, walks, and runs scored. His 24 home runs were the most hit in a season by a major leaguer in the 20th century to that point, and would remain so until eclipsed by a certain Boston outfielder four years later.

Game one opened with Alexander matched up against Shore before a crowd of 19,343. Both pitchers were particularly sharp, and going into the bottom of the eighth with the score tied at one, Shore was working on a three-hitter. The Phillies however, managed to push across two runs that inning on two walks and two infield hits. With one out in the top of the ninth, Ruth was sent to pinch hit for Shore, and grounded out to Phillies captain, first baseman Fred Luderus. He advanced Olaf Henricksen to second base in the process, but when Hooper, the next batter popped out to first, the Phils 3-1 victory was in the books. With his appearance in that game, Ruth became the second youngest player ever to participate in a World Series. Heinie Zimmerman was but three days younger in his first series appearance with the Cubs in 1907.

Rube Foster got the start in Game Two the following day and was opposed by 21-game winner Erskine Mayer. President Woodrow Wilson and his fiancee were among those in attendance, and this would mark the first time that a President was on hand for a World Series game. Foster put on a show for the chief executive, hurling a complete game three-hitter, going three for four at bat, and driving in the winning run in the top of the ninth for the 2-1 win. With the series tied at a game apiece, the teams took a Saturday night train ride up to Boston, enjoying Sunday off in preparation for game three at Braves Field on Monday.

With 42,300 fans jammed into the new ballpark on October 11th, a new series game attendance record was established, shattering the previous high set in 1911 at New York's Polo Grounds by nearly 10,000. It was of course the first World Series game ever played at Braves Field, and exactly 33 years later to the day, the very last series game ever held there would take place, with the Braves hosting Cleveland. Prior to the start of game three of the '15 series, the first ball was thrown out by Dorothy Lannin, the young daughter of the Red Sox owner. Ballplayers have been known to be a superstitious bunch, but Joe Lannin himself was apparently not one to tempt fate. Reportedly, he had recently cut up a new felt cap because he believed it to be a jinx. He then took to wearing a new soft cap and planned to keep it on during the series.

The new chapeau seemingly helped to produce the desired effect, as lefty Dutch Leonard spun a masterpiece every bit as impressive as Foster's the game before. Like Foster, Leonard also gave up only three hits and one run, as Duffy Lewis singled home Hooper in the ninth for a thrilling 2-1 win.

Though game four, held the following day, October 12 would have appeared to have been Ruth's turn to pitch, Carrigan opted to go with Shore. When the game's leadoff hitter Milt Stock singled, and Phillie shortstop Dave Bancroft walked on four pitches, Carrigan wasted no time, ordering Ruth and Foster to begin warming up. Shore settled down though and went the distance for Boston's third 2-1 win in a row, as they now held a commanding three games to one lead.

Once again, Ruth was passed over as Foster got the nod to start Game Five on Wednesday, October 13. The capacity crowd of 20,306 at the Baker Bowl would be disappointed to learn that their ace Alexander was unable to start due to a sore arm, and Foster was opposed by Erskine Mayer, his rival from Game Two. Though Foster did not quite duplicate his performance from the second game, he pitched well, but it was Harry Hooper who turned out to be the hero. It was in Boston's third inning that Hooper, leading off, drove a home run into the auxiliary seating in centerfield. Then, with one out in the ninth inning and the score tied 4-4, Hooper drove another solo homer into the same area, which would stand as the winning run for a series clinching victory. Carrigan was reportedly ready to give Ruth the ball to start Game Six, and though that appearance did not occur, he would earn more post-season distinctions by age 23 than most would in a career.

In the years to follow, it was often suggested that Carrigan purposely withheld Ruth from the 1915 series to keep his ego in check. In the *Boston Daily Record*'s 1943 interview with Carrigan, the former skipper addressed the question:

> "I don't know what effect keeping him out of that series might have had ... but it wasn't because I was thinking of his reactions that I didn't use him."

Carrigan went on to explain that he didn't use Carl Mays either, and that Shore, Leonard, and Foster were, in his judgment the right choices under the given circumstances. He finished by adding "Personally, I don't think Ruth could ever become fat-headed. There wasn't an ounce of conceit in his big frame".

≈

After wrapping up the series, the Sox returned to Boston surprised to find only one person at the station to greet them. The players were given two new baseballs and went about securing each others' autographs to bring home as souvenirs. After talking with Manager Carrigan, the players visited owner Lannin and said their good-byes. Each received a check for $3,825.80 as their series share. For Ruth, his share totaled approximately 109% of his 1915 salary of $3500. Babe was pleased to receive an additional $100 dollars which Carrigan had withheld from him because of insubordination in spring training.

The 1915 Red Sox were said to be the highest paid team in baseball, with a payroll of $125,000, but Lannin had clearly gotten his money's worth. The Red Sox' place atop the baseball world was due in large part to pitching and spectacular defense. Ruth would state in his autobiography with Considine that the 1915 Sox were, led by Speaker, the greatest defensive team he had ever seen. The pitching staff included the A.L. ERA champ in Smoky Joe Wood at 1.49; the top four finishers in winning percentage, Wood, Foster, Shore, and Ruth; the top three in fewest hits per nine innings; and the league leader in saves, Carl Mays.

The 1915 season had truly been a breakthrough year for young Babe, having gone from a borderline major leaguer in the early spring, to a vital member of a world championship team. He had established himself throughout the American League as a hurler with all the necessary weapons in his arsenal for stardom. Only eight pitchers in the A.L. exceeded Ruth's victory total of 18, and his ERA was a full half-run below the league average in that category. The areas in which he ranked amongst league leaders were: second in fewest hits per nine innings (6.82) behind only teammate Dutch Leonard; second in opponents batting average at .212; and fourth in the league in winning percentage.

Ruth's complete pitching record for 1915 follows:

W	L	Pct	ERA	G	GS	IP	R	ER	H	BB	SO	Sho	CG	WP	HBP
18	8	.692	2.44	32	28	217 2/3	80	59	166	85	112	1	16	9	6

Of course any review of Ruth's '15 season would be incomplete without also focusing on his batting achievements. He was becoming as well-known for his feats as a batsman as he was a hurler, and suggestions had already been made that Ruth take his place as an everyday position player to capitalize on that prowess. It is particularly interesting to note that while Babe hit his four home runs in just 92 at-bats, A.L. leader Bobby "Braggo" Roth hit seven in 384 at-bats. Roth was also the league leader in home run percentage at 1.8%, simply because Ruth at 4.3% did not have enough at-bats to qualify for the league leadership. If Ruth were to have maintained his 4.3% over the exact same number of at-bats as Roth, he would have totaled 17 round trippers.

Ruth's 1915 batting statistics:

G	BA	SA	AB	H	2B	3B	HR	HR%	R	RBI	BB	SO	SB
*42	.315	.576	92	29	10	1	4	4.3%	16	21	9	23	0

* 32 games as a pitcher, 10 games as a pinch hitter (1 for 10)

It would be 32 more years before the Rookie of the Year Award would be created, with Jackie Robinson its first recipient. For the first two years, 1947 and '48 only one award was given out rather than one in each league. Had the award existed in 1915, Ruth would have, without question been its winner in the American League. Being cheated out of postseason awards simply because they did not exist was a recurring theme in the early portion of Ruth's career.

᳇

After the conclusion of the '15 World Series, Red Sox players were scheduled to participate in a west coast tour of exhibition games arranged by the National Commission. The parties were unable to come to a suitable financial agreement for the tour, and the players ultimately did not become involved. At this time, Babe and Helen traveled back to Baltimore, where for the last time, they would spend the winter. Upon his return, he was instrumental in arranging an exhibition game to be held on Sunday, October 24 between St. Mary's Industrial School and the local Albrecht Athletic Club. About 8,000 locals would turn out, the largest crowd to witness a non-professional baseball game in the city, as Ruth pitched the entire contest for St. Mary's. As a brass band played, spectators completely encircled the field, and Helen greatly enjoyed the ovation given to her Babe.

Considered a homecoming for Ruth, the joy of the occasion was somewhat marred by one incident. While he was playing the game, he had one of the St. Mary's Brothers hold onto his brand new 2 1/2 carat diamond ring, which he had paid $500 for out of his World Series winnings. It was the first diamond ring Babe had ever owned, and unfortunately, he wouldn't own it for long. While attempting to keep the crowd from rushing onto the field, the priest lost the ring.

Another portion of Ruth's series money went toward investing in a new saloon for his father, George H. Ruth Sr. This establishment was located at the corner of Eutaw and Lombard streets, and presumably Babe was engaging in his last stint as an assistant saloon keeper over the winter. The big story out of the baseball world this offseason was the official demise of the Federal League. It was announced on December 22 that Organized Baseball had bought out the owners of the rival league, and with the disbanding of the eight teams, major leaguers now lost considerable leverage in terms of salary demands. Though Ruth's potential wages may have been impacted slightly, big stories were looming on the horizon for other members of the world champions.

▪Three ▪

1916: Forty Years Too Soon for the "Cy"

The 1916 season dawned with the National League celebrating its 41st year. Pundits spoke of the outrageous increase in the average salaries since the inaugural season of 1876. Babe Ruth's contract called for him to play for $3,500 dollars for the 1916 season, a fact that did not sit well with Babe considering he had asked for a doubling of his salary.

With the Federal League now a memory, there was talk of potential friction developing with those returning from the renegade league. There was also fear, amongst the players, that with their leverage gone, the salaries would begin to drop. Their fear was not unfounded.

In the trade of the winter, Connie Mack sold "Home Run" Baker to the New York Yankees for a reported $25,000. This made expendable the Yankees hard-hitting third baseman Fritz Maisel and the "Hot Stove" league had considerable grist for the mill. One rumor had Baker going to the White Sox for their recently acquired outfielder Joe Jackson. Another had him headed to the Red Sox for the World Series hero Dutch Leonard.

As the teams began to depart to the various spring training sites, the American League announced that they would cut in half the number of free passes to newspapers for the 1916 season.

In Boston, President Joseph Lannin ordered ticket prices at Fenway Park to be lowered for the coming season. The box seat price would drop to $1.00 from $1.25 and the grandstand price would go from $1.00 to $ .75 ($ .50 for the ladies). He revealed plans to construct a waiting room at Fenway Park. The *Boston Post* reported its intent was "solely for the ladies awaiting the arrival of their escorts". This would "relieve them of the oftimes embarrassing necessity of waiting in the crowded lobby or on the sidewalk in front of the stands". On the diamond, Lannin stated his intent to stand pat with the team that had brought him the 1915 world championship.

Tris Speaker, the star centerfielder of the Red Sox championship teams of both 1912 and 1915, became the first and most prominent victim of the defunct Federal League. It was widely reported that he could expect a cut from his $15,000 salary of 1915.

On February 19, the Sox' spring training plans were made known. The pitchers and catchers would report to Hot Springs on the 12th of March with the regulars joining them on the 19th. Leaving Arkansas on March 31, they would barnstorm their way north playing nine exhibition games before their opener at Fenway on April 12 against the "Mackmen" of Philadelphia.

Blizzard conditions existed in Boston when Carrigan and crew pulled out of South Station on Friday March 10. Stopping in Albany, the train rolled on to St. Louis, picking up Mr. and Mrs. Herb Pennock, Chet Thomas, Patrick Haley, and George and Helen Ruth. Half the population of Hot Springs turned out to greet the Sox upon their arrival. The townsfolk lined the train tracks and the main thoroughfare to cheer the reigning champs of the baseball world.

Babe was reported to be in better shape than the previous fall and the *Post* noted he was "crazy for the baseball season to begin". In reality however, Carrigan thought Babe was carrying about 25 excess pounds. He put Ruth in a rubber suit and worked him overtime to drop the weight. Carrigan warned him of the dangers of overeating and under-exercising. It was a problem that would plague Babe throughout his illustrious career.

It took but the first intrasquad game for the camp to be abuzz with tales of Ruth's bat. Ruth was on the hill for an expected unimpressive stint, surrendering five runs. But he gave the fans and writers enough to talk and write about with but one swing of his bat. With Red Sox centerfielder Olaf Henrickson holding down his post, Ruth sent a screaming line drive toward the gap in right center. Henrickson got a great jump on the ball and racing after it he just did catch up to it. The *Post* stated that, "the ball was moving at such speed" that Henrickson's momentum sent him crashing into the wooden fence, breaking three boards.

The intrasquad games found Ruth spending little time on the mound. Most of his time was spent in Speakers centerfield position. He knocked out a few hits and even had an assist. In the midst of all this, Carrigan announced to anyone who would listen, his plans to go ahead without his superstar centerfield. Was he viewing the 21-year-old Ruth as a potential replacement for Speaker? Although there is no hard evidence that this was the case, it is an interesting coincidence that while Speaker was holding out, Ruth's time on the diamond was spent almost exclusively in centerfield.

Midway through spring training, Speaker ordered his 1916 uniforms, (at his own expense), hopped a train and headed for Hot Springs. He arrived in time to play in the March 25 game. He went 4 for 4, with a home run, triple, and two singles. He remained unsigned but few worried, the general consensus being that his bluff had been called and it would be but a matter of time before he would be inked and in the fold.

As March drew to a close, Ruth toiled a bit more in centerfield before taking the slab one more time. It was the 29th of March when he made his final intrasquad appearance. Pitching for the "Yannigans" he blanked the "Regulars" in his three innings, allowing but two hits. In what the *Boston Post* described as united testimony, opponents stated that, "the husky southpaw had so much speed that they could not see the ball". This left little doubt that Ruth was ready for the season to begin.

April 6 would be the next time he would pitch. In a homecoming event in Baltimore, Ruth and Ernie Shore combined for a three-hit 5-0 shutout over Jack Dunn and his Baltimore Orioles. A disappointing crowd of only 800 people turned out to welcome home the Baltimorean, an indication of the state of the once thriving Oriole franchise.

The following day brought an inkling of the bomb that was about to drop in the Red Sox front office. It began as all "bombs" usually do, as a rumor. A report stated that Lannin was about to trade the disgruntled and unsigned Tris Speaker to the Yankees for the aforementioned Fritz Maisel and a sum of cash. A swift denial came out of the Red Sox office that categorically stated Speaker would not be sold or traded. It seems as if the proverbial vote of confidence even in 1916, was the precursor to the demise. The 28-year-old Speaker was traded the very next day, shipped to Cleveland for $55,000 plus 23-year-old pitcher "Sad" Sam Jones and Fred

Thomas. It is difficult to put into context the impact and furor raised by this trade, but upon evaluation it becomes unmistakably clear.

Since making his first appearance in 1907 at age 19, he had compiled a .345 lifetime batting average. This placed him on the same level with the likes of the formidable Joe Jackson and the incomparable Ty Cobb. As a defensive player, he was unparalleled. Truly one of the elite superstars of the game, his acquisition by the Indians prompted Connie Mack to comment, "it puts Cleveland in the race". A 28-year-old superstar with a .345 lifetime batting average, a gold glove-type fielder in a key defensive position who had just led his team to a world championship (its second in four years), it is little wonder that his trade would be front-page news throughout the country.

Speaker initially balked at the trade, saying he would not report to Cleveland unless he received $5,000 of the reported $55,000 Lannin had garnered in the deal. When all was said and done, Speaker was in Cleveland playing for the same $15,000 salary he had played for in 1915. It was never reported if he ever received the $5,000 he demanded from Lannin. His presence in the lineup excited Indian fans enough to show up in record numbers for their home opener. His performance on the field did not diminish, in fact by season's end, he would depose Ty Cobb as American League batting champ; the first time that had been done in a decade.

It had been an interesting spring for young George Ruth. He had plied his pitching craft sparingly, played the bulk of his time in centerfield and appeared in all likelihood for the first time on the cover of a national sports publication.

The March 4 edition of *The Sporting Life* features a cover with Ruth throwing a baseball in his Red Sox uniform. The caption misidentifies him as Herbert "Dutch" Leonard, however the photo is unquestionably that of Babe Ruth. It is not known if the intention of *The Sporting Life* was to feature Babe's teammate Leonard or if they just misidentified Ruth. It is, however, both interesting and ironic that the most identifiable face in the history of American sports would be mistakenly identified in his first encounter with the national media.

Boston's cold wintry weather held the April 12 Fenway Park opening day crowd to around 5,000. Boston's bombastic Mayor John Michael Curley had to warm up for five minutes before he could throw out the first pitch. Ernie Shore was slated to open the Red Sox championship defense, but was a last-minute scratch. The gauntlet fell to the 21-year-old Ruth to step in. The ball never left the infield in the first inning and Babe was in control the entire day. He would have had a shutout were it not for his own ninth-inning throwing error. He had opened the ninth by walking A's rightfielder Jimmy Walsh on four pitches. Battling back, he struck out Amos Strunk bringing up leftfielder Rube Oldring. He hit a scorcher up the middle of which Ruth made a brilliant stop and an equally poor throw. Shortstop Everett Scott had moved toward second attempting to force Walsh. The *Boston Post* noted that "even if Scott were equipped with a net, he could not have bagged the throw".

When 40-year-old Nap Lajoie singled up the middle scoring Walsh and sending Oldring to third, Carrigan had seen enough. He called upon Rube Foster to, what the *Boston Post* termed, "the disgust of Ruth and the disappointment of the fans". With the tying run on third and the go-ahead run on second, Foster induced A's first baseman Stuffy McInnis to hit a comebacker. He quickly threw to third and caught Oldring leaning the wrong way. Larry Gardner slapped the tag on him for out number two. Only pinch hitter Billy Meyer stood between Foster and an opening day victory. He flied to center and the 28-year-old Foster had preserved the win for Ruth and the Red Sox. The opening day win took the sting out of a 1-0 embarrasing shutout the champions had suffered at the hands of Boston College just the day before.

	I.P.	H	SO	BB	R	ER
4/12/16 vs.						
Philadelphia	8 1/3	4	6	2	1	0

At bat: 0 for 2, sacrifice bunt

The Sox came right back the next day and won behind the twirling of Ernie Shore and Herb Pennock, 8-2. A New England snowstorm would cancel the next game. But Saturday's 2-1 win completed a three-game sweep of the A's and set up the first confrontation of the season between the 21-year-old Baltimorean and the Washington Senators' Walter "Big Train" Johnson.

It remained unseasonably chilly in Boston for the first meeting of these two titans of the game. Over 3,000 spun the turnstiles that Monday afternoon at Fenway, with nary a hint of what was to transpire before their eyes. Who among them could have envisioned that in 20 years these two men would be among the first five men elected into the Baseball Hall of Fame?

It marked the first of what would be six head-to-head confrontations between the two in the season of '16. The day belonged to Ruth. He scattered eight hits in his eight innings on the hill, striking out six Senators, walking two and hitting one. He had it when he needed it, as the Senators, despite having men on base throughout the contest, could forge across but one run. Ruth's mates, on the other hand, pummeled the "Big Train" for five runs and 11 hits in only six innings. Babe even joined in with a double and would have had another if not for the slick fielding of Senator first baseman Joe Judge. He made a diving stab of a ball that Ruth seared right off the first base bag. The ball was hit so hard, that Judge had plenty of time to right himself and beat Ruth to the bag for the out.

Rain began to fall in the seventh inning, prompting Carrigan to appeal to the homeplate umpire R.F. Nallin to call the game. His appeal fell upon deaf ears until the eighth when Nallin called time. His intent was to wait the required 20 minutes and hopefully resume play. The Fenway Faithful, however, had another idea—they all went home! Within 20 minutes, the stands were completely empty. The game was indeed called, and Babe Ruth had his second win of the young season. The Red Sox were 4-0, and the royal rooting fans of Fenway had an assist.

The next day saw an eighth-inning rally fall short as the Senators defeated the Sox 4-2. It marked the first time that Washington had beaten Boston at Fenway in two years. Following a doubleheader split on Thursday, April 19, the Sox headed to South Station for the season's first road trip; a scheduled 11 games which would take them to Philadelphia, New York and the nation's capital.

Ruth opened the road trip on April 20 with a dominating 7-1 win over the A's. It was his first nine-inning complete game win of the year, as he surrendered five hits while walking three and striking out five. He also threw his first wild pitch of the season. His hitting woes continued as he went 0 for 4, but more importantly, he was 3-0 coming out of the gate.

Hitting woes or not, the next day Carrigan called upon Ruth for his first pinch-hitting assignment of the year. It was unsuccessful as the Sox lost their third game of the year, and at 6-3 were now in second place. Another failed pinch-hitting assignment and another loss at the hands of the Athletics dropped the Sox to 6-4.

Leonard would get them on track and back in first place with a 4-0 win in the last game of the series with Philadelphia.

It was on to the Polo Grounds and the initial battle with the Yankees. Ruth drew the task of pitching the opener and he proved a more than worthy selection. Going the route in a ten-inning 4-3 win, he gave up two earned runs on eight hits while striking out six and walking but two. He had another hitless outing, however Carrigan could hardly be disappointed with the April performance of his young southpaw. It was his final pitching appearance for the month of April. If the award for pitcher of the month existed in 1916, one would have been hard-pressed to find a more deserving candidate than the Red Sox lefty.

	IP	H	SO	BB	R	ER
April pitching stats:	35 1/3	25	23	9	6	4

He was 4-0 with an E.R.A. of 1.02. His strikeout-to-walk ratio was better than two-to-one and his opponents hit a paltry .191 against him. He would pinch-hit two more times in the month of April without success, closing out April 1 for 16 (.062). The one hit was a double off of Walter Johnson. May dawned with the Red Sox in Washington to face the Senators in an early-season battle for first place.

Ruth opened the series and the new month brought with it his first defeat of the season. It was basically self-imposed, as Ruth walked nine batters. Four of them would score as the Senators took the game 5-3. Ironically, when he could find the plate, Ruth was virtually unhittable. He yielded but five hits in his 7 2/3 innings, all of them singles. Unfortunately three of them came in succession following a walk in the second inning allowing Washington to surge ahead 2-0.

The Sox would battle back, taking the lead 3-2 in the fourth on a bases-loaded two-run single by Ruth himself. This was only his second hit of the season and his first two runs batted in. Buoyed by his offensive contribution, he settled down through the middle innings, taking a 3-2 lead into the home half of the eighth. With one out, it all unraveled. Babe threw eight consecutive balls putting men on first and second. When he threw yet another on the first pitch to the next hitter, Carrigan came to the mound to change catchers, perhaps thinking a new target would help his struggling ace. It proved no help at all, as Ruth walked the bases full.

Carrigan returned, this time summoning Leonard to the hill. Leonard promptly served up a bases clearing double to catcher John Henry, and Ruth was saddled with his first loss of the year, 5-3. His nine walks turned out to be a season high and would equal his total walks for the entire month of April.

When Washington beat Ernie Shore the next day, it was the Sox third loss in a row and left them longing for home cooking and the friendly confines of Fenway Park. They had lost six of ten on the road trip and four out of their last five. When they returned home on Thursday, May 5, Carrigan handed the ball to Leonard to get his men back on track.

Leonard was equal to the task, shutting out the Yankees, 3-0. Success was short lived as Wild Bill Donovan's crew took the next three games leaving the Red Sox reeling. They had now lost seven of eight and fallen below the .500 mark for the first time. Things were not going well for the local nine. The newshounds began lamenting the absence of the inimitable Tris Speaker in centerfield.

In the midst of this horrific streak came Ruth's first no decision of the '16 campaign. It occurred on Friday, May 5. It was a raw 50-degree day in Boston when the teams took the field. Ruth's mates staked him to a 3-0 lead in the first inning. Surviving his own erratic pitching, Babe took a 4-0 lead in the seventh. The Yankees got on the board with two in the seventh by virtue of a single, a double, a walk, a fielders choice, and a double steal.

Leading 4-2 in the ninth, Ruth allowed a leadoff double to pinch-hitter Paddy Baumann. When he went 3 and 0 to another pinch-hitter, Charlie Mullen, Carrigan called upon Carl Mays. (This was Mays' first appearance of the year, having had his tonsils removed in the spring). He walked Mullen (charged to Ruth) then caught Maisel looking. Home Run Baker then singled in a run, making it 4-3.

It looked as if the Red Sox would prevail when second baseman Joe Gedeon hit a ground ball to Larry Gardner at third. However, Gardner's throw pulled Hoblitzell off the bag at first. Although he still had time to get back to the bag, Hoblitzell opted for a sweep tag. He missed, and the score was tied at four. It would remain that way until the 13th, when the New Yorkers would score four, taking the game by an 8-4 count.

	IP	H	SO	BB	R	ER
5/15/16 vs. New York	8	7	6	6	4	3

Suddenly beset with control problems, Ruth was still looking for his first win in the month of May.

That evening, the local Elks club held a reception for the Red Sox, providing dinner and entertainment. Some members of the Yankees were also in attendance. There are no published reports of any outrageous behavior. No sightings of Ruth cruising the streets clad only in a lampshade. There are no records of any disturbances that called for the local authorities to become involved. This is remarkable, given the fact that the Red Sox had dropped a very tough decision only hours before this gala event, and that they were in the midst of a terrible streak. Add in the fact that Ruth was not pitching very well and would probably not see any action for a couple of days, it could be safely assumed that the Babe was home and tucked in bed long before his curfew, resting up for his next start . . . .

The prospects for the Red Sox did not look any brighter. Cleveland was on its way into town. Sporting an eight-game winning streak, they now sat atop the American League. The city murmured with excitement at the return of Tris Speaker as 15,000 turned out to pay tribute to him. The Red Sox presented him with a "large fez" and a jeweled badge. Enthusiastically cheered all day long, Speaker sent the crowd into a frenzy when he left the field following an inning and by force of habit ran into the Red Sox dugout. The day belonged to Speaker.

> "The outpouring showed the deep regard and esteem of which no player in either league, but Speaker could be the object"
> *Boston Post* 5/10/16

The game, however, belonged to Leonard and the Red Sox 5-1. Ruth sat and watched from the dugout, waiting for his chance to face his former teammate. It would come the very next day.

How many baseball fans would turn out today to watch Babe Ruth in a head-to-head confrontation with Tris Speaker? Would the LA Coliseum be large enough to hold them all? The significance of the matchup was apparently lost on Boston fans as only 4073 showed up at Fenway on this spring afternoon to witness the first battle of these former mates.

Speaker and the Indians fared much better on this day. They jumped right out in the first inning on singles by third baseman Terry Turner and Speaker, and a two-run double by first baseman Chick Gandil. Cleveland was never truly challenged, adding single runs in the second and third innings on their way to a 6-2 victory. Speaker emerged the victor in this head to head match up. He went 2 for 3 with a walk and three runs scored. His most significant play came in the field. With two outs in the bottom half of the seventh, Ruth stepped to the plate. There were two outs, two on and Cleveland was clinging to a 4-2 lead when Ruth sent a shot towards the gap in right center. Speaker, moving with the swiftness which the Fenway fans had become accustomed, reached the ball at full speed and hauled it in robbing Babe of a triple which would have tied the score.

It was the third disappointing start in a row for Ruth, and he began to be chided in the local sports pages. Paul Shannon of the *Post* made reference to his "obvious increased waistline" and further referred to him as "more than a little overweight." In his column of May 15, he wrote:

> "Ruth is overweight and when he gets rid of that surplus poundage he will be the same tough proposition of last year, to solve."

Whatever the reason, Ruth was clearly struggling. His brilliant April had melted in mediocrity in May. After three starts, his line for the month looked like this:

IP	H	SO	BB	R	ER
24 1/3	22	12	17	15	13

He was 0-2 with a no decision, an ERA of 4.81 and his opponents were hitting .301 against him.

The Red Sox and Indians split the final two games of the series. When Cleveland left town, the Sox were losers of seven of the ten games they had played in May, and were 12-13 overall. The question on the lips of Red Sox fans throughout New England was not only "What's the matter with Babe Ruth, but what's the matter with the Red Sox?"

Chicago came into town for a four-game set to begin on Saturday. Boston won the battle of the hoses, returning them to the .500 mark. The Ides of May brought with it torrential rain to Boston, causing cancellation of the final three games of the series.

The rains finally ended, but the Red Sox woes did not. The Browns of St. Louis came into town and proceeded to thump them 7-1 and 5-1 in the first two games of the series. Boston was now two games below .500 and mired in fourth place. The rains returned to Boston causing a delay of one hour and forty-five minutes before Babe's next start. Many a bag of sawdust and sand was scattered around the infield to make it playable for Ruth and his mates.

Ruth walked the leadoff hitter and many began to wonder if they were not in for another Ruth-induced walking parade. No damage was done, however, and Babe began to mow them down. He struck out two men in the third, and entered the fourth frame scoreless, when his control problems returned.

He walked leadoff hitter Burt Shotton. Upset at not getting a couple of close calls, Ruth's mates began to chide Umpire Nallin. When shortstop Ernie Johnson was passed, catcher Chet Thomas exploded, making several references to Nallin's heritage, which caused his ejection from the game.

Sam Agnew replaced him behind the plate and George Sisler stepped into the box with no outs and two on. He quickly sacrificed, putting men on second and third for rightfielder Ward Miller. He hit a ground ball to Jack Barry at second base who made a heads-up throw to home to nail the sliding Shotton. This left runners at the corners with two out, bringing up second baseman Del Pratt.

What then transpired was signature baseball of the teens. On the very first pitch, Miller broke for second base, and Thomas threw down as Ernie Johnson broke for home. The return throw was not in time, and the Browns had a run and the lead without the benefit of a hit. Boston battled back to take a 2-1 lead in their half of the fourth and it remained that way as St. Louis came to bat in the top half of the sixth. Ruth immediately put himself in trouble once again, and after the third walk of the inning and the bases now full, Carrigan strolled to the mound. Carl Mays was ready in the bullpen and after a brief discussion, Carrigan called for the submariner.

Ruth left the game without incident, no dirt kicking, no jawing with the manager or umpire, no outward signs of anger or frustration. From all indications he flipped the ball to the manager and headed for the clubhouse. What appears unusual about all of this is the fact that when Ruth left the diamond with two outs in the fifth inning, he was throwing a no-hitter. If such an incident were to take place today, it would be mentioned in every sports page in every major league city. On May 21, 1916 it bore hardly a mention. Buried deep in the account of the game the *Boston Post* wrote,

> "Ruth did not give his opponents the semblance of a safe hit and was taken out merely because he put the issue in jeopardy by a seeming inability to get the ball across the plate".

Other papers made note:

> "It is pretty hard to tell what would have happened had Babe Ruth been permitted to finish out the game against the Browns, he had gone well into the 6th inning without a hit being made off him". *Boston American* 5/21/16

> "No-hit Babe Ruth took his balloon ascension, jammed the bases by a hectic spell of wild flinging and was accordingly removed". *Boston Herald* 5/21/16

Mays was formidable in his relief stint, holding the Browns to two hits in the final 3 1/3 innings saving the win for Ruth and the Red Sox.

	IP	H	SO	BB	R	ER
5/20/16 vs.						
St. Louis	5 2/3	0	4	7	1	1
At bat: 0 for 2						

Ty Cobb and the Tigers were next to besiege Fenway Park as they came in for a four-game set to close out the homestand. A ninth-inning two-out single by shortstop Hal Janvrin drove in the winning run, giving the Red Sox the first game of the series and bringing them back to .500. It was the first time they had won two in a row since the last week of April. The rains returned the next day, forcing the fourth postponement of the homestand.

On the 24th, Ruth took to the hill for his final start of the month. Over 6,000 patrons occupied the stands on this Wednesday afternoon as Ruth took on Cobb, Bobby Veach, and the hard-hitting Detroit Tigers. Detroit went out one, two, three in the first inning, but threatened in the second. Bobby Veach opened the inning with a single that was quickly followed by another from future Hall of Famer Harry Heilmann.

When Ruth walked first baseman George Burns, the fans became edgy. Ruth got the next two batters on a pop-up and a strikeout, bringing his counterpart, Jean Dubuc to the plate. Dubuc hit a wicked shot that appeared to be heading for the rightfield corner. First baseman Dick Hoblitzell made a diving stop, righted himself and beat Dubuc to the bag to end the inning. It was the first of six brilliant defensive plays that Ruth would get behind him throughout the day. The other five belonged to Harry Hooper.

Harry's first virtuoso came in the third off the bat of shortstop Donie Bush. He made a fine running catch in the gap, robbing Bush of a triple. This saved a run as two batters later Cobb singled for his only hit of the game. The Sox would get on the board in the bottom half of the third, when Ruth doubled in Janvrin who had singled to start the inning. This proved to be the only run Babe would need as the Sox went on to win 4-0, however, Harry Hooper was just warming up in rightfield. He made two more nice running catches off the bats of Harry Heilmann and Oscar Stanage in the 4th and 5th innings, respectively. However, he saved his best effort for the 7th inning:

> "Veach, the first man at bat, got hold of one of Ruth's fastest offerings and drove it far down the rightfield corner. It was a 10-1 shot that it was good for at least 3 bases, and to many it appeared that it would clear the fence and go for a circuit drive; but Hooper, running like a deer, gathered the ball in with his *ungloved hand* and prevented what might have been a dangerous rally for the next man landed a hard one in right." *Boston Post* 5/25/16

This effort left Veach frustrated and the crowd, according to Paul Shannon, "screaming themselves hoarse." Hooper's exhibition ended two batters later when he ran down a line drive off the bat of a second baseman Ralph Young, stranding Harry Heilmann at third.

The outing was Ruth's best in over a month. He threw his first shutout of the season, had a double to knock in the first run of the game, added a single and scored yet another run. He held the powerful Tigers to only four hits, all of them singles. It would seem that Babe was the star of the game. Nevertheless, the 6,081 patrons left talking about, what Shannon called "the most spectacular outfielding" in the four year history of Fenway Park, courtesy of Harry Hooper.

	IP	H	SO	BB	R	ER
5/24/16 vs.						
Detroit	9	4	2	3	0	0

The following day, Boston concluded a sweep of the Tigers behind the pitching of Ernie Shore. It was their fourth straight win and marked the first time since May 1 that they were at least two games over .500. After the game, the team headed to South Station to board a train for New York where the Yankees lay in waiting. The Sox would play four games in three days and then return to Fenway to face the Senators. Friday was not a good day, as the winning streak came to a screeching halt as they lost both ends of a double-header by one-run margins, 2-1 and 6-5 in ten innings.

Saturday, Ruth again took to the hill. For the second time in this young season, he was called upon with two days' rest. He pitched well enough to win, but unfortunately he received little backing on the field, and virtually no support at the plate. Under a headline that read: "BABE RUTH PITCHES GREAT GAME, BUT IS NOT GIVEN SUPPORT NEEDED TO WIN", Paul Shannon wrote:

"the big southpaw would have shut his opponents out had he been properly supported .... Had every one of the Boston team worked with the same spirit as the Boston pitcher the story of this game would read differently." *Boston Post* 5/28/16

The final score was 4-2. New York scored one in the first, three in the second and Boston never led. The Red Sox could muster but three hits off of New York pitcher Ray Keating. Two of them were by Babe Ruth.

	IP	H	SO	BB	R	ER
5/27/16 at						
New York	8	8	4	2	4	3

At bat: 2 for 4, two singles and one run scored

It was their third loss in a row and once again dropped them below the .500 mark at 17-18.

This brought Ruth's erratic May to a close. What started out horrendously, ended on a much more positive note. Although Babe lost his third game in five May decisions, the signs were indicating that the Ruth of April was about to re-emerge.

Ruth's line for the month of May looked like this:

IP	H	SO	BB	R	ER
47	34	22	29	20	17

His record for the month was 2-3 with one no decision. His ERA was 3.25 and his opponents had hit .194 against him.

His season to date, read like this:

IP	H	SO	BB	R	ER
82 1/3	59	45	38	26	21

His record was 6-3 with one no decision. He was toting an ERA of 2.30. He had one shutout to his credit and his opponents were hitting at a .193 clip against him. His bat came to life a bit with the warmth of Spring. He went 5 for 18 for a .278 average. He drove in his first three runs of the season and whacked out his second double of the campaign. As a pinch hitter he was called upon but once in the month and would fail in that singular attempt. The hitting line to date was 6 for 33, .182, two doubles and three RBIs. His slugging percentage was a non-Ruthian .242 and as a pinch hitter he had been called upon four times without success.

Boston grabbed the last game of the New York series on the strength of a brilliant pitching performance by Carl Mays. The sub-mariner, making his first start of the year was virtually unhittable as he blanked the New Yorkers on three hits, 3-0. Another losing streak had been stopped, and the Red Sox headed home where Walter Johnson and the first-place Senators awaited.

The first three games of the series went to the Red Sox. Ruth and Johnson were set for their much-anticipated rematch in game four of the series; it was the second time in six weeks that Ruth and Johnson faced each other. Festivities were set before the game as the Red Sox were raising their 1915 American League championship banner. A local marching band was on hand to entertain the crowd, equipped with a drum major twirling a bat. The two teams marched to centerfield and watched as Old Glory and the championship flag were hoisted high. They then walked back to the dugout to grab their gear and the battle began.

There are occasions in baseball when something special takes place. When the fans leaving the ballpark are aware that they were privileged to have been in attendance. When the best of the best rise to extraordinary heights as to redefine greatness. June 1, 1916 was such a day at Fenway Park in Boston. The Red Sox, behind Ruth, prevailed this day, 1-0. They scored the only run of the game in the bottom of the eighth, on a heads-up baserunning play by second baseman Mike McNally. He scored all the way from second on an infield force out to literally steal the victory. The story of the game, however, was in the pitching.

> "The wonderful speed and alertness of Mike McNally breaking through the stonewall defense of Walter Johnson in the eighth inning of yesterday's spectacular pitching duel between Johnson and Babe Ruth gave Boston the single score needed to win .... McNally's leg run decided the greatest struggle of the year at the Red Sox ball park. For seven long innings both teams had been playing at the highest tension, the Senators fighting, as they always do, behind their great twirler while the Red Sox battled as the Sox have seldom fought before this spring".
> *Boston Post* 6/2/16

It took but the third batter of the game for Ruth to impress the crowd. Centerfielder Clyde Milan hit a bounder back to the box, the ball seemed destined for centerfield, however Ruth had other ideas. Leaping, what the *Boston Herald* called, "a mile or so in the air" and what the *Post* referred to as "a record high jump", Ruth turned it into a one-to-three on the scorecard. The pitchers cruised into the third inning, when Senator first baseman Joe Judge stepped to the plate:

> "Judge's cranium slightly impeded Babe Ruth's wild pitch ... and umpire 'Silk' O'Loughlin escorted him to first base". *Boston Post* 6/2/16

The *Boston Herald* added a bit more detail:

> "After getting struck Judge walked out toward Ruth. The latter came in to apologize, but the Griff first-sacker would not have it. Before any damage was done O'Loughlin and the players stepped between the men". *Boston Herald* 6/2/16

It is difficult to determine what exactly was the content of Ruth's apology. Regardless of what transpired, the bad feeling would erupt again in exactly one month when these two teams met again in Washington. It is interesting to note that 11 years later, September 30 1927 at Yankee Stadium, Joe Judge was the Senators' first baseman who watched Ruth round the bases after clouting home run number 60.

With O'Loughlin able to maintain peace, the duel between Johnson and Ruth resumed. Until McNally's heroics in the eighth, there were only two frames in which the "Big Train" allowed two men to reach base. Ruth was equally as dazzling. With the exception of the third and sixth innings, no two Senators occupied the bases at the same time. When the dust cleared and settled on the 1-0 Red Sox victory, the respective lines looked like this:

	IP	H	SO	BB	R	ER
Johnson	8	4	6	2	1	1
Ruth	9	3	6	1	0	0

At the plate, both moundsmen went 0 for 2 and each struck out twice.

For the second time in six weeks, Ruth defeated Walter Johnson. On this day, the 7,934 who were in attendance, left knowing they had witnessed two prodigious pitching performances.

Ruth's troubles of early May had vanished. He had won two of his last three starts, both of them shutouts, and had pitched well enough to win the other. It is not exactly clear if he went on a crash diet and dropped all that "excess poundage" or if he simply found the plate again.

It may have been at this time that Harry Hooper spotted something in his delivery that telegraphed his curveball. Babe used to stick his tongue out of the corner of his mouth every time he threw the curve. Hooper, after studying Babe intently, noted it and passed it on to the coaching staff who worked with Babe until the problem was corrected. A photo in an April 1916 edition of the *Boston Sunday Post* shows Ruth in his delivery with his tongue clearly sticking out of the corner of his mouth. Nevertheless, all of the comments pertaining to his girth vanished from the local sports pages. In truth, he was simply winning again.

Friday was a travel day. The Sox headed for Cleveland and the first leg of a western swing that would also take them to Detroit, St. Louis, and Chicago. A scheduled exhibition game in Buffalo was rained out, so the train bearing Carrigan's men headed directly to Cleveland where Tris Speaker and the first-place Indians awaited their arrival.

The winning streak came to an abrupt end courtesy of old friend Speaker. He went 3 for 4 with a double and two triples, knocking in five runs to lead the 11-2 drubbing of Leonard and Herb Pennock. The drubbing continued the next day with Mays and Foster the victims in a 9-3 loss. Cleveland had widened their lead to four games over the Red Sox with the Senators and Yankees sandwiched in between.

Carrigan handed the ball to Ruth to start the third game of the series and for the second time in five starts, Ruth was the stopper. Babe shutout the Indians 5-0, allowing six scattered hits. Only two Clevelanders reached third in the contest and the rampaging Tris Speaker was rendered impotent by the sinewy southpaw. Twice Speaker came to the plate in crucial spots and was dispatched by Babe, the key one coming in the sixth inning when, with the bases loaded and two outs, Ruth induced him to pop to Duffy Lewis to end the inning. He had them beating the ball into the ground all day, as first-baseman Dick Hoblitzell gathered 15 putouts for his day's work. At the plate, Ruth continued his surge, going 2 for 3 with an RBI and a run scored.

The Babe of April was back and then some. With back-to-back shutouts, he was in the midst of a 24-inning consecutive scoreless streak and three of his last four wins were shutouts.

	IP	H	SO	BB	R
6/5/16 at Cleveland	9	6	4	1	0

They left for Detroit in fourth place at 23-20. Slated to play four games at Navin Field, they would then head to Sportsman's park for five games with the Browns.

Losing the opener 3-0, Carrigan's crew received a break from the heavens. Rain washed out games two and three to the delight of the Sox skipper. With pitchers Shore and Foster nursing tender wings, second baseman Jack Barry headed back home with a bout of neuritis, Harry Hooper and third-baseman Larry Gardner still ailing, it is of little wonder why Carrigan welcomed the rain. This would allow Hooper and Gardner the extra time to mend and get back in the lineup when the series resumed.

Despite Ruth's outstanding pitching of late, his hitting remained the topic of conversation among pundits and fans:

> "The American League brotherhood of right-handed twirlers has passed resolutions forbidding any one of its members serving up any fast balls to the Baltimore Babe. One of the Tiger team declares that all the managers of teams who have played here this season have given rigid instructions to their pitchers to feed the big southpaw a continual diet of slow ones". *Boston Post* 6/9/16

On Friday, June 9, Ruth was on the mound to face the Tigers in an attempt to salvage a split of what was now a two-game series. Detroit drew first blood in the second inning when Bobby Veach and George Burns connected for back-to-back doubles, ending Babe's consecutive scoreless inning streak at 25. Two fine defensive plays by Hoblitzell at first prevented any further damage, and thus when Ruth stepped to the plate to leadoff the third, he trailed only 1-0.

> "Ruth evened the score by ushering in the third with one of the longest drives ever made in the big ball yard. The ball landed far up in the right-field bleachers. the drive was such a tremendous one that neither Cobb nor Heilmann made any attempt to go after it". *Boston Post* 6/10/16

Navin Field in Detroit was now added to a rapidly increasing list of ball parks in which Babe Ruth had hit the longest ball ever seen. It was his first home run of the year and the fifth of his career. Babe settled down on the mound allowing but one hit through the middle innings and taking a 4-1 lead into the eighth.

Cobb opened the frame with a single and was immediately forced at second by Bobby Veach. Following an error by second baseman Mike McNally, George Burns tripled making the score 4-3. Switch-hitting second baseman Ralph Young then singled home Burns, knotting the score at four. Ruth rounded out a 3 for 3 day with a leadoff single in the ninth. He was forced on an attempted sacrifice by Hooper who in turn was forced by McNally, but the venerable Lewis tripled allowing Ruth and the Sox to take a 5-4 lead into the ninth.

Obviously out of gas, Babe surrendered back-to-back singles to third baseman Ossie Vitt and Ty Cobb. Carrigan went to the bullpen calling upon Carl Mays to save the game. The first man he faced was Veach, who sacrificed.

With the tying run on third and the winning run on second in the person of the fleet-footed Cobb, Harry Heilmann dug in at the plate. He hit a shot toward first which Hoblitzell fielded and then gunned a throw home nailing the sliding Vitt for the second out. Heilmann immediately stole second but it appeared for naught, when Burns hit a soft liner toward McNally at second. For some inexplicable reason, he did not come up with the ball as Cobb and Heilmann both scored, making losers of Carl Mays and the Red Sox 6-5. Once again Babe had pitched well enough to win but came up empty.

	IP	H	SO	BB	R	ER
6/9/16 at						
Detroit	8	7	2	2	4	3

At bat: 3 for 3, homerun, RBI, and two runs scored.

After dropping two in Detroit, the Sox opened in St. Louis with a 4-2 victory in ten innings. Where Mays had failed against the Tigers, he succeeded in St. Louis, where taking over for Leonard, he got credit for the win in extra innings. The ensuing day brought another day off perpetrated by midwestern summer rains. When the skies cleared, and the teams took the field on the 12th of June, Vean Gregg was twirling for Boston.

In the Red Sox seventh inning with two men on and one out, history unfolded as Carrigan sent Ruth in to pinch hit for Hal Janvrin. The result was a:

> "mighty home run swat . . . a telling crash which hung up all of Bostons three runs and put the Red Sox really in the game".
> *Boston Post* 6/13/16

It was Babe's first successful pinch hit of the season, his first pinch-hit home run of his career and the first time he had hit home runs in successive games.

It tied the game 3-3 but the Sox would eventually lose it in the ninth, 4-3 dropping them to 24-23.

Ruth was wielding a blistering bat for the month of June. He was 6 for 9 with two homers and four RBI. Once again talk began to surface and expand regarding his future as a baseball player and where, on the diamond, that future should be.

"Some one of these days Babe Ruth may become an outfielder. Carrigan, Gregg and others think that with the proper training the Baltimore slugger should make a whale of a player for the outer garden. Babe can murder almost any kind of pitching . . . . He would like nothing better than to be allowed to stroll up to the plate everyday and take a shot at the opposing moundsmen. The days that he is not listed to pitch Babe cavorts about the outfield chasing singles rapped out by Vean Gregg". *Boston Globe* 6/12/16

Under a headline which read: "Ruth may get an outfielder's job" Paul Shannon of the *Herald* wrote:

"Effective as a pitcher as big Babe Ruth really is, there is hardly a man on the Red Sox team but is anxious to see him converted into an outfielder, where he could play everyday and provide the team with the badly needed punch. All over the American League circuit they are calling him one of the most dangerous hitters in baseball. The Senators and the Tigers all declare that were he with either team he would be quickly shifted from the pitching slab to the outfield. Ruth is a wonderful natural ball player, has a real baseball instinct and a superb throwing arm. With men on bases and Ruth at bat, no infield in the American League will willingly close in. When they are forced to do this as a last resort, everyone of the quartet is thinking of his life insurance policy and saying his prayers at the same time. He hits left-handed pitchers just as successfully as he does the other variety. At the present time Manager Carrigan has not given the subject of putting Babe in there very serious consideration but if the other Red Sox pitchers come through as they should, and the batting of certain parties does not improve, big Babe Ruth may soon be a fixture in the Boston outfield".

Suggestions notwithstanding, the following day found Ruth on the hill. Pitching 5 1/3 innings, he was the victor in a 5-3 win. His old roommate Ernie Shore picked up the save. The talk after the game was once more about his hitting. Going 2 for 2 with two RBI, he again homered deep into the rightfield stands. It was his third of the year and his third in three games, prompting the *Taunton (MA) Daily Gazette* to later note:

> "seems Babe Ruth has a wicked way of feeding baseballs to rightfield bleacherites. Doesn't he know that the pills are $1.25 per?". *Taunton Gazette* 6/20/16

	IP	H	SO	BB	R	ER
6/13/16 at St. Louis	5 1/3	4	5	6	1	1

Following this 2 for 2 effort, and with June half over, he was now 8 for 11 with three home runs and five RBI for the month. On the mound, he was 3-0 with one no decision.

The local scribes continued the talk of the big burly Baltimorean in the outfield:

> "Babe is such a great hitter that Bill (Carrigan) wants to have him in the lineup daily if possible. So fans at home don't be a bit surprised if Ruth soon becomes one of the Red Sox outfielders". *Boston American*   6/13/16

Arthur Duffey of the *Post* wrote:

> "When Babe Ruth gets tired of twirling on the mound it looks as if there were an outfielders job waiting for him. The way he has been hitting that pill shows that he is one of the most natural hitters in the game".

St. Louis took the last game of the series 8-5 and the Sox headed to Chicago for a four-game showdown with the White Sox. Boston took the opener before losing the second game of the series 7-4. Ruth saw two pinch hit appearances in those three games and was unsuccessful in both attempts. He was on the mound in the third game of the series and took a 5-0 loss, his first in the month of June. His cause was not helped by the fact that twice his mates had men on second and third with less than two outs and came away empty handed. Ruth's inconsistency prompted Paul Shannon of the *Post* to write; "His erratic work (made) him look like a world beater at one time and like the veriest busher another."

	IP	H	SO	BB	R	ER
6/17/16 at						
Chicago	8	12	7	1	5	5

The loss dropped Boston into sixth place, the lowest place they had occupied all season.

The road trip came mercifully to a close with a Red Sox victory enabling them to salvage a split in the White Sox series. They did not win a series on their four-city Western swing and were 5-8 overall. They returned home in fifth place, five games off the pace.

Getting home was no easy task as their train nearly derailed. They were 15 miles west of Buffalo when the mishap occurred. Apparently, a driving wheel broke free and smashed a connecting rod, causing the train to nearly shake right off the track. Swift action by the engineer averted disaster and after a two-and-a-half hour delay, a special hook up came and got the two cars containing Carrigan and his men, on their way.

The Red Sox woes continued as they dropped the first game of the home stand to New York, 4-1. Babe failed in a pinch-hit attempt in the eighth inning. His teammate, Everett Scott had entered the game late as well. The box score shows Scott going 0 for 0. He did however, participate in a 4-6-3 double play. The significance of this seemingly insignificant note in a box score is this: Everett Scott would not miss another game until May 6, 1925 when he would be replaced as the shortstop of the New York Yankees. Babe Ruth was a teammate of Scott's in both the first and last games of his 1,307 game streak. This would be the record until broken by Lou Gehrig on his way to 2,130 consecutive games. Coincidentally, Babe was on the field for the first game of that streak as well. It bears mentioning that Gehrig's sacred streak was broken by Cal Ripken at Camden Yards whose centerfield area was the former site of Ruth's father's saloon.

No one in attendance at Fenway Park that Monday afternoon had any inkling that they had witnessed Everett Scott begin a trek into history. However, the 4,523 present the very next day, left knowing they had seen history in the making. Twenty-eight-year-old Red Sox right-hander Rube Foster, who had been nursing a lame arm, threw the first no-hitter in the history of Fenway Park. He had a perfect game through five and then walked a man in each of the next three innings on his way to his historic achievement. When

Foster entered the clubhouse after the game, he learned that Red Sox president Lannin had left word for him to come to his office and pick up a $100 bonus check. Lannin also had gold handled pocket knives engraved and handed them out to each member of the team to commemorate Foster's feat.

In the wake of Foster's no-hitter, Babe took to the hill. He very nearly duplicated Foster's effort, surrendering but three paltry singles while orchestrating a magnificent 1-0 shutout victory. Wally Pipp singled to lead off the second inning and was summarily erased on the front end of a 1-6-3 double play. Ruth faced the minimum of fifteen batters through the first five innings. Singles in the sixth and ninth innings accounted for New York's total of three hits as Ruth was in total command all day. Only one New Yorker got as far as third base. The crowd of 3,889 witnessed the shortest game of the year, as Ruth disposed of the Yankees in 1 hour and 18 minutes.

	IP	H	SO	BB	R	ER
6/22/16 vs.						
New York	9	3	2	1	0	0

At bat: 1 for 3

Ernie Shore continued the magic the next day when, he blanked Philadelphia by the same 1-0 count. The Sox staff had now thrown three consecutive shutouts and were in the midst of 31 straight scoreless innings.

On Saturday, the "Mackmen" ended the streak at 34 innings when they scored two in the fourth inning in the first of two. That was all they could muster, however, as Boston took the opener 3-2. They won the nightcap as well, 7-3 behind a complete game victory by Carl Mays, who had also notched a save by pitching the ninth inning of game one. Ruth made one appearance in the doubleheader, flying out in a pinch-hitting role for Leonard in the eighth inning of the first game.

Going into the last week of June, the Red Sox were riding the crest of a five-game winning streak, perhaps spurred by Lannin's offer to purchase each player a $50 suit when the team reached first place. Whatever the reason, things were looking good for the crimson hose. Five wins in a row, back in third place within two-and-a-half games of first and "No hit" Rube Foster scheduled to start against the A's. Any suspense regarding back-to-back no-hitters was immediately alleviated when leadoff hitter Whitey Witt singled. Things did not get any better as five Boston pitchers were knocked around in an 8-5 loss.

On the 27th of June, Ruth pitched his final game of the month. For the third time this month, he proved the stopper. Surviving early control trouble, he yielded two runs in the first inning and then simply slammed the door. The *Post*'s Paul Shannon referred to him as "the same old puzzle he always is when absolutely right." He struck out a season-high ten batters in shutting out the A's over the last eight innings. It ended the brief homestand with the Sox winning six of eight and they left for Washington 33 and 28.

Two losses in a row in the nation's capitol dropped them back into fifth place. Ruth was relegated to one pinch-hit appearance at which he failed.

The month of June ended on an uproarious note when a near riot erupted at Griffith Stadium. The fray resulted in Red Sox catcher Sam Agnew knocking out Senators manager Clark Griffith with a right cross. Two Washington policemen came down from the stands and arrested Agnew right on the spot. He was led off the field and left the stadium in handcuffs.

Bad blood had been brewing between these two teams since way back in April. The Senators charged that Shore deliberately "beaned" Henri Rondeau. The flame was fueled with the aforementioned Babe Ruth-Joe Judge incident in Boston on the 1st of June. Tempers were flaring from the very start of this game. Both Carrigan and Ruth were ejected early in the game for disputing a call by base umpire Tommy Connolly. As Ruth left the field, the *Post* reported, "he was booed and baited by irresponsible fans who pushed through the box of the official scorer to tell him what they thought of the Red Sox." Senators beat writer Paul Eaton recalled the episode later in an October 26 column in *The Sporting News*:

> "An amusing incident occurred here in last summer's near battle between the Washington and Boston teams. A few fans rushed on the field... and the smallest of them wanted to pick on George Ruth. Luckily for him, Babe is well known for his good nature and only laughed at the fan, whom he could have shut up like a penknife and put in his pocket."

The bizarre was commonplace on this last day of June as another strange incident took place in the home half of the seventh inning. With Senator centerfielder Clyde Milan at the plate, homeplate umpire Brick Owens was crouched ready to call balls and strikes. The pitch was delivered by Carl Mays and Milan just got a piece of it, fouling it back. The ball struck Owens right in the throat, causing him to swallow the wad of tobacco he had in his cheek. He nearly choked to death, and it took him about 15 minutes to gather himself and resume his duties. The Red Sox won the game 6-1 closing out the month with a record of 34-30.

Ruth had re-emerged in June, as his line would indicate.

IP	H	SO	BB	R	ER
57 1/3	42	36	16	12	11

He was 5-1 with an ERA of 1.73. His strikeout-to-walk ratio was back to better than two-to-one and opponents were hitting .196 against him. He spun three shutouts and three of his five victories came following Red Sox losses. Once again, he would have to be considered for American League pitcher of the month.

At the plate he went 9 for 21, a .429 clip. He had slugged three home runs in three consecutive games and knocked in four runs. Ironically, those three homers would be his only round-trippers of the year, each of them leaving an indelible mark upon all of those who witnessed them.

Babe pitched the Red Sox July inaugural and had one of his most perplexing outings of the year. He mowed down the first nine men he faced and in the top of the third, he had staked himself to a 1-0 lead with a sacrifice fly. Boston added another run in the top of the fourth, allowing the Babe to take a 2-0 lead into the bottom half of the inning. He got leadoff hitter Danny Moeller for the second time in the game and he had now set down ten in a row. Suddenly and inexplicably, the wheels came off. A walk, a single, another walk, two more singles and Babe was headed for the showers, trailing 3-2 and responsible for runners on first and third. Foster replaced him and when catcher John Henry doubled, the line on Ruth was complete in his 4-2 loss.

	IP	H	SO	BB	R	ER
7/1/16 at Washington	3 1/3	3	5	2	4	4

At bat: 0 for 0 with an RBI on a sacrifice fly.

The first Sunday in July was a travel day. The Red Sox left Washington, losers of three of their last four games. They were bound for Philadelphia for a four-game series with the A's. Ruth saw no action in the Philly series as the Sox won three in a row. It was now home to face Cleveland for three games before Chicago would come in for a grueling seven games in four days.

They took the opener, winning for the second time in three days in their last at bat. The score was tied at five when the Red Sox came to bat in the last of the ninth. Everett Scott led off with a single and was sacrificed to second by Chet Thomas. Ernie Shore was due next, and the crowd began to chant for Ruth to bat for the right-handed pitcher. A few isolated voices grew to a groundswell as the fans wanted to see the Babe swing the bat. Carrigan did not yield to the demands of the crowd and sent Shore up to hit, who then fanned. The crowd's disappointment at not seeing the Babe hit quickly melted into euphoria when Jack Barry lined the first pitch over the leftfielder's head giving the streaking Sox their fourth in a row.

Ruth started the next game and began right where he had left off in Washington. First-inning singles by Graney (the first major leaguer Ruth ever faced, and whom singled off him in that at-bat, July 11, 1914), Speaker and Gandil gave Cleveland a 1-0 lead. A great throw by Hooper in rightfield nailed Speaker going to third. This ended the inning and saved Babe from any further damage.

He righted himself and was in command the rest of the way, allowing but one hit through the seventh inning and walking only two. Interestingly, he was lifted for a pinch-hitter in the Red Sox half of the seventh. With one out and the bases full, Olaf Henrikson was sent up to hit for Ruth. He walked to force across the tying run, but the rally ended there and the teams went to the eighth tied at one.

Less than one month before, the city was filled with talk of Ruth moving to the outfield to utilize his bat. Now in a key situation, he was pinch hit for by a reserve left-handed hitting outfielder. Although there was no mention of any words exchanged between

Carrigan and Ruth, and there were no apparent signs of controversy surrounding this move, one is left to wonder. Knowing Babe's
fiery nature and his competitive drive, it goes without saying that
this could not have sat very well with him. His efforts on the mound
ended in a no decision.

	IP	H	SO	BB	R	ER
7/7/16 vs.						
Cleveland	7	4	2	2	1	1
At bat : 0 for 2						

The Red Sox won the game with a run in the eighth and had
now won five in a row. For Ruth, July was now a mirror of May, with
his first two starts of the month garnering a loss and a no decision.

Babe had another failed pinch-hitting effort the following day
as the five-game winning streak came to an end. The heat and Chicago both came to town on Monday, the 10th of July. Chicago came
to play seven games in four days: two on Monday, two on Tuesday,
two on Wednesday and a single game on Thursday. The heat came
to test the stamina of both teams throughout the most rigorous
week of the season.

With the temperature and humidity both in the 90s, Chicago
took round one, sweeping Monday's doubleheader, 4-0 and 3-0. The
home team could muster but eight hits throughout the day, six of
them coming in game one as left-hander Reb Russell threw a two
hitter in the nightcap.

Tuesday brought the opposite results, as it was Boston's turn
to sweep, winning 5-3 and 3-1. Despite the oppressive heat, Ruth
started both games of the twinbill. He lasted only 1/3 of an inning
in the first game, but pitched a complete-game 3-1 triumph in the
twilight game.

Rube Foster was slated to start the first game, but by game
time was not sufficiently warmed up. Ruth stepped in and filled
the vacancy, retiring the first batter. He then gave way to a warmed-
up Foster who completed the victory. Ruth would be involved in a
similar, much more celebrated incident in a little less than one year.

The second game was scoreless when Ruth opened the third
by plunking catcher Ray Schalk, who came around to score on a
two-out single by Happy Felsch. It was the only run that Chicago
would score. Babe was in trouble in the sixth, seventh, and eighth

innings but wiggled out of it each time. Scenting the victory, Ruth retired them in order in the ninth to ensure the sweep.

	IP	H	SO	BB	R	ER
7/11/16 vs. Chicago	9	6	5	1	1	1

At bat: 1 for 3

At midnight, July 12, the temperature in the city of Boston was 80 degrees. By game time that afternoon, the street-level temperature outside Fenway Park had reached 100, as the marathon battle of the Sox' entered its third day. The Red Sox prevailed again behind complete games by Ernie Shore (game one, 2-1) and Leonard (game two, 3-1). Maintaining yet another four-game winning streak, they looked to close out the series with a simple single game on Thursday. Thunderstorms swept through Boston, bringing relief from the death grip in which the heat had held the city, giving the Red Sox a break from the rigors of a relentless schedule.

St. Louis came into town and Friday's matchup pitted Carl Mays against the Browns' 23-year-old left-hander, Ernie Koob. Amazingly, 17 innings later, the contest had ended in a 0-0 tie. While Mays would last 15 innings, Koob remarkably would last the entire 17.

On Saturday, the two went at it again in yet another doubleheader. It was Boston's fourth doubleheader in six days, and their one single game of the week was the 17-inning affair. St. Louis ended the drama of another long scoreless game when they jumped on Rube Foster for two runs in the first inning. It turned out to be all they would need as the Red Sox' inability to score runs extended into the eighth when Tilly Walker doubled in Jack Barry with Boston's first tally in 28 innings.

The second game belonged to Babe Ruth and Boston. The Red Sox bats came out of their slumber and pounded four Browns pitchers for 18 hits in a 17-4 thumping. Every regular had a hit but shortstop Everett Scott. Babe was in command . . .

"Babe Ruth, who made monkeys of the visiting batsmen and might have had a shutout had there been any necessity for it." *Boston Post*, 7/16/16

He left the game after six innings, leading 13-2, giving way to a recently acquired 24-year-old right-hander named Weldon Wyckoff, who had a rather nondescript career. Pitching in parts of six seasons for the Athletics and the Red Sox, he compiled a 23-35 record. But on this day he stepped to the mound and for the first of two times in the '16 season, relieved Babe Ruth a story that doubtless was told and re-told throughout the remaining 45 years of his life, to family and friends in his hometown of Williamsport, Pennsylvania.

	IP	H	SO	BB	R	ER
7/15/16 vs. St. Louis	6	3	4	2	2	2

At bat: 1 for 4.

The marathon week had finally and mercifully come to a close. Boston had played nine games in six days and on this particular week, must have been very happy that the city of Bostons' Blue Laws prohibited the playing of baseball on Sunday.

In modern day baseball, this week would have constituted the "All-Star" break. After the epic week that the Red Sox had just survived, surely Carrigan would have welcomed a three-day vacation for him and his men. However, Carrigan would have had to manage an All-Star game had it existed, and going with him would have been his 21-year-old hard hitting left-handed pitcher.

Babe's line through the mid point of the season looked like this:

IP	H	SO	BB	R	ER
165 1/3	101	97	61	46	41

He reached the halfway point at 13-5 with an ERA of 2.23. He had tossed four shutouts, three of them in a row, and four of his wins had come after Red Sox losses. There was no doubt that the burly southpaw was a pitcher of all-star caliber. The reality was, however, that following the customary Sunday day off, the wars would resume on Monday the 17th of July. Ninety-eight innings had been thrown by Red Sox pitchers in only six days.

Boston won another one-run game on Monday, and on Tuesday, Ruth was chosen to close out the five-game set. With the exception of the 17-4 game on Saturday, the games had been decided by one run. This one would be no exception.

Babe was in trouble all day beginning in the first inning when he allowed two runs on three hits. He showed his tenacity all day long, as he walked the leadoff man in the second, fourth, sixth and seventh frames, yet not one of them came around to score. In the fourth, his leadoff walk was followed by a double, putting Browns on second and third with no one out. He bowed his back, however, and remained unscathed, inducing a pop-up, a strikeout, and a weak ground ball to second.

Offensively, he was in the midst of the fray with a triple and a walk in four at bats:

> "The burly Babe had his troubles in a good many innings, for he was a little bit short on control. He more than made up for this by his prowess at the bat and his ability to butt his way into a victory. Ruth cut quite a figure in the clash aside from his hurling. He made two of Red Sox runs, he got one of the shortest three baggers ever made at Fenway Park, and he raced across in the third inning with a run that was badly needed before the close, sprinting home from third on an infield bounder and scoring only by reason of his ability to put catcher Severeid down and out for the count. The force of the collision which Babe took head first knocked Severeid unconscious and caused him to drop Lavan's (the shortstop) perfect throw. Ruth showed good speed on the bases and this helped us a whole lot."
>
> *Boston Post* 7/19/16

St. Louis catcher Hank Severeid left the game, a victim of a vicious hit by Ruth. There were no fights, no bench clearings, or even a Red Sox hit batsmen in retaliation. Browns backup catcher Grover Hartley simply put on his gear and went in to catch.

The Sox and Ruth were 4-3 winners and now awaited the Tigers to complete the homestand with six games in four days.

	IP	H	SO	BB	R	ER
7/18/16 vs.						
St. Louis	9	7	4	5	3	3
At bat: 1 for 3						

The Tigers arrived in town fresh off a 4-0 win in New York, a win that had brought the Red Sox within one game of the Yankees. New York still held on to first place by virtue of two more wins than Boston, but in the proverbial all important loss column, they were even. Things got off on the right foot when the Sox completed a sweep of the doubleheader series opening, 4-2 and 9-5. The Yankees also swept two , leaving the standings the same.

Thursday found Rube Foster giving way to Babe Ruth in the ninth, after pitching eight innings of admirable baseball. He left the game knotted at two and it remained that way until the unlucky 13th. Ruth then fell victim to the speed of Ty Cobb and his own throwing error. With one out, Ty beat out a chopper to the mound. He took second base on Babe's errant throw. Bobby Veach then popped back to Ruth and with two out and a man on second, the dangerous Harry Heilmann was intentionally passed. The strategy went for naught when Ralph Young singled Cobb home with what would prove to be the winning run.

	IP	H	SO	BB	R	ER
7/20/16 vs.						
Detroit	5	5	4	2	1	1
At bat: 0 for 2						

Friday's rain delivered another day of rest to Carrigan's overworked and fatigued pitching staff.

The largest crowd of the year swarmed Fenway Park on Saturday to watch the Sox and Tigers bring the 19-game homestand to a close. On tap was what had become commonplace, a doubleheader. The teams traded one-run victories, with Detroit winning the first one 4-3 and Leonard spinning a brilliant 1-0 shutout to close out the homestand in fine fashion.

The homestand had been an extremely successful one. The Red Sox went 12-6 and added one tie. They left for Cleveland in second place only a game-and-a-half behind the Yankees. It was as exhausting as it was successful. Boston had endured six doubleheaders, a 17-inning 0-0 tie, a 13-inning game and five "normal" nine-inning outings (three of which came in the first three games of the homestand).

Since Chicago had arrived in town on July 10, Boston had played two single games of nine-inning duration only twice in 15 games. The Red Sox hurlers had thrown 156 innings while playing 16 games in 12 days. The pending train ride to Cleveland must have appeared like a vacation by comparison.

On the way, the team stopped in Toronto to play an exhibition game against the minor league Maple Leafs. The teams played to a 5-5 tie. With Canada's involvement in the war raging in Europe, the two Red Sox players with names of German ethnicity were leery of taking the field. Fearing the possibility of reprisals, first baseman Dick Hoblitzell opted not to play, and Heine Wagner went by the name Richardson. Ruth was scheduled to open the road trip in Cleveland on Tuesday, and did not see action that day.

Babe started game one, and once again had first inning difficulties. Cleveland jumped out 1-0 on a two-out single by Tris Speaker followed by a double by Braggo Roth. The Sox tied it in the second, but the Indians took it back in the third when Babe issued a leadoff walk that eventually came around to score on a double by Speaker.

Boston threatened all day, including loading the bases with no one out in the fifth and coming up empty. They were finally able to crack through in the sixth when the Babe himself delivered a two-out, two-run single giving him and his mates a 3-2 lead. He carried that into the eighth when a leadoff walk sounded his death knell. An error put men on first and third with nobody out, and when Speaker spanked out his third hit of the game, the score was tied at three and Babe was done for the day. Foster came in to relieve him and proceeded to hurl his first pitch at the backstop allowing the lead run to score.

The next batter was Braggo Roth, who had doubled in the first run of the game, and he delivered once again, singling in Speaker with Cleveland's fifth run. It proved to be the game winner as Boston got one back in the ninth. It was Ruth's second loss in a row. He had pitched good enough to win, but fell victim to every pitcher's Achilles heel, the walk. Two of the four men he passed came on to score, and that was the difference in the ball game.

	IP	H	SO	BB	R	ER
7/25/16 at Cleveland	7	4	0	4	5	4

He had faced three men in the eighth and all of them had reached and would eventually all score. At bat he was 2 for 4 with two RBIs.

The next two days found Boston on the upside of two one-run victories. In the third game of the series they found themselves battling something else besides the Indians. A brass band had taken up residence in the ballpark and was intermittently playing throughout the game. They began to play in the second inning:

"The band that had continued to play in this inning, despite Umpire O'Loughlin's remonstrance, was finally persuaded to knock off work after "Silk" had called time." *Boston Post* 7/28/16

They continued to play and only the threat of a Cleveland forfeit finally silenced them permanently.

"Pandemonium reigned during most of the contest, and at one time Umpire O'Loughlin threatened to forfeit the game to Boston unless the band, which persisted in playing while the Red Sox team was in the field, could be silenced."
Boston Post 7/28/16

The series was concluded with Boston winning their third game in a row, 3-2. It was their seventh consecutive game decided by one run. When erroneous reports of a Yankee loss circulated out of Chicago, it appeared as if Boston was in first place. Lannin made good on his promise and issued $50 checks for the boys to purchase new suits. It was later learned that New York had rallied in the ninth and the Sox were still in second place a half game out. Lannin let them keep their checks. He may have regretted his decision the next day when his team dropped a double header to the Tigers 10-8 and 7-3.

The losses were attributed in part to the heat and travel as the team had taken a boat across Lake Erie, from Cleveland to Detroit.

"This however, was probably due in a great measure to the excessive heat and exhausted condition in which the team got here this morning. Leaving Cleveland after midnight on the boat which was supposed to afford the cool night's sleep, the players were forced from their staterooms by the stifling atmosphere and many of them sat up on deck until long after two o'clock in the hope of getting relief." *Boston Post* 7/30/16

Not so coincidentally, Ruth had his worst outing of the season. He faced only six batters surrendering a walk, three hits and one who reached on an error. He had lasted one-third of an inning and for the first time in his career, he lost three games in a row. He did, however, notch his second successful pinch-hit of the season when he tripled (and scored) for Jack Barry in the eighth inning of the second game. Thankfully, they remained only half a game out, as the Yankees were just as inept in St. Louis.

By virtue of Carl Mays' 9-3 win the day before and the St. Louis Browns' sweep of the Yankees, when Babe Ruth took the mound on Monday he was pitching for the first-place Boston Red Sox.

He was as brilliant as he had been pitiful in throwing his sixth shutout of the year, closing out the Tigers, the month of July and his personal losing streak in exquisite fashion with a magnificent two hitter. He allowed only two men to reach second base as he completely dominated the potent Tiger lineup.

	IP	H	SO	BB	R	ER
7/31/16 at Detroit	9	2	6	2	0	0

At bat : 2 for 4 with 2 viciously hit singles to rightfield.

Great plays by Sam Crawford saved extra bases on both hits and he was robbed of another by first baseman George Burns. In the words of Paul Shannon of the *Boston Post*: He was "slugging the pill in his old familiar style."

The dog days of August dawned with the Red Sox perched atop the American League. Closing out the Tiger series with two wins kept them there as Babe was relegated to but a single pinch-hit appearance in those two games, at which he failed. It was on to St. Louis to face a sizzling St. Louis Browns team that had won 12 games in a row. Having been firmly entrenched in seventh place, they were now only four games from the first division. A $5,000 bonus awaited each member of the Browns if they could rally and capture the flag.

The Browns extended their winning streak to thirteen games and dropped the Red Sox out of first place by winning the series opener 3-2. Ruth drew the assignment of getting them back to first place. In his way stood 40-year-old future Hall of Famer Eddie Plank. It was a battle of left-handers won by the crafty veteran 6-1. Babe was flat as he was knocked around for nine hits in only five innings as he became the Browns' 14th victim in a row.

	IP	H	SO	BB	R	ER
8/4/16 at						
St. Louis	5	9	3	4	5	5
At bat: 0 for 1						

Boston stopped the winning streak at 14 when they won the first game of a doubleheader behind Ernie Shore, 4-1. The Browns got right back on track when they took the nightcap, 6-3. Babe was called upon to pinch-hit in the seventh inning of the second game and for the tenth time this season failed in the role. He was now 2 for 12 on the year as a pinch-hitter. On Sunday, Rube Foster pitched his best game since his no-hitter when he threw a three hit 1-0 shutout. The game was highlighted by a classic donnybrook between Browns third baseman Jimmy Austin and Red Sox catcher Chet Thomas.

The Red Sox boarded a train north to Chicago to play a four game set with the White Sox. At stake was first place, as the Red Sox arrived trailing the Chisox by a half game and .002 percentage points. Boston took three of the four games and headed home back in first place. They now led Cleveland by a full game and the White Sox by a game and a half. Babe did not make an appearance in the big series but was slated to open the homestand against Walter Johnson and the Senators.

There were 16,557 partisans who poured into Fenway on that Saturday, August 12. Most of them were anticipating yet another matchup between Boston's young southpaw and Washington's esteemed right-hander. The last time they had squared off, Boston had won 1-0, and many in attendance expected more of the same. The game, however turned out to be a clash of left-handers as Clark Griffith sent his own 21-year-old southpaw Harry Harper to the hill to face Babe. In an ironic twist, both Ruth and Johnson pitched in the game, though not against each other. Babe had a superb outing, yielding only two hits in his seven innings of work. He allowed a run in the fourth on a sacrifice fly and in the sixth, he pitched his way out of a bases-loaded situation without giving up a run. He was removed in the seventh inning with two on and two out when Carrigan sent Hal Janvrin in to pinch-hit. Ruth had trouble with the Senators lefty who had struck him out twice. Carrigan's strategy nearly worked as Janvrin hit a fly ball to the gap in right center.

Washington centerfielder Clyde Milan ran it down with a fine running catch to end the inning.

Walter Johnson came in to pitch in the Boston eighth. He made two errors himself, which did not hurt him and he went into the ninth needing only three outs to preserve Harper's 1-0 victory. He failed as the Red Sox scored two to take a 2-1 win.

	IP	H	SO	BB	R	ER
8/12/16 vs.						
Washington	7	2	4	4	1	1
At bat: 0 for 2						

With the two teams taking the mandatory Sunday off, the series resumed on Monday with Washington turning the tables by eeking out their own 2-1 victory. On Tuesday, 5,467 fans clicked the turnstiles at Fenway and they were delighted to learn that Johnson would be pitching for the Senators. Opposing him, coming back on just two days rest, was Babe Ruth. The meager crowd was treated to one of the finest pitching duels ever exhibited at Fenway Park. It was a duel of such magnitude, that it was elevated from the sports page to the front page of local newspapers.

The formidable foes battled for 13 innings before Boston emerged victorious with a single run in the 13th. Up until that time, Johnson had actually outpitched Ruth, allowing only five hits. Ruth, on the other hand, had struggled early, but after the seventh inning had given up only an infield single to Clyde Milan in the eleventh. Milan would prove a further thorn in Ruth's side when in the home half of the 12th, he ran down Babe's blast to right center and pulled it out of the bleachers, robbing him of a game-winning homer. In the Washington 13th, an error and a balk put the lead run on second with one out. A line shot to first base resulted in an inning-ending double play and brought the Red Sox up in what would be the last inning.

"Never until the thirteenth were the champions able to find him[Johnson] for more than one hit to an inning. It seemed almost tragic that such a great slabster had to work so brilliantly for a team that could not make any runs behind him. Big Babe Ruth twirled a game that was hardly a whit inferior to that provided by the tall Senator. Babe was hit by the same number of safeties as his opponent, but he was in more trouble than was

Walter and in two or three instances things looked very threatening for the Red Sox. Happily in spite an occasional slip up in
fielding, the Red Sox defense came to Ruth's support at critical
times, and in this way the dreaded score was averted." *Boston
Post* 8/16/16

It marked the third head to head confrontation of the season
between Ruth and Johnson. Ruth was now 3-0 and two of those
wins were by 1-0 counts. In the other, Babe had yielded a single
run. Playing against the best the game had to offer brought out the
best in Babe.

	IP	H	SO	BB	R	ER
8/15/16 vs.						
Washington						
Ruth	13	7	2	3	0	0
Johnson	12 2/3	8	5	5	1	1
Ruth at bat:	1 for 4, double					

Following the game, word came from Lewiston, Maine that
Bill Carrigan's father-in-law had passed away. The impact of his
death would be felt by Ruth and the Red Sox but not until the 1917
season.

Chicago followed the Senators into town and partook in the
Red Sox second flag raising ceremony of the year. Between games
of a scheduled doubleheader, Mayor James Curley would raise the
1915 world championship banner. Nearly 26,000 turned out to
witness the event as well as take in two crucial games in the American League pennant chase. The flag raising was delayed as the first
game went 16 innings before Boston scored on a two-out throwing error by third baseman Fred McMullin, giving them a 5-4 win.
Babe appeared as a pinch-hitter with two outs in the ninth and the
winning run on second. and he grounded out to second to end the
inning. The Red Sox used 21 players during the game, believed to
be a record at the time.

"Shoeless" Joe went 4 for 7 in the game, banging out a double
and three singles. His most interesting at bat came in the second
inning. As he dug in against Leonard, catcher Chet Thomas flashed
Leonard the sign. He looked up and noticed something different
about Jackson's bat—it was flat! Thomas asked for time and pointed

out this discrepancy to umpire "Silk" O'Loughlin. Jackson was sent back to the dugout by O'Loughlin to get a new bat and the game resumed.

Darkness shortened the second game, which was called after six innings and it allowed the Red Sox to complete a sweep. Their 2-1 victory lengthened their lead to three-and-a-half games.

Chicago battled back to take the next two games of the series and as Ruth and his teammates prepared for Tris Speaker and the Indians, six of the eight teams in the league were within five games of the lead.

Babe got the nod from Carrigan to open the series against Cleveland. He was 1 and 2 against the Indians on the season, that win being a 5-0 shutout back in June. He was in command and cruising along, having retired the first nine batters in a row, when Jack Graney led off the fourth inning with a single. The normally sure-handed Duffy Lewis bobbled the ball allowing Graney to take second. A sacrifice bunt and a sacrifice fly later, the Indians had a 1-0 lead. It was still 1-0 in the sixth when opposing pitcher Joe Boehling led off with a single. As the ball was relayed back to the infield, Babe suddenly seemed unsteady on his feet. This brought second baseman Jack Barry to the mound.

> "Barry came to the mound . . . as Babe looked hurt. Barry asked that he be allowed to throw a couple of warm ups. He was allowed and finished the inning." *Boston Herald* 8/20/16

Conflicting reports cloud the true nature of his illness or injury. The Boston Globe reported that the heat was responsible for his early exit. Other reports hinted of something of a far more serious nature.

> "Ruth was overcome with a sudden attack of heart trouble, which had overtaken him on Thursday night and was directly responsible for his not working on Friday against the White Sox as per schedule." *Boston Post* 8/20/16

There is no definitive answer on what, if any, "condition" caused Babe's removal from the game. There is no definitive answer on the essence of his physical problems. However, there is substantial evidence that he was experiencing some sort of difficulty. He'd had a tough outing back on the 4th of August in St. Louis, having been hit very hard in only five innings of work. He missed his next start and went only seven innings versus the Senators on August 12th. He did pitch brilliantly for 13 innings on the 15th of the month, but then came the dizziness which caused his next start to be pushed up a day and his sixth inning removal from this game. With no medical reports indicating the existence of heart trouble or any other malady, it is not easy to determine the nature of Ruth's difficulties. It does, however, seem unlikely that the heat was the source of his illness.

The cause of his illness was open to speculation. Perhaps he had escaped the watchful eye of manager Carrigan one too many times on the recent road trip. Or perhaps he had gobbled down a dozen hot dogs for lunch just before game time. Maybe he had just been partying a bit too much and the dog days of August simply jumped up and bit him. Whatever the reason, Babe himself wanted to make it clear to the fans of Boston that he did not have a heart condition. In so doing, one week later, he shed a bit of light on the nature of his ailment.

> "Big Babe Ruth wants the general public to understand that it was not any affection(SIC) of the heart that caused his removal from the game .... Babe has no wish to be considered an invalid and grew rather warm under the collar when he saw that he had been accused of having heart failure. He merely wrenched the muscle in between his fifth and sixth ribs but declares it is all right now." *Boston Post* 8/27/16

Runs in the sixth and ninth innings earned the Red Sox a 2-1 victory as Babe registered only his sixth no-decision of the season.

	IP	H	SO	BB	R	ER
8/19/16 vs. Cleveland	6	3	1	1	1	0

At bat: 0 for 2

Babe's declaration hardly seemed necessary at the time that it came. For on Wednesday the 23rd, he made his first appearance since he had left the game early with dizziness. He relieved Leonard in the eighth inning with Boston in front 6-3. He gave up a lead off single to Braggo Roth and then struck out Wambsganss, Gandil, and Chapman in succession. He then doubled and scored in the Red

Sox eighth before retiring the side in order in the ninth to record his first and only save of 1916. The win completed a four-game sweep of the Indians and put some breathing room between the Red Sox and the rest of the league.

	IP	H	SO	BB	R
8/23/16 vs.					
Cleveland	2	1	3	0	0

At bat: 1 for 1, double, run scored

He came back the very next day to open the series against the Tigers. It was a dark and gloomy day in Boston, so dark it caused the *Boston Post* to comment "that speed pitching would be most effective." Babe must have had the speed on this day as he blinded the Tigers on three hits as he fired his seventh shutout of the season. He shut down the heart of the Tiger order as Cobb, Veach, and Crawford went hitless and Detroit did not manage a hit after the third inning. Babe suffered streaks of wildness as he walked five but as was his custom, he was at his best when he needed it most as he did not allow one of them to score. It was their fifth win in a row and the daylight between them and the rest of the league was increasing.

	IP	H	SO	BB	R
8/24/16 vs.					
Detroit	9	3	3	5	0

At bat: 1 for 2 with a single

He made pinch-hit appearances in the next two games, both of them 2-1 losses to Detroit. He was successful in one attempt as he doubled in the ninth inning of the final game of the series. It was his fourth straight appearance and in fact since his "illness" he had: notched his first save with two innings of shutout relief; fired a three-hit shutout the very next day; and gleaned his third successful pinch-hit of the year. His bat was coming back to life as he was three for his last five at-bats with two doubles. It therefore seemed superfluous that Babe would have to convey to Red Sox fans that he was not an invalid suffering from a heart ailment. As was always the case with him, his performance on the diamond had spoken for itself. There was never another mention of him suffering from a heart condition.

Detroit left Boston in second place trailing the Red Sox by five full games. Cleveland was in sixth place, six-and-a-half games back and St. Louis, Chicago and New York were sandwiched in between. Carrigan's men appeared poised for the stretch drive and the fans of Boston seemed assured that the Red Sox would be returning to the World Series. However the streakiness which had characterized them throughout the year was about to re-emerge.

Rain on Monday forced a postponement of the series opener with the Browns causing a doubleheader on Tuesday. Leonard started the first game and lasted only a third of an inning. Ruth came in to relieve him with two men on and retired the two men he faced. However, Boston came to bat trailing 2-0. They grabbed the lead with three runs of their own in the third and that's the way it remained until St. Louis came to bat in the sixth. With one out, Babe walked two men in a row and then booted a ground ball to load the bases. Carrigan made the call to Carl Mays in an attempt to hold the Browns at bay. An infield out tied the game and placed men at second and third where they both scored on a single, giving the Browns the lead and the game, 5-3.

It was a most interesting outing for Babe, as he allowed only one hit in his five full innings of work. Yet he was saddled with his tenth loss of the year, a victim of his own wildness and fielding error.

	IP	H	SO	BB	R	ER
8/29/16 vs.						
St. Louis	5	1	1	4	3	0
At bat: 0 for 1						

His mates fared no better in the second game as the Browns thumped three Boston pitchers for an 8-2 win. The comfortable lead of just a few short days ago was evaporating and the Red Sox were once again streaking, only this time it was in the wrong direction. In an effort to stem the tide, Carrigan called upon Dutch Leonard. Having been blasted out after facing only five batters the day before, some had to be wondering about the wisdom of his choice. On this day the crusty Boston manager proved a genius.

"Hubert "Dutch" Leonard is himself again. Baseball can now add the Californian's name to the list of those accomplished twirlers who are ranked forever in the Hall of Fame. For yesterday the portly southpaw from the coast, abused and banished by the Browns only the day before, gave one of the finest pitching performances ever seen at Fenway Park, not only whitewashing Fielder Jones' exasperated batsmen but likewise twirling a no-hit game." *Boston Post* 8/31/16

Leonard had a perfect game going until he walked catcher Hank Severeid with two outs in the eighth inning. Another walk in the ninth accounted for the only St. Louis baserunners as Babe watched the second member of his pitching corp throw a no-hitter. Most importantly, it halted the losing streak at four. As Foster had before him, Leonard received, from Lannin, a crisp new $100 bill for his efforts.

Just as he had started the game following Foster's no-hitter, Babe was on the mound following Leonard's masterpiece as well. He had followed Foster's no-hitter with a three-hit shutout and although he was not quite as sharp in this outing, he certainly pitched well enough to earn a victory. Unfortunately, the Red Sox could muster but one run, and Babe fell to the Browns 2-1. Ruth himself made the last out of the game, popping out to George Sisler at first to end it. He had closed the month as he had opened it, with a loss. The Red Sox now had five teams nipping at their heels.

	IP	H	SO	BB	R	ER
8/31/16 vs.						
St. Louis	9	7	5	2	2	2

At bat: 2 for 4, double, run scored

His 2 - 3 record for the month of August did not reflect how effective he had been. His ERA was a microscopic 1.29, his opponents hit but .196 against him, and he had notched what would be his only save of the year with a two-inning relief stint in which he struck out three of the six men he faced. In his two no-decisions, he pitched a combined 13 innings in which he allowed only five hits and one earned run. His two wins were both shutouts, one of them the 13-inning gem against Walter Johnson. At the plate, he was 6 for 22 for a .272 average and as a pinch-hitter he was 2 for 5. Four of his six hits were doubles. He carried a 17-11 mark into

September and was ready to lead the Red Sox down the stretch toward another World Series.

The September run began in New York. A split of the first two games of the series brought Ruth to the mound to start the first game of a Labor Day doubleheader. Babe was in command throughout the day as no New Yorker reached first base until the fourth inning, when the first two batters got on but did not score. Boston scored five in the seventh inning to bust open a 1-0 game and give them a 6-0 lead. When Ruth walked Wally Pipp leading off the Yankee seventh, it would cost him his eighth shutout of the year. Pipp scored the only Yankee tally in a 7-1 Red Sox victory.

It proved to be a vital victory when Boston dropped the second game in the ninth inning 4-3. The once very comfortable five-game lead the Red Sox had enjoyed a scant week before had nearly evaporated as Detroit was now a single game back.

	IP	H	SO	BB	R	ER
9/4/16 at						
New York	9	5	5	1	1	1
At bat: 0 for 4						

After the game they headed straight to Grand Central Station to catch a train to Philadelphia where another doubleheader awaited them on Tuesday.

Boston trailed the opener when Babe registered a pinch-hit single batting for Ernie Shore in the Red Sox fourth. The Sox added a run in that inning, and when Ruth entered the game to pitch in the home half of the fourth, Boston was trailing 3-2. Babe pitched admirably, especially taking into account his complete-game win only 24 hours earlier. Four of the seven hits he allowed were bunt singles, as the A's went on to win the game 5-2. The Red Sox rallied back to take the second game 7-1, gaining them their second split in as many days and keeping them one game ahead of the charging Tigers.

	IP	H	SO	BB	R	ER
9/5/16 at						
Philadelphia	4	7	4	1	2	2
At bat: 1 for 3						

Two more wins in Philadelphia and Carrigan led his men further South to take on the Senators. Rain in the Nation's capital on Friday washed out a game in the sixth inning with the score deadlocked at 0-0. This forced the third doubleheader of the week and set up, for the fourth time this season, a matchup between Babe Ruth and Walter Johnson. Their three previous encounters had resulted in Ruth victories: 1-0, 1-0 and 4-1. This one would not be very different. Washington jumped right away with a single, a walk and a double to take a 1-0 first inning lead. From that point on, Ruth was virtually unhittable, surrendering only two singles and two walks the rest of the way. The Red Sox touched Johnson for eight hits but could plate only two runs. It was enough, however, to earn Ruth his 19th victory of the season and his fourth win, without a loss against Cal Griffith's venerable gentleman.

	IP	H	SO	BB	R	ER
9/9/16 at						
Washington:						
Ruth	9	4	5	3	1	1
Johnson	9	8	6	0	2	2
Ruth at bat:	1 for 3					

Washington won the second game, 4-3, in ten innings and for the third time in five days, the Red Sox had split a doubleheader. In Washington, as in Boston, baseball was not allowed to be played on Sunday. Both clubs welcomed the day off as they prepared to resume the series on Monday. Boston won on Monday, 4-2, setting up yet another Ruth-Johnson matchup to conclude the series on Tuesday.

In a move, which by today's standards would be termed nothing short of "Herculean", Ruth and Johnson squared off for the fifth and final time of the 1916 season with both of them coming back on only two days' rest.

Walter Johnson was the first baserunner of the game when he singled with two outs in the bottom of the third. This came after Ruth had ended the Boston half of the third with a long fly ball that Senator centerfielder Clyde Milan ran down, robbing Babe of a home run. It was the second time this season that Milan had robbed the Boston slugger of a homer. They battled 0-0 into the seventh, when Boston scored two runs on a two-out error by third baseman Ken

McBride. Leading 2-0 going into the ninth, it appeared as if Ruth would once again get the best of Walter Johnson. However, Babe faltered, yielding a two-out basses-loaded double to John Henry, which knotted the score at two. Mays came in to register the third out and when Boston scored in the top of the tenth, it looked as if the Sox would prevail against Johnson for the fifth time in the 1916 campaign

It was not to be, as the Senators rallied for two in their half of the tenth making a 4-3 winner of Johnson. The Washington fans had, for the second time in three days, witnessed a pitching duel between the best right-handed pitcher in the American league and the 21-year-old left-hander who was about to stake his claim as the league's best southpaw.

	IP	H	SO	BB	R	ER
9/12/16 at Washington:						
Ruth	8 2/3	6	7	3	2	2
Johnson	10	7	5	0	3	1
Ruth at-bat:	0 for 3					

The book on Ruth and Johnson was closed for the 1916 season. Five times they had faced each other with Babe winning four. Johnson was the victor in their last matchup with Ernie Shore taking the loss for Boston. Each of them threw four complete games in their five outings. Johnson departed after six innings in their first encounter in April while Ruth left after 8 2/3 in their last duel in September. Ruth was not beaten by Johnson once all season.

RUTH VS. JOHNSON COMPOSITE FOR THE 1916 SEASON

	G	IP	H	SO	BB	R	ER	ERA
Ruth	5	47 2/3	28	26	12	4	4	0.76
Johnson	5	45 2/3	38	23	7	13	11	2.17

The Senators hit an infinitesimal .196 against Ruth while the Red Sox batted a hefty .277 against Johnson. There was one instance where they both appeared in the same game but did not face each other, Babe starting and leaving after seven and Johnson entering in the eighth. There was no doubt whatsoever that Babe relished competing against the best and one need look no further than this matchup for profound evidence of that fact.

Wednesday was a travel day as the Red Sox headed west where they would play two games in St. Louis, three in Chicago and three in Detroit before heading back east through Cleveland and four games with the Indians. The pennant would be decided in these 12 games on the final western swing. Carrigan was confident.

> "My club has convinced me that it can play just as good ball on the road as home, and I see no reason why we should not split even or better on the coming western whirl, which means that we will be up there when the old bell rings . . . . I have four pitchers ready to take their regular turn in the box. They are Shore, Ruth, Leonard and Mays, with George Foster able to work about one game a week, and I am confident that this staff of mine will carry me through on top with colors flying." *The Sporting News* 9/11/16

While the Sox were traveling, the Tigers were winning to get within percentage points of first place. They split the series with the Browns and when they dropped the opener in Comiskey Park, they suddenly found themselves looking up from third place, trailing Detroit by a game and the White Sox by a half game.

On Sunday afternoon, September 17, over 40,000 fans turned out to watch the White Sox future Hall of Famer Red Faber pitch against Boston's Babe Ruth.

> "a crowd of real World Series proportions, a gathering that packed every available inch of space in Comiskey's mammoth ball park, overran right, left and center fields, fringed the fences and clung like flies to trestles and cross pieces in the grandstand . . . ." *Boston Post* 9/18/16

They roared with delight when Ruth issued a walk, three singles and a wild pitch after two were out in the first inning, staking the White Sox to a 2-0 lead. The Red Sox responded with three of their own in the second including one on a bases loaded fielders choice by Ruth himself. From that juncture on, Ruth tamed "Shoeless Joe" and the White Sox. He surrendered just two hits the rest of the way and allowed another runner to reach on a walk. The crowd proved to be more of a threat to him than the White Sox as they repeatedly encroached upon the field throughout the contest.

> "In the eighth and ninth rounds the fans saw defeat staring the White Sox in the face and they did their utmost to help the home players by tactics which were a disgrace to any big league city. The fans in centerfield pelted Walker with cushions and surrounded him so that the police had to force them to give him elbow room. Lewis was pushed and shoved by the frenzied fans on all sides of him and when the last man flied out to short left Duffy could never have caught the ball as a dozen maniacs rushed out and interfered. Happily for Boston, Scott was able to get under it." *Boston Post* 9/18/16

Through it all, Ruth was throwing harder at the end of the game than he was at the beginning, retiring the side in order in the ninth to secure his 20th win of the season. He became the third Red Sox left-hander to accomplish that feat.

	IP	H	SO	BB	R	ER
9/17/16 at						
Chicago	9	5	6	2	2	2

At bat: 0 for 4, RBI

Boston reclaimed first place the following day on the strength of Ernie Shore's 4-3 victory. This coupled with the Tiger loss to Philadelphia put the Red Sox back in first by .003 percentage points as they headed for Navin Field and a three-game showdown with the Tigers. While Cobb and company prepared for the Red Sox, Tiger president Navin prepared for the World Series as carpenters were constructing new bleachers in centerfield.

Victories in the first two games of the series put some breathing room between the Red Sox and their pursuers. By the time Babe took his turn on the mound, their lead was a game-and-a-half over Chicago and two full games over Detroit. Scoring two in the first inning, Ruth and his mates had a 7-0 lead before Detroit scored their only two runs of the game in their half of the fourth. The 10-2 drubbing all but eliminated the Tigers from the race as they now trailed Boston by three full games and five in the loss column. Babe was not as effective as he had been, but was as good as he needed to be. It had been since mid-July that he had pitched with such a lead. By the time the Red Sox left town, the construction·on the centerfield bleachers had ceased.

	IP	H	SO	BB	R	ER
9/21/16 at						
Detroit	9	7	4	4	2	2

At bat: 2 for 4, triple

Only Cleveland lay between the Red Sox and the familiar surroundings of Fenway Park. They continued their roll, taking the first two games of the series, 4-1 and 5-3. A fluke cost them their seven-game winning streak when Indian second baseman Marty Kavanaugh hit a ball through a hole in the outfield fence that wound up going for a grand slam home run.

Carrigan handed Babe the ball to close out the 23-game road trip and he closed it in fine fashion. Hurling his eighth shutout of the year, he scattered seven hits and was only in trouble once, that coming in the sixth when he pitched out of a first and third no-out situation. He chipped in with the bat as well, providing himself with an insurance run with a sharp RBI single to right in the fourth. The 2-0 win closed out one of the most successful western swings in Red Sox history and reduced Boston's magic number to five. Carrigan's prediction proved prophetic as his team captured nine wins on their 12-game western whirl.

	IP	H	SO	BB	R
9/25/16 at					
Cleveland	9	7	5	2	0

At bat: 2 for 3, RBI, single

His eight shutouts in a season set a new mark for Boston lefthanders and tied a major league record as well. Only three other lefties had thrown that many shutouts in a single season: Eddie Plank (1907), Ed Killian (1905), and Rube Waddell (1904, 1906)

At the Polo Grounds on the very same day, John McGraw led his New York Giants to a doubleheader sweep of the St. Louis Cardinals. It was the Giants' 20th and 21st consecutive victories, breaking a major league record held by the Providence Grays since 1884.

The train ride home was a gratifying one and as they pulled in to Back Bay Station, only the Yankees and the A's stood between them and their second straight trip to the World Series.

They split the first two games with New York. With five games left to be played and the pennant still in doubt, Babe took the mound for the third game of the series. His opponent was Yankee Bob Shawkey, who himself had 24 wins in 1916. The Red Sox scored three runs in the second inning, which would prove to be the only runs produced throughout the afternoon. Babe held the Yankees at bay and, once again, only once during the contest was he in any difficulty. He extricated himself from trouble with some outstanding defense. He opened the eighth inning by walking his counterpart Shawkey and Lee McGee followed with a double. Paddy Bauman was called upon to pinch-hit and scorched one back up the middle. Shawkey, sure it was a base hit, broke for home and was nailed by Babe who had made a sensational stop. This left runners on second and third with one out when Donovan countered with another pinch-hitter, sending Les Nunamaker to bat for Wally Pipp.

"The first ball that Ruth served up was allowed to pass by for a strike. The second was a hard foul tip, but the third was met squarely and went like a rifle shot till Ruth intercepted it in mid-air. Hanging on to the fierce drive Ruth pegged to third and doubled McGee before he could dash back to the bag, and thus the visitors one best bet was killed." *Boston Post* 9/30/16

New York went down one, two, three in the ninth and Babe had his 23rd win of the season. It was the second time during the year he had thrown back-to-back shutouts and this one established a new major league record for shutouts in a single season by a left-handed pitcher, becoming the first major pitching record held by Babe Ruth. Thirty years would pass before another pitcher (Bob Feller) would throw more shutouts in a single season and 62 years would pass before another American League left-hander(Ron Guidry) would equal the task. No American League left-hander has ever surpassed the mark.

	IP	H	SO	BB	R
9/29/16 vs. New York	9	5	4	4	0

At bat: 0 for 3

In what was becoming characteristic, Babe saved his best for when everything was on the line. With the Red Sox in the thick of a pennant race and in danger of blowing a five-game lead, Ruth was nothing short of spectacular. He was unbeaten for the month while winning six games and he never surrendered more than two runs in any one appearance. His opponents hit but .187 against him and down the home stretch he'd hurled back-to-back shutouts. In a September issue of *The Sporting News*, a note was made: "When the final test comes, it will be the good arm of Babe Ruth on whom Boston's fate depends, and it is some arm." Some arm indeed. If there had been any previous doubt, it was now eliminated, Babe Ruth was the unquestionable ace of the Boston staff.

His September line follows:

IP	H	SO	BB	R	ER	ERA
66 2/3	46	40	20	10	10	1.35

The next day, Dutch Leonard threw a 10-inning 1-0 shutout at the New Yorkers, clinching a tie for the American League pennant. The pennant would be clinched while the Red Sox were enjoying their customary Sunday off in Boston and Cleveland was defeating the White Sox. With the last three games with Philadelphia now meaningless, the Red Sox announced that the final two games of the season would be played at Braves Field to give the team a chance to familiarize themselves with the ballpark in which they would defend their title of world champions.

With the pennant in the bag and the Red Sox just staying loose in their preparation for the series, Ruth pitched the final game of the season. Ordered by Carrigan to make sure the outfielders "got a workout", Babe pitched what amounted to a glorified batting practice and was beaten by the A's to bring his final record for the year to 23-12.

	IP	H	SO	BB
10/3/16 vs. Philadelphia	5	11	1	1
At bat: 0 for 2				

The World Series was set to begin on October 7 at Braves Field. Fifty cents would purchase a seat in the bleachers and five dollars would garner a box seat. The grandstand section would cost a patron two or three dollars depending upon location. Record crowds were expected for the 13th edition of the Fall Classic. With four days to prepare for the start of the series, some of the Red Sox traveled to Worcester, Massachusetts, about 90 miles west of Boston to play in an exhibition game against the A's. All proceeds would go to a fund to purchase a gravestone for late umpire John Gaffney, which was to read, "King of the umpires". Babe did not make the trip because speculation had it that he or Ernie Shore would open up for the world champs in game one of their title defense.

The oddsmakers made the Red Sox 10-7 favorites to repeat as champions. Ty Cobb, Grover Cleveland Alexander, and Red Sox second baseman Jack Barry had all signed on with the *Boston Post* to "report" the series. Citing pitching and defense, Cobb picked the Red Sox to win. Citing lack of pitching experience, Alexander picked Brooklyn. For personal reasons, Barry picked Boston as well.

Brooklyn manager Wilbert Robinson, to the surprise of many, announced that Jack Pfeffer, a 25-game winner, would be in the bullpen for the first two games of the series. He named left-hander Rube Marquad to open the series and 25-year-old southpaw Sherry Smith to go in game two. Robinson made it very clear that this was not a reflection on Pfeffer's ability or his confidence in him. Rather, he felt it the best way to neutralize the left-handed bats of Dick Hoblitzell, Larry Gardner and Harry Hooper. The book on the Red Sox was that they were susceptible to left-handed pitching. Carrigan stated that he would decide on game day who would start for the Red Sox. Jack Barry suggested that the weather would be a factor in determining which Boston hurler would start, stating that an overcast sky would favor the harder throwing Ruth. Arthur Duffey of the *Boston Post* spoke to Ruth about the possibility of him starting the World Series.

> "Big Babe Ruth was the most unconcerned of the whole bunch. You would think that pitching in the World Series was an ordinary occurrence for the huge Southerner. When I asked Babe if he was going to pitch the opener, he replied,' well it makes no difference to me. If the big boss(Carrigan) says the word I'll be there for I never felt better in all my life.'" *Boston Post* 10/7/16

Whether the sunny weather played a part in Carrigan's decision is not known. But on October 7, 1916, Ernie Shore was pitching as the Red Sox opened their title defense. Boston scored the first run of the series in the third inning on a two-out double by Duffy Lewis which scored Hoblitzell who had tripled before him. So much for neutralizing their left-handed bats. Brooklyn came right back to tie the game in the top half of the fourth when Casey Stengel, who had led off with a single, scored on a triple by Zack Wheat. Brooklyn would have had more were it not for the defensive exploits of Harry Hooper.

Second baseman George Cutshaw followed Wheat to the plate and hit a blooper to short rightfield. Hooper charged the ball and slipped while doing so. From the sitting position, he reached up and made the catch. Wheat tagged at third and dashed toward home. Hooper sprang to his feet and threw a perfect strike to catcher Hick Cady who tagged the sliding Wheat completing the double play. It was, to that point, the greatest catch anyone had ever seen in World Series play. The Red Sox took a 6-1 lead into the ninth inning and nearly blew it as Brooklyn scored four runs and had the bases loaded when Jake Daubert grounded out to Everett Scott to end the game. Carl Mays saved the game for Shore and Boston had the series edge, one game to none.

Boston's "Blue Laws" were not suspended for the World Series and as a result it took an immediate hiatus.

The series resumed on Monday as 5,000 people gathered outside the gates at Braves field by 10:25 a.m. waiting for the gates to open. As the players prepared for the game, Carrigan walked to the bullpen with coach Heinie Wagner, catcher Sam Agnew and pitchers Ruth and Carl Mays. With Agnew catching Ruth and Wagner catching Mays, Carrigan watched, still not sure who he'd name to start the second game. It was not until 2 p.m. when Babe strolled dinktoed to the mound that the partisan crowd of 41,373 knew Carrigan's decision. Babe threw a few warm-up tosses and plate umpire Bill Dineen yelled "Play ball." Finally Ruth was starting in a World Series game and history was waiting to be made.

Babe's first pitch to Jimmy Johnston was a fastball for a called strike and when he swung and missed the next one, the crowd was already on its feet and cheering. He would eventually fly out to Tilly Walker in center and after Jake Daubert fouled to Larry Gardner at third, Brooklyn centerfielder Hy Myers stepped to the plate. He took ball one outside and then nailed one to the gap in rightcenterfield. Hooper raced for it and gave it an outstanding diving effort but it got by him and rolled all the way to the wall. By the time Walker reached it and fired to Everett Scott, Myers was sliding headlong into home with the first run of the game. Wheat followed with a drive to the same spot but higher and Hooper was able to amble under it and make the catch to end the inning. Ruth's first inning of World Series ball was behind him, and the Sox came to bat trailing 1-0.

Great defense and a baserunning error kept Brooklyn from taking a 2-0 lead in the third. With one out, Smith lined one down the rightfield line for what was a sure double, but the Brooklyn pitcher never stopped at second and was gunned down—Hooper to Walker to Gardner. The mistake proved costly when the next batter, Johnston, lined a single up the middle. He was thrown out trying to steal on a perfect throw from Thomas to Janvrin. Brooklyn had a double and a single in the inning and not even a left on base to show for it.

Babe himself would register the RBI that tied the game in the Red Sox half of the third. Scott led off with a triple over the head of Zack Wheat in left. Chet Thomas followed and hit the first pitch toward the middle, but second baseman George Cutshaw—short hopping the ball, holding Scott at third and flipping the ball to Daubert at first in time to get Thomas. Ruth then stepped to the plate and also swung at the first pitch hitting the ball to the same place. This time, however, Scott broke immediately for home. Cutshaw, in his haste to get Scott, momentarily bobbled the ball. He recovered in time to get Ruth at first, but the Sox had tied the game. The significance of that eked-out run grew as the afternoon melted into twilight.

The game remained 1-1 going into the ninth with each team having had their chance to take the lead and failing to do so. Boston's best chance came in the fifth when, with two out, Chet Thomas hit a line drive into the leftfield corner. As he was rounding second, Thomas slammed into Brooklyn shortstop Ivy Olson and fell to the ground. As he was crawling, Thomas was yelling to Umpire Quigley, pleading for an interference call. He got it, as Quigley, despite the protestations of the entire Brooklyn infield, awarded the Red Sox catcher third base. Home plate umpire Bill Dineen had to come between Olson and third base coach Heinie Wagner, as an exchange of words brought Wagner out to shortstop.

Order was quickly restored and Ruth stepped to the plate. He took the first offering from Smith for a strike and then took two successive "Ruthian" swings that found nothing but air and the score remained tied going to the sixth.

Brooklyn's chance came in the eighth. Mowrey led off with a single that brought Olson to the plate. Soundly booed by the partisan Boston crowd, he executed a perfect bunt moving Mowrey to second and when Hy Myers singled for his second hit of the game, the Brooklynites had men on first and third and one out.

Next up was pitcher Smith. With the infield drawn in, Smith hit a 0-1 pitch sharply on the ground to Scott at short who quickly fired home, catching Mowrey in a run down. Thomas ran him back toward third before flipping the ball to Gardner. Mowrey dashed toward home only to find the six-foot plus frame of Babe Ruth standing there with the baseball. In an attempt to jar the ball loose, he slammed into him. Babe held his ground—and the baseball—as Mowrey was tagged out. The Boston pitcher did sustain a bloody nose and play was held up for a bit as Babe was tended to on the third base line until the bleeding ceased.

Babe then returned to the mound to face leadoff hitter Jimmy Johnston with two out and runners on second and third. With the count one ball and no strikes, Johnston hit a high bouncer that appeared earmarked for centerfield. Ruth leaped high in the air to snag it and instead of a two-run single, it was out number three. As the Red Sox left the field, the 41,000 plus roared their approval.

Boston went one, two, three in their half of the eighth as did Brooklyn in the ninth. The game nearly ended in the Red Sox ninth when a double and an error put men on first and third with nobody out. Hoblitzell then lined to Myers in centerfield who threw a perfect strike to the plate to get Janvrin who had tagged up. When Larry Gardner fouled out to the catcher following an intentional pass to Lewis, the game headed into extra innings for the ninth time in the series' 13-year history.

Ruth, as he had done all year long, grew stronger as the game wore on. He issued a two-out walk in the tenth and then set the side down in order in the 11th and 12th, striking out Daubert to close the 11th and Myers to open the 12th. This accounted for half of his strikeout total for the game. Mowrey reached on an error by Gardner leading off the 13th but Babe easily disposed of Olson, Miller and Smith, thus setting the record for innings pitched in one

World Series game. Only two Robins had reached base since the eighth inning; one on a walk and the other on an error. Sherry Smith tied the record when the Red Sox went down one, two, three in their half of the 13th inning.

Twilight was upon Braves Field as Babe strolled to the mound to face Brooklyn in the 14th frame. All in attendance knew that this would be the last inning. The darkness that was creeping upon the city would claim this game, if none of the combatants did. N.J. Flatley, a sportswriter for the *Boston Herald* wrote,

> "Down there in the lonesome gloom of nightfall, Babe was pitching as only great pitchers can." *Boston Post* 10/10/16

It took Ruth but nine pitches to retire Brooklyn in the 14th, reestablishing the record Smith had just tied, and setting the stage for the dramatic finish. Dick Hoblitzell, Boston's steady first baseman, led off the 14th for the Red Sox. The darkness was thickening, and some even wondered if plate umpire Dineen might call it at this juncture.

Smith threw "Hobby" only five pitches and he was on his way to first base; it was the fourth time that Hoblitzell had walked in the game. Though the three previous passes had not caused Smith and his mates any damage, this one would prove fatal. Duffy Lewis bunted the first pitch and sacrificed Hoblitzell to second, which brought up Del Gainer to pinch-hit for the left-handed hitting Larry Gardner. Gainer took the first pitch for a ball, when suddenly Carrigan sprang from the dugout beckoning Dineen for time. Time was granted and Carrigan, after a brief consult with Heinie Wagner in the third base coaching box, yelled out to the bullpen for Mike McNally to run for Hoblitzell at second. Gainer swung and missed the next pitch before taking Smith's one and one offering on a line into leftfield for a base hit. McNally was off at the crack of the bat and by the time Wheat fielded the ball, he was well past third. Wheat made a throw, but had no chance of getting the sliding McNally as the crowd erupted with a victorious cheer.

Boston now held a two-games-to-zero lead in the World Series. No team had ever been beaten after capturing the first two games of the world championship series.

As the venue for game three moved to Ebbets Field, the pundits dissected the record setting 14-inning contest. Paul Shannon wrote:

"After the score had been tied and Ruth was assured that the air tight defense(SIC)which Boston boasts would not falter, he comforted himself with the usual brilliant style, and his pitching and fielding gave the quietus to the critics who said he could not prevail against the National League champions.....Babe pitched with all the craft of Waddell and the speed of Johnson in the last half dozen rounds." *Boston Post* 10/10/16

Smith pitched equally as brilliant. Some, Grover Cleveland Alexander among them, thought he even pitched better than Ruth. It was the longest game in the 13-year history of the World Series as Babe Ruth set the record for the longest complete game victory in World Series competition. Over 80 years has passed and over 400 World Series games have been played; a longer game has yet to be played, and Babe's record still stands. Someday two pennant winners will engage in a World Series contest that will go longer than 14 innings, but it remains extremely unlikely that one pitcher will remain on the mound for the entire game. Given the time and circumstance, this may have been Babe's finest pitching performance.

	IP	H	SO	BB	R	ER
Ruth	14	6	4	3	1	1
Smith	13 1/3	7	2	6	2	2

Carl Mays and Jack Coombs squared off in game three as Brooklyn finally captured a win. Staked to a 4-0 lead, Coombs cruised into the sixth before a walk, a triple and a single cut his lead in half. When Larry Gardner homered with one out in the seventh inning, Robinson immediately summoned his ace, 25-game winner Jack Pfeffer from the bullpen. Pfeffer shut the door, retiring eight Red Sox in a row, striking out three of them and saving the win for Coombs.

Game four saw another battle of lefties as Robinson went back to his game one starter, future Hall of Famer Rube Marquad. Carrigan countered with Leonard. Buoyed by their win in game three, Brooklyn came out smoking as their first two batters tripled and singled giving them the quick, early lead. A walk, a wild pitch, and an error led to another run and when Boston came to bat in their half of the second, they trailed 2-0. They hit right back in the second; Hoblitzell walked, for the fifth time in the series, and Lewis doubled. Gardner stepped in, and on the first pitch lined one into the gap in left centerfield. It rolled all the way to the wall and the Red Sox third baseman had his second home run of the World Series, giving his team a 3-2 lead. The Red Sox would not relinquish the lead, adding single runs in the fourth, fifth, and seventh. Leonard settled down after a rocky first inning, only allowing three hits the rest of the way as Boston took game three, 6-2. They boarded a train for home, needing only one win in three games to retain their title of world champions.

Facing elimination in game five, Robinson went to his ace, Jack Pfeffer, to keep them alive, while Carrigan countered with his game one starter Ernie Shore. A new World Series attendance record was set, as 43,620 turned out hoping to see their Red Sox crowned champions on this day. Brooklyn again scored first, forging across a run in the second without the benefit of a base hit. A leadoff walk, a sacrifice bunt, an infield out, and a passed ball gave the Robins a 1-0 lead. Boston countered with a Lewis triple and a sacrifice fly to tie the score in their half of the second. Boston added two more in the third when they sandwiched two singles between a walk and a double error by Brooklyn shortstop Ivy Olson.

It was all that Shore would need as he allowed the Robins but three hits throughout the afternoon, giving the Red Sox the game and the series and allowing them to join the Chicago Cubs and Connie Mack's A's as the only teams to win back-to-back world championships.

Ruth made no other appearances in the series, but as was always his style, he left his indelible mark on the 1916 World Series. Only Shore pitched more innings and no one touched his series leading ERA of 0.64. Although he went 0 for 5 at the plate, he did have a very big RBI in game two that enabled the game to go to extra innings.

The following day, the players met at Fenway Park to divide up their share of the World Series money. A full share for the winning Red Sox was $3,910.26. This was $410.26 more than what Babe's contract for 1916 had called for, so he was happy to double his salary. It was the second largest purse in World Series history, surpassed only by the $4,024.68 each member of the 1912 Red Sox champions had received. The smallest piece of the pie was the $15.00 the players gave to the lad that tended the "auto gate" at Fenway Park.

The players then made their getaways. Del Gainer and Larry Gardner headed to the Scott Gun and Fishing Club just outside of Quebec. Herb Pennock took an early train bound for his home in Philadelphia, while Jimmy Walsh hit the rail north for Syracuse. Vean Gregg had the farthest to travel to his farm in the wilds of north-western Canada. Sam Jones left South Station bound for his home in Ohio, while Agnew and Foster headed to their respective homes in Oklahoma and Mississippi. Carl Mays announced plans to drive his new automobile to his home in Portland, Oregon. His expected arrival date was "around Thanksgiving." Ernie Shore remained in Boston to have his tonsils out, as Carrigan and Heinie Wagner made plans to head toward Carrigan's home in Lewiston, Maine. As the manager prepared to leave, he announced that he was through with baseball. Although rumors would persist throughout the winter about Carrigan's return, he had managed his final game for the Boston Red Sox.

Jack Barry had rounded up a barnstorming crew that was scheduled to play in New Haven, Connecticut on Sunday the 15th of October and then in Laconia, New Hampshire on Tuesday the 17th. Babe was on the team and was a large part of the reason that over 3,000 fans showed up at Lighthouse Point to watch baseball on that Sunday afternoon. Another reason was that Ty Cobb was both managing and playing first base for the local entry from New Haven.

Babe pitched the full nine innings for the "Red Sox," surrendering three runs and six hits, while walking three and striking out five. He had only a single in four trips to the plate, but it was a key hit in the game. It came with his team trailing 3-2 in the fifth and would eventually provide the tying run. He moved to second base on a fly ball and then following a strikeout, stole third base, scoring on an errant throw by the catcher. It tied the score and that is how it remained. Ty Cobb had touched Ruth for a single and a double, scoring a run in the fourth when the Colonials scored all three of their runs. The patrons left happy and considered it a moral victory that the local nine had held the world champs to a 3-3 tie.

On their way from New Haven to Laconia, they made a brief stop in Lowell, Massachusetts to be greeted in a reception by the sportswriters of the city before heading on to New Hampshire. The trip to New Hampshire was a mixture of business and pleasure, as John Maynard, co-founder and owner of the Draper-Maynard Sporting Goods Factory in Plymouth, New Hampshire, had extended to

Barry and his mates an invitation to visit the factory and then head out to his cottage on Squam Lake.

Several Red Sox players visited the factory every fall from 1915-1918, many times making suggestions on the manufacturing of different gloves. The factory was experimenting with a new "padded" glove and welcomed the input of the Boston players. It is said that Babe may have even named the Draper-Maynard's "Lucky Dog" model that he subsequently used for many years.

Before visiting the factory, the team would play in Laconia. Barry and the Boston players were feeling pressure as American League president Ban Johnson and the National Commission had issued statements that the world champs were in violation of league regulations by playing in exhibition games. They were informed that they would be admonished if they continued to do so. The result of the warning was a day that the local Laconians still talk about.

In an attempt to circumvent this league regulation Barry and his men scrambled the teams. When nearly 2,000 townsfolk showed up at the Pearl Street Grounds on that chilly Tuesday afternoon, they were delighted to find that Babe Ruth was pitching for the local nine. Chet Thomas caught Babe and although his mates knocked him around pretty good, he electrified the crowd with his bat, going three for four with a double and a homer as he led the Laconia nine to an 8-6 victory. After the game, the Red Sox visited local New Hampshire landmarks before being entertained by Mr. Maynard at the Lake Gorge home of a wealthy Red Sox fan.

The townsfolk turned out again the following day as the Red Sox toured the Draper-Maynard facility and greeted the coeds from the Plymouth Normal School. The Plymouth Normal School was a two-year facility for young women to prepare to become teachers. Today it is known as Plymouth State College. Babe was the hit of the day; bedecked in his full-length raccoon coat, his autograph was the most sought after item of the day. Although members of the Red Sox visited the factory for several years, none of the visits generated the hoopla and holiday atmosphere that welcomed the 1916 world champs.

That afternoon, the contingency headed to Lake Squam for a little relaxation. While out at the lake, a couple of the boys donned some boxing gloves and began to play around. To no great surprise, Babe was in the midst of it all. Arthur Duffey, the *Boston Post* columnist traveling with the team wrote,

"Not content with pulling down some of the big pitching hon-ors, big Babe Ruth would like to be a real white hope champion. He has a sneaky suspicion that he can fight." *Boston Post* 10/24/16

Visions of heavyweight championships danced in Babe's head. Spotting boxing gloves hanging on the wall, Babe immediately donned them, all the while urging his teammate Mike McNally to do the same. With some coaxing from the rest of the gang, McNally obliged. Three inches shorter and roughly 40 pounds lighter, "Minnooka Mike" was clearly at a physical disadvantage. However, before too much time had elapsed, it became clear that McNally could hold his own as he "was bouncing 'em right and left off Babe's beezer". Babe did not take too kindly to this and things got a bit out of hand, and the aspiring pugilists had to be pulled apart by their teammates.

Not happy to retire with a loss, Babe coerced a Y.M.C.A. in-structor who was with the group to put on the gloves and the two proceeded to go at each other "hammer and tongs". Babe emerged the victor in this one and upon his return to Boston, he took his one and one amateur record to the gym of George Byers in the old West End of Boston. His boxing career under Byers lasted but a few days of training. However, his fascination with the fight game would remain with him and talk of his becoming a boxer would re-emerge off and on throughout his career.

While the Red Sox team scattered from New Hampshire, Babe and Helen remained for an extended visit, sightseeing and taking in many local events. Babe did some hunting and fishing as the young couple began a routine that would last approximately seven years. They would make an annual visit to the Meredith area, where Helen was believed to have been born and lived before migrating to Bos-ton when she was 15 years old.

In the early years of their marriage, they were often seen en-gaging in many activities together. They would attend dances at the local town hall, ice skate, coast upon the snow-covered hills and hike the mountain trails. One night at a dance, a number of the local "toughs" were milling about the floor when one of them made a remark to Helen that Babe just happened to overhear. Babe was on him in an instant and reportedly shook the kid by the collar until he was blue in the face. This convinced the lad to apologize to

Helen, after which Babe turned to the remaining dozen or so of the toughs and informed them that each of them would suffer the same fate if any of them tried any more "rough stuff." Throughout the remainder of the evening, none was reported.

Following Helen's tragic death in a fire in 1929, the *Meredith News* recalled one of their early visits to the mountains of Hew Hampshire. "Mrs. Ruth and the immortal Babe made Meredith quite a visit during the winter about ten or twelve years ago. They were guests at the home of Mr. and Mrs. Durant [at the corner of Main and Plymouth Streets] and indulged in coasting and other sports. Both made many friends while here."

Babe and Helen would continue their visits following their move to New York. But as their marriage began to unravel and eventually extinguish, so to did their trips to the mountains. It is likely, however, that for the young married couple riding the tails of Babe's rapidly rising star, these were among the happiest times they shared. Today, the town of Plymouth, New Hampshire still recalls with warmth and pride a time when it called Babe Ruth one of its own.

Meanwhile, back in Boston, the rumor mill was churning. One had Joseph Lannin pursuing Connie Mack to manage the Red Sox. This rumor would surface more than once during Ruth's tenure with Boston. Another had the players preparing to strike over contract issues regarding injuries incurred while playing.

Yet another had a Boston sportsman named John McCarthy attempting to buy the Red Sox. Among his investors was said to be a Boston banker, Joseph P. Kennedy. The son-in-law of former Boston Mayor "Honey Fitz" Fitzgerald, Kennedy would soon become a father for the second time. His wife Rose was seven months away from giving birth to their second son, John F. Kennedy.

One rumor turned to reality when on November 1, 1916 the announcement was made that Joseph Lannin had sold the Red Sox to a "theatrical firm" headed by Harry H. Frazee and Hugh Ward. The reported purchase price was $750,000. Frazee immediately issued a statement in which he let it be known that he hoped that Carrigan would stay on as manager. This prompted Carrigan to declare again his intent to retire from baseball. Citing his banking interests in Lewiston, Maine, he stated he would not consider any offer to return to the game.

Frazee and Ward would be unanimously approved on the first day of the owners meeting in Chicago on December 13. But Frazee didn't wait that long to create fan interest and excitement.

Arriving in Boston on December 8, Frazee and company went immediately to Fenway Park to watch a football game. After watching Somerville(Massachusetts) High defeat DePaul Academy of Chicago 7-0, he left for what would become the Red Sox' new executive offices on the seventh floor of the Dexter building at the corner of Washington and Winter Streets in downtown Boston. It was from these offices that he made his first baseball move. It was a call to Clark Griffith of the Washington Senators to offer him $60,000 for Walter Johnson. Although his offer was denied, Frazee's gesture had brought instant endearment from the fans.

By the time Frazee had arrived in Chicago, he was in firm control of the Red Sox. He was now the youngest owner in major league baseball and the *Sporting News* of November 9 reported: "He is a 'human dynamo' who will bring something in the way of activity and legitimate sensation it[baseball] has never known before. He has ideas that in their working out will probably add an interesting chapter in the game's history." These words proved prophetic and their echoes reverberate in the ears of generations of Red Sox fans.

In diamond news, the *Sporting News* announced its plans to begin selecting a major league all-star team. The writers would choose a player from each everyday position, four pitchers and two utility players. The first writer polled was Irving Sanborn of the *Chicago Tribune*. Scratched on his ballot was the name of Babe Ruth of the Red Sox. He would likewise appear on the ballots of Cleveland correspondent Henry Edwards and the legendary Grantland Rice.

On December 14, the *Sporting News* released the pitching statistics of the American League hurlers. Babe's line for the year looked like this:

G	IP	AB	H	R	ER	BB	SO	ERA
44	323	1,146	230	83	63	118	170	1.75

He hit eight batters, threw three wild pitches and balked once. Forty of his 44 games were starts, which led the league. Twenty-three of those starts were complete games, ranking him fourth in the league. His actual innings pitched totaled 323 2/3, ranking him third in the league. His ERA led the league as did his nine shutouts. Defensively, he shone as well as his 24 putouts would indicate. This tied him with Cleveland's Jim Bagby for the league lead in that category.

His opponents hit but .192 against him with Ty Cobb having particular difficulty with Ruth's offerings. Cobb hit only .263 against Babe and although that is .62 points higher than the rest of the league touched him for, it was .108 points lower than his league average of .371. The article accompanying the stats trumpeted Ruth's sterling season: "Babe Ruth of Boston was the premier pitcher of the American League in the 1916 season and no one can question his rights to the honors. He made the high record for effectiveness and did it pitching more innings than any other pitcher bar two".

In only his second full season, Babe Ruth had begun to sketch his place in baseball history. With the Cy Young Award not created until 1956, it had all occured 40 years too soon to receive such honors.

His reward for his post-season accolades was a notification from the National Commission that he, along with nine other Red Sox players, was being fined $100 for playing in the exhibition games following the World Series. Ty Cobb was fined $50 for his infraction.

As the curtain was being drawn on 1916, Jack London passed away and Ethel Barrymoore left her stage career to pursue a career in the new motion picture industry. Ban Johnson met with Jake Ruppert in French Lick, Indiana discussing plans to erect a new 50,000 seat stadium in New York. The projected cost was $1 million, and they hoped to have it open for the 1918 season.

George Foster retired from the Red Sox and Harry Frazee traveled to Lewiston, Maine to meet with Bill Carrigan in an attempt to pursuade him to return as manager of the Red Sox. George and Helen Ruth drove to Baltimore to spend the holidays with Babe's father, where they were involved in an auto accident, in what was becoming a growing list of mishaps behind the wheel. Thankfully, he and Helen escaped without a scratch.

It was during late 1916 and early 1917 that he began to make regular trips to the Boston suburb of Sudbury. Located at the end of Harness Lane off of Butler Road in West Sudbury, nothing but an old foundation and a dug well exist where Babe made his first appearance in this outlying town with its rolling hills and wide open spaces.

Willis Lake was a popular retreat for celebrities and professional athletes as they regularly rented lakeside facilities to partake in fishing, hunting and an occasional party or two. Taken there for the first time by a friend, Babe fell in love with the area and he became a regular visitor, eventually purchasing a farm there.

The farm that today bears the address 558 Dutton Rd. was actually not purchased by Babe until June 26, 1923. The land was roughly 160 acres and was called Hudson Rd. Babe himself did not own the property for very long, as he conveyed it to his soon-to-be estranged wife Helen on October 16, 1925. At that time a mortgage of $6,000 was held on the property by the First National Bank of Marlboro. Exactly six months later, on April 26, 1926, Helen sold the farm to Mr. George H. D. Lamson of Weston, Massachusetts. Babe's attempt at becoming a gentleman farmer was over.

However, there is evidence that Babe was active in Sudbury long before his actual purchase of the farm. An entry in the journal of the Wayside Inn (made famous by Henry Wadsworth Longfellow) tells the tale of Babe coming to the aid of stranded travelers. Dated only 1917, the journal relates that a Mr. and Mrs. Allen of Cambridge, Massachusetts had missed their train at the Wayside Inn Station and were hitchhiking back to Cambridge when they were picked up by a stranger in "a long, expensive motor car". The Allens asked if he were a professional driver, and the stranger replied that he was a baseball player. It was not until the next day, when they saw a picture of their benefactor in the morning paper, that they realized it was Babe who drove them home.

Other yarns are spun of his antics in this rural suburb, which he alternately called home for nearly a decade. There was a time on Willis Lake when he is alleged to have thrown a piano into the lake during a quiet get together with some of his teammates. It is not known whether the piano was out of tune or had offended Babe in some other way. Perhaps after imbibing a beer or two, some macho contest of strength developed that entailed the carrying of a piano to the side of the lake and tossing it in. The piano was never recovered.

Other reports had Babe distraught over the fact that he was not allowed to shoot squirrels. He commented to a friend that he could have a full-length coat made of squirrel tails if he were only allowed "to shoot the damn things". He did enjoy shooting and he had found the perfect place to do it. One account noted that "every tree within 100 yards" of Babe's house had a bullet hole in it. Babe never did anything in a small way.

Although Babe didn't purchase his farm until 1923, he may have rented it during his time with the Red Sox. References were made to Babe coming into Boston from his farm to meet with Red Sox officials. Babe himself commented during the winter between the 1918 and 1919 seasons that he was "working on my farm" to stay in shape.

Living nearby at the time was a family with two young boys. Merton Haskell and his younger brother Clarence were often guests of Babe's and spent time fishing and hiking through the local woods with the young Boston baseball star. Clarence was 83 years old when in 1994 he shared his memories of Babe with Rudy VanVeghten of the *Meredith News* in Meredith, New Hampshire.

With a vivid clarity and warmth, Haskell recalled some of his adventures with Ruth. "Babe Ruth did a lot of good things... On more than one occasion, Babe would arrange with an orphanage in Roxbury to have a busload of boys come out to the farm for a day in the country. The boys played ball with Babe, went fishing in a nearby pond and visited with the animals ... a cookout provided food for all as Helen always saw to it that the boys were well fed. She also took care of any scratches and bumps..."

Another favorite activity was for Babe to hit golf balls with a baseball bat. Stationing the boys hundreds of yards away in an open field, Babe would hit them at times so high they would go out of sight. The boys would gather them up, run them back and the exercise would begin anew.

When it was time for the boys to go, Babe would give the high sign to Merton, who would roll out a wagon with a canvass cover over it. As the boys entered the bus, Babe rolled back the cover and reveal bats, balls and gloves and each boy received one of each. The balls he would personalize with an autograph. These events took place two or three times a year and at Babe's request the media was never present.

There are no census records that show Babe Ruth ever claimed anywhere in Boston or its surrounding towns as his legal residence during his playing days in Boston. However, in his early years of stardom and fame, it was Sudbury where the boy in him roamed the fields, walked the woods and fished the creeks.

Four

1917: A Most Unusual Perfect Game

After weeks of speculation by the press, Bill Carrigan informed new Sox owner Frazee the first week of January that he would not be returning to manage the team. Between growing tired of traveling, and business interests in his hometown of Lewiston, Maine, he opted to walk away a winner.

Babe, who was losing the best manager he would ever have, couldn't be too disappointed in the choice of replacements. Though Harry Hooper, Dick Hoblitzell, and Heinie Wagner were reportedly considered, Frazee announced on January 6 that Jack Barry would be his new player-manager. The Sox second baseman would be paid $10,000 per year, and Frazee stated that money would not be spared in fielding a championship team.

One of Barry's first official acts as manager was to contact shortstop Everett Scott in Indiana and order him to stop playing competitive basketball. Reporters wondered aloud, however, if Barry would be able to handle temperamental lefties Babe and Dutch Leonard as well as Carrigan did

Babe and Helen drove back up from Baltimore in his new auto and arrived in the Boston area on Saturday, January 13. He stopped by the Red Sox executive offices and visited with team secretary Johnny Lane, and was said to appear in great condition. He enthusiastically stated to a *Herald* reporter "I have a new gun that can shoot three miles, and I am going to try it out around here."

It was also reported in the local papers that Babe was attempting to learn how to ice skate. He spent the afternoon of January 17 on Boston's Jamaica Pond, receiving instruction from teammates Gardner, Henriksen, and Janvrin. N.J. Flatley of the Boston *Herald* wrote the following day:

> "A good time was had by all, except Babe. According to him, skating is harder than hitting a left-hander's hook. The ice, he admits, also is fairly hard."

Herman Nickerson, in his weekly *Sporting Life* column noted: "He is a better pitcher than skater, and if he doesn't break either his arm or his neck, he will be lucky."

❧

One of the dominant sports stories over the winter of 1916-'17 was a proposed major league players strike. The Players Fraternity, as it was called, was headed by 40-year-old David Fultz, a former outfielder who had spent seven seasons in the majors between 1898 and 1905. The union was seeking to abolish the ten-day clause, which allowed teams to cease paying an injured player after he had been out of action ten days. Fultz and company were also looking to have minor league teams pay traveling expenses to spring training for their players.

On January 18, Fultz arrived in Boston for a meeting with the players at the Hotel Touraine, on the corner of Tremont and Boylston Streets. Babe, likely sporting a few bumps and bruises from his skating excursion the day before, was a Red Sox representative, and was joined by more than a dozen fellow ballplayers. After three hours of discussion, the players were convinced that their case was strong. Fultz had been urging players not to sign contracts for the upcoming season, yet Ruth himself was already under contract, having signed a two-year deal before the '16 season. It would have been interesting to have heard Babe's input in what was likely his first union experience.

In late January, in his own attempt to help avert the strike, Frazee invited all of the Sox players' wives to attend spring training at Hot Springs. His thought was that the wives would not allow their husbands to hold out, causing them to miss a month-long vacation at the resort. Ruth and several Boston players immediately contacted Frazee's office to inform the team that their wives would be attending. Though talk of the strike continued, more and more players were signing contracts to play for 1917. Struggling to maintain the fight, Fultz finally called off the strike in New York on February 14, just days before the deadline. Organized Baseball officially severed relations with the union at this time, and ballplayers were once again without representation.

Ruth's contract for 1917 called for a raise of $1,500, bringing his salary up to $5,000 for the year. His National League counterpart Grover Alexander was, at this time embroiled in a bitter contract dispute with the Phillies, demanding $15,000 for the season. *The Sporting News*, in its "Scribbled by Scribes" column of February 8 took exception to Alexander's demands:

> "With Babe Ruth drawing only $3,500 last year, where does Grover Alexander get off demanding $15,000? Babe is the best pitcher in the country today."

Burt Whitman of the *Herald*, expounding on the matter called Ruth "one of the best drawing cards of all pitchers." He added:

> "[Ruth's] popularity is due to his tremendous slugging ability rather than his ability to pitch airtight baseball ... if you go out to Braves Field and see Alexander pitch ... then go to any out-of-Boston ballyard where Babe Ruth is pitching, you'll see the difference."

In the end, Alexander would settle for a reported $12,500 weeks later, a full two-and-a-half times the amount paid to Ruth.

Six weeks before spring training was to begin, Barry had invited a few of the Red Sox who lived locally to come up to Worcester to work out with him. Babe became a regular visitor to the Barry home around this time, and the *Herald* of February 1 told of the two men arriving in Boston via auto the previous day for a visit. Jack and Babe were engaging in daily workouts at the Holy Cross University athletic facility known as "the cage". When Burt Whitman visited Worcester on February 5, Barry said of Ruth "You know the big reason he is up here with me. He feared a natural tendency to put on weight."

Babe's stay included more ice skating at the city's Elm Park, and years later the Barrys also shared an interesting recollection regarding their guest's peculiar eating habits. It seems that Mrs. Barry was about to prepare hamburgers for dinner, and a ravenous Babe said, "Don't bother cooking mine, I'll just eat it raw" as he proceeded to gobble up the uncooked meat. Mrs. Barry, a schoolteacher, was undoubtedly charmed.

Ruth was apparently enjoying his stay in Worcester, as an item from the *Boston Herald* of February 23 would indicate:

> "Big Babe Ruth is looking for a house in Worcester. The gigantic left-hander wants to be near manager Jack Barry and other great friends he has made of late in Worcester. It's a good bet that Barry would like to have Ruth up where the two would have an easier time chumming."

On Saturday, March 3, the Red Sox contingent departed from South Station for its annual trek to Hot Springs for training camp. The Ruths and the Barrys boarded together in Worcester, and the group arrived at its destination on March 5. The Sox' adversaries from the previous fall's World Series, Brooklyn, would also be training in the Arkansas resort town this spring. Frazee and Dodger owner Charles Ebbetts had recently agreed that their teams would engage in a ten-game barnstorming tour beginning in late March and proceeding northward into early April.

On the first day of camp, March 6, Frazee, reminiscent of Joe Lannin, couldn't hide his enthusiasm and grabbed a bat and began hitting grounders. On the third day, Ruth slugged two prodigious home runs in practice and the *Herald* reported, "It was Frazee's first chance to see big Babe in action and he got the surprise of his life."

Ruth was said to be in the best shape of any of the pitchers in camp. The *Herald* wrote that Babe ended one of the early workouts by "shooting some of his cannonball speedsters over the plate." He was progressing quickly, but Barry, who didn't want him working too hard, ordered Babe to lay off putting anything on the ball. Away from the field, there were as usual, other activities to engage in at Hot Springs, as Ruth golfed with teammates, went bowling with Helen, and wagered on horses at Oaklawn Park.

On March 15, Ruth saw his first action in a "Regulars-Yannigans" scrimmage, and three days later the Sox and Dodgers played the first of two games at Majestic Park in what was informally called the "Hot Springs World Series". Babe came in to relieve, allowing six safeties in the fourth through sixth innings as the Dodgers prevailed over the champs 7-2. Ruth started the second and final matchup March 25, and in his four innings pitched, Brooklyn only managed one hit. The subsequent relievers pitched poorly, and with an 11-2 win the Dodgers reigned as "Hot Springs Champs". It was said at this time that Ruth and Sherrod Smith, adversaries in the classic 14-inning game from the '16 series had become quite friendly.

The Sox and Dodgers wrapped up camp on March 27, embarking that date on their seven-city tour. The teams traveled together in four special Pullman train cars, arriving first in Memphis for a game on the 28th. Brooklyn owner Charles Ebbetts came up with the idea at this time that the players on each team should sport numbers on their uniforms so that unfamiliar fans in non-major league cities would be able to identify them. The Red Sox would be wearing their numbers on a red and white band on the sleeve of the uniform. It is generally believed that Ruth first wore a uniform number in 1929, yet this in fact occurred a full 12 years earlier.

The second stop of the tour brought the two teams into Little Rock, Arkansas on the 29th of March. Ruth was given the start in the exhibition, and in his five innings of work, he held Brooklyn scoreless while allowing only two hits. Later, the Dodgers pushed across the only run of the game for their third win in four contests. Before the following game in Oklahoma City on the 30th, Ruth and his mates were featured in a large parade through the city streets. They rode in open cars with the crowd cheering wildly, and the Mayor and other dignitaries greeted them at the park. It was not often that outposts such as Oklahoma bore witness to such major league baseball exhibitions.

After a stop in Kansas City, Missouri, Ruth made his third appearance against Brooklyn in Davenport, Iowa on April 2. He came on in relief of Leonard in the fourth and pitched four effective innings in the Red Sox' 5-1 win. The tour continued on the next afternoon to Peoria, Illinois, birthplace of Sox owner Frazee. The crowd was squarely in Frazee's corner, and the owner felt greatly embarrassed by Boston's 13-5 loss.

The final game of the series, scheduled for April 6 in Columbus, Ohio was canceled due to bad weather. The two teams then parted company, Boston having prevailed in five of the nine exhibitions staged.

As the Red Sox began to work their way toward New York for opening day, they stopped in Toledo for a two-game set versus the local American Association club. Making his last pre-season appearance, Ruth started the first game on April 7 and went the first six innings. One interesting sidenote is that Ty Cobb, on a brief leave from the Tigers, played outfield for Toledo in both games against Boston. Ruth, it was said in the *Herald*, pitched far below standard, and was easy to hit, as well as wild. It was included that when Toledo began to pile up a lead, he appeared to be taking the situation as a joke. This could not have endeared him to the hyper-intense Cobb.

On the front pages of the newspapers of the day was a story of great international and historical importance. President Wilson had proclaimed war as the country was on the verge of full-scale involvement in the European conflict. As a show of patriotism and support, major league teams would be performing military drills before games. American League President Ban Johnson reportedly offered a cash prize of $500 to the team best skilled at competitions held later in the season.

One final exhibition game had been scheduled for Scranton, Pennsylvania on April 9, but the cold would not allow it. The Red Sox moved on to New York City, checking into the Ansonia Hotel at 7:30 that evening. The team would be holding one final practice the following day at Fordham University Field. In its opening day preview on April 11, the *Boston Herald* speculated "The Boston pitching selection will very likely be Ruth, for he has shown the best form in the preliminary games."

By and large, the Sox would be opening the season using a three-man rotation of Ruth, Leonard, and Shore. Smoky Joe Wood, who was attempting to come back from arm woes could not reach a contract agreement with Frazee and was sold to Cleveland just before spring training. Unfortunately, Wood suffered more arm trouble in 1917, appearing in just five games for the Indians that year. Ruth's pitching arm was in fine shape however, likely due to his off-season conditioning, but curiously, his bat had been conspicuously silent. In the five non-scrimmage games Babe had appeared in, he had no hits in seven at-bats.

Nearly 17,000 fans filed into the Polo Grounds on Wednesday, April 11, braving the freezing temperatures. It had snowed two days before in New York City, and six inches had to be cleared from the field in preparation. The Yankees performed their military drills before the game for U.S. Major General Leonard Wood, however the Red Sox did not, as they hadn't practiced and simply weren't prepared.

The *Boston Herald* of 4/12/17 reported:

> "The band struck up martial tunes, dozens of flags and pennants began to flutter from the stands, and out onto the field marched the Yanks ... and proceeded to get thoroughly and undeniably walked all over by the Boston Red Sox, champions of the planet."

Babe impressed all with a complete game three-hitter, all three hits being singles, as Boston cruised in the opener 10-2. In his four at-bats, he chipped in with a scratch single in the ninth, but his at-bat in the seventh caused the *Herald* to comment: "Babe Ruth was struck out in the seventh inning, and he was so perturbed about it that he gave [umpire] Connolly a look which would melt a stone."

After the three-game series in New York, the Red Sox had a Sunday exhibition scheduled in Meriden, Connecticut, birthplace of Jack Barry, but the local authorities refused to allow the game to take place; Sunday baseball was still frowned upon in many northeast cities. The team then trekked over to Philadelphia where Ruth pitched the opener against the A's on Monday, April 16.

> "Jack [Barry] assured the success of the undertaking when he sent Babe Ruth to the hill. Ruth was as effective as Connie's trio of hurlers were ineffective, which is saying a pageful." *Boston Herald* 4/7/17

Seven Athletics went down on strikes, and the only run they would score was unearned. The Sox went on to take three of four from Philadelphia, and then headed home for the Fenway opener. Ruth was said to have moved in at this time to an apartment at 20 St. Stephen St., in the shadows of Symphony Hall, just a short trolley ride from Fenway. The opener came on Saturday, April 21, against the Yankees, and before the game, the Sox Royal Rooters presented the team with a giant horseshoe of roses that each player ducked through for good luck. Boston's Mayor Curley threw out the first ball, and the Fenway crowd proceeded to witness a fine all-around performance from the 23-year-old Babe.

"For with the gigantic and herculean George "Babe" Ruth forever in the limelight, the Sox beat the formidable and chesty Yanks 6 to 4 ..." *Boston Herald* 4/22/17

Aside from his fine pitching, allowing nine hits, striking out three in the complete game, Babe put on a display with the bat. Going 3 for 3, he muscled out a triple and two doubles, and also scored one of the Red Sox runs. In a *Sporting News* column dated April 23, Burt Whitman wrote:

" ... Ruth and Hubert "Dutch" Leonard are in remarkable condition ....These three hurlers [Ruth, Leonard, and Shore] are, as a body, the equal of any three on any other club in the game."

On Wednesday, April 25, Clark Griffith brought his Washington team to town, and Ruth was scheduled to be opposed that day by fireballer Walter Johnson. An attack of indigestion would keep Johnson from making the start, and one could only guess how many pitchers might just wish for just such an attack rather than face Ruth the hitter or the pitcher. Babe had his ups and downs, but ultimately came away with another complete-game victory, topping the Senators 5 to 4. Again his batting was worthy of mention as his single in the fourth inning, which drove in a run for a 3-2 lead, was his fifth hit in five straight at-bats.

	IP	H	SO	BB	WP
4/25/17 vs.					
Washington	9	6	5	7	1
At bat: 2 for 4 (2 singles)					

After Washington left town, Philadelphia came in, and as he would so many times that season, Ruth was given the ball to start the series. Though he again completed the game as Boston doubled up on the A's 6-3, the sailing was far from smooth. In the headline from the *Herald* of May 1: "Ruth wins fifth straight game but is hit hard by Mackmen batters". He was pounded for ten hits, five of which came in the last two innings, but again his bat aided the cause. "Ruth had to battle for the victory, and it took Babe's good stickwork as well as some good twirling in the pinches ...."

He also benefited greatly from good fielding by Walker, Hooper, Scott, and Barry. Babe was in fact suffering somewhat from the unseasonably cold Boston weather, and it became necessary for Sox trainer Doc Green to massage his fingers and arms between innings.

4/30/17 vs. Philadelphia At bat: 2 for 4, 1 run

At the conclusion of the Athletics series, both teams left town on the same train, with Philadelphia returning home, and the Red Sox traveling down to Washington. Ruth was set to open the series, and this time his rival, Johnson, would be available, setting the stage for an absolutely classic pitcher's duel. Johnson was masterful, not allowing a baserunner until shortstop Scott singled in the sixth, and gave up only four hits in all. As fine as the veteran hurler's performance was, young Ruth's would be better.

Babe yielded only two singles, and no Senator baserunner would reach second the entire game. He also played a part in the one lone run the game produced. After Scott doubled in the eighth inning then advanced to third, Ruth sent him home with a sacrifice fly. Of the numerous occasions Ruth and Johnson would square off, this was among the most classic. It marked the third time in the young career of Babe Ruth that he bested Walter Johnson by 1-0 count.

	IP	H	SO	BB	R
5/7/17 at Washington					
Ruth	9	2	3	1	0
Johnson	9	4	7	1	1

In a *Sporting News* column of the same date, Burt Whitman stated that in the opinion of Jack Barry, Ruth is due for a wonderful year. Whitman wrote:

> "The big gent is aiming for a mighty record this year. He [Ruth] openly states that he feels capable of winning 30 games and opines that he may run the total up to 35 ....Today he is one of the most picturesque figures in the game".

Whitman also added that Ruth's fastball was the key to his success, and when he's right, he "just whizzes them by the batters and that's all there is to it".

The Sox had moved on to Detroit, and Babe notched his seventh straight victory with a complete game effort on May 11 by a slim 2-1 margin. He was touched for only five Tiger hits and sent six back on strikes.

Late in the game, yet another interesting incident occurred involving Ty Cobb. With the Sox ahead 2-1, Cobb led off the ninth by bunting his way on. The next batter, Bobby Veach, grounded to Gardner at third, whose only play was to first base. Cobb rounded second, and without hesitation, continued on to third. When the Sox realized it, shortstop Scott ran over to cover third, but Ruth was already there taking the throw from first baseman Del Gainer. Cobb was sliding in feet first and Ruth tagged him so viciously in the ribs that the Georgian couldn't get up for nearly two minutes. Cobb had been ridden hard by the Boston dugout after having been struck out by Ruth earlier, and now he had fallen victim to his own brutal brand of baseball.

5/11/17 at Detroit   At-bat: 2 for 4 (double)

As the western swing moved on to Cleveland for four games, Ruth saw his first action of the season as a pinch hitter in game one on May 14. He went up for Scott in the eighth inning, striking out, as the Indians came out on top 7-6. In his *Sporting News* column from this date, Burt Whitman stated that with all due respect to Grover Alexander, Ruth is the biggest drawing card in the game. He also observed that Babe would often win the first game of a series, which seemed to give the team a big psychological boost.

The day after Ruth's pinch-hitting stint in Cleveland, Barry gave him the start against the Tribe, and a controversial scoring decision would result. It was the first start of '17 that Ruth failed to complete, as he surrendered nine hits and was given the hook with two out in the fifth in favor of Leonard.

The *Post* reported that "Babe was wild and ineffective from the start, and good fielding alone saved him from damage earlier". Boston was clinging to a slim 6-5 lead when Babe came out, and with Leonard pitching scoreless ball for 3 1/3 innings the score ended that way.

The *Post* also reported that Ruth was given credit for the win, when in fact official scorer Henry P. Edwards, a Cleveland beat writer, awarded the victory to Leonard. Edwards, in his judgement, decided that even though Ruth was leading when pulled, Leonard was more deserving due to his superior performance. Ruth was not pleased, and maintained that it should have been his win, which would have brought his total to eight straight. Ultimately, the decision was reversed and Babe was given credit for the victory.

He would finally break into the loss column however, in the first game of the White Sox series on May 18. Wildness again proved costly as he walked three and allowed four earned runs in just 2 1/3 innings of work. Reliever Lore Bader was summoned from the pen, and Boston went on to lose 8-2. The *Post* sportspage announced "Ruth's winning streak stopped", but was clearly overshadowed by the front page headline which blared "PRES. ORDERS ARMY TO FRANCE". Twenty-five thousand men were to be deployed as America's involvement was on the verge of becoming full scale.

The final two games of the Red Sox-White Sox series in Chicago were wiped out by rain. The Red Sox were visited at the Hotel Metropole by U.S. Army Sgt. A. B. Hoffman, who met with Ruth and his mates in a banquet room to begin instruction in military drills.

Ruth got back on track with a win a few days later, May 24 in St. Louis. In the Thursday afternoon tilt at Sportsman's Park, he held the Browns to eight hits, striking out five and walking just one in the 4-2 win. He also got into the act with his bat, slugging a triple in his one official at-bat.

The *Sporting News* of this date featured two significant references to Ruth. On the front page appeared a photo of Babe and fellow pitcher Ernie Shore under the title "One Investment That Has Paid". The item stated that the price Boston paid for the two (the inflated $27,000 price) was well worth it and should continue to pay dividends.

Also in that issue's Detroit Tigers weekly column by H.G. Salsinger dated May 21, Senators manager Clark Griffith, who had just been in town with his team told reporters that Ruth is the hardest and best hitter in baseball, and that he could earn just as much playing a position, however the Sox need him as a pitcher.

‰

The 24-day road trip was about to conclude where it started, with back-to-back doubleheaders in the nation's capital. After watching Leonard score a complete game 2-1 victory in the first game of the first day, Ruth topped the performance by spinning a 9-0 shutout.

	IP	H	SO	BB	HBP
5/29/17 at					
Washington	9	6	7	3	1

At bat: 1 for 4 (single)

The Sox not only swept that day's doubleheader but the following day's as well. Back to Fenway on the final day of May, Carl Mays handled the Indians easily, 5-1, for Boston's tenth straight victory. The next day, Ruth had the chance to extend the streak to 11 games, and he subsequently engaged in a pitcher's duel with Cleveland's Guy Morton. When Ruth stroked a solid single over second base in the eighth, it would be the only hit that Morton would allow. Babe himself only allowed one hit until the ninth, when the Indians got to him and prevailed by a 3-0 score.

Later on in the Cleveland series, Ernie Shore's complete game 2-1 win leapfrogged the Red Sox over Chicago into first place. The Indians left town and were replaced by the Tigers, and Boston embarked on a stretch of eight games in which they would only win one. The lone win belonged to Ruth, however two of the losses did as well. He opened up the Detroit series on June 6 and was anything but sharp. Ruth allowed three earned runs in the first inning and although he closed the door the rest of the way, that was all Cobb and company needed for a 3-0 win.

	IP	H	SO	BB	WP
6/6/17 vs.					
Detroit	9	10	4	7	1

At bat: 1 for 2 (single)

Three days later, a then season-high 15,000 fans came to Fenway for the Tiger finale. In the heartbreaking 1-0 Ernie Shore loss, Babe pinch hit for catcher Cady in the ninth, drawing a base on balls. When he reached first, something occurred that he was slightly unaccustomed to—he was pinch run for by Mike McNally.

Ruth helped to break up what could have been an extended losing streak with one of his finest outings of the season on June 13. In the first game of a Wednesday doubleheader against the Browns at Fenway, he engaged in another pitcher's duel that would see a total of six hits. Ruth's own double which hit the top of the left-field fence in the seventh, accounted for one of Boston's three hits, and the Red Sox' two runs would be the difference.

	IP	H	SO	BB
6/13/17 vs.				
St. Louis	9	3	5	4

The following day, also against St. Louis, Ruth, who was colorfully referred to that week in the *Sporting News* as the "infant from Baltimore" pinch hit for Leonard, singling in the eighth inning of a 3-0 loss. The *Post*'s Paul Shannon observed in the next day's column that Ruth "Seems able to clout no matter who is twirling".

On the 16th, Babe took his turn at trying to break the slump, and like Shore, Leonard, and Mays before him, he failed. Joe Jackson of the first place White Sox went 3 for 5 with two doubles, and though Ruth went the full nine innings, Boston went down 7-2. The Sox had now scored a total of six runs in the previous six games.

Two days later, Boston swept a doubleheader from the rival Sox, as Ruth pinch hit unsuccessfully for Scott in the eighth inning of the second game. His next pitching appearance came on June 20 in the second game of a doubleheader at New York's Polo Grounds. Babe's performance prompted the *Post* to write that he "gave a grand exhibition of twirling in the fourth", as he displayed superb control in this complete game 3-1 victory, striking out six and issuing no walks. One of the umpires of this game, Brick Owens would become involved in a unique and well-documented incident involving Ruth just three days later.

The Red Sox were back at Fenway after a brief three-day road trip to New York, set to take on Washington on Saturday, June 23 in a doubleheader. Ruth was given the start in game one, set for an afternoon of work as Senators leadoff hitter, Baltimore native Ray Morgan stepped into the right batter's box. Three pitches later, the count was sitting at three balls and no strikes with Ruth objecting strenuously from the mound. He and Owens had a verbal exchange, and Babe finally returned to the rubber to deliver the fateful fourth pitch. As the umpire called, "ball four", Ruth stormed off the mound, and the *Post* of the following day reprinted the heated dialogue, or more likely a sanitized version:

Ruth: "Keep your eyes open!"

Owens: "You get back there and pitch or I'll run you out of the ballpark!"

Ruth: "If you run me out of the ballpark, I'll take a punch at you on my way!"

Owens: "You're out now!" (waving his arms in a gesture of banishment)

Ruth completely lost his head and charged in at the umpire, and versions of what transpired next differ slightly. He delivered a blow with his right hand that some said glanced off Owens' cheek; others said it landed behind his ear; and still others claimed it hit him on the neck. In his *Sporting News* column from the June 28 issue, Burt Whitman offered:

" . . . Whether the blow landed full or not does not matter, nor does it matter whether Owens invited combat—the result is the same. Ruth is in for a long suspension no doubt . . . . "

Chet Thomas joined his incensed left-hander when he was also banished from the game. Manager Barry turned to Ernie Shore, seated on the bench, who had pitched two days earlier in New York, and asked if he could fill in until another pitcher warmed up. Once action resumed, Morgan immediately tried to steal second and was nailed to record out number one, and Shore subsequently retired the next 26 batters without one reaching base. Ruth's tantrum had contributed to the most unusual perfect game in baseball history.

American League President Ban Johnson announced two days later from his Chicago office that Ruth was suspended indefinitely, and gave no indication of the amount of the fine that would surely go along with it. Comparisons were being made to a recent incident involving Giants manager John McGraw, who was fined $500 and suspended 16 days for a similar offense. It was thought at the time that Johnson might wait until the Red Sox traveled to Chicago to meet with Ruth, which was not scheduled to occur for three more weeks. In the July 5 issue of *The Sporting News*, several writers commented on the incident, most actually treating Ruth surprisingly kindly.

"No apologies are offered for Ruth, except he is the last player one would expect to indulge in the brainstorm habit, [?] and is noted among his friends and associates for good nature and an easygoing disposition." *Senators* column - Paul Eaton

"There are many, many things that are meaner, baser, and more vile than an honest punch delivered in the heat of the moment (and not altogether without provocation) by one able-bodied young man to another young man by no means deficient in tongue or muscle." "Scribbled by Scribes" column

Paul Shannon editorialized that Boston had been a victim of bad umpiring all season, and that Sox players had concluded that there was a bias against them. He added:

"Ruth, who is normally one of the best-tempered fellows in the world, has done alot of kicking about the way that the umpires behind the plate have been judging them lately."

Days after Johnson's initial announcement regarding Ruth, he settled on what amounted to a nine-day suspension and a fine of $100. Many baseball columnists seemed to believe that Johnson was far too lenient on Ruth, while others scoffed at the suggestion that he should be banned for the season. Umpire Owens had reportedly spoken out on behalf of Babe during the investigation, and *The Sporting News* speculated that the league took the interests of the Sox team into consideration and did not want to spoil their pennant hopes with a long suspension of their ace pitcher.

Another interesting incident was taking place at this time, as the National Commission chose to become involved in a personal money dispute between Ruth and Charley Deal, a third baseman for the Chicago Cubs. Deal submitted a claim to the Commission for $100 against Ruth for the balance of the price of a car Babe had purchased from him over a year before. The board ruled that by not contesting the case, it was an admission of the debt and he would not be eligible to play until it was paid. It was soon discovered however, that the debt had already been paid. The National Commission apologized to Ruth, and he was declared back in good standing with the league on July 2.

Burt Whitman wrote that "(The Sox) proved that there are other pitchers on their staff besides Babe Ruth", as Boston won six and lost only three in his absence.

While on suspension, Babe kept his throwing arm sharp by working out before games in the Fenway bullpen before the umpires showed up. On Tuesday, July 3, he finally made his return, at home facing the Philadelphia Athletics. For the third time in less than five weeks, Ruth suffered a complete game 3-0 defeat. In the next day's *Boston Post*, Arthur Duffey wrote: "... give Babe another day or so in which to get his bearings and he should be the same old terror on the mound."

The Red Sox headed out on Thursday evening, July 5 for a two-and-a-half week western trip, and stopped in Buffalo for an exhibition game the next day with the International League club. The crowd of 3,000 on hand howled their disapproval at the fact that few regulars played, calling in vain for Ruth, Hooper, Gardner, Scott, and others.

The following day Ruth opened up in Cleveland, and again experienced a nearly complete lack of support. The *Post*'s Paul Shannon observed that he had great speed and a wonderful curve that day, and "In spite of the southpaw's really excellent pitching, the Red Sox lost 3-1." Scott made a crucial error at shortstop in the fifth that allowed Cleveland to go ahead. Ruth singled to lead off the sixth but couldn't get beyond second. The final game of the Indian series on July 10 was washed out by rain, allowing the Red Sox to catch a 2:35 train to Detroit, setting the stage for what Shannon called the "greatest pitching performance that the southpaw has ever achieved".

Babe dominated the formidable Tiger lineup, taking a no-hitter into the eighth inning. After retiring the first batter of the frame, Detroit shortstop Donie Bush slapped a line drive up the middle, which Ruth lunged at, deflecting towards Scott at short. Scott picked it up and fired to first, but Bush had crossed the bag safely. The general belief was that if Ruth had not deflected the ball, Scott likely would have gotten the throw over on time, preserving the no-hitter.

Bush's scratch hit would remain the only Tiger safety, and in his own four trips to the plate, Babe collected a triple, single, and a walk. Still, Boston went into the ninth without having scored a run. Outfielder Chick Shorten, pinch hitting for Ray Agnew, tripled, driving in Tilly Walker as Ruth then completed his 1-0 masterpiece.

Forty-two years later, Shorten commented on Ruth to a Pennsylvania newspaper, *The Scrantonian,*

> " You'd see Babe only at game time.....as soon as it was over he'd take off for a party and have more fun. It never seemed to affect his ability and there was a saying among the Sox that 'He does everything right on the ballfield and everything wrong off it.' "
> 12/20/59

Indeed, Ruth seemingly lived life as if he expected two burly men in uniform to approach him and inform him that he would have to return to St. Mary's.

⋄

The third stop of the western trip brought the Red Sox into St. Louis, and Ruth again opened the series, hurling the first game of a July doubleheader. He came through with another superb outing, and though it took ten innings, Babe completed the 4-2 win. With the exception of a shaky seventh inning, he was virtually unhittable otherwise. His pitching record was now listed as 14 wins, six losses, and he was ranked second in the league in hitting at .373, albeit with only 63 at-bats.

The only other action Ruth saw in the St. Louis series was a pinch-hitting appearance on July 16. The unsuccessful attempt came in the seventh inning in place of Scott. A five-game series with the first-place White Sox began on the 19th, and the second-place Red Sox opened with Ruth on the trip's last stop. He was reported to be pitching wonderfully for the first seven innings, but weakened considerably and was hit hard in the eighth and ninth. Little damage was done, however, as Chicago only scored one each in the fifth and ninth, and Ruth notched a complete game 3-2 triumph.

	IP	H	SO	BB	R	ER
7/19/17 at Chicago	9	8	5	5	2	2

At bat: 1 for 4 (single)

Two days later in the third game of the important series, Ruth was called on to relieve for the first time of the 1917 season. Leonard had started the Saturday afternoon contest and gamely hurled ten innings. Ruth came on and yielded only three hits and no earned runs in five innings, as the game was called due to darkness tied 5-5 after the 15th. The Red Sox lost the final two games to Chicago, finishing the road trip with six wins in 16 games, and placing further distance between the top two teams.

Back in the friendlier confines of Fenway Park, Ruth cruised to an easy 11-2 win over St. Louis in the first game of a doubleheader on July 26. He shined in all phases of the game, going 2 for

3 with a sacrifice bunt, and his five fielding assists drew rave reviews from the *Post*'s Arthur Duffey regarding his glovework. There was also very nearly a fight between Ruth and Browns' shortstop John Lavan, who after a close pitch thought Babe was trying to bean him. Lavan threw his bat at the mound, but no punches were thrown, and the two later shook hands.

It was now Boston's turn to host Chicago, as the top two teams squared off for four games beginning Monday, July 30. Ruth, who won the only game for Boston in the series the two teams had played a week and a half before, was anxious to pitch two games, hoping to come back on two days' rest for the closer on Thursday. With 12,000 fans pulling hard for him, Babe had "twirled invincible ball" according to Paul Shannon, and came out on top, 3-1. He was said to be at his very best except in the third when Chicago garnered three of their four hits on the afternoon. Joe Jackson's triple drove in the only White Sox run, and behind Ruth, the Red Sox had now won their sixth straight game.

Ruth did not pitch again in the Chicago series as he had hoped, but instead started the first game of the Cleveland series on Friday, August 3rd. Once again he pitched superbly but was given meager support by his mates, dropping a complete-game decision, 2-1.

	IP	H	SO	BB
8/3/17 vs. Cleveland	9	7	0	1

The Red Sox' offensive woes continued further in the following game two days later when right-hander George Foster threw a one-hitter, but lost to Cleveland 2-1. Ty Cobb and company came into town after the Indians departed, and Ruth took the mound on August 10 in the first of a twin bill. Just a day before, it didn't appear that Babe would be in any shape to pitch at all, the victim of a severe sunburn received on the team's outing on Cape Cod a couple of days before.

"Early yesterday the eminent physician Dr. Charles Winslow Green, busy at work on his charges, trying especially to get big Babe Ruth in some sort of shape to work. Babe was a groaning invalid, for his shoulders were little better than a mass of blisters." *Boston Post* 8/10/17

Somehow sufficiently recovered, Babe got the sluggish Red Sox, winners of just two of their previous seven games, back on track with a complete game four-hit 5-4 win. Ruth made the difference with his first home run of the season, an incredible drive to deep centerfield that was said to be the longest ever slugged at Fenway.

> "Ruth ... drove the ball into the centerfield bleachers, halfway up and on the fly, for the most terrific wallop ever made at Fenway Park." *Boston Post* 8/11/17

In that week's *Sporting News*, Burt Whitman's column stated "Babe Ruth persists in pickling the ball most wickedly while he is throwing it with class...."

The day after Babe's titanic blast, he was tabbed to pinch hit for Scott in the seventh inning of the Detroit finale, drawing a base on balls. It was the fourth time he batted for Scott in six pinch hitting appearances thus far in 1917. The next day it was back out on the road, and the team stopped off in Connecticut to play an exhibition versus Waterbury College on August 12. The 6-1 Red Sox win was noteworthy in that Ruth went in to play rightfield in the seventh inning.

The tour continued on to Philadelphia, Cleveland, St. Louis, Chicago, and Detroit. Lack of support was once again the story in Ruth's start against the Athletics on August 14th. Again he went the distance, but with his pitching lapse in the third, he had only a loss to show for the 3-1 game.

	IP	H	SO	BB
8/14/17 at Philadelphia	8	8	1	3

At bat: 2 for 4 (2 singles)

Offensive support finally came in abundance for Babe on the 18th in Cleveland as the Sox applied a 9-1 shellacking behind Ruth's five-hitter. Ruth did not have old teammate Tris Speaker to challenge, as the superstar missed the entire series due to a beaning he received several days earlier. Two days later, now in Chicago, Ruth saw action, albeit limited in both games of a doubleheader. In game one, he had an unsuccessful pinch hitting appearance for Barry in the ninth inning; and in the second game he came in from the bullpen with one out in the eighth to relieve Mays. He pitched a brief two-thirds of an inning, getting both outs via strikeout and yielding no hits. The first strikeout victim, Joe Jackson went down on three straight pitches, and the save Ruth earned was the first of two in 1917. Back in Boston, pennant fever was rampant, and many were writing to the team to be considered for World Series tickets.

Rain wiped out the second game of a scheduled doubleheader at Comiskey Park on August 21, and Ruth may have wished the first game was scrapped as well. Allowing only two runs, he clearly pitched well enough to win, but the Boston bats, including Ruth's own, remained silent. He was on the losing end of the pitcher's duel, 2-0.

The next stop of the tour brought the Red Sox into St. Louis' Sportman's Park, where on the 25th, Ruth made his final relief appearance of the season. He came on to start the ninth in place of Foster and allowed no hits to earn the save in the 3-2 victory. Before the game, the Sox lined up in formation and performed military drills that were judged by U.S. military expert Lt. Col. Raymond Sheldon. In the league-wide competition, Boston placed fifth out of the eight teams, with St. Louis capturing the first-place prize of $500.

The disturbing trend of Boston's offensive failings continued in Ruth's next start, August 27 at Detroit's Navin Field. Partially on the strength of Ty Cobb's 3 for 4 afternoon, the Tigers handed Babe a 5-1 complete game loss. Ruth managed to stroke one double in four trips to the plate, and *The Sporting News* of that week made reference to his already legendary power. In a weekly feature entitled "Questions and Answers", a reader asked, "Who holds the record for the longest hit ever?" The response was that Ruth had recently hit the longest drive ever, though there was no real way of telling.

Back at Fenway on August 31, Ruth scored his first victory in two weeks against Mack's Athletics in game one of a double bill. He hurled exceptional ball this day, surrendering only six hits, striking out five, and walking none. Babe was said to be pitching his very best until he wrenched his ankle in the eighth inning, but was able to continue. The 5-3 victory was yet another of his 35 complete games of the season, and also marked his 20th win.

The Red Sox were said to be doing very well attendance-wise at this time, and most loyal fans seemed to be hoping for a Boston-New York Giants matchup in the World Series—a repeat of 1912. Ernest J. Lanigan of *The Sporting News* predicted that if the two teams met, the Sox would prevail. Pessimists however, were speculating more on a "city series", a consolation exhibition series that might be played between the Red Sox and Braves if neither qualified for the Fall Classic.

On the final day of the brief homestand, September 4, Ruth followed up his fine win over the A's with another impressive outing. In an hour and twenty minutes he dispatched the visiting Yankees in the first game of a doubleheader, holding them to just five hits and one base on balls. The Red Sox headed back out on the road for one final trip, an eastern swing that would take them to Philadelphia, Washington, and New York.

Babe went unused in Philly, but drew the start in the opening tilt of the Monday doubleheader. In D.C. Ruth held up his end, going all the way, giving up just six hits and two runs, but a 2-1 loss was the result. An interesting incident occurred in Boston's 13-7 loss in New York on September 13, as bad umpiring caused a near riot on the Sox bench. It appeared as though Ruth and umpire Moriarty might come to blows when the ump dared him to repeat the Brick Owens incident, but nothing developed.

Ruth gave another outstanding showing at New York's Polo Grounds on the 15th, though he suffered a slight letdown near the game's end. Babe took an 8-0 lead into the bottom of the ninth, and promptly allowed three Yankee runs, settling for an 8-3 complete game win. Ruth was applauded loudly by the New York crowd each time he stepped to the plate, and he did not disappoint, slugging a homer, his second and last of the '17 season.

	IP	H	SO	BB
9/15/17 at New York	9	6	4	2

At bat: 2 for 4, HR, single

Boston was playing winning baseball in September, but were failing to gain significant ground on the first-place White Sox. In Burt Whitman's *Sporting News* column dated September 17, he stated that Boston fans were resigned to the fact that the Red Sox would not be making their third consecutive World Series appearance. Many, in fact were now looking forward to the proposed Braves exhibitions.

The Red Sox arrived back home for their final homestand, opening with Detroit on September 19. The Tigers' 5-2 victory in the first game was due in large part to eight Red Sox errors. In the sixth inning, Ruth was called on to bat for starter Shore and drew a base on balls. The following day, Ruth's start was an all-too-typical example of what had occurred to him so many times in the past few months. The Tigers were able to get to him for only six hits—all singles, with their only run scoring in the seventh inning. The Red Sox hitters, including Ruth, produced virtually nothing as the classic 1-0 heartbreaking loss would be slapped on Babe.

It was the fifth time of the season he suffered a complete game shutout loss while allowing the opponents three runs or less. On four other occasions, Ruth allowed three runs or less with Boston scoring just one run. It seems that a combination of an overwhelming lack of offensive support, and a measure of misfortune prevented Babe from making good on his prediction of a 30-win season.

On the day following Ruth's 1-0 loss to Detroit, the Red Sox hosted the league-leading White Sox. In the bottom of the tenth inning trailing 2-1, Ruth was sent up to pinch hit once again for Scott. With one out, Babe bounced into what was described as a thrilling game-ending double play, and the victory officially clinched the pennant for Chicago. Ruth hurled the final game of the White Sox series on the 24th, showing great form and dominating the A.L. champs in a 3-0 shutout.

A day later, with Cleveland now in town, the Sox and the Tribe staged a 13-inning affair with Shore working the entire game. The Indians came up with one run in the top of the 13th to take a 3-2 lead, and in the bottom half of the inning, Ruth was to make his final pinch-hitting appearance of the season, subbing for Ray Agnew. He drew a walk, and Boston pushed two runs across to capture a thrilling 4-3 win.

A review of Babe's pinch-hitting performances for 1917 show ten plate appearances with three walks and just one hit. Anytime Ruth stepped to the plate, awesome displays could result, however, during the early portion of his career, his pinch-hitting attempts tended to be fruitless far more often than not. His overall career record in this role up to this point was 6 hits in 37 at-bats for a disappointing .162 average.

ॐ

A benefit exhibition game was held at Fenway Park on Thursday, September 27, to aid the family of the late dean of Boston sportswriters Tim Murnane, who had died suddenly in February. A longtime writer for the *Boston Globe*, he had also served as president of the minor league New England and Eastern Leagues, and had played for Boston and Providence of the National League in the 1880s. The contest was arranged as a Red Sox versus "All-Star" team, with the gate receipts going to the large family he had left behind. Appearing on the squad of "All-Stars" was an impressive array of mostly American League stars, including Walter Johnson, Rabbit Maranville at shortstop, and a hard-to-match outfield of Cobb, Speaker, and Joe Jackson.

Just prior to the game, various athletic contests were held among the players, such as throwing for distance as well as accuracy, and racing around the bases. Ruth won the fungo-hitting contest with a drive that measured 402 feet. The long distance throw was won by Jackson with an incredible toss of 396 feet.

Over 17,000 fans piled into Fenway that day and saw Ruth faced with the unenviable task of starting against the collection of legends. Babe however, was more than equal to this task as he gave up just three hits and no runs in his five innings, and Boston prevailed over the stars 2-0. More importantly, over $14,000 was raised to assist the family of the beloved scribe who, incidentally had predicted big things for a young George Ruth nearly three years before.

ॐ

With just one day of rest after the exhibition, Ruth started the second game of a double-header in Boston against the Browns on September 29. He cruised just about as easily as he had all year, and turned in a noteworthy all-around performance. As if completing the 11-0 shutout on six hits and five strikeouts wasn't enough, he also went 3 for 3 (double, two singles, three runs) and added five fielding assists and a putout in his final victory of the season.

The campaign's final series commenced at Fenway on October 2 with a doubleheader against Washington, Boston's 26th twin bill of 1917. Ruth's final appearance of the year occurred the following day, going head to head with Walter Johnson. It was billed as "Soldier Day" at Fenway, and a group of the many military men on hand presented Johnson with a silver trophy. It truly was his day as he brightly outshone Ruth on the mound, holding Boston to just seven hits in the 6-0 shutout. Ruth was tagged for 11 hits, and in the seventh allowed his pitching rival to double with the bases loaded.

Ruth's season thus ended with an earned run average of 2.01, and a better performance that day would have allowed him to finish under 2.00 for the second straight year.

The Red Sox season came to a close the next day, October 4th, and with a record of 90-62, had to settle for second behind Chicago and their 100 wins. Some observers of the team were critical of Barry's managing, but most felt that he did well under the circumstances. Centerfielder Tilly Walker had not performed as well as in '16 when replacing Speaker; first baseman Hoblitzell's batting had dropped off; and Carrigan was missed not only on the bench but behind the plate. Boston had occupied first place at various times during the season, but the majority of the year was spent in the runner-up spot. Chicago bumped them out for good on August 19.

Though Ruth's pitching did not quite equal the level of domination of 1916, he did attain what would be career highs in victories, complete games, and innings pitched. Among American League hurlers he ranked first in complete games; second in wins behind White Sox ace Eddie Cicotte; third in both fewest hits per nine innings and innings pitched; and fifth in winning percentage and strikeouts. A couple of months after the season, *The Sporting News* named an unofficial major league All-Star team for 1917. Though Ruth was not named to the squad, he was acknowledged as the most valuable left-handed pitcher in the American League.

Ruth's 1917 pitching statistics follow:

W	L	ERA	G	GS	CG	IP	H	BB	SO	ShO	Sv
24	13	2.01	41	38	35	326.1	244	106	128	6	2

As a hitter, Babe further cemented his reputation as an offensive force in 1917. Though he only connected for two round-trippers, his batting average ranked fourth in the league among players with a minimum of 100 at-bats.

Ruth's 1917 batting statistics looked like this:

G	AB	R	H	2B	3B	HR	TB	SB	BB	SO	BA	SA
52	123	14	40	6	3	2	58	0	12	18	.325	.472

 za

The World Series of 1917 opened up at Chicago's Comiskey Park on October 6. After splitting the first four games, Chicago clinched in game six at the Polo Grounds on October 13. Almost exactly three years later, eight members of this world championship team would be banished from the game for life for their role in the 1919 series scandal.

While gathered at the World Series, White Sox manager Clarence Rowland and several of his players were engaged in baseball talk with reporters. The question was proposed to those gathered "Who is the hardest hitter in the game?" The names of Joe Jackson, Zack Wheat, Bobby Veach, and Wally Pipp were offered, but when Ruth's name was suggested, all present unanimously agreed that he could outhit them all for distance.

Frazee had decided by season's end that the Sox would not be engaging in the proposed "city series" with the Braves. He seemed to feel that there wasn't sufficient interest to stage such a matchup, though much of the Boston baseball public was displeased with the decision. Frazee was referred to in print as "far from popular", however his players seemed to like him, and were actually quite supportive of him. They were particularly pleased with his policy of allowing $3.50 a day in meal money on train trips, which was the highest rate in the majors. If a player went over his allotted $3.50, which Ruth no doubt did from time to time, Frazee would often tell him to make it up with a good performance on the field. This might lead one to wonder how many of Ruth's stellar games were motivated by payback due to his ravenous appetite.

Babe was said to be wintering just outside of Boston in Sudbury, attempting to stay in shape by working out in local gymnasiums. About a month after the season ended, he made headlines for his unfortunate involvement in an auto mishap. Vehicular incidents were obviously not an altogether uncommon occurrence with Babe, as *The Sporting News* filed its report under the title "Ruth's annual auto affair". It seems that while driving near Fenway Park, he attempted to negotiate between two trolley cars and his vehicle was twisted into a shapeless mass of metal. Ruth was unscathed, but the unidentified young lady who was with him was taken by ambulance to the hospital.

Several Red Sox players had enlisted in the military by the fall of 1917 due to America's involvement in Europe. Among those activated by mid-November were Ernie Shore, Chick Shorten, Mike McNally, and most importantly, manager Jack Barry. The prevailing belief was that unless the conflict ended by the spring, the enlisted players would likely not be granted furloughs for the baseball season, which had actually been discussed. Throughout November and December, rumors were rampant in the press as to whom Frazee might have take over the Red Sox reins. Included were well-known names such as Nap Lajoie, Johnny Evers, and Hugh Jennings, as well as first baseman Dick Hoblitzell and minor-league manager Jack Hendricks.

Frazee had pulled off a fairly large player transaction around this time, acquiring pitcher Joe Bush, Amos Strunk, and catcher Wally Schang from the Athletics in return for Chet Thomas, Vean Gregg, and $60,000 cash.

Meanwhile, Ruth's future would be indirectly affected by a December meeting of International League team owners. The magnates voted to cut the salary of longtime league president Ed Barrow from $7,500 per year to $2,500, prompting him to resign almost immediately. Speculation began as to what position Barrow might be in line for within Major League Baseball, and when the dust had settled, Babe Ruth's career would be in for some changes.

⸺ ▪ Five ▪ ⸺

1918: A Banner to Last a Lifetime

The war was raging in Europe, and as 1918 opened, many wondered why baseball players were receiving special privileges. Several members of the Red Sox were already in the military service or working in a war-related industry —among them was manager Jack Barry. Ruth was preparing for spring training, having registered for the draft in his hometown of Baltimore and been granted a marital deferment.

A report out of Washington indicated that a Massachusetts congressman "acting on behalf of the owners of the Boston American League Club" had asked the Navy department for a furlough for Barry so he could manage the team during the 1918 season. This was met with a hailstorm of criticism and when Frazee was contacted by a local writer he stated, "I don't understand it, there's some mistake somewhere." Rectifying the "mistake" or responding to the criticism, five days later Frazee hired Ed Barrow to pilot the 1918 edition of the Boston Red Sox. He was Babe's fifth manager in his fifth year in professional ball.

Babe's managers included: Jack Dunn, Babe's first manager with the Baltimore Orioles, Wild Bill Donovan with the Providence Grays, and Bill Carrigan, Jack Barry and Barrow with the Red Sox. Each of them had a remarkable connection linking them together. Dunn was a teammate of Donovan's with Brooklyn in 1899, and later they managed simultaneously in the International League. Donovan and Carrigan both managed teams owned by Joseph

Lannin in 1914, and while Donovan managed the Yankees, he and Carrigan would oppose each other 40 times during the '15 and '16 seasons. Carrigan worked with Dunn regarding Ruth's sale to Boston in July of 1914, was a college teammate of Jack Barry's in 1906 and managed him (Barry) on the Red Sox. Barry was managed by both Carrigan ('15 and '16) and Barrow (1919) while playing for the Red Sox. Barrow's hiring completed the link in the chain as he managed Donovan on the Detroit Tigers in 1903 and 1904. He was also President of the International League when both Dunn and Donovan were managing there. They would now be inexorably linked as men who managed Babe Ruth.

Of course, the hot stove league, as always, provided interest and speculation as to who was going where for the upcoming season. The often-held Ty Cobb sweepstakes had the Tiger outfielder bound for the Yankees, again.

Frazee, reacting to a shortage of players and a disappointing 1917 finish, was very active during the winter. Taking advantage of another Connie Mack fire sale, he purchased the contracts of pitcher Joe Bush, outfielder Amos Strunk, and catcher/utility man Wally Schang, for a reported $60,000. He then traded Larry Gardner, Tilly Walker and Hick Cady to the A's for Stuffy McInnis. In each instance, Frazee beat Yankee owner Jake Rupert to the punch and in the minds of many, Boston was now clearly the decided favorite to depose the 1917 champion Chicago White Sox.

Speculation ran high that Connie Mack would soon be coming to Boston to manage. It ran so high that Ban Johnson issued a statement insuring that Mack would remain in Philadelphia. It was also reported that Frazee had made an offer to the Tigers for the services of Cobb. Although no figures were published, it was said to have been a figure "far in excess" of what Cleveland had paid Boston for Tris Speaker, ($55,000).

In February, the owners settled the suit brought against them by the long defunct Federal League to the tune of $500,000. A $55,000 payment was made, with the settlement calling for the National League to make yearly payments until 1936. Rumors persisted that after the war baseball would become an international sport as " far-sighted" men envisioned the league expanding to Europe.

On January 11, 1918, Babe signed his contract for the upcoming season. Receiving a $2,000 raise, he would play for $7,000 in 1918, over five times what he played for in his rookie season of

1914. The terms of the contract were not revealed at the time, however Babe's ability to put people in the stands was not lost on Frazee, the media and certainly not on Babe himself. His unique style and brash, yet likable manner—not to mention his 47 wins in two years—had endeared him to the hearts of baseball fans throughout the country.

> "Ruth's power as a turnstile clicker is well known over the A.L. circuit.... the Baltimore boy is a trifle temperamental. He does things in a 'different' manner from most ballplayers. He has a walk all his own. He has a way of talking all his own. When he comes to bat the outfielders drop back to the far barriers usually with their backs up against the walls and fences. He is the type over which the small boy and the tired businessman go wild.... Everyone knows how strong he is. He bends things of metal in his hand as if they were switches and he has a hand grip which crushes you when he puts on full pressure. *Boston Post* 1/12/18

In three full seasons with the Red Sox, he had compiled a record of 65-31. He had clearly established himself as the premier left-handed pitcher in all of baseball and one of the best pitchers in the major leagues, yet it was a chance to see him swing the bat that brought the fans to ballparks throughout the country. He had batted only 351 times and was yet to play a game at any other position but pitcher and he was already redefining the game of baseball with the power of his bat.

A week after signing his contract, a story circulated that Babe, along with fellow southpaw hurler Herb Pennock and the newly acquired Stuffy McInnis were about to embark on an off-season basketball career. Although nothing ever came of it, the mere possibility was enough that owner Frazee went on record to remind the players that a clause in all their contracts expressly forbade such an endeavor. Bob Dunbar of the *Boston Herald* worried more about what might happen to the other players and the gym should Babe take up the winter sport, when in the January 18, 1918 edition he wrote:

> "This colossus can take care of himself, but what about the basketball players he might bump up against and how about the building if he should slap up against the wall in earnest?"

In early March, Babe made his way to the Red Sox downtown offices in the Dexter building to meet with new manager Barrow and prepare travel arrangements for Hot Springs and spring training. Three days later on the 9th of March, the first Red Sox contingency headed south from South Station. Babe was the only player in the group as he accompanied coach Dan Howley, traveling secretary Larry Graver, and newsmen. The train was scheduled to make its customary trip taking three days and picking up players with stops in Albany, Buffalo, and St. Louis.

Babe was an immediate hit with a group of soldiers from the local Army base at Camp Devens. They were on their way home for the weekend and Babe mingled, made merry and handed out cigars. A blizzard in the Berkshires slowed the arrival into Albany where the train picked up Frazee, Barrow, coach Johnny Evers and pitcher Dick McCabe before proceeding on to Buffalo. In Buffalo, the train picked up a mass of recruits from the aviation school in Ithaca, New York and many more in Akron, Ohio bound for Texas.

The Red Sox car was on the way to the dining car allowing every soldier access to Babe and his mates. Ruth was the object of the bulk of the attention from Uncle Sam's boys, and accommodating as he was, he was not all too pleased when the distractions caused him to miss a couple of "openers" in the five and ten card game that he had originated. Nonetheless, many a hand was shaken and autographs signed.

The players awoke at 8:30 on the morning of March 12 and spring training was officially underway. As had become their custom, the team walked to and from the field (a distance of about three miles) as part of their regimen to get in shape. Their opponent for spring games were the Brooklyn Robins in a rematch of the 1916 World Series. They would travel to Texas to play them in Austin, Houston, and Dallas as well as playing them in Hot Springs. Ever mindful of contributing to the war effort, Frazee announced that they would also play them in a five-game series at Camp Pike in Little Rock where 4,200 draftees were stationed.

Spring training was a glorious time for Babe. Everything he did was cyclopean. Dubbed "The Colossus" by *Boston Herald* sportswriter Burt Whitman, the moniker fit perfectly. His every action was huge. From merely washing up in the morning which was described as a "savory and vigorous affair" to his "titanic" home run exhibitions in batting practice. From his unbridled enthusiasm in leading the team to the field, to the exuberance he brought to just shagging fly balls. Having just turned 23, he was not only the ace of the Red Sox pitching staff, but he was now clearly established as the best left-handed pitcher in the game. His performance in the spring of 1918 would leave Barrow with a dilemma. What to do when the best pitcher on your team is also the team's best hitter.

Babe wasted no time feeding Barrows' quandary when in the first exhibition game against Brooklyn he belted two home runs in only two at bats and played first base like a seasoned veteran, as the Red Sox romped over Brooklyn 11-1.

Playing first base when he was not pitching, Babe would add to Barrow's conundrum with his powerful hitting performance throughout the spring of 1918. He hit four home runs that spring, accounting for nearly half of the 9 hits he had in 21 at-bats. One was a grand slam which a writer stated, "broke the game into fragments." When not blasting homers, he was pitching and winning as he was developing a "slow ball" with some effectiveness in keeping hitters off balance.

Just as he was leading the team to the field in the morning, and on the field during days of workouts and games, he was leading the team in off-field recreation as well. Regularly visiting the local race track, one morning Babe received a note at the Hotel Majestic on a tip at the track that afternoon. Sharing his good fortune with his mates and playing the horse "Bellboy" to the limit as his tipster had so instructed, Babe collected various amounts of money from several of his teammates and headed for the track. "Bellboy" jumped out to an early lead and did nothing but gain at the quarter and half mile marker before coming up lame down the stretch and losing. It is hard to determine whether Babe was more upset at having to report back to his mates of their collective bad luck or the fact that he had dropped 20 bucks on the horse himself. In all likelihood, his reaction to his money lost was most probably that there was more where that came from, for he always spent it as if there was a never-ending supply. And why not, he was 23 and the world was his.

Two days later, another track-related event of a more serious nature nearly cost Babe and several teammates their lives. Following an afternoon at the races, Babe, Harry Hooper, Everett Scott, Joe Bush and Wally Schang engaged a chauffeur of a "big touring car" (a forerunner to a taxi) to take them back to the hotel. The driver reached speeds of 50 miles an hour through the city before coming to a screeching halt in the center of town. He demanded that they pay him and leave the car. He wanted to return to the track to pick up more fares and if he took them all the way to the hotel, he would not get back in time to do so. A heated argument ensued and the players found a policeman to settle their dispute. After the policeman ordered the driver to take them to their destination, he became irate and told them he was going to tip all of them out first. He then proceeded to accelerate and in an attempt to do just that, driving into a horse and smashing into a wagon. He finally stopped the vehicle when Harry Hooper grabbed him and threatened to punch his lights out. Following a delay while the owner of the horse and wagon collected autographs, the driver returned to his senses and the trip was resumed. All arrived safely.

On March 30, Babe made what would turn out to be his last pitching appearance in Hot Springs, Arkansas as a member of the Boston Red Sox. He entered the game in the fifth inning with Boston trailing 1-0. He proceeded to surrender a two-run homer to Otto Miller in the seventh and when Ruth's battery mate, Sam Agnew led off the bottom of the eighth, the Sox were down 3-0. Agnew hit one over the leftfield wall for a home run and Babe stepped to the plate. He drilled the first pitch over the rightfield fence, "a mile away" but foul by a few inches. The next pitch was also hit over the rightfield fence, only this time it was fair and the fans in attendance cheered wildly as they had witnessed a rarity of the times, back-to-back home runs.

Brooklyn took a 3-2 lead into the ninth. Hoblitzell opened the frame with a single to left which was abruptly followed by a double by George Whiteman. When Bobby Fisher, batting for Evers, blooped a single to left, the score was tied at three, bringing Agnew up, with men on first and third and nobody out. Agnew forced Fisher at second while Whiteman was held at third bringing up Ruth. As Babe made his way to the plate, Robinson made his way to the mound, calling for left-handed pitcher, "Lefty" Mitchell. Once again Babe jumped on the first pitch, sending it sailing over centerfielder Hy Myer's head allowing Whiteman to trot home with the winning run.

The fans left knowing they had seen a great battle for this particular time of year, but as the two teams prepared to take their show on the road to Texas, Alabama, and Tennessee before heading North to start the season, the fans could not have known that they had seen the last of the Babe in red stockings.

Before leaving Hot Springs, Babe purchased an alligator to take home with him as a pet. There are no reports on what happened to the gator. Whether Babe gave it away, let it loose, ate it, or turned it into a suitcase is not known. What is known is that there were no reported sightings of Babe in Boston, or any other major league city, cruising the streets with alligator in tow.

Babe terrorized Brooklyn pitching throughout the spring of 1918, to such an extent that the fans, according to the *Boston Herald*'s Bob Dunbar are "disappointed when they don't read that big Babe Ruth hit a home run." It wasn't just the home runs, either. It was the way he hit them out in batting practice and the long fly balls he hit for outs during the games. It was the way the opposing outfielders ran to the fences and stayed there, their backs against the outfield walls waiting for him to hit. He was the premier left-handed hurler in the game and one of the very best hitters in all of baseball.

In the past two seasons, he had started 78 games and completed 58 of them. He was 47-25 for a winning percentage of .653. He had hurled 15 shutouts and had a two-year combined ERA of 1.89. Yet despite it all, it was his bat, "Black Beauty" which fans all over the country heard about, talked about and wanted to see. His legend was building as he stood on the verge of taking the game of baseball to a place it had never seen.

The team pulled out of Hot Springs and headed to Texas. They played in Dallas on the 1st of April and beat Brooklyn 2-1. The following day matched Babe against Rube Marquad. Boston won the game 7-6 in 16 innings, but by then both left-handers were gone. The Red Sox had thumped Marquad for four runs on ten hits in only five innings. Brooklyn touched Babe for a run in the fourth and two in the fifth, before he gave way to Dick McCabe.

The talk of the day, however, was Babe's bat, or lack of it. His first time up, Marquad fanned him on three easy slow curve balls. Babe was so frustrated that he threw his bat out into rightfield in an attempt to throw it out of the ball park. When he came to bat the second time he decided to try it right handed. He was equally unsuccessful as Marquad again sent him down swinging. This time he did not heave the bat, but returned to the dugout. It marked his first and only recorded right handed at-bat for the Red Sox.

From Dallas it was on to Waco, Austin, and Houston before heading for New Orleans. The Red Sox were fortunate that they remained in the jazz city for only one night or they may have lost

Babe forever. There were no reports of any transgressions on the part of the prized southpaw, but it is logical to assume that the wild side of the city of New Orleans suited Babe just fine.

Rain on the sixth forced a postponement of a scheduled game that was played the following day. Babe was again matched up against Marquad and he wowed the crowd in batting practice when he knocked one clear out of the park and into a railroad yard. He went 2 for 4 on the day and surrendered 12 hits and three runs in nine innings of work. Brooklyn won the game 4-3 in 12 innings but the fans left happy for having seen Babe hit one out in batting practice. During the game, home plate umpire Joe Hart announced the name of every player to the crowd as they came to bat. The loudest and most raucous cheer was reserved for Babe.

From New Orleans it was time to head north. There would be a stop in Mobile, Alabama where the Sox and Brooklyn played a 13-inning 6-6 tie in which Brooklyn made 11 errors. Then it was on to Birmingham where the frigid weather forced an early end to a seven-inning contest, played in only 35 minutes, that saw Brooklyn win 3-1. It was then time to head toward Fenway with one more stop in Chattanooga, Tennessee. When the game there was called due to snow, Barrow and the boys headed home. Opening day was five days away, and Barrow let it be known that either Carl Mays or Babe Ruth would get the call as the starting pitcher.

The team limbered up in workouts at the Harvard University batting cage and their lineup was set. McInnis had won a spot at third base and another acquisition from Connie Mack, Amos Strunk, would open the season as the Red Sox centerfielder. 40-year-old Dave Shean, reacquired from the Cubs during the winter, won the starting assignment at second base. Frazee's moves in the off season had placed the 1918 edition of the Red Sox in a position to contend following their disappointing 1917 finish.

When opening day finally arrived, it was Babe Ruth who was standing in the middle of the diamond with the ball. Barrow's dilemma was temporarily solved as he went with his left-handed ace to start the season. It was the third year in a row that Babe had been the opening day pitcher and as he had done in the previous two, he pitched the Red Sox to victory.

❧

An enthusiastic crowd of 7,180 was in attendance at Fenway, none of them aware that before the game, old friend Heinie Wagner was reinstated as a coach, replacing Johnny Evers. A personality conflict with Barrow ended the future Hall of Famer's brief tenure in a Red Sox uniform. The teams marched out to centerfield before the game, where captains Hoblitzell and Oldring together raised a new flag up the centerfield pole. They walked back to home plate displaying a plea for the fans to subscribe to the third edition of Liberty war bonds, and awaited the ceremonial first pitch from Boston Mayor Andrew Peters. Before the first pitch, the mayor met Frazee and Hoblitzell at home plate, and on behalf of the Royal Rooters, presented them with flowers.

Peters was flawless pitching the first ball to catcher Agnew, and the 1918 baseball season, once thought an impossibility, was underway. Opposing Ruth was a 6'4" 27-year-old right-hander named Willie Adams, who had not pitched at the major league level since 1913 with the Browns. He had pitched 15 games for Pittsburgh in the Federal League in 1914 and since then had bounced around in the minors. With the war depleting the league of players and Connie Mack in fire sale status in Philadelphia, Adams was the designee to open the '18 season for the A's.

Both pitchers were flawless in the first, and the A's actually drew first blood in their half of the second. George Burns led off with a single and advanced to second when old friend Tilly Walker grounded out to short. Babe then grew wild walking "Wickey" McAvoy and "Red" Shannon. This loaded the bases for Joe Dugan who proceeded to rip a vicious line drive to right-center. It appeared to be headed for the gap and at least two bases when Strunk made a diving, tumbling catch and came up firing to third. A run scored, but Amos had kept the damage contained and the newly acquired centerfielder was an instant hit among with the Fenway crowd. Babe helped himself in the Boston half of the inning when with two outs and men on first and third, he lined a single to right in his first at bat of the season. This scored George Whiteman with what proved to be the winning run.

The rest of the day belonged to Ruth and the Red Sox. Babe settled down, allowing only three hits throughout the remainder of the contest. He even added another RBI with a long sacrifice fly to leftfield in the fourth. Three runs in the seventh sealed the fate of the A's and accounted for the 7-1 final. The Red Sox were off and running in their campaign to recapture their lost championship.

The consensus was that all newcomers had acquitted themselves well in their respective debuts.

	IP	H	SO	BB	R	ER
4/15/18 vs.						
Philadelphia	9	4	3	2	1	1

At bat: 1 for 3,   2 RBI, sac fly

They continued their mastery over the A's when Carl Mays carried a no-hitter into the eighth the following day. Losing the no-hitter, Mays then had to concentrate on getting the win as the Sox came up in the ninth with the score tied at zero. His mates came through for him when Scott singled in McInnis who had doubled, making him a 1-0 winner.

With Hollywood film star Mary Pickford in attendance, the Red Sox completed the three-game sweep in dramatic fashion. The A's had gone ahead 4-3, scoring two runs in the top of the ninth. A walk and a double put runners on second and third with no one out and Ruth stepped in to pinch-hit. Amidst jeers from the crowd, he received an intentional walk, which brought up another Barrow pinch-hitter in the person of Wally Schang. Schang then delivered a two-run single to win the game. Mack and the A's left town 0-3, and in each game a player whom Mack had dealt to Boston played a key role in a Red Sox victory. It was the first series of the season, and Harry Frazee looked like a genius.

The Yankees came to town to begin a five-game series with a Patriots Day doubleheader on Friday the 19th. Rain had forced the postponement of the final game of the A's series, pushing Babe's start back to the second game of the twinbill. It was the first doubleheader of the year, and in game one Joe Bush made his Red Sox debut. As effective in his debut as his mates had been in theirs, Bush four-hit New York on his way to a 2-1 win before a little more than 3,000 fans. Babe's strength as a drawing card was once again illustrated when just under 14,000, braving the afternoon chill, showed up to watch him start the second game.

The game was deadlocked 1-1 when the Red Sox came to bat in the bottom of the fifth inning. Agnew led off with a double to right center bringing up Ruth. Before singling, (Agnew stopping at third) Babe hit a foul ball behind first base. Yankee second baseman Derrill Pratt drifted into foul territory to make the catch. Burt

Whitman wrote in the *Boston Herald* the next day: "Ruth ... sent up the highest foul I ever saw, so high that it came down with snow on it, slippery, so slippery Pratt muffed it." Hooper then dropped a bunt single giving Boston the lead, 2-1. The lead was extended when Pratt made his second and third errors of the inning, first by booting Dave Shean's easy ground ball and then by throwing wildly to second base, allowing Ruth and Hooper to score. In all, five runs came across and the Red Sox had a 6-1 lead.

They added to the lead on the strength of a Babe Ruth sacrifice fly. The unusual was becoming commonplace for Babe, and so it was with his RBI in the sixth. With Everett Scott on second base and one out. He lofted a towering drive to deep rightfield. Many in the crowd thought it would find its way into the bleachers. Yankee rightfielder Frank Gilhooley raced back, making an outstanding catch, taking the ball off the wall. Scott tagged up at second and never stopped at third, racing all the way home from second on a sacrifice fly. Many thought that Scott could have scored from first, so high and deep was the fly ball. Once again, Babe's bat had treated the fans to one of baseball's most unusual feats as he provided the most spectacular hit of the entire afternoon, a fly ball out to rightfield. He was furious at the ball being caught, and that may have led to a lapse in concentration as New York added two runs in the seventh to make the score 7-3. Boston got the two right back in their half and had the game salted away. The final score was 9-5, as Babe surrendered 13 hits in the contest. Not particularly effective in this start, he was typical Babe, surrendering the bulk of the runs when the game was all but decided in his team's favor.

	IP	H	SO	BB	R	ER
4/19/18 vs. New York	9	13	4	3	5	5

At-bat: 1 for 3, RBI, run scored

He had wowed the crowd with a mammoth pop foul and a gargantuan sacrifice fly. He now was making outs in a larger way than had been done before.

The next day, Carl Mays won his second game of the season and the Red Sox were 6-0 coming out of the gate. Sunday was an off day and on Monday, New York handed the Red Sox their first loss of the young season, 11-4.

On Tuesday, April 23, Yankee pitcher Herbert Thormahlen, a victim of horrendous defense just four days earlier, carried a no-hitter into the ninth. Early in the game, Babe mentioned to Barrow the he would like to have a chance to bat against the young Yankee left-hander. "I think I can hit him," Babe had told the skipper, and when Strunk singled with one out in the ninth, Barrow summoned Ruth to bat for Hoblitzell. "Can I play first if I get a hit ?" Babe asked. "You can," Barrow replied, and Babe strolled to the plate and promptly singled, sending Strunk to third. McInnis was intentionally passed, bringing up George Whiteman, who flied to Ping Bodie in shallow leftfield. In his haste to get Strunk at the plate, Bodie dropped the ball, and Amos scored the winning run. For the second time in four days, the 21-year-old Yankee left-hander had been victimized by shoddy defense. The ninth inning win had delayed Ruth's debut at first base.

It was on to Philadelphia for the first road trip of the season and the home opener for the A's. The pre-game ceremonies included gifts for the former A's who were now members of the Red Sox. Bush received a diamond badge from the local Elks club, McInnis a chest of silver. Wally Schang was given flowers and a cane while Amos Strunk picked up a new set of golf clubs.

On the mound it was another battle of lefties as Ruth squared off against old teammate Vean Gregg. Both pitchers were equal to the task, carrying a 0-0 game into the bottom of the eighth. With one out, Babe walked switch-hitting left-fielder Manny Kopp. This brought up Larry Gardner, who hit a perfect double play ball to second base. Shean, however, booted the ball and there were runners on first and second. George Burns stepped in and with the count one ball and no strikes, Ruth grooved a pitch that "had nothing on it but Ban Johnson's signature" and that was the ball game. It was Babe's first loss of the season.

	IP	H	SO	BB	R	ER
4/24/18 at Philadelphia	9	5	1	3	3	2

At bat: 1 for 3

After winning the next three games, Boston boarded a train bound north where a four-game series with the Senators awaited. First they would stop for an exhibition game in Bridgeport, Connecticut in which Babe played first base. The Red Sox won 7-0 despite an error by Babe and an 0 for 1 performance at the plate. While the Red Sox were playing in Connecticut, the city of Boston was enjoying its first ever Sunday baseball game as over 28,000 showed up at Braves Field to watch Camp Devens defeat the Commonwealth Pier team 6-2.

Returning to Boston, the Red Sox defeated the Senators in the first game of their series, 2-1. The next day the city was abuzz; not over the sensational 11-2 start of the Red Sox, but the headlines in the *Boston Herald* sports page.

"GREATEST VALUATION IN THE HISTORY OF BASEBALL PLACED ON BABE RUTH."

Burt Whitman outlined the details of the story:

"Since the start of the championship season Owner Harry Frazee of the Red Sox has been offered more than $100,000 for one ballplayer and of course his name is George H. "Babe" Ruth, colossal southpaw pitcher and hitter most extraordinary. The magnate turned down the offer saying: 'I might as well sell the franchise and the whole club as sell Ruth. The sum named was three times as much as was paid for Tris Speaker, and of course is far and away bigger than any figure that has been used in baseball. But it is ridiculous to talk about. Ruth is our big ace. He's the most talked of, most sought for, most colorful ballplayer in the game.' "

Speculation at the time had the offer coming from either Charles Comiskey or Jake Ruppert. It would be learned within a couple of weeks that the Yankee owner was the one who made the colossal offer for the "colossus." In a little less than two years Ruppert's offer would not seem as "ridiculous" and in a little less than five years Frazee's comment that he " might as well sell the franchise" would come hauntingly true. For that is exactly what he did, to the Yankees, a player at a time, and the remains he sold to Bob Quinn.

Already the best left-handed pitcher in the game; already redefining the art of hitting a baseball, already the new, most popular drawing card in either league, Babe now was redefining the relative worth of a player to his team's owner. He also brought new meaning to the term "worth one's weight in gold." At 200 pounds and the price of gold at 20 dollars an ounce, Babe's weight in gold was a paltry $64,000. Babe was worth more than twice his weight in gold.

High, fluffy clouds filled the sky as the sun cascaded down on Fenway Park, bringing the month of April to a close. It was as warm as it had been frigid just a week before, as the first shirtsleeved crowd of the year gathered at Fenway to watch Babe pitch against the Senators. The gentle breeze provided refreshing reprieve to those who watched from the sun-drenched bleachers. Babe was the topic of conversation among most of the 2,300 plus in attendance, all talking about the recent revelation. Frazee himself reconfirmed the figure to be in the $150,000 range.

Belying any of his skeptics present on this afternoon, Babe totally dominated the game. Doubling in two official at-bats, he knocked in a run and scored two. He stole second in the eighth inning, allowing Scott to come home when the catcher's throw went awry. He was brilliant defensively; starting a double play, covering first on a ground ball to second after Hoblitzell fell going after the batted ball, and knocking down a screaming line drive off the bat of Howard Shanks, which turned a sure hit into an easy out. His mates, as they often did, elevated themselves to another level behind him as the Red Sox rolled 8-1. The *Boston Post* thought Babe "a little off form" on the mound, but the general consensus was that Babe "looked like a million," rather than a mere $150,000. That would be tough to dispute after having watched him excel on the mound, at the bat, and on the field.

	IP	H	SO	BB	R	ER
4/29/18 vs. Washington	9	5	1	3	1	1

The Red Sox ended the month with a record of 12-2. It was the best start any Red Sox team had ever enjoyed. Nearly 80 Aprils later, it remained the best month of April in the team's history. Babe was off to another good start at 3-1 for the month, with an ERA of 2.25. His opponents hit .200 against him, with a good portion of those hits coming in a game in which his team was leading 9-1. In three of his four starts, he surrendered two earned runs or less and in one of those he suffered his only loss.

His line for the month of April looked like this:

IP	H	SO	BB	R	ER
36	27	10	11	10	9

May dawned with the Red Sox facing Walter Johnson. Without his nemesis opposing him, the "Big Train" threw a four-hit 5-0 shutout at Barrow's crew. The only ones to solve him on the day were Hooper (3 for 4) and McInnis (1 for 4). The Fenway fans were clamoring for Babe to pinch-hit in the ninth, but to no avail. With the game lost, Barrow said he did not want to waste him.

The following day Hooper and McInnis continued their torrid hitting as Hooper pounded out three doubles in five trips to the plate, and McInnis went 3 for 3 as Boston romped 8-1. It was now on to New York, the Yankees and the Polo Grounds. The face of major league baseball was about to be changed forever.

In the opening game of the three-game series, Bush went 11 strong innings and Hooper continued his torrid hitting, going 2 for 5, but it wasn't enough as the Sox succumbed to New York 3-2 in 11 innings.

Babe was on the mound for the second game facing fellow Baltimorean Allen Russell. New York decided to test Boston's new third baseman, Stuffy McInnis, and the fielding prowess of Mr. Ruth as they paraded one bunt after another down the third base line. Their strategy worked as Babe made two throwing errors that led to three Yankee runs. Babe ended the day with nine assists, but when the stands emptied at the Polo Grounds, it was not his errors on the field or his nine assists that were on the minds and lips of those who had witnessed the game. It was his bat!

Ruth and Russell were natural rivals who took great delight in striking each other out. In Babe's first at-bat, he went down on three straight Russell "spitballs". Russell laughed at him, and as the teams changed positions, Babe walked past the right-hander and said, "Don't get chesty, I'll be up a few more times this afternoon and I may not look so funny."

Russell had remained virtually unhittable throughout the day when Babe came to bat in the seventh. Trailing 4-1 with two outs and Everett Scott on first, he strolled to the plate. On the first pitch, he drove a rising line drive into the upper deck that was "foul by six inches." Disappointed but not defeated, he picked up his bat and as he was walking back to the plate he said to home plate umpire Billy Evans, "I'll hit this one right back, Bill, and it will be fair by such a wide margin there will be no doubt about it." The very next pitch he drilled even further into the upper deck and there indeed was no doubt about it as it landed about 100 feet fair. Though his famous "called shot" has been disputed, his first, on this day appears indisputable. The crowd was stunned, amused and appreciative as the score was now 4-3.

The Yankees got one back in the eighth, taking a 5-3 lead into the ninth. When Hoblitzell and Scott went out in the ninth, many of the 15,000 in attendance headed for the exits. Then Sam Agnew doubled, bringing up the tying run in the person of Babe Ruth. The fans all scurried back from under the grandstand as Babe stepped up to the plate. Once more Babe offered at the first pitch and sent it deep into the upper deck, once again just foul. This brought Yankee manager Miller Huggins out to talk to his pitcher. As the brief war council came to a close, the outfielders backed up, and Babe resumed his position in the box. Yankee rightfielder Armando Marsans was nearly back to the wall, but it didn't matter as Babe tore into one that shot over his head and off the wall for a double. Evans said it was his hardest hit ball of the day.

Agnew scored making it 5-4, bringing up Harry Hooper with Ruth on second. Hooper, who had eight hits in his previous 14 at bats, grounded out to end the game and the Sox had lost their second in a row and third of their last four. Babe was now 3-2 on the year.

	IP	H	SO	BB	R	ER
5/4/18 at						
New York	9	8	0	3	5	2

At bat: 2 for 4, double, home run, 3 RBI

During the game, first baseman, Dick Hoblitzell injured his finger. It did not seem like a major injury at the time, and in fact was nothing that would cause any long-term damage or require him to be sidelined for any extended period of time. However, Sunday's day off was not enough time for it to heal, and he would be scratched from Monday's line up.

When manager Barrow rambled to the plate with his lineup card on May 6 of 1918, Carl Mays was written in the ninth spot as the starting pitcher. Batting sixth and playing first base was Babe Ruth. Gathering all the attention around the first base bag during warm ups, Babe was tickled to be in the lineup and for the very first time in his major league career, he was starting in a game at a position other than pitcher.

The game was scoreless until Ruth came to bat in the fourth inning. With Stuffy McInnis on first, Babe duplicated his effort of the previous day and lofted one high into the upper deck in rightfield. Scott lined a double and scored on a single by Agnew, giving Mays and the Red Sox a 3-0 lead. The lead was short lived, however, as Ping Bodie lined a two-run single that coupled with two throwing errors tied the score. Bodie feasted on Mays and Jones, going 3 for 4 with a double, two singles, five RBI, and a run scored. A journeyman player who played parts of nine seasons with three teams and never even hit .300, Francisco Stephan "Ping" Bodie could forever claim that he had stole the thunder from Ruth in Babe's first game as an everyday player. New York won 10-3 to sweep the series.

The Red Sox had dropped three in a row and four of their last five, but the talk throughout Boston and New York was the bat of Babe Ruth.

"Babe Ruth continues to thrill the New Yorkers with his potential batting strength. They scoffed along Broadway when we sent them the story that there had been a $150,000 offer for Ruth. Now thy (SIC) appreciate his worth. He'd be a better investment for the Yankees than would be Ty Cobb. How the Babe would maltreat that rightfield stand, the upper tier and the none too distant barriers." *Boston Herald* 5/7/18

Bob Dunbar's words were not lost on Jake Ruppert.

It was on to Washington to face Walter Johnson and the Senators. With Hoblitzell still nursing an injured finger, Babe again got the call at first base, only this time he was inserted in the cleanup spot in the order. Johnson was in control throughout the day, surrendering only four hits in a 7-2 victory. One of them was by Ruth, and it came in the sixth inning. Following an infield hit by Amos Strunk, Babe stepped up and "got hold of a fast one and gave it wings. It sailed on and on over the garden wall, messing up a war garden and scaring a mongrel pup half to death." It was Babe's first career home run off Walter Johnson and the second time that he had hit three home runs in three successive games. His efforts were appreciated by the Senators fans as he received a large ovation as he trotted around the bases. Having witnessed Babe's home run against Johnson, Bob Dunbar of the *Boston Herald* remarked; "My idea of a hard hit ball is Babe Ruth crashing into Walter Johnson's fastball for a home run, such as the Colossus scored off the Kansas catapult in the district yesterday."

The Red Sox woes continued the following day, as the Senators clubbed three Boston pitchers for 17 hits in a 14-4 romp. Babe was again at first base and in the cleanup spot. He scored the first run of the day in the first inning when he hit a changeup off the scoreboard in right for a double and came home on a single by McInnis, extending his hitting streak to nine games. Boston had actually led 4-0 going into the bottom of the fifth, when Washington erupted for eight runs. Barrow had announced that Ruth would be the starting pitcher the following day as the Sox would attempt to break their five-game losing streak.

Thursday's game was moved up an hour to 3:30 so the Red Sox could catch the Federal Express out of Washington to get home to face the Browns the next day. It was Babe's first start since April 29 when he had beaten the Senators 8-1 at Fenway. To say that Babe answered the bell would be an understatement. Pitching and batting fourth, he came to the plate in the first inning with two outs and nobody on and laced a triple to the scoreboard in right. He died at third base, but still led 1-0 when he took the mound.

It remained that way until the seventh inning when the usually reliable Harry Hooper made a two-base throwing error that cost Boston two runs and the lead. In the eighth inning there were two outs and nobody on, when Babe stepped in. He was 3 for 3 having singled to lead off the fourth and doubled to center with one out in the sixth. He again hit one to the gap in right center for his fourth hit and second double of the day. This time, however, he was not stranded as George Whiteman singled him home to knot the score at two. The Red Sox went ahead in the ninth when Wally Schang, running for Hoblitzell, scored on Hooper's sacrifice fly. Washington tied it in kind when Walter Johnson, pinch-hitting for pitcher "Doc" Ayers, scored Ray Morgan with a sacrifice fly of his own.

Going to the tenth, the Senators now had Walter Johnson on the mound. Strunk, Ruth, and McInnis were due up for Boston. No one left the park, remembering the prodigious blast that Babe had hit off Johnson two days before. Johnson disposed of Strunk and readied himself to face Ruth. Babe lashed one to the scoreboard in right for his fifth hit of the day and his third double. Unfortunately for Boston, Babe was cut down trying to steal third, and the game ended 4-3 in favor of Washington. Despite Babe's five-for-five day (the first five-hit game of his career), he had lost the game to Walter Johnson.

He certainly had pitched well enough to win. Washington's 11 hits had been scattered, and two of their runs were unearned. The other two came home on sacrifice flies. He did fall victim to the walk, as his leadoff pass in the ninth to Ray Morgan led to the eventual tying run, preventing Babe and his mates from winning the game in nine. He certainly had hit well enough to win as well; unfortunately, he never came to bat with men in scoring position, and thus his five hits could produce no runs. His unique role of pitcher and cleanup hitter was not lost on the pundits, as *The Sporting News* noted in its May 16 issue:

> "It is a strange setting to find a pitcher batting fourth in the line up of one of the best clubs in baseball. It savors much of college or school baseball where often times the pitcher is the big gun of his team every way one looks at him. Needless to say, Ruth is the rumble in the Red Sox family."

To watch him everyday was to realize his value and understand why Frazee had turned down an offer to sell him, even for an exorbitant price.

	IP	H	SO	BB	R	ER
5/9/18 at Washington	9 2/3	11	1	5	4	2

The Red Sox were now mired in a six-game losing streak and had dropped into second place for the first time in the young season. Babe's record was 3-3, and his hitting streak was at ten games. It was home to Fenway to begin a 20-game homestand against the St. Louis Browns.

Two streaks came to an end in the first game of the homestand. Boston ended their six-game skid with a 4-1 win. Babe played his first game in the outfield, patrolling "Duffy's Cliff" in leftfield. He went 0 for 5 to end his ten-game hitting streak. His only other hitless game came in the second game of the year when he was intentionally passed as a pinch-hitter, with men on second and third and two outs in the ninth.

His debut as a leftfielder was a success. Lamenting that it was "lonesome out there", that "it's hard to keep awake", and that there was "nothing to do" he made a "fine impression" as a left-fielder. Bob Dunbar wrote:

"He handled three base hits which went to his district . . . in the fielding style which recalls Tris Speaker. He drove home the impression, already rather general, that he is a natural born ball player. Before the end of the season he may be playing shortstop or catching."

Perhaps responding to Babe's boredom in left, Barrow had him back at first base the next day. His bat scintillated again as he had three "screaming" hits in four at-bats, including a long double to right center which only the wind prevented from being a home run. He displayed his prowess around the first base bag in the sixth when he made a sensational stab of a line drive heading down the line turning a sure double into an out. It was all for naught as the Sox lost again 4-2.

In the seven games between May 4 and May 11, Babe hit at a .483 clip, going 14-29. He had hit three home runs and knocked in seven runs. On the year, he was leading the majors with a .487 batting average, three home runs. a triple and seven doubles. This had clearly been the best streak of his career.

Sunday was an off day, and with Babe scheduled to pitch on Tuesday, Barrow gave him Monday off as well. The Sox won 7-5 before the last game of the Browns series was rained out, pushing Babe's start back to the opener of the four-game set with Detroit.

The Tigers took an early 3-0 lead when Frank Walker reached Babe for a bases-loaded triple. Boston added a single run in the fourth and Babe himself scored in the fifth when Harry Hooper followed his double with a single to rightfield. Detroit added an unearned run in the fifth before Boston added another single score in their sixth and the Tigers lead 4-3 going into the ninth.

With one out, Schang batted for Thomas and walked. Scott followed with a single and Barrow went to his bench for another lefty, sending up Hoblitzell to bat for Sam Agnew. "Hobby" singled and tied the game as Schang ran through third base coach Heinie Wagner's stop sign. The throw home allowed Scott and Hoblitzell to advance to second and third, bringing up Ruth.

The crowd was now humming with excitement. Babe had already doubled to deep right center and taken centerfielder Frank Walker all the way to the wall with a huge shot in the third inning. Tiger pitcher Hooks Dauss wasted no time in issuing an intentional pass to the Boston pitcher. But it only delayed the inevitable as Harry Hooper hit one over the head of a pulled-in Bobby Veach in

Babe's first manager, Jack Dunn, who signed him to his first pro contract and sold him to the Red Sox in July of 1914. *(National Baseball Hall of Fame Library, Cooperstown, NY)*

A playful 19-year-old Babe with his first pro team, the Baltimore Orioles of the International League, 1914. *(Courtesy Babe Ruth Museum, Baltimore, MD)*

Babe in team photo with Orioles, seated in front row middle, next to mascot
(Courtesy Babe Ruth Museum, Baltimore, MD)

Ruth in his Providence Gray's uniform. His last minor-league stop, he pitched for them in August and September of 1914, and was a factor in the team winning the league championship. *(National Baseball Hall of Fame Library, Cooperstown, NY)*

Young and full of confidence, Babe is shown here shortly after his meteoric rise to the majors in 1914. *(Courtesy Babe Ruth Museum)*

On August 15, 1995 in the centennial year of Ruth's birth, the city of Providence, Rhode Island dedicated a plaque at the former site of Melrose Park. Babe played his home games here as a member of the Grays of the International League shortly after being purchased by the Red Sox.

Boston's Back Bay Railway Station as it appeared in 1914 when Babe emerged onto the city's streets for the first time. *(Courtesy Boston Public Library)*

Boston's Brunswick Hotel located in Copley Square at the corner of Boylston and Clarendon Streets, where Babe stayed when he first arrived in town. He was a frequent guest in years to come. *(Courtesy Boston Public Library)*

Babe (at left) and fellow Red Sox at his first major league training camp at Hot Springs, Arkansas in 1915. Owner Joseph Lannin is seated in the middle (in street clothes) with Manager Bill Carrigan to his immediate left. Carl Mays is shown in upper right corner. *(Courtesy Robert Wood)*

Photo of newlyweds Babe and Helen as it appeared in the *Boston Post* on March 15, 1915. *(Courtesy Boston Public Library)*

Manager Bill Carrigan and his wife at spring training in Hot Springs, Arkansas circa 1915. Babe would later say that Carrigan was the best manager for whom he ever played. *(Courtesy Robert Wood)*

Babe's first appearance on a baseball card, from a *Sporting News* set of 1916.

Ruth's first World Championship team, the 1915 Boston Red Sox. *(Courtesy John Hooper)*

Raising the 1915 World Championship Banner at Fenway Park on June 1, 1916. Babe appears third from left. *(Courtesy Boston Public Library)*

Photographer Babe taking photo of several teammates at Fenway Park, circa 1916. *(National Baseball Hall of Fame Library, Cooperstown, NY)*

Babe on a tour of the Draper & Maynard Sporting Goods Factory in Plymouth, New Hampshire, October of 1916. To Babe's left is Duffy Lewis. *(Courtesy Plymouth, New Hampshire Historical Society)*

Babe (in full-length raccoon coat) and teammates greet co-eds from the Plymouth Normal School on the 1916 New Hampshire trip. *(Courtesy Plymouth, New Hampshire Historical Society)*

Babe dons the boxing gloves with teammate Mike McNally at Lake Squam in Plymouth, New Hampshire. Babe came up on the short end of what became a little more than a playful exchange. *(Courtesy Plymouth, New Hampshire Historical Society)*

Harry Frazee, who purchased the Red Sox in November of 1916, will forever be remembered as "The Man Who Sold Babe Ruth". *(Courtesy National Baseball Hall of Fame Library, Cooperstown, NY)*

Jack Barry, who managed the Red Sox in 1917. Ruth and Barry became close friends and Babe had an extended stay at the Barry household in early 1917. *(Courtesy National Baseball Hall of Fame Library, Cooperstown, NY)*

The farmhouse Ruth rented and eventually purchased, located at 558 Dutton Road in Sudbury, Massachusetts. *(Courtesy Linda Ruth Tosetti)*

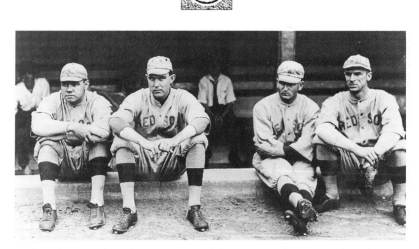

Ruth (left) seated on the top steps of the visitors dugout with (left to right) Ernie Shore, George "Rube" Foster, and Del Ganer circa 1917. *(Courtesy National Baseball Hall of Fame Library, Cooperstown, NY)*

Ruth posed for a photographer during spring training at Hot Springs, Arkansas circa 1918. *(Courtesy John Hooper)*

Ed Barrow managed the Red Sox from 1918 through 1920. Ruth made the transition to an everyday outfielder during his tenure. *(Courtesy National Baseball Hall of Fame Library, Cooperstown, NY)*

THE BOSTON RED SOX 1918

LAWLER MILLER JONES THOMAS RUTH HOOPER MAYS SHEAN KINNEY STRUNK M'INNIS BARROW
SCOTT DUBUC BUSH WHITEMAN SCHANG MAYER WAGNER AGNEW COFFEY
MASCOT & BATBOY

The 1918 World Championship Red Sox team. Although they had just won their third championship in the previous four seasons, no man in this photo would live to see the team win another. *(Courtesy Sports Museum of New England)*

The 1918 World Series Emblem presented to family members of that year's championship team, on September 4, 1993. The players were originally denied their emblem due to their threat to strike before Game 5 of the series. Ruth's emblem was accepted by step-daughter Julia Ruth Stevens.

Boston Red Sox
1918 World's Series Emblem
Presented September 4, 1993

NAME					BIRTH DATE	BIRTH PLACE
D	RUTH, GEORGE BABE		4515		2-7-94	BALTIMORE
ADDRESS					AGE WHEN EMPLOYED 24	NATIONALITY AMERICAN
WHEN EMPLOYED						

HEIGHT	WEIGHT	EYES	HAIR	EYESIGHT	SINGLE WIDOWER	TRADE
6-2	200	BROWN	DARK	GOOD	XXX DIVORCED	BALL PLAYER

HEARING	HERNIA	VACCINATED	HEART	SKIN	DEPENDENTS	
GOOD	NO	YES	GOOD	WHITE	IN UNITED STATES	IN FOREIGN COUNTRY

USE INTOXICANTS   MARKS

No

WIFE YES

IN CASE OF DISABILITY NOTIFY

MRS. RUTH, SAME ADD

CHILDREN UNDER 16

PREVIOUS SICKNESS OR INJURIES

No

CHILDREN OVER 16

REMARKS:

OTHER

ACCEPTED

REJECTED   101

(SIGNATURE OF APPLICANT)   (SIGNATURE OF EXAMINER)

Bethlehem Steel Company   Physical Examir   Form 2062-50m-5,17,18 BS.Co.

Babe's timecard for his brief employment at Bethlehem Steel Plant in Pennsylvania. Note incorrect birthdate, and rather suspect denial of "Use of Intoxicants". *(Courtesy Lebanon, Pennsylvania Historical Society)*

Red Sox Manager Ed Barrow, former major leaguer and Evangelist Billy Sunday, and Ruth in Tampa, Florida for spring training 1919. *(Courtesy John Hooper)*

Historical marker commemorating the home run Babe hit at Plant Field, in Tampa, April 1919.

BABE'S LONGEST HOMER

At Tampa's Plant Field on April 4, 1919, "Babe" Ruth, playing for the Boston Red Sox against the N.Y. Giants, smacked a 587-foot home run that set a record in a pre-season game. 4,300 screaming fans saw the feat. Famed Evangelist Billy Sunday, an ex-major leaguer himself, who was conducting a tent revival on the Florida Fair grounds nearby, had pitched the first ball of the game, and The Bambino's pace-setting ball was presented to him. Ruth played from 1915 to 1935. He is regarded as the most popular player and greatest slugger in history. One year, he hit 60 homers.

Babe demonstrating his swing for a photographer circa 1919. *(Courtesy National Baseball Hall of Fame Library, Cooperstown, NY)*

Ruth posed with future Governor of Connecticut John Trumbull before an exhibition game in Hartford in 1919. *(Courtesy National Baseball Hall of Fame Library, Cooperstown, NY)*

An editorial cartoon as it appeared in the *Boston Post* on August 15, 1919 after Babe broke the American League single-season home-run record. *(Courtesy Boston Public Library)*

Babe, with Helen at his side, accepting tokens of appreciation on "Babe Ruth Day" at Fenway Park on September 20, 1919. *(Courtesy National Baseball Hall of Fame Library, Cooperstown, NY)*

NO WONDER BABE RUTH PELTS THE BALL OVER THOSE DISTANT FENCES

The Home-Run King is a Favorite Among the Movie Folk and in This Picture Shows the Strength of His Arms and Shoulders That Sends the Well-Known Old Apple Riding Over Far-Away Barriers

While on a trip to Hollywood in the Fall of 1919, the *Boston Herald* published this photo of Babe demonstrating his strength by holding up two young actors. *(Courtesy Boston Public Library)*

Front-page headline of the *Boston Post,* January 6, 1920. *(Courtesy Boston Public Library)*

Herald cartoon published the day Ruth's sale became public. *(Courtesy Boston Public Library)*

Cartoon that appeared in the *Boston Herald* the day after Ruth's sale to Yankees. *(Courtesy Boston Public Library)*

Babe left Boston in 1920 for the ultimate urban playground, New York. He is shown here in one of his many subsequent forays into high society. *(Courtesy Babe Ruth Museum)*

Painting of Ruth that hangs in the Sports Museum of New England, signifying his induction into the newly created Boston Red Sox Hall of Fame in 1995.

rightfield, making winners of the Red Sox and Ruth, 5-4. Babe was now 4-3.

	IP	H	SO	BB	R	ER
5/15/18 vs.						
Detroit	9	9	1	1	4	3

Babe had pitched well, as he kept the Tigers beating the ball into the ground all afternoon. McInnis had 15 putouts at first base, with Babe himself fielding four comebackers and registering four assists of his own. At the plate he was 1 for 3, with his double and run scored.

The next three games found Babe in leftfield and batting in the clean-up position. Although he only had two hits in those three games, he continued to electrify the crowd with huge towering shots to the outfield. Twice he flied out to deep center, hitting balls that "would have been home runs in other ball parks."

Playing with reckless abandon, he nearly "tore down the leftfield grandstand" going after a ball hit by Tiger pitcher Bill James.

"Babe almost made a sensational catch of this but missed, and it is a wonder he did not muss up the entire stand by the force of his impact. He himself was unhurt. He is one of those heaven sent athletes who . . . instinctively handle themselves well in a jam . . . escaping injuries which make life a series of horrors for performers less natural, less agile." *Boston Herald* 5/17/18

The game was temporarily halted as Babe assisted rearranging the seats he had bowled over.

In the third game of the series, he gathered in four flies for putouts and added two assists. On one of the assists, he hooked up with third baseman Chet Thomas to nail Ty Cobb who was "sleeping" with his head down walking back to the first base bag. Cobb had singled on the ground to leftfield and when Babe quickly gathered the ball in, Ty walked back towards first, not knowing that Ruth had swiftly relayed the ball to Thomas. Thomas whirled and fired the ball to first, nailing Cobb. With all this activity in left, Babe no longer felt lonely and bored patrolling Duffy's old grounds. Three straight wins completed a sweep of the Tigers and the Red Sox had now won five in a row.

The Sunday off brought the first summer weather to Boston, and Babe headed north of the city to spend the day at Revere Beach. He was not alone, as an estimated 175,000 people swarmed to the beaches in and around the city. Ignoring the sore throat that had been bothering him for a few days, Babe romped in the surf and played ball on the beach. By the time he arrived home that night, he was suffering from a temperature of 104. He showed up at Fenway Park as he was scheduled to pitch against Cleveland, but after a brief meeting and exam by the unofficial team doctor Oliver Barney, Babe was convinced that it was more than a mere sore throat and was ready to take the recommended four or five days of bed rest.

Babe accompanied the doctor to a Back Bay drugstore, seeking medication for the ailment. While waiting in the drug store, Babe collapsed and was taken immediately to the Massachusetts Eye and Ear Infirmary. His condition was reported as serious, but by the evening he was termed "out of danger."

He was diagnosed with an edema of the larynx and he was being treated by a well known throat specialist, Dr. George Tobey. Bed rest and complete silence were the primary elements of his treatment and he was also keeping ice on his throat. Initially the hospital stay was expected to be at least ten days, which left Barrow looking towards sometime around the 5th of June before Babe would be back in the lineup.

Babe's hospital room rapidly filled with flowers from well wishers. Among them were his teammate Dick Hoblitzell and his old manager Bill Carrigan. As to be expected, sitting around all day was not something Babe took well. He was frustrated not knowing what was going on at Fenway as it was happening. The evening was his favorite time, because he would get the results of the day's action. There was even some talk of attempting to hook up a dictaphone to allow him to listen into the dugout during the games. This idea was scrapped when it was decided there would be no way of screening from the nurses the rather salty language that had a tendency to be uttered in the Red Sox dugout.

While Babe lay in his bed, an announcement came from Washington that would have a profound effect on major league baseball and the 1918 season. Secretary of War Newton D. Baker announced that the occupation of baseball player was declared "non-useful." All baseball players would either be drafted or employed in an occupation deemed "essential" to the war effort. All draft deferments were rescinded as those players with wives and children did not have to be drafted, but could be employed stateside for the war effort. All this was to take effect on July 1, but several owners, Frazee among them, saw a glimmer of hope in the fact that people in the theater industry were exempt. The reason was that the War Department felt that entertainment should not be curtailed and was essential to the morale of the country. Frazee and others saw a chance for baseball to complete its season.

Babe was discharged from the hospital on Sunday, May 25. Leaving with Helen on his arm, he was advised by his doctors to forget about baseball and get complete bed rest for a few days at home before rejoining the team. Barrow, in an attempt to keep Babe away from the park, announced he would not use his left-hander until the team was in Detroit the following week. He was kept out of uniform, but when Monday's game was announced as a benefit for the Red Cross, Babe was among the 4,284 who showed up to watch his mates battle the White Sox.

With all gate proceeds and the Daughters of Mercy volunteer nurses passing the hat, Frazee donated $6,700 to the war effort. Babe enjoyed the day, signing autographs and bantering with the fans. He did not enjoy the outcome, however, as Chicago won 6-4. The Red Sox were now 3-3 since Babe had been hospitalized. Not happy with the way things were going, Babe told Burt Whitman of the *Boston Herald* that, "he would make up for his enforced absence as soon as he is able to swing the old hickory again."

Perhaps it was Babe's presence or perhaps it was just their streaky nature, but the Red Sox reeled off four wins in a row before Babe made his official return to the lineup. It came in a pinch-hitting role in the eighth inning of the last game of the homestand against the Senators. It was the second game of a doubleheader and Washington led 4-0. As Babe emerged from the dugout swinging two bats, the 11,000 began to cheer. By the time he'd stepped into the batter's box, they were all on their feet according him a resounding ovation. Babe was back.

The month of May came to a close, and the Red Sox were in first place, two games ahead of New York and four-and-a-half ahead of the third-place Browns. It was on to Detroit and four games with the Tigers, where for Babe there would be one more pinch-hitting assignment (a ninth-inning strikeout in a 4-3 loss) and then he would return to pitch the second game of the series.

Ruth's rustiness was evident as the first pitch he threw was laced for a double by shortstop Donnie Bush. After getting the next batter, Bobby Veach lined the first pitch into rightfield for a single, and Detroit led 1-0. Babe fell victim to his own wildness in the second when he walked two men with the bases loaded, staking the Bengals to a 3-0 lead.

The lead lengthened to 4-0 in the fourth on a walk, a single, and an infield out before the Sox began to battle back. There was one out and no one on in the Boston sixth when Babe stepped up. In his two previous at-bats in the series he had fanned, and he quickly went into the hole with two strikes. He then poled one high and deep to right into the bleachers and Boston was on the board. They added single runs in the seventh and ninth, and in fact had the tying and winning runs in scoring position when the game ended in a 4-3 Detroit win.

It went in the books as a loss for Babe, but his performance, though shaky at the outset , showed that he was indeed back. That was great news for Barrow and the Red Sox.

	IP	H	SO	BB	R	ER
6/2/18 at Detroit	9	9	2	3	4	4

At the plate he was 1 for 3 with his fourth home run of the year. His solo homer in the sixth accounted for his RBI and run scored. He would be back in the outfield the next day and he was on the verge of once again redefining the art of hitting a baseball.

Monday, June 3, 1918 brought two more firsts in the career of Babe Ruth. He started the game in centerfield between Harry Hooper in right and George Whiteman in left, and found himself batting third in the lineup for the very first time. Starting in center due to the twisted ankle of Amos Strunk, Barrow reaped immediate dividends from inserting him into the third spot in the order.

With two on and nobody out in the first inning, Babe hit another towering drive to rightfield, which landed in nearly the exact same spot as the day before. The Red Sox led 1-0, and it was all they would need. This day belonged to Leonard; he walked Bobby Veach with two outs in the first inning, and that was the extent of the Tiger baserunners for the day. The next 25 men went down and Leonard had the second no-hitter of his career. Babe had once again hit home runs in successive games, and there was more to come.

The following day found Babe again in centerfield and batting third. For five innings, the Red Sox were held hitless by Tiger pitcher Bill James. Mays had surrendered three singles, but the score was knotted at zero when the Red Sox came to bat in the sixth. A single by Hooper followed by a stolen base and another single by Dave Shean brought Ruth up with one on, none out, and one in.

In the fourth inning, Babe had laid down a perfect sacrifice bunt after Shean had walked. James half expected him to bunt again and laid one in to him, but Babe planted it high and deep into the rightfield stands and the Red Sox led 3-0. For the second time that year, he had hit home runs in three successive games.

The Red Sox edged out a 7-6 victory as the early pitchers' duel turned into a slugfest, with the Sox barely hanging on. Babe had now so captivated the fans with his thunderous bat that the query often was not "Did the Red Sox win?", but, "Did Babe hit a homer?" His latest exploits caused Bob Dunbar to comment on Babe's projected value as a Yankee.

> " Just think how often he would 'find' that rightfield stand, or the leftfield bleachers at the Polo Grounds. In no time at all he'd be running George Cohan a close race for premier honors in the Broadway Popularity League." *Boston Herald* 6/5/18

Mr. Dunbar was a soothsayer.

Having taken two of three from Detroit, it was on to Cleveland for five with the Indians. For the third straight game, Ruth was in center and batting third as Joe Bush went against Cleveland's 28-year-old right-hander Jim Bagby. Cleveland had scored in the first and it remained 1-0 until the sixth, when once again Babe stepped in with a man on, a man out, and a man in. For the fourth time in as many games, he lofted one high and deep toward right. The ball carried clear out of the ball park, the first of the year to do so at Lee Field. With this blow, he became the first man in baseball history to hit four home runs in four successive games. The Red Sox now led 3-1. Babe did not see a pitch to hit for the rest of the afternoon as he was intentionally passed in the eighth and in the tenth. Five errors eventually did in the Sox, as Cleveland won 5-4 in ten innings.

His home run streak came to an end the next day, but he did please the crowd in batting practice by driving a blast out of the park, which broke two windows across the street. In the game, he went 0 for 4 but drove in the only run with a bases loaded shot up the middle in the tenth inning. Second baseman Bill Wambsganss made a great stop behind the bag to get a force at second but Hooper came across with the tally and Boston won 1-0.

Six Boston pitchers, including Babe, were clubbed for 13 hits and 14 runs as Cleveland won the next game, 14-7. Babe had been playing leftfield and had a single, a triple, two RBIs, and a run scored to his credit when he volunteered to go in and pitch in the seventh inning in the midst of a Cleveland rally. He faced just two men, walking them both. They went on to score the tying and winning runs, thus saddling Babe with his fifth loss of the season. His record was now 4-5.

	IP	H	SO	BB	R	ER
6/7/18 at						
Cleveland	0	0	0	2	2	2

He also received his third intentional pass in two games.

They split the last two games of the series and then headed further west for four games with Chicago, then four with St. Louis before they would return home to Fenway. The fans in Chicago cheered him and hoped they would get to see one of his long, high home runs. It was not to be, as Babe cooled a little, getting only an RBI single in ten at-bats in the three games he played. The White Sox were pitching around him when the situation called for it, even intentionally walking him one time. The Red Sox took three of the four games, with all their wins being shutouts. Their pitching was back on track.

At this time, Ruth received a letter from Frazee stating he would receive a $1,000 bonus if he won 30 games. Next, it was on to St. Louis where the Browns and their fans waited. They too, were anxious to see the man whose legendary tales preceded his arrival. L.C. Davis, a St. Louis beat writer had written of Ruth, "Babe hits that pill so hard that the infielders duck even when he gets a base on balls."

Back in leftfield and the cleanup position, Babe's bat came back to life in St. Louis. He had a single and a double in four at-bats in the opener, driving in three runs in what was a 5-4 St. Louis victory. He provided the difference in the second game of the series with a long three-run homer in the rightfield bleachers breaking a 4-4 tie with two outs in the seventh. He added an RBI single in the ninth to account for the 8-4 final.

On Sunday, the Browns squeaked out a 2-1 win. Babe was back at first base and the box score officially lists him as 0 for 1. He batted four times in the contest, three of them with a man on second base. On all three of those occasions, he received an intentional walk, moving Bob Dunbar to write, "this compliment was never paid to any modern day slugger, not even Cobb." His hitting prowess was now redefining the way pitchers and managers handled certain game situations.

Monday's game brought more of the same, as Babe was intentionally passed his first two times up. That made it five intentional walks in a row, unprecedented in baseball history, and extremely frustrating to Babe. He did get a double later in the game, which was an 8-0 Sox win, but his frustration at not being able to take his cuts was obvious.

"If Babe doesn't get his chance to swing, he'll start swinging at them[pitchers]." *Boston Herald* 6/18/18

Babe went 5 for 15 in the four-game series. He had two doubles, a home run and seven RBI. He received five intentional passes, which had manager Barrow thinking that he might put Babe back in the pitching rotation and save his bat for a swing in each game, only with the bases loaded. Then they would have to pitch to him. Players and managers were thinking of the game in ways and in terms never thought of before. Babe's big black bat was casting shadows across every ball park and every opposing dugout in the league.

It was home for a quick five-game set with the A's, and a strange series it turned out to be. All the games were shutouts. Philadelphia grabbed the first two, 5-0 and 2-0. The Red Sox took games three and four, 3-0 and 13-0 and the fifth game was rained out. Babe went hitless in the series until the fourth game, when he singled and tripled. Mack's boys made seven errors in that contest, and Carl Mays fired a one hitter. Babe exhibited some defensive prowess and showed some of his powerful arm strength when he gathered in Larry Gardner's line drive and nailed Rube Oldring at the plate in the first inning of the first game of the series. No one attempted to run on him for the rest of the series.

☙

During the brief homestand, Babe was involved in yet another motor vehicle mishap. The *Boston Herald* reported the incident:

> "If they were giving automobiles to the 'most' players in the two big leagues this season, it's a certainty that Babe Ruth would get the A. L. buggy. It's equally certain that there would be little left of the machine by the start of the next season. Babe can hit telegraph poles as hard as he hits the horsehide. But we love him just the same."

They loved him indeed. Babe was nearly as much of a menace to his fellow drivers on the road as he was to American League pitchers.

≈

The Federal Express barely had time to let her engines cool before the Red Sox were back on it bound for New York. The Sox and the Yankees would play four games in a battle for first place. Babe was not in the lineup for the first game as he watched the Yankees score two in the ninth to steal a 3-2 win. New York had made six errors, but the Red Sox could not capitalize on their miscues. Babe's absence from the lineup left some to speculate that he might take a turn in the rotation. However, he may have been a little sore from his encounter with a Massachusetts telegraph pole.

Babe was back in centerfield as Amos Strunk was nursing a tender leg he had injured sliding in Monday's game. The Babe wasted no time there in thrilling the New York fans. Always a favorite among the fans at the Polo Grounds, Babe received a remarkable ovation when he stepped up in the first inning with George Whiteman standing on first. Miller Huggins' 24-year-old right-hander Allen Russell tried to sneak a fastball by Babe. It was letter high and over the outside corner. Babe crushed it, somehow pulling it high and deep to rightfield. Described as a "colossal clout" and a "tornadic thump", it landed in a box in the upper deck and the fans of New York cheered as he rounded the bases. It was his ninth home run of the year and his third at the Polo Grounds—all of them had reached the upper deck. Staked to an early lead, Sam Jones cruised, and Boston won 7-3 to remain in first place.

July had not even arrived, and Babe already had as many home runs as Wally Pipp had hit in 1917 to lead the league. The following day, he had a double in four at-bats and scored the only Red Sox run in a 3-1 loss. He injured his wrist on a slide into second base and would re-injure it the same way the next day. He had developed a bad habit of putting his hands down as he slid, and it was a cause for concern. Although he had not pitched in several weeks, his career as a pitcher was not over. Barrow had made that clear only a week before when he spoke of re-inserting Babe into the rotation. His current mode of sliding could cause serious injury to his pitching hand. Jammed wrist or not, he went 2 for 5 with a single and a double in the closing game of the series. He and his mates pounded out 17 hits, but it was not enough as the Yankees captured the game and first place with a 7-5 win.

It was on to Washington for four with the Senators and then to Philadelphia where they would celebrate the 4th of July with a doubleheader against the A's.

The opener belonged to Harry Harper and the Senators as the 23-year-old left-hander dazzled the Sox throughout the afternoon. He walked one and had not allowed a hit until Babe stepped to the plate in the seventh inning. He lofted one deep into the rightfield stands for his tenth home run of the year, tying the score 1-1. Washington added two in the eighth to give Harper his sixth win in a row, 3-1.

The Red Sox reversed the 3-1 score and won the game on Saturday, setting up a Sunday afternoon clash between Carl Mays and Walter Johnson. A huge crowd was on hand as the Senators had 2,000 soldiers attend the game as their guests. Four hundred of them received bats as gifts before the game got underway, and a large contingent of Boston rooters were among the festive crowd. The expectation that the season could end any day, coupled with Walter Johnson pitching, and of course, the presence of Ruth, added a holiday atmosphere to the proceedings. It was now wildly accepted and unquestionably true that Babe Ruth had surpassed Ty Cobb as the number one drawing card in all of baseball.

The biggest event of the night on U.S. war ships was the relaying of baseball scores at 23:00 hours from the wireless out of Arlington, Virginia. The Red Sox results were always the last score given and the final transmission was if Babe had slugged another homer or not. His exploits were a source of great interest to the men on the front as well.

" The story of Babe Ruth's mighty hitting, his homeric smashes, kindles a glow in the hearts of all those who know baseball. In Italy, in Normandy, in Alsace and in a hundred camps along the firing line, men meet and ask the latest news of the gifted hitter of home runs. The story of each succeeding circuit clout is received with acclaim. It lightens and breaks the dangerous tension of a soldier's duty and it is not stretching a point to say that in his own inimitable way the colossus is contributing a worth while gift to the morale of Uncle Sam's fighting men both in the new and old world. He is the hero of all present day baseball . . . ."
Boston Herald 7/1/18

Even rain could not dampen the spirit of this rare Sunday crowd. It began to fall in the third inning and three times during the game home plate umpire Hildebrand halted the game. The crowd refused to leave, and the game was played in a constant drizzle that sometimes became a heavy rain. The Red Sox had scored a run in the third, and even though they had touched Johnson for nine hits, they took a slim 1-0 lead into the Senators ninth. Three singles tied the score, and the game headed to extra innings.

The rain had abated as the Red Sox came to bat in the tenth, and after two were out, Dave Shean singled to rightfield, bringing up Ruth. The clouds were breaking as he stepped in, and for the first time all day, the sun peeked through the gray Washington sky. On the first pitch, "the slugger swung with all his strength" lofting the ball high and deep toward rightfield. Washington rightfielder "Wildfire" Schulte watched as it sailed over the fence, giving the Sox the lead, the win and first place back.

It was the second time during the year that Ruth had reached Johnson for a home run and the sixth time he had homered in successive games. It was not yet July, and Babe's 11 home runs already exceeded the totals of nine American League home run champs since 1900. Incredibly, Babe's 11th home run of the year had come on only his 139th at-bat.

The month came to a close and with no official word from the War Department in Washington, the games went on although the Sox and Senators enjoyed an unusual Monday off.

Red Sox third baseman Fred Thomas was the first to fall victim to the non-essential ruling when, on July 1, he received notice to report to his draft board in his hometown of Weekwonago, Wisconsin. As his mates were enjoying a day off in the Nation's capital, Thomas packed up and caught a train to begin the long trek home.

Carl Mays was reclassified, making him eligible to be called at any time and popular shortstop Everett Scott had an appeal pending to maintain his deferment; he was married with two young children. Leonard and Hoblitzell were already gone and many were just waiting on Washington to end the season.

Tuesday marked the last game of the series, and the Senators again threw Harry Harper at Ruth and the Red Sox. Washington grabbed an early lead when, in the first inning, Babe made a costly error that led to a pair of runs. He had a chance to redeem himself when he came to the plate in the third with two on and one out. He swung and missed three straight pitches, and the crowd roared with delight as Babe walked back to the dugout. The Senators added a run in the third and were leading 3-0, when Babe came up to bat in the sixth. The crowd again went into a frenzy when Babe struck out a second time as Harper threw a curve ball that had Ruth falling backward as strike three hooked across the plate.

Babe did not emerge from the dugout again as the Sox went down to Harper by a 3-0 count. The story line was that he was bothered by stomach trouble, and as a result, had to leave the game. The reality was decidedly different.

On Monday, Babe had been given permission to visit his hometown of Baltimore. Expected back early on Tuesday, he did not show up until just before game time. Barrow, though chafed at his tardiness, refrained from saying anything to him and inserted him in the lineup. Babe's first inning error did nothing to endear him closer to the heart of his already irate manager. Swinging and missing three straight pitches and then nearly falling out of the batter's box on called strike three was all that Barrow could handle. When Ruth returned to the dugout, fireworks erupted. Babe explained his version to the *Boston Post*:

> "The whole fuss was started over a play on the field. I hit at the first ball and he said something about it being a bum play. Then we had some words and I thought he called me a bum, and I threatened to punch him. He told me that would cost me $500 and then I made a few more remarks and left the club." *Boston Post* 7/3/18

> "I got mad as a March hare and told Barrow then and there that I was through with him and his team. I knew I was too mad to control myself, but suiting the action to the word, I did leave the team and came home." *Boston Herald* 7/4/18

At 11:20 that night, Babe wired Frank Miller, manager of the Chester Shipbuilding Company baseball team of Delaware County. He was inquiring as to the best terms available under which he could play for his team. Miller sent a representative to Babe's home, and by 3:30 the next afternoon Ruth had come to contract terms that would place him on the mound for the Chester team July 4. When Babe did not show up for the scheduled game with the A's, Frazee sent him a telegram asking him to come to Philadelphia to confer with him. Barrow dispatched Babe's longtime friend and mentor, Heinie Wagner to Baltimore to speak to Ruth and convince him to return. Frazee threatened a suit and had begun plans for a civil action against the Chester Shipbuilding Company. He said he would seek an injunction preventing Ruth from playing for the Chester team.

> "Frazee said that if it takes every cent that he has invested in baseball he will bring Ruth to his senses and put a summary stop to those who are inducing players to go back on their legal contracts ...." *Boston Post* 7/3/18

Fortunately for all concerned, Wagner's trip was successful and he returned to Philadelphia with Babe in tow at two A.M., the morning of the fourth.

Babe was in uniform for the morning game, but Barrow not only did not speak to him, but did not use him at all during the Red Sox 11-9 win. This rekindled the heat under Babe's 17-inch collar. Miffed at not being welcomed back with open arms, Babe changed out of his uniform and was reportedly on his way home again when some mates interceded and coerced him to stay.

A half-hour before the second game began, Babe approached Barrow and made his peace with him. Barrow let Babe know in no uncertain terms that he was to follow instructions just like everybody else. Babe and Barrow shook hands and the hard-hitting lefty was in centerfield and batting third in the second game. He singled in the Red Sox' only run, tying the score 1-1 in the eighth. The Sox lost 2-1 in 11 innings, but the prodigal son was home.

Babe's actions were not well received by writers, players, fans, and least of all owner Harry Frazee. The events ignited some animosity among teammates.

"Not a single player on the team is in sympathy with him and the Red Sox first and last are disgusted with the actions of a man whom they say had his head inflated with too much advertising and his effectiveness impaired by all together too much baby-ing." *Boston Post* 7/3/18

Bob Dunbar wrote in the *Boston Herald* of July 4, 1918:

"Babe Ruth is a distinct Boston big league product, and all Hub fans feel a propriety interest in the huge fellow and hope that he will not make them feel ashamed of their enthusiasms of other days."

The Sporting News stated the discord was caused "because the Babe is only a big boy, views things through youthful lens, and is utterly reckless of consequence." Frazee steamed, and a rift opened between the owner and the greatest player in the game. The rift would never be closed.

 ❧

The final game of the series found Barrow naming Ruth to pitch and bat fourth. It was his first pitching appearance since he'd walked the only two men he faced on June 7 and took the loss. It was his first start since he had beaten the Tigers 4-3 at Navin Field on the second of June. As was so often the case, Babe surrendered a run in the first inning, giving the A's a 1-0 lead. The Sox countered with single runs in the second, third and the eighth, taking a 3-1 lead into the ninth. Babe had given up but two singles since the first inning, but was greeted by old friend Tilly Walker with a lead-off double. Walker would eventually score on a single by Joe Dugan, and when Babe hit leftfielder Manny Kopp with the bases loaded, pinch-runner Jimmy Dykes came across with the tying run.

With two outs and nobody on in the Red Sox tenth, Babe came to the plate. He walked and scored immediately on a long triple by McInnis. Buoyed by regaining the lead, Babe set the A's down in order in their half of the tenth, earning him his fifth win of the season.

	IP	H	SO	BB	R	ER
7/5/18 at Philadelphia	10	7	3	4	3	3

Although he was hitless in three official at bats, he scored the winning run after walking in the tenth.

It was now time to head home where they had played only four games since the first of June. Cleveland, Chicago, St. Louis and Detroit would provide the opposition for the 15-game homestand. The fans were anxious for the team to get home, anxious to see Babe at bat, and anxious to view his exploits, as most of them had occurred on the road.

They would not have to wait very long. Sitting out of the first game of the series with Cleveland because he had pitched ten innings the day before, Babe came up as a pinch-hitter for third baseman Walter Barbere (who had been picked up from the minors when Thomas was drafted). There were men on first and third with nobody out in the bottom of the sixth and the Indians leading 4-2. A huge roar from the crowd welcomed Ruth at the plate and he responded by ripping the first pitch down the rightfield line that rolled all the way to the wall. Whiteman and Scott scored easily and as Babe was heading into third, the relay came from rightfielder Bobby Roth to his second baseman, Bill Wambsganss. In his haste to nail Ruth at third, Wambsganss made a bad throw, allowing him to score. A thunderous clamor reverberated throughout the park as Babe crossed with what would prove to be the winning tally. The Red Sox were back in first place.

Babe's performance and the response of the fans at Fenway Park inspired Paul Shannon of the *Boston Post* to write: "unmistakably ... there is still but one Babe Ruth in fandom." It was hard to believe that a mere 48 hours before, Babe was slated to pitch for the Chester Shipbuilding team of Delaware County Delaware.

ॐ

Monday turned into a doubleheader to make up a game that was rained out in May when the Indians last visited Fenway. Babe was in leftfield, and batting fourth for both games. When he came to bat in the first inning of game one, the fans rose and gave him an ovation. It was clear that all was forgiven, at least from the perspective of the fans. The first game featured a classic pitching confrontation between Boston's Sad Sam Jones and future Hall of Famer Stan Coveleski. The game was scoreless when Babe led off the eighth and lined a single to rightfield. He took second on a bunt by McInnis, but died there. Into the tenth they battled, until Amos Strunk singled with one out bringing Babe back up to the plate.

"The Colossus of Clouters came up swinging his two, heavy, new bats. The crowd yelled loudly and long for a home run. Babe took his stance, made his bid on the very first pitch, a curve ball, and zowee how it traveled . . . up into the realm of eagles, high and higher, far and farther." *Boston Herald* 7/9/18

Rightfielder Bobby Roth quickly turned on the ball and then stopped watching as the ball sailed three quarters of the way up into the rightfield bleachers. It was the longest Fenway Park home run anyone had ever seen.

It was the first ball that Babe had hit out of Fenway Park all season. His 11 previous homers were hit on the road. The irony of it all is that to this day it still stands in the record books as a triple. For in 1918, the rules were such that in instances such as this, the game officially ended when the preceding runner scored. Because Strunk was on first base, Babe gets credit for a triple. If Amos had been on third, Babe would have only been given a single for his colossal clout. It wasn't until 1920 season that this rule was changed.

Cleveland captured the second game, 4-3, to salvage a split of the doubleheader. Although Babe went 0 for 4, he did make a great running catch in the second inning. It prompted the *Boston Herald* to remark, "he can do something other than hit three base hits which ought to be home runs." The *Herald* even went so far as to suggest a way that Babe could have been given credit for a home run. It went to great lengths to explain how Strunk just had to miss third base and Babe could have completed his trip around the bases. Amos would have been the second out and Babe's run would have made it 1-0, and he would have had home run number 12. Once again he was changing the way people looked at the game.

Tuesday found Babe back at first base as McInnis was suffering from an attack of the boils. In yet another pitchers' duel, Joe Bush outlasted Cleveland right-hander Jim Bagby as the Sox won 1-0 in 12 innings. Babe went 1 for 3 and nearly put another one into the rightfield bleachers, but former Sox Joe Wood hauled it in with his shoulders against the wall. Not to be outdone by an ex-mate on this day, Babe too, would shine on the field.

In the third inning of the game, he placed his leg between the first base bag and a sliding Jack Graney. Graney's spikes caught Babe between the knee and thigh, tearing his pants and causing a slight flesh wound. He later survived a collision, on the same knee, with Ray Chapman. At one point, he collapsed during the game but following a brief pause, continued to play. Despite it all his performance around the first base bag was described as "remark-ably fine" and his toughness added the moniker "Cave-man" to his growing repertoire of nicknames. Bob Dunbar of the *Boston Herald* even suggested it "a good idea to insure Babe's physical equip-ment for the contents of a sub-treasury or two."

The third game of the series was a rained-shortened five-in-ning affair in which Babe was once again the principle player. Af-ter striking out in his first at-bat in the first inning, he came to bat in the fourth with a man on first and lofted one high off the wall in left centerfield. By the time Speaker caught up to it, Babe was stand-ing on third, and the Red Sox had a 1-0 lead. Babe rode home on George Whiteman's single, accounting for the 2-0 final. It was the third Red Sox win in a row that was decided by a Babe Ruth triple. They had taken four out of five games from the Indians and now were in first place by two-and-a-half games. All this he accomplished with a bruised and battered knee. He was so wounded, in fact, that his insistence to play had manager Barrow calling it "the gamest thing" he had seen in all his years in baseball.

Chicago was next in town, and incredibly, Babe was about to turn his game up yet another notch. At morning batting practice before the game, Barrow was giving Babe some tips on how to hit the ball to the opposite field. In a matter of minutes Babe was bang-ing the ball to leftfield at will.

This proved an invaluable lesson that was quickly applied. With White Sox knuckleballer Eddie Cicotte pitching Babe outside all afternoon, Babe took him three times into leftfield for doubles. This led one of the local pundits to comment that the only time Babe stopped at first base was when he played there.

On this day, he played like few before him had ever played at first. Stretching and saving throws, leaping and pulling down high bounders or merely making the routine play, the day belonged to Red Sox first baseman Babe Ruth. He finished the day with 20 putouts at first and he saved the best for last. With one out, Chicago had the bases loaded and Shano John Collins at the plate. Collins hit a scorching bounding ball toward the rightfield corner. Babe scooped it up and noticed that the runner on first had hesitated. He dashed toward him, tagged him and then ran toward first, slid-ing in just ahead of Collins to complete the unassisted double play. The final score was 4-0, giving the Red Sox their third shutout in a row and their fourth in five games.

The second game of the series brought the return of summer rains to Fenway. Dark clouds hovered throughout the day. Thunder boomed in the distance and lightning flashed, creating an almost mystical setting around the ball park. Burt Whitman of the *Boston Herald* wrote, "It was the perfect setting for the battering Babe to hammer out a few of those extra base specialties of his." Hammer them out he did—a bloop double in the second, a triple to deep left center in the fourth, and a triple to the rightfield corner in the sixth. In all, he accounted for four of the Red Sox' six runs in a 6-3 victory. At first base it was more of the same, diving stops, sensational stretches or just routine plays—Babe was everywhere. His ten putouts gave him 30 in the last two games. When the rain finally ended the contest, it was Babe who was the most disappointed. He was convinced that his next time up, he would have hit one out of the park. Who was to doubt him?

If Babe Ruth were alive today, and he were asked to pick one week out of his entire career that epitomized him as a baseball player, it is entirely possible that he may have chosen the week from July 4 through July 11, 1918. For in the one week since his return from his 36-hour hiatus in Baltimore, he had 12 hits in 30 at-bats for a .400 average. Five of those hits were triples, and four of them were doubles, propelling him to a slugging percentage of .867.

He had hit the longest home run anyone had ever seen at Fenway Park—which went into the books as only a triple—and he had sparkled defensively at his favorite position, first base. He had authored an unassisted double play and had registered 20 putouts in one game. He also pitched a ten-inning complete game victory. Much of this having been accomplished with a knee so injured that the fact that he could even play had his manager marveling at his gameness. There has never been a more proficient utility player in the annals of baseball.

He had elevated the game to mythical proportions heretofore unseen. Burt Whitman of the *Boston Herald* said it best:

> "The more I see of Babe and his heroic hitting the more he seems a figure out of mythology or from the fairyland of more modern writers. He hits like no man ever has, truly the master man of maulers." Standing out "like an Ajax and knock[ing] the living daylight out of the delivery . . ." 7/13/18

On Saturday, the White Sox turned the tables by shutting out the Red Sox 5-0. Babe played first base again and went 0 for 4. The crowd left disappointed not so much in the fact that the home team had lost, but because "big Babe didn't hit one of his destructive drives." The new utterance heard among those leaving the ball park after the game was "give me back my money, Babe Ruth didn't get a hit."

On Monday, the Red Sox stats were posted. Babe was leading the team in hitting with a .315 batting average. Of his 57 hits, 37 were for extra bases, giving him a slugging percentage of .685. He was leading the league in home runs with 11.

Tuesday was the last game of the White Sox series and the Red Sox emerged victorious, 3-1. This marked the return of Babe as a "normal batter" as he went 2 for 3 with only two singles in the game. The "normal batter" was now hitting .321, fifth best in the league.

Wednesday brought the Browns into town for the first of a three-game series. Babe was again on first, as McInnis was still down with the boils. Ruth tripled, leading off the second, to deep left centerfield, as he once again just took the outside pitch the other way. He scored when Whiteman singled and Sam Jones had a 1-0 lead that he would take into the ninth.

George Sisler led off the St. Louis ninth with a single and he came around to score with the aid of a sacrifice bunt, a wild pitch and a sacrifice fly. It was now time for more Red Sox heroics, only of a bit of a different nature. Dave Shean led off with a single and was immediately sacrificed to second by Amos Strunk. This brought up Babe, who was to no one's surprise, intentionally passed. With Whiteman at the plate, Shean and Ruth took off from their respective bases, which caught the Browns totally off guard. When catcher Les Nunamaker's throw sailed into leftfield, Shean got up and dashed for home with the game winner. Babe had chalked up one of his six stolen bases of the season.

The following day found Babe back on the mound, pitching the second game of a doubleheader. It was his first pitching performance at Fenway Park since the 15th of May. In the first game, he played leftfield and batted in what was now his customary fourth position. He went 1 for 4 with a single in Joe Bush's 7-0 shutout win, and once again he had people talking about a failed at-bat in glowing terms. In the second inning, he popped up to Joe Gedeon at second base. In what would have appeared in the official score book as a meager PO-4, Burt Whitman wrote: "Babe's fly to Gedeon in the second went up so high, it came down covered with stardust."

Babe remained batting in the cleanup spot in the second game, despite the fact that he was pitching. Barrow reaped immediate benefits from that decision when he doubled in two runs in the first inning. It turned out to be all that Ruth and the Red Sox would need as he shut the Browns down on only four singles. The game was played under an ominous dark cloud, with thunder rumbling throughout the contest and lightning intermittently dancing across the sky. Babe was in the midst of another two-run rally when he doubled and scored one of the two Sox runs in the third. With the dark clouds becoming more foreboding, the Red Sox began to deliberately run into outs on the base paths. Leading 4-0, they wanted to do everything in their power to get five innings in to assure that the game would be official.

St. Louis had two outs, a run in and a man on second when the skies opened in the top of the sixth inning. The teams never retook the field, so the game reverted back to the last completed inning, giving Babe a shutout with an assist from the heavens. It was his first shutout of the season and the 17th since he had debuted in 1914. What the 9,000 fans in attendance did not realize as they left the ball park, was that they had witnessed the last regular season shutout of Babe Ruth's career. He was now 6-5 on the year.

	IP	H	SO	BB	R
7/17/18 vs.					
St. Louis	5	4	2	1	0

At bat: 2 for 2, 2 doubles, 2 RBI, run scored.

During the week Babe received another letter from Frazee. Dated July 12, it cancelled the conditions of his letter in June and gave Babe an instant bonus. He further stated that another $1,000 bonus awaited Ruth if the Red Sox were to win the pennant. This was a fair-minded gesture from Frazee as he realized, with urging from Babe, that his lack of pitching appearances would preclude him from winning 30 games.

Babe went uncharacteristically hitless in St. Louis' 6-3 win on Friday. He did almost kill Browns second baseman Joe Gedeon with a searing line drive, but he slapped it down and recovered in time to throw him out at first. The fans felt somewhat cheated as Bob

Dunbar noted in his column, "Babe didn't even make a long fly out yesterday, he'll surely make up for it today." People just wanted to see him hit, it didn't really matter if he hit safely, just as long as he hit them high and far. No one else in all of baseball could please the fans with the way they made outs. He was redefining the expectations of the fans who came out to the park.

Dunbar was right, he did indeed "make up" for it the next day. Detroit was in town, and they would be without the services of Ty Cobb for the first game, as he had missed the train. Babe led the Sox to a 5-0 win with a single and a triple in three official trips to the plate. He drove in a run and scored two as Carl Mays dominated the Cobb-less Tigers, allowing them only three singles.

During this game, the ruling came down from Washington D.C. Secretary of War Newton Baker, officially stating baseball was a "non-essential" industry, and as the players left Fenway Park for home, they were informed that American League President Ban Johnson ruled the season would end following the games of July 20. There was one game left in the season.

Red Sox owner Harry Frazee sprung into action. Not at all pleased with the way major league baseball had been represented in Washington, Frazee telegraphed baseball's National Commission asking them to implore Washington to allow the season to be concluded after 100 games and a World Series had been played. He issued a statement in which he outlined why baseball should be allowed to continue, and how he felt it aided the war effort. He even spoke of taking the Red Sox (if they won the pennant) to France and replaying the World Series against the National League Champions, for the boys at the front.

Both league presidents issued statements that they would comply with Baker's order and the players readied themselves for the last game of the season. On Saturday July 20, Babe played leftfield, went 0 for 3, and the Red Sox beat the Tigers 5-1. Frazee worked frantically to keep the game alive, and why not?— his Red Sox were in first place, five games up.

Word was received that Monday's games could be played, and the Red Sox and Tigers decided to close out the series. Moving Tuesday's game to Monday, they played a doubleheader. A heat wave blanketed the city, sending the temperature soaring to 98 degrees. Despite the oppressive heat, 10,000 showed up for what some thought might be the last baseball played at Fenway for quite some time. The Red Sox swept two games from Detroit, 1-0 and 3-0. The pitching staff had now pitched five shutouts in their last seven games. Babe went 0 for 7 in the doubleheader and was now hitless in his last ten at-bats. Was it the heat, the enormous distraction or perhaps, as some suggested, the presence of Cobb that had him pressing? It mattered not, but what did matter was whether or not the season would continue. From a Red Sox perspective, Washington could not have picked a worse time to shut down the game.

John Tener, National League President, appealed on behalf of Major League Baseball to continue playing until such time as the particulars of the stoppage could be worked out. Among them were provisions for a World Series. The request for clarification brought new life to the game as Baker agreed to review Tener's appeal. While Baker reviewed, the games would go on.

How long they would go on was anybody's guess. Some thought the season would be concluded, some thought the end was near. Thus, amid reports of fishing boats being sunk 65 miles off the coast of Maine and of crowds gathering on Cape Cod beaches to watch the salvage of vessels sunk by German U-boats; with the state of New York looking at the possibility of cousins Teddy and Franklin Roosevelt running against each other for Governor; and the United States government announcing it was taking over control of the Cape Cod canal, Babe Ruth and the Red Sox boarded a train for Chicago and hoped to play the White Sox.

Harry Frazee was in Washington, along with Ban Johnson and others presenting to Baker a petition to postpone the "work or fight" order until October 15, 1918, which would allow the season to be completed. He called Barrow on the phone expressing optimism that the season would proceed. While Barrow was in Chicago, preparing his men to fight the White Sox, word came from Washington that a decision had been reached. Frazee's optimism proved somewhat correct. In a compromise decision released on July 25, Secretary Baker gave Major League Baseball until September 1 before the ruling would take effect. Baseball had five weeks.

Chicago, the defending World Champs, were mired in fifth place with no chance of catching the Red Sox, especially now that only five weeks remained in the season. This did not deter them, however, as they beat Boston three out of four games. Babe showed signs of his bat coming back to life even though he was only 2 for 16 for the series. Eddie Collins robbed him with a great play at second on a line drive that Babe had hit in the opening game of the series, and centerfielder John Collins had tracked down a long fly to center in Chicago's' 7-2 win in the second game of the set. Carl Mays was pounded in the final game of the series and complained to Barrow about being tired. With his pitching ace suffering from a weary arm, Barrow had but one place to turn to aid his weary staff.

He tapped Babe to open the series in St. Louis. Batting fourth, Babe knocked in the first run of the game in the first inning. Stepping in with two outs and Hooper on first, he showed his opposite field power when he tripled to the wall in left. He then proceeded to take to the mound where he performed as if he'd been pitching all year. He did not give up a hit until the fourth inning, and allowed just four Brown hits all day; three of which came in the sixth when St. Louis scored their two runs. In six of the nine frames, Babe set them down one, two, three. His fastball rising, he had the Browns popping the ball up all afternoon as only five ground balls were fielded by his infield. He was now 3-0 in July and 7-5 on the year.

	IP	H	SO	BB	R	ER
7/29/18 at St. Louis	9	4	3	2	2	2

At bat: 1 for 4, triple, RBI

On Tuesday it was back in leftfield for Babe as he went 3 for 4 in an 11-4 Red Sox drubbing of the hapless Browns. He came within a few feet of a home run when he drilled one just to the right of the foul pole in right. His bat was coming back to life, despite the report in the *Boston Herald* that said he was "held" to three singles. He now could go 3 for 4, and yet fall short of expectations. Pundits were redefining his own success in terms of what they knew to be his awesome capabilities. Babe himself may have contributed to this attitude when in an interview with *The Sporting News* he stated:

> "I'd rather make one home run than six singles, because I think it's a circus to watch the other fellows chasing the ball around the ball park. I guess it's just a case of the old saying that what a man likes to do, he does best."

While they were playing in St. Louis, Babe gave an interview with *The Sporting News*. In it he answered several questions about his hitting prowess and gave an interesting insight into his feelings and ideas about hitting and pitching. It also revealed his playful and somewhat boastful nature.

He began the interview with a classic Ruth answer to a question he would be asked countless times over the years:"What's the secret to your ability to hit ?" "There isn't any secret Bud, I just live to hit," he answered. More often then not he referred to people as "Bud","Kid" or "Pal" due no doubt to his utter inability to remember names. Delving into his philosophy on hitting, he explained his propensity for the long ball: "I have tried to specialize on long hitting, because I'm not fast, and then too, if a fellow gets out and pitches he hasn't much in reserve to beat out bunts and such." Probing deeper, Babe was asked about pitching and playing regularly.

"While I have done it this season, I don't think a pitcher can show to best advantage if he plays regularly. Pitching will affect one's batting, there's no doubt about it. It's a tiresome business and when a fellow's been through nine innings of it, he doesn't feel much like getting out the next day and handling low throws at first or chasing flies in the outfield."

Explaining his preference for fastballs because one did not "have to swing nearly as hard to get distance to your drives", Babe also revealed that Reb Russell of the Chicago White Sox was the toughest pitcher for him to hit."I've tried to figure what he is going to throw, but Reb's my idea of a smart pitcher."

Concluding the interview, Babe gave an indication of his persona when he said,

"I'd like to tell you what kind of a ball [pitch] I'm weak against but I don't know myself. I've tried to find out so I could practice hitting that kind."

He then flexed his muscle and implored the interviewer to "feel", saying:"there'll never be a steel shortage in this country with Babe around."

The Red Sox continued their dominance over St. Louis with an 8-4 win on Wednesday. Babe went hitless in three at-bats as the day belonged to Sox pitcher Joe Bush. Taking a page from Ruth's book, he pitched a complete-game victory, and went 4 for 4 with two doubles and two runs scored.

With the dog days of August now doubling as the stretch run, Babe made his second start in three days. It was the first time he had taken a regular turn in the rotation since mid-May. It was like he never left. Dazzling St. Louis for the second time in four days, he held them scoreless until two were out in the ninth when they scored their only run on an infield out. Surrendering five hits, he won 2-1 for his fourth win in a row. He was now 8-5 on the year, and he had Barrow breathing a little easier. With Ruth back in the rotation, his team was ready to make the stretch run.

They headed for Cleveland for a first-place showdown, leading the Indians by five full games.

	IP	H	SO	BB	R	ER
8/1/18 at						
St. Louis	9	5	4	2	1	1
At bat: 0 for 4						

It was on to Cleveland where the Sox and Indians would battle for first place while the American League magnates met to hammer out their ideas for the World Series. Conflict had arisen as the National League owners announced plans for a World Series to begin on September 2. Meanwhile, American League President Ban Johnson issued a statement: "I personally will not be a party to a baseball game played after September 1."

While the Red Sox were doing their level best to let Cleveland back in the race by dropping the first two games of the series, the American League owners were voting down Ban Johnson's proposal. Coming out in concurrence with the National League plan, they voted to end the season on September 2 and begin the World Series on September 3 or 4, all of course, pending approval from the government.

On the field, Babe was scheduled to pitch the first game of a Sunday doubleheader. With Cleveland now only three games back, they could close the gap to one with a sweep of the twinbill. Over 20,000 fans, Cleveland's largest crowd of the year, jammed Lee Field to watch the biggest doubleheader of the year.

Just as he had in his previous start, Babe drove in the first run of the game in the first inning. He lined a single to right with two outs, scoring Amos Strunk from second and giving himself a 1-0 lead. Taking the mound in the bottom of the first, he totally dominated the Indians all afternoon. Taking a 1-0 lead into the eighth, Cleveland tied it on two singles sandwiched between an infield out and when neither team scored in the ninth, the contest headed into extra innings. Babe was brilliant, not allowing a baserunner as the game remained tied into the 12th when Babe's battery mate singled in third baseman George Cochran with the go-ahead run. Setting down the Indians in order in their half of the inning, Ruth had secured a huge victory for himself and his mates. They now were assured of leaving Cleveland no worse than three games in front.

Given the time, place, and circumstance, this was one of the finest games Babe pitched for the Red Sox. Going the distance in a 12-inning game, he yielded only four hits, and two of them came in the eighth inning. He walked no one and after the Indians had tied the score, he did not allow another one of them to reach base. It was his fifth win in a row and he was now 3-0 since his return to the rotation. Had the Red Sox lost this game, Cleveland would have been but two back with a chance to cut it to one by winning the second game. The magnitude of this victory was intensified by a 2-0 rain-shortened loss in game two.

	IP	H	SO	BB	R	ER
8/4/18 at Cleveland	12	4	2	0	1	1

At the plate he went 1 for 4 with his RBI single in the first inning. He also received an intentional pass in the 11th with Strunk on second and two out. In the seventh he came within a few feet of hitting his 12th homer when he drove one just foul down the rightfield line.

Babe welcomed Monday's day of travel as the team headed to Detroit to wrap up the road trip. Sweltering heat greeted them upon their arrival, and the temperature read 115 degrees as the Sox and Tigers took the field for the first of three games.

The Red Sox were trailing 4-1, when Babe came to bat in the eighth inning with men on first and third and no one out. He had aided in the Sox first run, in the fourth, when he moved along Amos Strunk with an infield hit. Amos then scored on a sacrifice fly. The first pitch from George Cunningham was a spitter, and Babe went right after it. He came within about two feet of tying the score as the ball caromed off the screen in front of the rightfield stands. Shean scored, and Strunk went to third as Babe cruised into second with a double. He would eventually score the tying run on a bases-loaded walk and the game went into extra innings. Three Sox runs in the tenth gave a win to Carl Mays, who pitched a complete game in the stifling Detroit heat.

A single, a double, an RBI, a stolen base, and a great shoe string catch by Babe could not help the Sox on Wednesday as Detroit scored six in the first inning and never looked back en route to an 11-8 win.

Babe was on the hill on Wednesday and before he even fired a warm-up toss, he was leading 3-0. Taking full advantage of two walks, a sacrifice, and two doubles, the Red Sox had all they would need before they even took the field. Although he was not as sharp as he had been in his previous three starts, Babe was more than adequate as he held Detroit to one run on seven hits while registering his tenth win of the season. The win closed out the road trip and allowed the Sox to finish the Western swing with eight wins and seven losses. It was the only time the Yankees beat him at Fenway.

	IP	H	SO	BB	R	ER
8/7/18 at Detroit	9	7	3	4	1	1

At the plate he went 1 for 4 with an RBI single in the seventh inning.

He was now 10-5 on the year and he had completed every one of the 14 games he had started. He had six wins in a row and since his re-insertion into the starting rotation on July 29, he was 4-0 with an ERA of 1.15 while his opponents were hitting a scant .146 against him. His line for those four games looked like this:

IP	H	SO	BB	R	ER
39	20	12	8	5	5

His re-emergence on the mound caused Paul Shannon of the *Boston Post* to write, "His pitching performances of late have been just about as sensational as his earlier achievements with the willow."

It was home to the confines of Fenway Park where the Yankees would begin a homestand that would encompass 19 games and take them to the end of the month. A Saturday doubleheader opened the stand, and the Sox came out on the short end of both by 5-1 and 4-1 counts. Babe was 2 for 7 in the two games, playing both of them in leftfield. His two strikeouts on ferocious swings in the first game caused home plate umpire Billy Evans to comment, "Babe swinging and missing is like the cooling wind off the Atlantic."

Sunday was an off day and when Monday morning brought the publication of the Red Sox statistics, Babe was leading the team in hitting with a .305 batting average.

On Monday, Babe took his fifth consecutive turn in the pitching rotation. Facing him was National League reject Hank Robinson. Having not pitched in the big leagues since 1915, Robinson's opportunity at rebirth came as a result of the war. Allowing only three singles and one run, he beat Babe 2-1, handing him his first loss since June 7. There was no doubt that Ruth pitched well enough to win, but his mates could do nothing with the 28-year-old lefty who, until his death in July of 1965, would be able to tell one and all about the day he outpitched Babe Ruth and held him hitless in three official at bats. In fact, Babe flied out to end the game, after which he heaved his bat beyond second base in frustration. The Sox had now dropped three straight and were suddenly only two games in front.

	IP	H	SO	BB	R	ER
8/12/18 vs. New York	9	4	1	4	2	2

Chicago was next in town, and even though the Red Sox looked rather listless, they were able to take two out of three from their pale counterparts. Babe sat out the first game following his pitching turn, and managed a double and a single in eight trips during the next two games. This set the stage for the arrival of the Indians, and for the second time in less than two weeks the Sox and Cleveland would battle for first place. Speaker led his team in for three games, trailing Boston by only two.

Babe was on the mound to open the series, opposing Cleveland right-hander Guy Morton. The largest crowd of the year, more than 15,000, turned out at Fenway to watch the battle. Cleveland drew first blood when in the top of the fourth Tris Speaker doubled following a triple by Jack Graney. Speaker, however, died at second, and the Red Sox came up in their half of the fourth, down 1-0.

Both Babe and Stuffy McInnis reached Morton for infield hits and scored when Hack Miller singled and leftfielder Jack Graney threw wildly home. It remained 2-1 until the Boston eighth. Bagby came in to pitch and surrendered two hits, a sacrifice, an intentional pass to Babe, and a two-run single to McInnis. Cleveland got one back in the ninth, but once again, Babe made sure that the Red Sox would be in first place at the end of the Cleveland series.

	IP	H	SO	BB	R	ER
8/17/18 vs.						
Cleveland	9	5	3	3	2	2

At bat: 1 for 2 , run scored, 2 intentional walks

On Sunday, Babe made the trip to New Haven, Connecticut to play in an exhibition game against the New Haven Colonials. He played his favorite first base position and hit a home run as the locals beat the Red Sox 4-3. It left sports columnist Arthur Duffey wondering where Babe had been hiding his home runs. He had not hit one since June, and Duffey mused that he was perhaps saving them for the World Series.

The series with Cleveland resumed on Monday with Sam Jones shutting out the Indians for the third time this season. He yielded but two hits and struck out five, as the Sox lengthened their lead to four games with 14 to go. Babe contributed a double, two runs scored and a "phenomenal" catch in left to the 6-0 win. He also received yet another intentional pass.

Babe was back on the mound on Tuesday, despite the fact that he had pitched just three days before. He exhibited considerable defensive prowess on two different occasions, which left the fans cheering. In the second inning, Cleveland catcher Steve O'Neill hit a high pop-up between the mound and home plate. Babe moved in and backed off when his catcher Wally Mayer called for the ball. The ball popped in and out of Mayer's mitt, but Babe caught the ball before it hit the ground. In the sixth, Ray Chapman laid a beautiful bunt down the first base line. Seeing that McInnis was not in a position to field the ball, Babe sprinted after it and scooped it up on the dead run, before continuing his sprint to the bag in time to beat Chapman and register the put out.

It would all prove for naught however, as Babe's teammates were not as adept defensively on this particular day and Babe did not have his best stuff on the mound. Two errors and two balls lost in the rightfield sun led to four Cleveland tallies. Babe himself was racked for two doubles and two triples among the 13 hits he surrendered. It was the first and only time all year that he did not complete a start. He was now 11-7.

	IP	H	SO	BB	R	ER
8/20/18 vs.						
Cleveland	7	13	2	2	8	6

To add to his frustration, Babe went 0 for 3 with still another intentional walk.

That same day, the National Commission met in Chicago to solidify plans for the World Series. All was set as they emerged with a decision to begin the postseason event on September 4, pending official word of approval from the War Department.

Cleveland left town three games behind the Red Sox and Barrow's men prepared to welcome the Browns. Carl Mays put the Red Sox back on their winning ways, beating the St. Louis contingent 4-1. Babe was in leftfield contributing a single in two official at-bats and scoring a run. He received two more intentional passes, leaving many to wonder if he would ever again be pitched to with men on base and first base open.

That evening he headed North to the suburban town of Revere to watch the "motor-paced" bike races. He had become quite a fan of this younger version of dirt bike races. They were held every Wednesday and Saturday night, and when the Red Sox were home, he was very often found in the front row of the grandstand "rooting like a dyed-in-the-wool bleacherite."

Thursday afternoon found him back in leftfield, and just to show that he could play baseball the customary way, he displayed some of his traditional baseball skills. Leading off the second inning, Babe laid down a perfect bunt. Completely fooling the Brown's infield, he was safe at first, with no play being made on him. Moving to second on McInnis' infield out, he tried to score from second on Everett Scott's infield hit. Seeing George Sisler all but turned around at first base as he moved to his left to snare Scott's shot down the line, Babe saw a chance to score. Sisler, however, righted himself and made a perfect throw home to nail the sliding Ruth. It was the closest the Red Sox would come to scoring, as Dave Davenport stopped them on five hits winning 1-0.

The two teams resumed the series on Friday with Sam Jones on the mound for the Red Sox. Babe was in what now could be called his customary leftfield position. In the first inning, he saved a run when he ran down a ball in the gap off the bat of George Sisler. Making a one-handed "circus" catch, he deprived the Browns' first baseman of at least a double and kept them scoreless as the Red Sox came to bat in the first. He then put them ahead when he smashed a line drive off the scoreboard in left that scored Dave Shean who had singled and advanced on Strunk's infield out. The ball was hit so hard that it ricocheted right back to leftfielder Jack Tobin, making Babe an easy out trying to reach second.

The game was tied at five when the Red Sox came to bat in the ninth. It had gone back and forth as the Red Sox never trailed, but could not seem to shake the Browns. St. Louis had been behind 2-1, 4-1, and 5-4, and three times tied the score. With one out in the Red Sox ninth, Dave Shean singled. He was forced at second by Amos Strunk, and Ruth came to the plate. Ever cautious and aware of his dangerous bat, Browns hurler Duke Houck, pitched around Babe and walked him, sending Strunk to second and bringing up McInnis. Stuffy never got a chance to swing as both runners broke on the first pitch. St. Louis catcher Hank Severeid threw to third in an attempt to get Shean, and the ball sailed into leftfield. Shean jumped up and scored easily with the winning run. It was the second time in a little over a month that Ruth and Shean had combined on a double steal to win a ball game.

Babe was on the mound to close out the St. Louis series. There was still more in his repertoire that he had not shown, and on this day it would be revealed. A single, a sacrifice, a throwing error by Babe and another single put St. Louis ahead 1-0 in the second inning. The Sox struck right back in their half of the second, and to no one's surprise, Babe was in the midst of it.

Barrow had Babe batting seventh. It was the first time since early May that he was not in the third or fourth spot in the lineup. It proved an ingenious move when the events of the second inning unfolded. Miller, batting clean up, led off the inning with a single. McInnis laid down a bunt and when the throw went to second too late, everyone was safe. Everett Scott then successfully sacrificed putting men on second and third with Babe at the plate. Infuriated at yet another intentional pass, Babe was about to run the bases with "reckless abandon".

After a strikeout, third baseman Jack Coffey (recently acquired from Detroit) blooped a single to score two runs and put Ruth on third. On the first pitch to Harry Hooper, Coffey broke for second, and as soon as Nunamaker released the ball, Babe dashed for home.

The return throw home was too late as Babe slid hard into the St. Louis catcher. His leg twisted under him and his left hand was cut, but Babe had the first steal of home of his career.

Limping throughout the remainder of the game and with his pitching hand showing his wounds, Babe allowed only three singles the rest of the way as he won his 12th game of the year, 3-1. He saved his best for the eighth when with two outs and two on, he struck out George Sisler on three pitches.

	IP	H	SO	BB	R	ER
8/24/18 vs.						
St. Louis	9	5	4	2	1	1

At bat: 0 for 2, two walks.

In Chicago, word came down that the Secretary of War had extended the "work or fight" order to September 15, and thus there would be a World Series, set to begin on September 4. Now all the Red Sox had to do was hang on.

That night back in Babe's hometown of Baltimore, George Ruth Sr., Babe's 45-year-old dad, was killed in a fist fight with his brother-in-law. The whys of the family tragedy remain sketchy and shrouded in mystery. The facts of the incident however, are clear.

On the night of August 24, 1918, Benjamin H. Sipes, the 30-year-old brother of Mr. Ruth's second wife Martha, entered Ruth's saloon and had a heated exchange with one of the patrons. He left the saloon and went across the street where he stood for several minutes in front of a cigar store. Sipes then came back from across the street and was standing in front of Ruth's saloon when, witnesses stated, Ruth came out of his saloon, walked directly up to him and struck him in the face. He staggered back, and as he was about to recover himself, Ruth struck him again. He fell to the ground and was then kicked by his assailant. Sipes rose to his feet and struck back, catching Ruth in the face and knocking him back on the sidewalk, where he hit his head on the curbstone. He was carried back into his saloon, and when an attempt to administer first aid did not revive him, he was rushed to the hospital. He died the next morning as a result of a fractured skull.

The patron with whom Sipes had the heated exchange was a man named Oliver Bleefelt, who was married to the sister of Ruth's wife. Mrs Ruth's sister had been staying with them, having recently been discharged from a hospital. Bleefelt and his wife had been estranged for some time, and only a few weeks before he had been arraigned on charges of assaulting and enticing a 16-year-old girl from her home.

On the evening in question, Sipes had come to visit his sister, and while he was there she began to weep as she recounted to him how Bleefelt had been mistreating her. Sipes told police that he then went into the saloon and began to rebuke him. A harsh exchange of words followed and Sipes removed himself, walking across the street. He returned to the front of the saloon when Ruth emerged and struck him.

A coroner's inquest took but two days to determine that Sipes had "delivered the fatal blow in self-defense," and was therefore cleared of all charges.

It is not clear why Ruth struck him. The reasons for his ac- tions the elder Ruth took to his grave. On Wednesday, August 28, George Ruth was buried in Baltimore's Louden Park Cemetery. Stand- ing at his graveside as he was lowered into the ground was his son. The "Colossus of Clouters", the "Mauler", the "Cave-Man", the "Babe", the best player in the game of baseball was now truly an orphan.

While Babe was away, the Sox split two games with the Ti- gers, losing on Tuesday 2-1 and winning on Wednesday, 3-0. Thursday's game was rained out, and the Tigers left town while the Sox prepared for a Friday doubleheader with the A's.

Babe was back in the lineup on Friday, batting in his familiar number-four spot and playing leftfield, he went right to work. Com- ing to bat in the first inning with men on second and third and one out, he lashed a double to rightfield, giving Carl Mays a 2-0 lead. It was all the right-handed submariner needed as he shut out Mack's boys 12-0. Babe added a single to the hit parade but the game be- longed to Mays, as he went 3 for 3 with a double and two singles, and two runs scored while registering his league-leading eighth shutout of the season.

Mays was the starting pitcher in the second game and he fared equally as well. He again went the distance allowing but five hits and also went 2 for 3 at the plate as the Red Sox completed the sweep, 4-1. On the day, Mays had thrown 18 innings and allowed but one run. He also went 5 for 6 with his bat. It was a performance reminiscent of Ruth, who was 0 for 2 officially in the second game with two walks, one of them intentional.

As Babe Ruth toiled in leftfield at Fenway Park, on this 30th day of August 1918, 25-year-old May Williams toiled in childbirth 3,000 miles away in San Diego, California. At 12:20 p.m. Pacific time, while the Red Sox game was in progress, she gave birth to a baby boy. She named him Theodore Samuel, and 21 years later, he too would take his place in Fenway's leftfield.

The Red Sox were now one win away from reclaiming their American League championship. Just as he was on the mound when the season began, Babe was on the hill with a chance to clinch the pennant. The opponent, as it was on opening day, was the Philadelphia A's.

The A's scored first, pushing across a run in the opening frame, but that was all they would muster against the offerings of Ruth. Babe stymied them throughout the day allowing only three hits. He also had an RBI double in the fifth that, if not for the wind, would have carried into the centerfield bleachers. It seemed fitting and proper that George Herman Ruth should be the pitcher of record on the day that the Red Sox reclaimed the American League pennant, for the 1918 baseball season had indeed belonged to him.

	IP	H	SO	BB	R	ER
8/31/18 vs. Philadelphia	9	3	3	1	1	1

At-bat he was 2 for 2 with an RBI. With the win, he finished the year 13-7.

Babe made an appearance in the second game, playing centerfield in the last four innings. He went 0 for 2, but none of that mattered. It was now time to prepare for the National League Champion Chicago Cubs. The Red Sox would appear in their third World Series in four years.

It was on to New York where a Labor Day doubleheader would end the regular season. Babe played leftfield in the first game, going 1 for 3 in a 3-2 Red Sox win. He was plunked on his left arm in the very first inning by the Yankees' hard-throwing, somewhat wild left-hander Slim Love. The thud could be heard all over the grandstand and was initially a cause for consternation on the part of Barrow. Babe shook it off and trotted to first base. He walked in the third inning and beat out an infield hit in the fifth, which was particularly gratifying to Ruth as it assured that he would hit .300 for the year. It was his only hit of the game and did leave him at an even .300 for the 1918 campaign.

In the seventh inning, Babe nearly hit one clear out of the Polo Grounds. It was foul and bounced off the back wall of the upper deck. It was one of his patented rising line drives that Babe loved to hit. Even though it was nothing but a long strike, the Polo Grounds fans left feeling they had gotten their money's worth because they saw the Babe tie into one. New York captured the second game 4-3, as Babe watched from the dugout.

On Tuesday the Red Sox pulled out of Grand Central Station in New York bound for Chicago. There would be little time for preparation as the series was to start on Wednesday the 4th. Some favored the Cubs to win because of their dynamic left-handed duo of Hippo Vaughn (22-10) and Lefty Tyler (19-8). The Cubs' right-handed ace was no slouch either, as Claude Hendrix was 20-7 on the year to lead the National League with a .741 winning percentage. Chicago had outhit the Red Sox by 16 points as a team, so it is of little wonder that manager Fred Mitchell was confident that his Cubs would prevail.

> "We will outhit the Sox and outfight them…and I believe…our pitching will stop Ruth's batting. The Sox are a one man team and his name is Ruth. But we have studied his ways and his mental processes so much this season that we will spike his guns."
> *Boston Herald* 9/4/18

Others saw Ruth as providing the difference. Yankee manager Miller Huggins thought the teams were pretty evenly matched but gave the edge to Boston because of the presence of Ruth. Red Sox manager Barrow thought his pitching staff was better balanced than that of the Cubs and flat out said that Babe was a better pitcher than Vaughn. Red Sox captain Harry Hooper, playing his captain's role superbly, stated:

> "I believe our experience and our proven ability to play our best ball when the battle is most fierce will help us pull out ahead."
> *Boston Herald* 9/4/18

Babe was ready and just anxious to play. Bemused at all the questions thrown his way regarding his "nervousness" on the eve of the World Series, he related to Burt Whitman of the *Herald* his inability to understand why anyone would consider the possibility that he would be nervous or worried.

"Why I'd pitch the whole series, every game if they'd let me....Of course I can do it. I used to pitch three games in one day when I was at school and didn't I pitch a 13-inning game one Saturday for Dunn while I was with Baltimore and then pitch a double-header the next day, Sunday with the second game another 13-inning one?"

Remembering his non-appearance in the 1915 series and the fact that he pitched just one game in the 1916 battle for baseball supremacy Babe stated:

"I hope I don't have to sit on the bench a single inning of the series." *Boston Herald* 9/4/18

It was made clear to one and all, the way Barrow saw Babe's role in the 1918 World Series, when he named the "Colossus" his starting pitcher in the first game and said he'd bat ninth. There was no question where Barrow wanted Babe's focus. His opponent would be Hippo Vaughn.

Wednesday, September 4 brought rain to the Windy City, causing the postponement of the opening of the World Series until Thursday. The weather remained cloudy and raw, which along with the fact that America's attentions were focused on the war, may have accounted for only 19,274 fans showing up at Comiskey Park to witness the game. This was nearly 13,000 less than had witnessed the opening game of the 1917 series in the same ball park. A report out of Worcester, Massachusetts, a suburb 50 miles west of Boston, stated that calls into their local telegraph office inquiring about the action during the first game were down 80 percent from the previous year. The minds of Americans were clearly centered on the war effort.

Red Sox rightfielder Harry Hooper was warmly cheered by the partisan Chicago crowd as he walked to the plate to begin the 15th World Series, and when he grounded out to first baseman Fred Merkle, the championship battle was under way. The Sox went quietly in the first, mustering only a bloop single to right by second baseman Dave Shean.

Max Flack, the Cubs' rightfielder, led off the game for Chicago and Babe made short order of him, catching him looking at a called strike three. Twenty-two-year-old left-handed hitting short-stop Charlie Hollocher, who had led the National League in hits and was the Cubs only .300 hitter, stepped up and promptly grounded out to second base. It looked like a one, two, three inning for Babe when left-fielder Les Mann's ground ball bounced toward Shean at second base, when it suddenly hit a pebble and hopped over his head into right for a single. Dode Paskert then singled sharply into the leftfield corner and took second when Whiteman attempted to nail Mann at third base. With runners on second and third and two out, Fred Merkle worked Babe to a full count before walking to load the bases. This brought up second baseman Charlie Pick, who had joined the Cubs late in the year and was batting for the first time in World Series competition. He flied to Whiteman on a two and one pitch and Babe and the Red Sox were out of an early jam.

The game was scoreless until the Red Sox fourth when Dave Shean walked to open the inning, and after Strunk popped out Whiteman looped a single into left with Shean stopping at second. He would not be there for long however, as he scored on a line single to left by Stuffy McInnis. Another pop-up and a strikeout ended the frame for Boston, who although stranding two baserunners, held a 1-0 lead.

Babe made it hold up as he surrendered only three hits the rest of the way. Chicago threatened again in the sixth with men on second and third and two out. However, they never scored as Babe registered his first shutout in World Series competition, becoming only the fourth man to hurl a 1-0 shutout in the World Series.

In a strange turn of events, Babe was cheered every time he came to bat. The crowd actually implored him to get a hit. Even though the Cubs were on the short end of a close 1-0 score, the fans still wanted to see Babe belt one. He was even redefining the way the fans rooted for the players.

The victory was crucial as the Sox jumped out and led the series one game to none. Only three times had a team come back to win the World Series after losing the first game. Twice it was the Red Sox, once in 1903 and again in 1912.

	IP	H	SO	BB	R
9/5/18 at Chicago	9	6	4	1	0

At the plate, he was 0 for 3. He lined out to centerfield in the third on a nice catch by Dode Paskert. He then twice went down on strikes, swinging and missing with his mighty swing.

During the seventh inning an event took place that would have a profound effect on the landscape of American sports. As the fans rose for the customary stretch in the home half of the seventh, the band played the National Anthem. While they played, the players stood and gave the civilian salute (right hand placed over their heart). Chet Thomas, who was on leave from the Navy to participate in the series, snapped to attention and saluted until the anthem was completed. A mighty cheer went up as the band concluded the song and an American tradition was born.

Before another small crowd of only 20,040, the Cubs came back in the second game, scoring three runs in the second inning and holding on for a 3-1 victory to even the series. Held scoreless into the ninth, the only Boston tally crossed when Strunk and Whiteman opened the final frame with back-to-back triples. Whiteman died on third, as the Sox went down without bringing him across. Babe sat anxious, hoping for a chance to swing the bat, however with two on and one out Barrow sent up right-handed hitting Jean Dubuc to bat for Thomas against the Cub southpaw Lefty Tyler. He fanned, and when Wally Schang popped out to short, the series was even.

The Cub victory in game two aroused a bit more interest among the locals as 27,054 showed up for the third game. In a move designed to keep Ruth out of the lineup, Cub manager Fred Mitchell started left-hander Hippo Vaughn again in the third game. It was successful in one respect as Babe once again did not play. His mates, however, scored two runs in the fourth and hung on for a 2-1 victory as Carl Mays put the Sox ahead two games to one. The game ended with a play at the plate when Cub second baseman Charlie Pick attempted to score from third on a pitch that had rolled away from catcher Wally Schang. Schang recovered however, and Pick was out two to five to two. The Red Sox headed to Fenway needing two wins to regain their title of World Champs.

Barrow named Babe to start the first game at Fenway before the teams left Chicago. With Vaughn having hurled game three, Mitchell named his other southpaw Lefty Tyler to pitch. The mere presence of Babe's bat kept Mitchell from going to his right-handed 20-game winner Claude Hendrix. It was four games deep into the series and the Red Sox had not even seen the pitcher who had the best winning percentage in the National League. Such was the size of the shadow cast by the bat of Babe Ruth.

Babe nearly took himself out of action with a mishap that occurred on the train back to Boston. Many biographies report that Babe played in game four of the World Series with a swollen finger on his pitching hand. Babe himself in his autobiography written with Bob Considine, tells the story this way:

> " We had a second string left-hander on our club by the name of Kenny. He and I used to go in for a lot of roughhousing ... we'd grapple and box and roll all over the floor. On the train ride back to Boston for the fourth game we started it again. I took a swing at Kenny, but he ducked and I hit the knuckles of my left hand on the steel wall of the car. The middle finger of my left hand became swollen to three times its normal size."

The "Kenny" Babe refers to is Walt Kinney, a 24-year-old rookie left-handed pitcher who appeared in five games, pitching a total of 15 innings.

With the particulars of the event open to speculation, the *Boston Herald* of September 9, 1918 sheds some light on what might have transpired. Amidst all of the articles and stories about the pending game four of the series, a small article appeared under a small heading which read "Ruth crashes into car window but is not hurt." Apparently, the train was just outside of Springfield, Massachusetts when the incident occurred.

> " He was standing in the aisle of the Sox car talking to Carl Mays when the train lurched, sending the Colossus spinning and crashing against a window. The heavy glass was shattered and fell clattering inside and outside. Babe did not know how seriously he had been injured , but he had the presence of mind not to put out his hands, and was fortunate enough to escape with only a small cut on his trousers."

There is no name of a writer associated with the report but in all likelihood it was Burt Whitman as the name Colossus was the name he always used for Ruth.

What had really happened? Had Carl Mays, never known for his bubbling personality, thrown Babe Ruth through the window in a fight? Had Babe and the 6'2" 186-pound rookie, Kinney, truly been just horsing around? Or had indeed the train lurched causing Babe to lose his balance? Was it possible that there were, in fact, two separate instances of near disaster on one train ride? No other newspaper in the city even carried an account of the event, and those who were present have long since taken the truth of the matter with them. The result was that Babe was going to face the Cubs in game four of the World Series at less than 100 percent.

A crowd of 22,183 assembled at Fenway to witness Babe take on the Cubs in game four, and they were not disappointed. Rooting with a "pre-war enthusiasm" the crowd was cheering from the moment Cubs rightfielder Max Flack stepped into the box to open the game. Although he was pitching, Barrow moved Babe up to the sixth spot in the batting order, hoping to get him an extra swing during the contest.

Chicago had men on base in each of the first three innings but were unable to get any of them across. Flack led off the game for Chicago with a single, and after Cub shortstop Charlie Hollocher lined out to McInnis at first, Agnew picked Flack off first. Leftfielder Les Mann popped out to McInnis at first, and the inning was over.

Two more hits were tallied by the Cubs in the second, but they were left stranded when catcher Bill Killifer hit a ground ball to Everett Scott, which ended the inning. Babe came up for the first time with two outs and nobody on in the home half of the second. "A storm of applause" greeted him as he stepped to the plate and the Chicago outfield awarded him due respect as they backed up "against the fences." Babe was retired when second baseman Charlie Pick made a one-handed stop of his sharply hit ground ball.

There were no hits by the Cubs in the third, but Babe did walk his opposing pitcher to lead off the inning. He was forced at second by Flack, and when Hollocher grounded unassisted to McInnis at first, Flack moved to second. He did not remain there long as Babe whirled and picked him off to end the inning. It was the second time in three innings that he had been picked off, which did not endear him to manager Mitchell. When the Sox went out one, two, three in the third, one third of the game was in the books and there was no score.

A slick play behind second base by shortstop Everett Scott aided Ruth in getting the Cubs in order for the first time in the fourth, and the Sox had the heart of the order coming up in their half of the inning. Shean led off with a walk, and after Strunk flew out to center, he stole second base. Whiteman then walked, followed by a fielder's choice by McInnis.

The fans were "wild eyed" as Babe stepped in with two outs and two on. Tyler threw two straight balls and then cut the corner for a strike. The next offering was wide, and Babe was up in the count three and one. He took a mighty swing and missed bringing the count full. Tyler glanced into the dugout, took a deep breath and stood on the mound. He tried to sneak a fastball by him, but Babe was thinking fastball all the way.

"A report like that of a rifle shot rang through the park" and the crowd rose as one. The ball sailed over Flack's head in rightfield landing at the base of the bleacher wall, and by the time the Cub rightfielder had retrieved it and fired it in, Babe was standing on third with the first World Series hit of his career, and the Red Sox led 2-0. The crowd, screaming with ecstasy, nearly "ripped the roof off the grandstand."

There was no scoring in the fifth, but Babe again walked Tyler to lead off the sixth, and the next three Cubs went out as did the Sox in their half of the inning.

Unbeknownst to anyone, Babe had just tied a World Series record. When the Cubs were retired in the sixth, Babe had hurled 28 consecutive innings of scoreless World Series ball. This equaled the mark Christy Mathewson had set with his three straight shutouts in the 1905 series, and one inning which was carried into the World Series of 1911. When Bob O'Farrell grounded into a double play to end the Cubs seventh, the record belonged solely to Ruth. He maintained until his dying day that it was his "proudest achievement".

Record or not, the Cubs battled back to tie the game in the eighth, ending Babe's streak officially at 29 2/3 innings. A single, a passed ball, a sacrifice, and an error allowed the Sox to retake the lead in their half of the eighth. Babe was lifted for Joe Bush, after yielding a single and a walk to the Cubs first two batters in the ninth. He finished the game in leftfield, as Bush recorded the save, and the Red Sox were now just one win away from another world championship. Babe had his third career World Series win and it proved to be his last. It would take 68 years before another Red Sox lefty would start and win a World Series game.

	IP	H	SO	BB	R	ER
9/9/18 vs.						
Chicago	9	7	2	6	2	2

Although Babe would appear in 37 more World Series games, he would not pitch another World Series inning. Thus his book was complete.

World Series:	IP	H	SO	BB	R	ER
1916 - '18	31	19	8	10	3	3

He won all three of his starts without a loss and compiled an ERA of 0.87. Among all World Series pitchers who have pitched 30 innings or more, only Harry Brecheen has a better ERA. Ruth's World Series opponents hit a collective .169 against him and he is one of only 16 men to throw a 1-0 complete game victory in the World Series. It would take over 40 years for Whitey Ford to break his consecutive scoreless inning streak in the 1961 World Series. To this day, he owns the World Series record for pitching the longest complete game victory as a result of his 14-inning 2-1 win in game two of the 1916 series.

❧

Game five was delayed by a 45-minute strike as the players were protesting their diminished World Series shares. Since 1910, the winners share of a World Series purse had averaged roughly $3,000. Due to, among other things, a new rule which had all players who played on first-division teams sharing in the purse, it became known that the winners' share for this series would be around $1,000.

Present in the crowd were many wounded veterans, and that may have been what ultimately saved the series. After considerable haggling between Ban Johnson and Garry Hermann of the National Commission and the players, Harry Hooper of the Red Sox stepped up and spoke for the players:

> "we'll play for the sake of the game, for the sake of the public ...
> and for the sake of the wounded sailors and soldiers who are in
> the grandstand waiting for us." *Boston Post* 9/11/18

While Ban Johnson sat blubbering in tears in somewhat of an intoxicated state, former Boston Mayor "Honey Fitz" Fitzgerald was at home plate telling the crowd that an agreement had been reached and the game would be played. Babe was in the dugout watching as his game one opponent, Hippo Vaughn, shutout his mates 3-0, drawing the Cubs to within a game of tying the series.

Arthur Duffey, columnist for the *Boston Post* had this response to the 45-minute strike in his column of September 11:

"professional baseball is dead ...The game has been dying for two years, killed by the greed of players and owners. Professional baseball, in the past four years, has only been a mad scramble for money."

On Wednesday September 11, 1918, the Sox and Cubs took to the field in what would prove to be the decisive game of the series. Vaughn and Mays hooked up in a duel that was decided by a third-inning two-out line drive to rightfield by George Whiteman. Cub rightfielder Max Flack could not handle it, and his error allowed both Mays and Shean to score. Chicago got one back in the fourth, and that concluded the scoring as the Red Sox captured the game and the championship. Babe was put in leftfield late in the game, and was there when the title was clinched. It was his third world championship in his five years with the Red Sox, and it was Boston's fifth world championship since the classic had begun in 1903. No other major league team had enjoyed such success.

History of a different sort was made this day, as for the first time ever, returns of a World Series game were transmitted as they happened. In the press stand were nine homing carrier pigeons from the Army base at Fort Devens, some 58 miles away. After each inning, a pigeon was sent up with a written message of the results of what had just transpired. It would take about 30 minutes to reach its destination, keeping Uncle Sam's boys abreast of the action at Fenway.

As the 15,238 fans left Fenway Park that day, they had no possible way of knowing how the game that they had just witnessed would be weaved into the folklore of their beloved Red Sox. Grandfathers attending the game with their grandsons had no idea that their children's children's children would be telling their young that over 75 years had passed since the Red Sox won the World Series. They could not have fathomed the concept of a 75-year-old grandfather of ten, who was yet to be born in 1918, sending a message, 1,500 miles through cyberspace to his son in September of 1996 that read, "The Sox are out of it, I'm running out of time." Indeed, their worries were much more immediate, for millions of young men were being called into the Army as the United States was preparing a force to go to a far off land and fight for freedom.

The next day Babe and his teammates met at Fenway Park to vote on World Series shares. A full share was $1,108, a substantial decrease from the $3,910 Babe had won in the 1916 series. The shares were dispersed in increments of $750, $500, $300, $100 and $25 for the clubhouse boys. What remained after the vote was $117.15, which was given to the gate keeper.

The end of the season brought what many thought would be the end of many baseball careers. With no indication of the duration of the war, players were making other plans. Ty Cobb, "Home Run" Baker, and Tris Speaker all expected that they had played their last games of professional baseball. In Boston, Jack Barry and Dick Hoblitzell were sure to be gone, and Harry Hooper actually announced his retirement. Babe was weighing offers from several steel plants and shipbuilding companies.

While deciding between Quincy, Massachusetts; Providence, Rhode Island; or Lebanon, Pennsylvania; Babe played in exhibition games in Hartford, Connecticut and in Springfield, Massachusetts where he made news when he struck out with the bases loaded. It was reported he received $300 for participating in that game, nearly one-third of what he had received for the entire '18 Series. From there it was on to Lebanon, Pennsylvania where he joined his old batterymate Sam Agnew on the baseball team of the Bethlehem Steel Company.

On September 25, 1918, Babe completed negotiations with "Pop" Kelchner, the physical director at the Lebanon plant, and immediately reported there for work. He and Helen moved into an apartment located at 718 Chestnut Street and Babe began practicing with the squad. He wasted no time in impressing the locals by sending one shot after another well over the right and leftfield fences. His first—and as it would turn out, his only game—was played on Saturday, September 28. On that day he struck out twice, was intentionally walked, and reached on an error. Scott Perry of the Philadelphia A's was the winning pitcher as Babe's debut with his new team ended in a 4-2 defeat.

The team played only four more games to close out the season and Babe was in the lineup for none of them. Accounts of the games indicate that Babe was missing due to his presence in Baltimore to take care of "business affairs". When the Lebanon team signed Rogers Hornsby on the 10th of October, the locals were very excited as they looked toward the 1919 baseball season. The last game of the year was played on October 12. Hornsby was in the lineup, but Ruth was not. Having not returned from Baltimore, in time, he missed the season finale, which was played against Babe's

World Champion Boston Red Sox. Wally Schang, Amos Strunk, Joe Bush, and Wally Mayer were the only members of the Red Sox on the squad as they beat the locals 1-0 in 11 innings. Bush stuck out 11 and surrendered but four hits in securing the win. Strunk, Bush, and Schang would each be fined $100 for violating Major League Baseball's rule prohibiting members of the championship team from barnstorming.

The presence of major league baseball players in this small steel town was not as well received as might be anticipated. Virtually every able-bodied man in Lebanon between the ages of 21 and 30 was in the Army or soon expected to be. Front-page news stories appeared regularly of Lebanon's sons who were killed or wounded abroad. The October 7, 1918 issue of the *Lebanon Daily News* ran a story under the headline "BALL PLAYERS LEAVE PLANT AT STEELTON". "Of the 15 or more big league players who drifted into the Steelton fold immediately after the work or fight order was issued, only three remain in the company's employ.... From this one might draw the conclusion that essential occupations become non-essential immediately after the baseball season closes..... Performances such as this will tend to reduce the interest in the various steel and shipyard leagues. The baseball public will begin to see that the players merely used the steel mills and shipyards as a shield for their personal ambitions."

The arrival of the 24-year-old Red Sox star was thought by many to be just another attempt by another ballplayer to avoid service. Babe greeted these criticisms the same way he had met them during the year, by simply stating, "all they've got to do is call me, and I'll go."

According to employment records, Babe worked at Bethlehem Steel until February 28, 1919, but the last reports of Babe in Lebanon were on November 13, two days after the armistice. He was recuperating from a badly wrenched knee that he injured during a baseball game he had played in Baltimore the week before. The injury was severe enough to require the use of crutches to maneuver around.

On the 5th of October, the National Commission announced that they were withholding from the Red Sox, their emblems signifying their championship season. In a letter written by Garry Herrmann of the Commission and published in the *Boston Post*, he stated the following:

" In utter disregard of their duties to patrons and their respective clubs, both the contesting teams planned to strike and terminate the World Series if their unjust, unfounded demands for compensation were not granted.... the United States government officials are on record as condemning the selfish, mercenary and anarchistic actions of the players on that occasion and it has been strongly intimated that official favors will not be again extended to them quickly."

It took 75 years before those "official favors" would again be extended as the descendants of the members of the 1918 Red Sox gathered at Fenway Park before a September 1993 game. There they officially received emblems recognizing the 1918 Boston Red Sox as World Champions. Babe's stepdaughter, Julia Ruth Stevens was on hand to accept on his behalf.

Despite suffering a serious bout with influenza that claimed a life-long friend and partner, Harry Frazee worked in an attempt to remove Ban Johnson from his position as President of the American League. Upset with Johnson's inaction with the War Department throughout the summer, Frazee had his own vision of how baseball should be governed. His vision was for one man, a commissioner, to oversee baseball. His idea received some support and at one point Frazee, acting unilaterally, even offered the position to William Howard Taft. The ex-president and retired chief justice of the United States supreme court was one of the most respected men in America. Taft rejected the offer, and Frazee never received the required support to bring his idea to fruition. It would take the scandal of 1919 before his fellow moguls would see the need for such a position.

Within three weeks after the Armistice, word came from the government sanctioning the return of baseball for the 1919 season. With most of the players facing discharge from the service, the Boston fans were excited at their prospects for 1919. With Barry, Janvrin, Lewis, McNally, and Pennock ready to rejoin the reigning champions, they had every reason to be.

As Christmas and the end of the year approached, many players contended that they were now free agents. They claimed that the season ending on September 4 had rendered the reserve clause ineffectual. Cobb used this reasoning to declare himself a free agent. The yearly rumors of Cobb to the Yankees again circulated throughout the game. A 140-game schedule for 1919 was agreed to, and in early December, Tiger owner Frank Navin was the first to announce plans for spring training. Baseball mourned the passing of umpire "Silk" O'Loughlin who fell victim to the influenza outbreak in Boston.

In Boston, Harry Frazee was burning up the wires with trade talks. On December 16 he offered Dutch Leonard to the Tigers for Bobby Veach. When Navin turned him down, he went to the Yankees and traded Leonard along with Ernie Shore and Duffy Lewis for outfielder Frank Gilhooley, catcher Roxy Walters who had hit .199 in 1918, 30-year-old right-handed pitcher Ray Caldwell, and $15,000 cash. The *Boston Post* reported: "It will take a lot of arguing to convince Boston fans that they got the best of this one."

Rumors were abound that the Red Sox were again for sale. This idea was being pushed by American League President Ban Johnson. Angered at Frazee for his attempt to create a position that would eliminate the National Commission, Johnson had surreptitiously come into Boston in November to look for local investors to buy the team. Frazee made the comment that it would take a "considerable offer" for him to listen, and then he turned down 1.2 million dollars. This was nearly twice what he was believed to have paid. The sale of the Red Sox seemed more of a hope of Ban Johnson's than a pursuit of Harry Frazee's.

Babe's 1918 performance resonated throughout baseball during the fall and into the early winter. Written and talked about, it was best encapsulated by umpire and sportswriter Billy Evans. In *The Sporting News* of November 28, 1918, Evans wrote: "When you recall the worthwhile baseball happenings of last summer, I am certain you will agree . . . the most talked about man in major league circles . . .without the slightest hesitation would be Babe Ruth of the Boston Red Sox." Evans even wrote a column urging a rule change as a result of Babe's home run that went as a triple in Boston back in July.

Who could argue with Evans? He had tied for the league in home runs and led the league in slugging percentage. He was tied for third in RBI, was second in doubles, fourth in triples and hit .300 on the nose. All this with roughly 100 to 175 less at bats than the rest of the field. If an MVP award were in existence, it would have undoubtedly gone to Babe. The vote may have even been unanimous.

On the mound he was equally effective, perhaps even more so. Winning 13 and losing 7, his ERA was 2.22, placing him eighth in the league among those who had hurled 100 innings or more.

Only three men allowed fewer hits per game and only Walter Johnson held his opponents to a lower on base percentage. His performance on the mound requires no more endorsement than manager Ed Barrow handing him the ball to open the World Series.

He played in 92 games, 20 on the mound, 13 at first base and 59 in the outfield. While playing first base in a game in July, he registered 20 putouts. This is two shy of the major league record, which is held by four first basemen. He played the outfield with what Billy Evans called "astonishing cleverness". In the Red Sox team picture that appeared in the *Boston Herald* at the end of the season, Babe's position is listed as "all around", and it's no wonder, for there has never been a "utility player" who was as adept and productive as Babe Ruth in 1918.

In the fall, Babe Ruth unofficially deposed Ty Cobb as the prototype major league baseball player. The St. Louis Cardinals signed a six-footer out of the Navy named Joe Doyle and announced to the world that they had signed the "Babe Ruth of the Navy." No longer were prospects "future Ty Cobbs"; the Babe now occupied that throne. "Smiling Joe" Doyle never played a game in the major leagues.

Babe and Helen were in Baltimore when the year came to a close. It had been a tough few months for Babe following the death of his dad. He had returned to Boston and performed brilliantly in the World Series. But from that point on it seemed to be one thing after another. A kitchen accident had left him singed and blistered before he reported to Lebanon and his steel mill job. His less-than-enthusiastic welcome in Pennsylvania was followed by a two-week bout with the flu. After his recovery came his knee injury, leaving him on crutches for several days. The holidays were a bittersweet time for Babe, as indeed the entire year of 1918 must have been as well. All of his success on the field, his wealth and fame was overshadowed by the death of his father, a man who in many ways, he had just come to know.

• Six •

1919: A New Home Run Record

The year 1919 opened with the country mourning the death of former president Theodore Roosevelt. Roosevelt was in office when the American League made its debut as a major circuit in 1901. The major leagues were looking forward to the first season in several years without impending or existing military involvement; the threat of a rival league; or a proposed player's strike. The Boston Red Sox were experiencing changes in the off-season, including the location of their upcoming spring training camp. In mid-January, owner Frazee accepted a letter of invitation from the city of Tampa, Florida, forsaking their longtime training site at Hot Springs.

Personnel changes were continuing at this time as Frazee purchased third base defensive specialist Oscar Vitt from the Tigers to round out the infield. In late December, he had sold Duffy Lewis, Ernie Shore, and Dutch Leonard to the Yankees in what would be the beginning of a long procession of players sent to New York in the coming years.

Several Red Sox players had yet to sign contracts for the 1919 season as of late January. It was widely anticipated that there would be a downward trend in salaries throughout the major leagues for the upcoming year. Team owners had voted to play a 140-game schedule for '19, and a roster limit of 21 players was instituted as a cost-cutting measure. Boston sportswriters speculated, however, that not only might Ruth be spared a cut, but would likely be one of the very few granted a slight increase. Ruth engaged in his first discussion on the matter with Frazee when the latter traveled to Boston from his New York office on January 21. Paul Shannon reported on the meeting:

> "Warned by the press that the Boston club owner was in town, Big Babe Ruth came up from his camp in Sudbury yesterday afternoon, had a long talk with his boss and then went back to the country. But Babe did not talk terms, and there is plenty of time between now and the start south to get down to business, neither man was very much concerned over the result." *Boston Post* 1/22/19

Ruth clearly believed by this point that he was the team's top star, and desired a salary commensurate with that lofty status. Evidence of Ruth's perceived superstar billing within the organization was apparent in connection with a relatively unimportant item that appeared in a Paul Shannon column in the *Boston Post* on January 19. In reporting that the Red Sox did not currently have an office downtown, he wrote: "...Babe Ruth and everyone else connected with the club will have to call at Fenway Park to do business." It is interesting to observe that the Red Sox organization at this time seemed to be divided into two basic categories: 1) Babe Ruth, and 2) everyone else.

გა

The *Post* featured a large article about Ruth on its sportspage, singing the praises of both his outstanding pitching as well as his phenomenal slugging ability.

> "During the past two years...his fame as a hitter began to prove a bigger drawing card than his skill on the rubber. Fans who seldom cared to witness a pitchers battle usually planned to take in the afternoon contest for the sake of seeing Babe pole one of his long drives to the fences." *Boston Post* 1/26/19

A very similar article appeared that week in *The Sporting News,* and included the following quote:

> "Ruth's ability to hammer the horsehide farther than any other man ever hammered it before in the long history of the game makes him a man apart." 1/30/19

Both articles featured virtually identical accompanying charts detailing his pitching and batting records. They were hailing Ruth's accomplishments in the opposite aspects of the game, just as Jack Barry had done in a *Post* interview two weeks earlier. He was quoted as saying, "If Babe had not shown such versatility [playing left-field, first base, and pitching in '18] the Sox probably would not have won."

Ruth's ability to be so versatile was beginning to wear on him, however. Three published items from early 1919 indicate his desire to discontinue the habit of spreading himself around. On January 19, Arthur Duffey stated, "Ruth refuses to be Jack of all trades on the diamond", and on February 11th, Paul Shannon's column included the line "Ruth recently stated he intends to play but one position this year". In a brief article in the January 23 issue of *The Sporting News*, Ruth had reportedly said that a ballplayer's life is short enough without being cut shorter by being worked to death.

Ruth was likely leaning toward playing an everyday position, as the notion of coming to the plate four times a day every day to swing his mighty bat was no doubt appealing to him. Babe and Ed Barrow were seemingly on a collision course on this issue as an article in the *Post* stated the Boston manager's intentions:

> "Manager Ed Barrow of the Red Sox has definitely decided to use Babe Ruth only as a pitcher and pinch hitter next season, and would like one more seasoned outfielder in the event that Hooper does not sign." *Boston Post* 3/1/19

Appearing in *The Sporting News* on February 13 was a brief piece entitled, "Tell Where They'd Play Babe Ruth". It claimed that among major league managers polled, the majority believed he should continue as a pitcher, performing occasional pinch hitting duties. In the following week's issue, Washington's Clark Griffith was listed among the minority, saying Ruth should play first base. Griffith believed that in time, he would be even better at the position than Stuffy McInnis. However, one month later, in the March 20 issue, Griffith praised Ruth's pitching, albeit in an odd sort of a way by saying "Babe Ruth is a joke pitcher. But the joke is usually on the batter."

It was around this time that Ruth had taken on a personal manager, a character by the name of Johnny Igoe. Babe seemed to be adopting the strategy that exploring other financial opportunities would create additional leverage when it came time to talk contract with Frazee. There was considerable talk in early '19 of Ruth entering the ring as a heavyweight boxer—an idea that was met with skepticism by the local media.

Paul Shannon:

"I see they're trying to make a boxer out of Babe Ruth ... (He) had better stick to baseball. He will make more in the national pastime than he ever will within the ropes .... Babe is big and husky and all that, but if he is wise he will get this prize fight bug out of his noodle in a hurry and keep in baseball right where he belongs." *Boston Post*, 2/19/19

Shannon recalled the incident from the 1916 fall visit to Plymouth, New Hampshire when Ruth and teammate Mike McNally laced up the gloves for a brief sparring session. Babe was rather embarrassed at being handled easily by McNally, over whom he held a considerable advantage in size. Ruth subsequently went to boxing trainer George Byers' gym on Howard St. in Boston, and failed to make a very positive impression.

The *Post*'s Arthur Duffey also weighed in on the topic:

"Talk about Babe Ruth becoming a world's heavyweight aspirant recalls that a couple of seasons ago Babe had the same bug, but it was a case of Babe's wife wouldn't let him then, and it comes pretty near applying just now." 1/25/19

Another venture that had caught Babe's fancy at this time was a popular indoor sport known as "Roller Polo", which could best be described as hockey on roller skates. Ruth and a prominent local businessman traveled down to New Bedford, Massachusetts on the evening of February 28 to check out the local franchise, which was said to have the finest rink in the league. He had previously attended several games and had become somewhat of a fanatic. The plan was that if the situation checked out well, they would purchase the team, and Ruth would be a great drawing card as the skipper of the club. It was also speculated that he and other well-known businessmen might organize a Maine State roller polo league next season.

Frazee had even heard rumors that Ruth was considering playing ball in the Delaware County League. He was not concerned however, going so far as to dare the independent league to challenge Boston's rights to Ruth and others in court. Frazee obviously put little stock in the notion that Babe would be doing anything other than playing for the Red Sox in 1919, as the following quote from the team's owner would indicate:

> "Lock every gate and bar every window at Fenway Park, and Babe Ruth would climb the fence, bust into the clubhouse, wrestle his way into his uniform and be in readiness to play that first game . . . just imagine that bird staying away from baseball and taking care of a garden! That's good enough to put in a book!" *The Sporting News,* 1/30/19

One of the first indications that Ruth's contract negotiations were not progressing smoothly came in "Arthur Duffey's Sport Comment":

> "Barrow claims that Ruth will have to come down off his high horse if he wants to play with the Sox, and Babe says 'Nothing doing under $15,000.' and there you are." 2/27/19

Arthur Duffey again on March 2:

> "Babe Ruth says $15,000 or bust; and Harry Frazee says 'bust.'"

Frazee was said to be offering $7,500, and the haggling continued through early March, yet the belief was that both Ruth and Frazee realized ultimately that they needed each other. Both were waiting for the other to blink, and were doing their share of posturing; Frazee saying Babe was only "spoofing"; while Ruth was saying "wait and see". It was even theorized that with Frazee having claimed to have been offered $150,000 for Ruth the year before, Babe now truly believed he was worth the $15,000 per year he was asking.

Negotiations came to a head by mid-March, and readers of the *Boston Sunday Post* of the 16th were taken aback by a column entitled:

"Ready to dispose of Ruth"
"Frazee says he's now ready to trade star"

Among Frazee's quotes to Paul Shannon:

> " . . . I have done everything possible to talk (Ruth) into a reasonable frame of mind, yet he . . . demands a contract that is

absolutely out of the question. If I cannot come to terms with Babe then I will ... see what other clubs will offer in the way of a trade. I will have no man on the team ... dictate terms to the management ... If Ruth doesn't want to work for the Red Sox at the handsome salary offered him, maybe we can make an advantageous trade for him ...."

The Red Sox group pulled out of South Station on Monday, March 17 bound for spring training in Tampa. Conspicuously absent was Babe, who was now officially a holdout. There seemed to be the belief that teams could not afford high salaries, and few of Ruth's teammates supported him in his demands. Frazee and Barrow openly felt that he had been ill-advised, and a trade was still an option, with Washington, Philadelphia, or St. Louis listed as possibilities.

The *Post* sportspage of Friday, March 21 contained another article with a truly attention-grabbing title: "Ruth may be traded for Walt Johnson". In the piece, Frazee indicated that something would occur within 48 hours if Ruth didn't hurry up and sign his contract. But as Bostonians were reading the threatening words from the owner, Ruth, who had taken the train to New York City, was sitting in Frazee's office. That day, he put his signature on a deal that was reported by some to pay him $10,000 per year for three years. Other sources, the *New York Times* among them, reporting the yearly figure to be $9,000.

The following day's *Post* reported that "Ruth was just as happy as a schoolboy as he emerged from Harry Frazee's office with the new contract tucked away in his pocket." The magnitude of the signing was indicated by Arthur Duffey who wrote: "Probably no event in local sporting circles had so much effect on the fans as the signing of Babe Ruth to a Red Sox contract."

Ruth had apparently not expected to sign a contract that day, as he had failed to bring along his luggage. After the meeting with Frazee, he telephoned a friend in Boston to bring his baggage to New York. Later that evening after his bags had arrived, he boarded a midnight train for Florida. As Ruth was signing what would be his final Red Sox contract, a 16-year-old youth from Michigan named Thomas A. Yawkey was inheriting a $10 million fortune from his recently deceased uncle. The late William Yawkey was a part-owner of the Detroit Tigers, and young Mr. Yawkey would one day become involved in the ownership of an American League franchise.

Upon his arrival, Ruth checked into the Tampa Bay Hotel where the team was staying. On his first day he broke two bats in batting practice, and the *Sporting News* noted that one of them was the one George Whiteman used for his World Series heroics the previous fall. Ruth was said to be fat and short of wind, but still clearly in possession of his batting prowess.

His first game action came on March 24 as he played leftfield and batted in the cleanup spot in an intra-squad exhibition. Pitcher Carl Mays now remained the lone holdout on the team, but he was in camp engaging in workouts. Ruth took batting practice against him on the 25th and was left exasperated at his inability to drive one out off Mays. The submarine-style right-hander was openly stating at this time that he would bet Ruth big money he couldn't hit a homer off him.

Back in Boston, Arthur Duffey reported in the *Post* on his brief encounter with Babe's wife Helen:

> "Ran across Mrs. Babe Ruth and Mrs. Dave Shean yesterday on Washington St. Both were just a little perturbed at being unable to accompany their illustrious husbands to the sunny south this season, but when I informed Mrs. Ruth that Babe was still busting the little old pill as usual she replied 'Oh good. I knew he was in fine condition before he left. I know he is going to be worth every cent that Harry Frazee paid him.'" 3/26/19

Though it was believed that Barrow still intended to use Ruth as a pitcher, Babe made no secret his preference for leftfield. The fact that there was a vacancy there due to Duffy Lewis having been traded, made Ruth long for the chance to show what he could do on a regular basis. There was even talk that the Sox might attempt to acquire a star leftfielder to eliminate the temptation for Babe. Those close to the situation expected the issue to be a sore spot as the spring wore on. Some of Ruth's teammates opposed his insistence on batting cleanup, feeling not only that he belonged farther down in the order, but that he should continue his role as a pitcher and occasional pinch hitter.

Barrow placed Ruth in somewhat of a leadership role on March 29 by appointing him captain of the "Battering Babes" squad, a group of Sox assembled to scrimmage against the "Regulars". The first of these matchups took place on March 30 with Ruth playing first base. In batting practice before the game, Babe drove two home runs completely out of the park, wowing spectators. They were hoping he might repeat the feat during the game, but he went hitless in his squad's 5-4 win. That evening he reveled in the spotlight again, as the master of ceremonies at a big dance held at the hotel. The following day's *Post* reported that "The southpaw has butted into society with a vengeance," a fact that Helen must have been thrilled to read back in Boston.

Babe showed no apparent ill-effects from over indulgence the following day as, again playing first base, he singled, doubled, and crushed a long home run over the rightfield fence. The blow was said to have broken the "long distance batting record for Tampa".

One amusing incident involving Ruth and Red Sox pitcher Joe Bush had occurred sometime during this portion of training camp. It seems that Bush had nicknamed Ruth "Tarzan", and never having heard the name before, Ruth asked what it meant. Bush explained that it was the name of a mighty hunter who was a great hero, and Babe seemed satisfied with that. Some days later, an early film version of the classic came to a local theater, and Ruth decided he would check it out. As the movie began and he saw a scantily-clad jungle man swinging from vine to vine, he became enraged at what he felt was an insult, and burst out of the theater. He ran directly back to the training camp, grabbed a bat, and proceeded to chase Bush around the field for half an hour until he disappeared from the area.

৯৮

On April 2, Ruth saw his first competitive action on the mound, splitting time between pitching and first base in the "Battering Babes" 2-0 win over the Regulars. In these early spring games, former major league player-turned evangelist Billy Sunday was acting as occasional guest umpire at Red Sox scrimmages. The "Billy Graham" of his day, Sunday had been making several appearances in the Tampa area, and even took a moment to pose for a photo with Ruth and Barrow. Though 56 years old and out of the majors since 1890, he also enjoyed working out and shagging flies with the Sox.

John McGraw brought his New York Giants to Tampa on April 4 to begin a seven-game exhibition series versus the Red Sox. Ruth played leftfield in the first two contests on the 4th and 5th, and brief items in the *Post*'s recap of each game gave an indication of the expectations he had created with his mighty bat: "Ruth slams out usual homer as Sox nose out Giants 5-3", and "He [Babe] had a bad afternoon, getting only two singles on which he drove in four runs and scored one tally himself."

The home run he had delivered in that first game on the 4th was particularly worthy of note, as he had apparently broken his own Tampa long-distance record. Many decades later, a plaque was erected at the site where the nearly 600-foot blast had landed, now part of the campus of the University of Tampa.

The Boston-New York spring series switched to Gainsville, Florida, the site of the Giants training camp on April 7. Ruth appeared in both of the games there, playing leftfield each day. After the second game on April 8, both teams boarded a train to continue the series in Columbia, South Carolina on the 9th and Spartanburg the 10th. The final game versus New York was rained out on the 11th, and the Sox continued on to Richmond, Virginia for three games against Colleges and semi-pro outfits. Boston's 18-0 massacre of Randolph-Macon College of Virginia produced the following passage in Paul Shannon's *Post* recap:

"Babe Ruth set the college boys aflame with enthusiasm by driving the ball over the rightfield wall and onto the fairgrounds, the longest hit ever in Richmond within the memory of its oldest inhabitants." 4/16/19

Babe had added one more location to the seemingly endless list of ballparks in which it was he who had hit its longest home run. Three days later, he put on a thoroughly awesome display in Baltimore against Jack Dunn's Orioles, and was said to have "set the fans of his hometown crazy". It may not be an exaggeration to claim this game as Ruth's most impressive offensively in a professional uniform to this point, as he clouted four home runs and walked twice in his six at-bats.

"Batting Babe Ruth, famed throughout the length and breadth of fandom as the greatest long distance hitter the game has ever known, eclipsed all minor league records this afternoon and set the slugging crown more firmly on his own head by driving out four home runs in as many times at bat ...." *Boston Post* 4/19/19

In the wake of that performance, future Hall of Fame outfielder Joe Kelley, star of the old National League Orioles dynasty of the 1890s was asked if Ruth could hit the ball as hard as 19th century slugger Ed Delahanty. Old-time ballplayers are generally partial to those of their own era, yet the former Baltimore star responded promptly "Ruth can hit a ball as hard as any man that ever lived".

One could barely pick up a sportspage without finding some flattering reference to the Red Sox superstar around this time. A Washington Senators weekly column in *The Sporting News* by Paul Eaton dated April 7 that told of Walter Johnson hitting two homers in one day at camp at Augusta was titled "Great Walter as a Babe Ruth". In the following week's issue, April 17, Ernest J. Lanigan commented "The Red Sox haven't lost any popularity and they have an extremely colorful athlete named George Herman Ruth to attract the populace".

Arthur Duffey indicated the widely held opinion that Ruth would be capturing his second straight home run crown:

> "Already they're betting even money that Babe Ruth will lead the four sack hitters for the 1919 season. From the way Babe has been hitting 'em in the spring training season it looks like a pretty safe bet." *Boston Post* 4/14/19

Working their way further northward Babe and the Sox stopped at Jersey City, New Jersey for two final spring tuneups against Wild Bill Donovan's International League squad. Boston shutout the minor leaguers 1-0 and 11-0, though Ruth contributed little with his bat. His lack of production prompted the Post to comment "Noteworthy Event: A day when Babe fails to hit out a homer."

Opening day had finally arrived, and expectations were high for the team, with several writers predicting them to repeat as champions. As for where Ruth would play to start the season, Harry Hooper, Everett Scott, and coach Heinie Wagner, along with Babe himself tried to convince manager Barrow to allow him to play the outfield. Reluctantly, the manager consented to allow him to try the experiment, but indicated that it was back to strictly pitching at the first sign of an extended slump.

Thirty thousand fans jammed into the Polo Grounds on April 23, said to be the largest crowd to attend an opening day game in New York City. For the first time since 1915, Ruth would not be the

Red Sox starting pitcher in the season opener, but rather found himself in his preferred leftfield, batting fourth. It didn't take Babe long to generate excitement, as on his first at-bat, with Hooper on base he slugged a scorcher over the head of new Yankee centerfielder Duffy Lewis. The ball rolled all the way to the wall, and Ruth recorded his first home run of 1919. The Yankees also couldn't touch the magnificent pitching of Carl Mays, who dominated the New Yorkers 10-0.

4/23/19 at New York: 2 for 4, home run, single, walk, 2 RBI

Each of the next three days' games were canceled due to New York City's cold, wet weather. The Red Sox left the city on Saturday evening for Washington, and Helen joined Babe as the two were reunited after five weeks apart. It was Sunday, the 27th that the team began a four-game series with the Senators, and with Sam Jones on the mound, Ruth again manned leftfield. His only hit was a triple, however he scored three runs, and the Sox ran away with it 8-0. Babe's impressive three-bagger warranted particular attention in the following day's *Post*:

> "Babe Ruth got the longest triple ever made on the local grounds, and had not Clyde Milan been playing almost out in Maryland for the ball, Ruth could have walked all the way home on the hit."

The second game of the series the following day featured a Carl Mays-Walter Johnson matchup, and Babe supplied his share of the offensive production. In his five plate appearances, he doubled, tripled, scored two runs, and was intentionally walked by Johnson, as the Red Sox won a squeaker 6-5. Their first defeat of the '19 season came the next day, dropping a 4-3 decision to the Senators at Griffith Stadium. Ruth was held hitless in his three at-bats.

The Red Sox were scheduled to wrap up their series in Washington on April 30, but Babe would not be available. A few hours before gametime, Barrow and Ruth had it out regarding the slugger's "training violations", and Babe was suspended indefinitely.

On the Wednesday night train ride home from Washington after the Sox 4-1 victory, Ruth was contrite, and promised to behave, and was re-instated immediately by Manager Barrow. The *Boston Post* found his return newsworthy enough to run a front page headline and accompanying story:

"Babe Ruth Plays Today"
"In spite of his flareup at Washington yesterday noon and the consequent suspension by Manager Barrow, Babe Ruth will positively appear in the Red Sox lineup on Thursday ... "

The team arrived back in Boston, poised for their Fenway season opener as defending World Champions versus the Yankees May 1. The pre-game festivities included the flag raising with the U.S. military's 101st Regiment in attendance. In his now familiar cleanup spot in the order, Ruth came up in the first inning, was given a great ovation, and slugged a double driving in old friend Jack Barry, who had returned from the Navy to his second base position. That would be Ruth's only hit on the day, and regarding his play in leftfield, the *Post* remarked that he "threw poorly on two occasions".

Carl Mays went the distance for Boston, but the 7-3 loss was his. The Yankees took the next day's game also, 3-1, and Ruth had an unproductive 0 for 4 day at the plate. In the second inning, his throwing arm was again an issue, and the *Post* reported: "The weak throwing arm of big Babe Ruth handed the visitors another tally ...."

Frazee announced after the loss that Ruth would take his regular turn in the rotation starting the next day, and only play left when Barrow saw fit. Babe seemed to accept the decision, and was referred to as "a good sport" who would "submit to the judgement of the management".

As promised, Ruth finally made his pitching debut for the season on Saturday, May 3, drawing the starting assignment against New York. Despite his limited mound work in the spring, Shannon would report that he " ... acquitted himself splendidly and showed that he is now practically ready to work with regularity on the rubber where he surely belongs." The crowd of nearly 16,000 fans saw him complete the come-from-behind 3-2 win.

Arthur Duffey commented in the *Post* two days after the victory, "Babe Ruth never worked harder to put the Sox back on the winning side of the sheet than on Saturday, which accounted for the score of 3-2." That same edition included Shannon's report: "Ruth's arm is strengthening every day, and Barrow is pretty nearly convinced by now that he must depend on Babe as a twirler rather than an outfielder. He does not peg as a regular outer gardener should do."

	IP	H	SO	BB
5/3/19 vs.				
New York	9	7	2	4

At bat: 1 for 3, double, run, RBI

After the usual Sunday off at home, Ruth found himself back in left on Monday, May 5, for the final game of the Yankee series. His only hit in three official at-bats was a triple in the fourth inning that very nearly landed in the bleachers in the deepest part of centerfield. He subsequently scored, preventing the Red Sox from being shut out in the 5-1 loss.

Washington came to town for a series to begin on May 6, and Ruth had a fairly uneventful hitless day as the leftfielder. He was far from alone as Boston could muster only two hits, Washington only three as Ray Caldwell notched a 2-0 victory for the Red Sox. Rainy, cold weather forced the postponement of the next day's game, and the teams would next meet on Thursday, the 8th with Walter Johnson hurling for the Senators. The day of rest due to the rainout likely prompted Barrow to trot Ruth out to leftfield again, as he singled in two at-bats, also reaching on an error. Johnson didn't make it past the sixth inning, and Sam Jones gave the Sox another shutout, 3-0.

Ruth was scheduled to start against the A's on Friday, May 9, but that game and the next day's game as well were washed out. The Red Sox traveled down to New Haven, Connecticut on Sunday and engaged in an exhibition with a local squad. They then came back to Boston where yet another game against the Athletics was rained out on Monday. The Red Sox left that night on a 22-day road trip that would take them to every other American League city except New York.

Ruth and company ran up against a tough opponent in Chicago in the trip's first stop on May 14. Carl Mays and Eddie Cicotte were locked in a magnificent duel, and Jack Barry's error gave Chicago the only run of the game. Ruth had no success against the former Red Sox/future Black Sox participant Cicotte, as he went 0 for 4 with two strikeouts while manning left, also popping out with Barry on base to end the game.

It had been nearly two weeks since Frazee declared that Ruth would return to pitching primarily, yet he had appeared in every game that Boston had played since then. Finally on the 15th in Chicago, it appeared that he would be watching the game from the dugout, however he was called upon early. With none out in the second inning, Sox starter Joe Bush was ejected by umpire George Moriarty after a heated argument, and Barrow tabbed Ruth to replace him. He warmed up quickly, and as the game wore on he was in and out of trouble. Employing a boxing metaphor, Paul Shannon wrote that he "reeled and staggered through the ensuing 11 rounds". It was in the top of the 12th inning that Stuffy McInnis doubled, scoring Barry for an eventual 6-5 victory for Ruth.

	IP	H	SO	BB
5/15/19 at Chicago	11	13	0	8
At bat: 0 for 4				

The Sporting News issue dated May 15 contained two flattering references to Ruth. Legendary sportswriter Grantland Rice had penned a rather lengthy poem that was essentially an ode to Babe's phenomenal slugging prowess. Contained in the poem were the lines:

" ... I've seen a few I thought could hit, who fed the crowd on four base rations, But you Babe are the Only It—The rest are merely imitations . . . ."

Also, an uncredited editorial item mentioned Barrow's chastising of Ruth for his extracurricular activities. It wondered however, that after seeing Ruth's performances on the field, why Barrow didn't encourage other players to engage in such activities.

Despite Babe's marathon relief stint of the 15th, he was back out in Comiskey Park's leftfield the following day. In his three at-bats he singled and scored a run, but Boston went down 7-4 in the final game of the White Sox series. The St. Louis Browns were the Red Sox' next host, and the only action Ruth saw in the first game, May 17 was a fruitless pinch-hitting appearance. He was sent up for pitcher Sam Jones in the eighth inning of Boston's 2-1 loss.

In the final game of the St. Louis series, Ruth got the start, but it was his bat that truly did the talking. His hurling that day was erratic and unsteady, but when he came to the plate in the second inning with the bases loaded, his drive over the rightfield fence was, in the words of Paul Shannon " ... one of those terrific wallops that have made the Hub's big southpaw famous". He hung on to complete the contest and collect the 6-4 win.

	IP	H	SO	BB	HBP	Balk
5/20/19 at						
St. Louis	9	9	1	4	1	1

At bat: 1 for 4, grand slam, 4 RBI

The Red Sox moved up to Detroit to begin a four-game set at Navin Field on the 21st. The road trip was on the verge of really going sour, as Boston dumped the opener 6-5. Ruth, back in left, was a non-factor, going 0 for 3 with a walk. He didn't play in the following day's game, which the Tigers won 6-3, dropping the Red Sox below .500 at 9-10.

The next day, Paul Shannon wrote in his *Post* column:

> "Chances of Babe Ruth being seen regularly in the left garden hereafter are very remote . . . he seems to be reconciled to the fact that he is a pitcher instead of an outfielder . . . the other members of the team have just about convinced our burly southpaw that it is on the rubber that the champions need him most."

He began the Detroit finale, May 24 on the bench, but Barrow called on him to bat for left-fielder Gilhooley with two out in the seventh. During that at-bat Hooper was picked off second, so Ruth led off the eighth inning, but was retired. He finished the game in left, though he didn't bat again as the Sox lost, 5-3.

The fourth stop on the western tour brought the Red Sox into Cleveland the next day for a three-game stint. Ruth's only hit in four at-bats was a vicious single that scored the first run of the game. Former teammate Larry Gardner drove in all three Indian runs in the Tribe's 3-2 win. The losses were mounting for Boston, and Babe was sent to the mound on the 26th to hopefully put a stop to it.

This would not be the day though, as Ruth walked in a run in the first, walking a total of four in the first two innings and allowing three runs to score. He was sent out to leftfield to start the third, and Ray Caldwell was brought in to relieve. None of the four Red Sox pitchers who worked were particularly effective this game, and the result was a 12-7 loss.

	IP	H	SO	BB
5/26/19 at				
Cleveland	2	2	1	4

At bat: 0 for 3, walk, run scored

The Red Sox season-high losing streak of six would be reached the next day in the last game of the Cleveland series. In the 6-4 loss, Ruth, playing left, had a noteworthy day with his mighty bat, adding another first to his resume. Already having singled, he came up in the ninth inning and smashed a tremendous triple that bounced off the screen in right centerfield. It was the first time in the history of the ballpark that a batted ball had ever struck this screen.

May 28 was a travel day, and on the way to Philadelphia the Red Sox stopped off in York, Pennsylvania and manhandled a local team in an exhibition game, 19-3. It was their first taste of victory of any kind in a little over a week, and there were many reports of dissension in the ranks. Some were saying that Barrow's personality was not appreciated, and several players were hopeful that Jack Barry would regain the managerial position. Given Ruth's run-ins with Barrow and his friendship with Barry, it is not hard to imagine him among this group. Ruth was even thought by some to be one of the roots of the problem with his continuing desire to play outfield instead of pitching. Duffy Lewis, and the spark he brought to the team, were clearly missed, and some players believed that if he were still around playing leftfield and Ruth were pitching and pinch hitting, the team would be better off. *The Sporting News* of June 5 wrote, "Ruth has found it is far more difficult to throw strikes from the outfield than it is from the box."

In the first game of the Athletics series at Shibe Park on May 29, Carl Mays turned in a fine performance. The submariner hurled a four-hitter in Boston's 7-1 win, and leftfielder Babe kicked in with a double, single, run scored, and two RBI in five at-bats. His last couple trips to the plate he faced former staffmate Walt Kinney, whom he had scuffled with briefly on the train during the '18 Series.

Despite the victory, the World Champions found themselves with a mediocre 11-15 record, floundering in sixth place. Friday, May 30 brought the annual Memorial Day doubleheader, and Ruth would get the ball for the start in game one. He would not earn any awards for his pitching performance, giving up 12 hits including a home run to Tilly Walker. He did hang on however, to complete the 10-6 win, helping the cause with his own bat. In the sixth inning, Ruth hit a tremendous foul ball that landed on the roof of a building on 20th St., bouncing on to Lehigh Ave. —the longest hit fair or foul ever seen there. In all, he had a double, two singles, a run, and an RBI in five at-bats.

In true ironman fashion, he trotted out to leftfield for game two of the twin bill and had an eventful game. In the first inning, Babe came up with two out and hit a pop fly to short rightfield that went so high Red Shannon grew dizzy waiting for it to come down. The second baseman, who would be Babe's teammate in less than a month, missed the ball completely and Ruth got credit for a double.

When Babe came to bat in the eighth, he was being razzed rather boisterously by the crowd, having struck out in an earlier at-bat. He proceeded to quiet the hecklers by depositing the ball over the rightfield fence, prompting Athletics beat writer James Isaminger to refer to him as, "King of the long-distance hitters". It was his third home run of the year, but surprisingly it was the first he had ever hit in Philadelphia. It didn't help the cause, though, as Boston lost 4-3.

On the final day of May, the Sox wrapped up their series in Philadelphia with a 6-4 complete game win by newly-acquired Bill James. With Manning in leftfield once again, Ruth chipped in with a double and a run scored in four at-bats. It was now on to Washington for the final leg of the extended road tour.

The team spent Sunday off in the Capital, and the outcome of Carl Mays' complete game in Monday's opener was a sharp contrast to his previous outing in Philadelphia. The Red Sox could only manage three hits off Senator Jim Shaw, who, like Ruth, had played on the Bethlehem Steel team the previous Fall. Ruth, with a single and a stolen base was the only Boston player to reach third base as they were blanked 4-0.

Rumors of a shakeup were beginning to surface, with Frazee reportedly anxious to make a deal to help get the team winning. He was said to be willing to sacrifice almost any one of the infielders for a hard-hitting leftfielder, likely with the idea of discontinuing Ruth's dual role.

Boston staged a ninth-inning rally against Washington on June 3 to pull off a 4-3 victory. Ruth was sent in to leftfield to replace Gainer in the ninth and did not get an at-bat. The next day in the final game versus the Senators he was more of a factor. He went 2 for 3 with a triple, scored two runs, and was hit by a pitch as Bill James recorded his second straight complete game win, 8-3.

The Tigers arrived in town for a series to begin on June 5, and the papers spoke of batting leader Ty Cobb holding court with the press in the lobby of the Brunswick Hotel, where Babe had spent his first days in Boston. Ex-Sox lefty Dutch Leonard was to oppose Ruth in game one, but a minor injury put a premature end to Ruth's game. After pitching the first three innings, he came to bat in the home half and beat out a grounder to first baseman Harry Heilmann. A couple of batters later he was on third, and when Dave Shean lined to second, he slid back into third to avoid getting doubled off. In the process, he wrenched his knee, and it was obvious he was in pain by the expression on his face as he was carried off the field. Frank Gilhooley came in to pinch run, and Mays relieved him as Boston went on to prevail 2-1.

	IP	H	SO	BB
6/5/19 vs.				
Detroit	3	3	1	1
At bat: 1 for 1, single, walk				

Ruth only missed one game due to the injury, and he returned to leftfield on June 7 for the final game of the Tiger series. He came to bat in the fifth inning with two runners aboard, and proceeded to hit the first pitch into the rightfield bleachers as a young boy stood up and caught it. Ruth also drew an intentional walk, and was taken out of the game in the seventh to rest his sore knee. During the game, Babe and his old roommate, pitcher Dutch Leonard had a verbal clash, and players stepped between them to prevent it from becoming physical.

It is entirely possible that after the game that night, Babe may have spent his Saturday evening as a spectator at the motorcycle races in nearby Revere, the track having just opened for the season a few days prior. It was fairly well known that he and Everett Scott were dyed-in-the-wool fans, and could be found perched in the grandstand every Wednesday and Friday when the Red Sox were at home.

The first-place White Sox arrived to start a four-game series on June 10, and Ruth was set to square off against Eddie Cicotte. Shoddy defense did Ruth in as four errors led to three unearned runs and a 5-3 loss. Among the seven Boston safeties was a double by Ruth, and though he displayed more stuff on the mound than any previous outing this year, the support and breaks favored Cicotte.

Barrow gave Babe a day off on the 11th, but he was back in leftfield the next day as Boston was opposed by White Sox future Hall of Famer Red Faber. Pitchers around the league had yet to find Ruth's weakness, and Faber was left frustrated as well. During his at-bat in the fourth inning, he tried to work him outside, but Ruth reached out and poked a double into leftfield, scoring two runs. It was his only hit on the afternoon, but it was more than enough, as Herb Pennock twirled a masterful three-hit, 4-0 shutout.

In the next day's White Sox finale, Ruth started off in left, but moved over to centerfield to replace Frank Gilhooley in the sixth inning. Babe had only a single in two official at-bats, but drew two walks and came around to score twice. Sam Jones' fine 6-1 win helped Boston split the series, but little headway was gained. Fans were becoming increasingly disgruntled, and were riding the team hard. The upcoming series, with Cleveland now in town, would only serve to exacerbate the bleak situation.

In game one of the series on Saturday, June 14, Ruth got the ball and was locked in a marathon affair with Cleveland's Jim Bagby. In the third inning, the Indians managed one run off Ruth, and did it without the benefit of a hit—two walks, a wild pitch, a sacrifice bunt, and a sacrifice fly. It remained that way until two outs in the bottom of the ninth with Ruth at the plate as Boston's last hope. He singled off Bagby and then scored on McInnis' triple to send the contest into extra innings. The two teams slugged it out until the 13th, when Cleveland plated two, and in the home half a Sox rally came up short. Hooper scored on Ruth's groundout, but Bagby allowed no more and won the error-free duel 3-2.

	IP	H	SO	BB	WP
6/14/19 vs.					
Cleveland	13	15	2	3	1

At bat: 2 for 6 , 2 singles, 1 run

After the Sunday off, Ruth was a leftfielder again on Monday with Carl Mays pitted against Stan Coveleski in what would be another duel. Mays' five-hitter was topped by Coveleski's three-hitter, and the Red Sox came up on the short end, 1-0. Ruth's only hit was a savage linedrive that knocked third baseman Larry Gardner off his feet, and he was also robbed of what could have been a home run when outfielder Jack Graney extended fully to pull one down with his back against the fence.

They would close out the Cleveland series with a double-header on Tuesday, June 17, with Babe in left for the entire 18 innings. His triple in the ninth, his only hit, drove the Indians' starter from the mound. Joe Wood, who had converted to an outfielder because of arm trouble, was brought in to make what would be his only pitching appearance of the year. He earned the save by nailing down the final two outs as Cleveland won, 4-3. Game two was slightly more eventful for Ruth, as he went three for four with a home run in the sixth off Morton, two singles, and a stolen base. The result, however, was the same, as Boston again lost, 3-2. They had been swept by Cleveland, losing all four games by a margin of one run, and the champions now sported a record of 18-24.

George Sisler and the St. Louis Browns arrived at Fenway the next day for four games. The opposing uniforms were different, but the result was the same—yet another one-run loss as the Browns prevailed, 3-2. Ruth scored one of the runs, had two singles, and swiped a base. Relief in the form of a victory finally came the following game, June 19, as Boston came out on top, 2-1, in their sixth straight one-run game. Babe, who was 2 for 3 in Mays' complete game, started a rally in the sixth with a double, and scored the first run. In a show of respect for Ruth's devastating power, Browns third baseman Jimmie Austin played halfway between third and left-field when he came to bat.

Taking a respite from his daily leftfield duties, Ruth was the starting pitcher against St. Louis in game three of the series on Tuesday. *The Sporting News* recapped that, "Babe pitched nice ball and was never in real danger". Although he put eight runners on base via walk and allowed nine hits, they were scattered, and he easily completed the 2-1 win. Though his triple in three at-bats was his only hit, it was he who scored both Red Sox runs.

"It was [Browns pitcher] Bert Gallia's turn to learn the might of Battering Babe Ruth's inhuman wallops yesterday and chiefly by the punch contributed by the Boston Battering Ram the Browns went down to a second defeat." *Boston Post* 6/21/19

The last game of the Browns series went a full ten innings, but because the Red Sox had to catch the train that Saturday evening to New York, the 3-3 deadlock was called. The game would not be reflected in the standings, but individual statistics would, and Ruth's infield single in the sixth inning extended his personal hitting streak to 20 games.

Ernie Shore put an end to the streak at the Polo Grounds the next day, holding Babe hitless in three at-bats. Another old mate, Duffy Lewis, helped the Yankee cause by going 3 for 3 with a home run. The Sox had traveled down to the city for a rare one-game series, lost 6-2, and came right back for a five-game set against Washington starting the following afternoon.

In the first contest on June 23, Ruth found himself in leftfield for the third straight day. He was hitless in his first two at-bats of the 12-3 loss, and was then was pinch hit for by Del Gainer, as he was scheduled to pitch the next day. However, Barrow sent him out to left one more day, and Ruth, who had failed to hit safely until the seventh inning, came up and hit the first pitch from Robertson out of the yard. His seventh home run of the year contributed to the Red Sox' 5-2 win.

Ruth took his turn in the rotation on the 25th in the first game of a doubleheader. Senators speedy centerfielder Clyde Milan had three hits off him, and Sam Rice hit a home run. Though he completed the game, not much went in his favor. Ruth allowed nine hits, five walks, and went hitless in his own four at-bats in the 8-3 defeat.

He came right back in game two to play leftfield, with Sam Jones opposing Walter Johnson. Ruth's single was one of only five hits off the great right-hander, but what resulted would occur to Johnson more than any other pitcher in history—a 1-0 defeat.

After this outing, Ruth issued an ultimatum to Barrow that from now on he would either pitch or play outfield, but not both. The dual role was clearly catching up with him, and some seemed to feel he was losing his fastball. Barrow relented this time, agreeing to use him, at least for the time being, as an everyday player. Babe was satisfied, but still a few of his teammates didn't believe he was experienced enough as an outfielder, feeling his place was still on the mound.

After Ruth's busy day against Washington, Barrow gave him a well-deserved day off. In the 12 games Boston had played in the previous ten days, Babe had played every inning; ten games as a leftfielder and two complete games on the mound. He would get an additional day off the following day as the first game of the beginning of their road trip in New York was washed out. That day the Red Sox announced a trade with the Athletics in which they would send Jack Barry and Amos Strunk back to the team they had broke in with, receiving slugging outfielder Bobby Roth and infielder Maurice "Red" Shannon. Barry, however, refused to report and subsequently retired, and Boston made up the difference to the A's with cash.

Friday's rainout necessitated a Saturday doubleheader, and circumstances created a new challenge for Ruth. An injury to Stuffy McInnis prompted Barrow to start Babe at first base in both ends of the twin bill. He responded by stroking a double, a single, and scoring a run in Carl Mays' complete-game 2-0 shutout. Remarkably, Mays came back in true ironman fashion and completed the second game as well, this time losing 4-1. Ruth also went 2 for 3 (2 singles) in this game, and had handled a total of 19 chances flawlessly at first base on the day. Filling in for McInnis again the following day, he singled and scored once in four trips in the Red Sox 5-2 loss at the Polo Grounds.

On Monday, the last day of June, the Sox played another doubleheader to close out the Yankee series. Playing first base for the fourth straight game, he had already singled when he came to the plate in the sixth inning with the bases full. Ruth got hold of a Bob Shawkey offering that landed in the upper rightfield pavilion, and prompted this headline on the *Post*'s sports page the next day: "Our Babe Thrills Gotham Fans by Smiting the Pill Into the Bleachers".

They took no chances with him in the eighth and walked him, and the grand slam had accounted for all the Sox runs as they lost 7-4. In the second game it was back out to leftfield for the first time in five days, and he went 0 for 2 as Boston lost, 4-2. The team had concluded a horrendous June in which they won but 12 of 28 games.

Amid cries of "What's the matter with the Red Sox?", the team moved down to Philadelphia for five games to close out the brief two-city trip. Ruth had begun a streak of 17 games in which he performed strictly as a leftfielder, and he had one of the only two Red Sox hits on July 1. In the first inning, his vicious single to right drove in Vitt, but he was nabbed at second trying to stretch it.

The following day, Boston reversed their fortunes briefly by beginning a modest four-game winning streak versus the Athletics. Though Ruth went hitless, he was walked twice and scored a run in Ray Caldwell's 4-2 win. He was experiencing slight knee problems at this time, as his kneecap was slipping in and out of place on nearly a daily basis.

The Athletics scored two runs in the first inning on July 3, but didn't score another as the Sox went on to an 8-2 win. Babe had only one single, but in the fourth he hammered a tremendous drive that Tilly Walker caught with his back against the centerfield scoreboard. Ruth himself robbed Joe Dugan of a home run in the sixth in what was called the most sensational play of the series. After the game, the two teams traveled together to Boston to begin another series, one that would see them play three doubleheaders in the coming four days.

The first would be the traditional 4th of July twin bill, and Boston would come out on top in both ends, 9-2 and 9-6. In the opener, Ruth stroked a double, two singles, walked twice, and scored once. He was also said to have made a pretty catch of the recently traded Strunk in the fourth.

The next day's doubleheader produced the opposite outcome with the Red Sox getting swept, 5-3 and 8-6. Ruth went hitless in the first game, and Philadelphia scored two in the ninth to win. With regard to game two, the *Post*'s headline included the line "Babe's Two Home Run Drives Only Consolation for Fans". The first came in the eighth inning, and the second in the tenth, but it simply wasn't enough. It was, however, the first homer he had hit over the leftfield fence. It also tied him for the major league lead with Phillie Gavvy Cravath with nine, and the *Post* speculated at this time that if Ruth played in a smaller park like Cravath did, he would hit a home run per day.

The two teams had a much needed day off on Sunday, July 6, but went right back at it for two more on Monday. Sam Jones was sharp in the first game, shutting out the A's 2-0, as Babe had two singles and a run scored in three at-bats. He also made a phenomenal running one-handed catch in left in the second inning.

Though he was experiencing more trouble with his knee in game two, he stayed in and had a double and a single in the 5-4 win. Having played 14 games in the previous nine days, the temptation to ease the burden on the pitching staff by using Ruth must have been strong. Barrow however, would stick to his agreement with Ruth for the time being.

After the game, the Red Sox set out for an extended western trip that would begin in St. Louis on July 9. Ruth's only time on base that day was a walk in four appearances, though he very nearly put one out. He hit a tremendous foul ball to rightfield, foul by just a few feet that caused quite a stir. Babe's ability to create excitement even in his failed attempts was already legendary. Commenting on this game, in which he was struck out twice by Browns pitcher Allen Sothoron, *The Sporting News* of July 17 stated, "Twice in one game he struck out—and there was as much commotion over it as if a World Series had been decided." The brief item, which was accompanied by a photo of Ruth also added " ... whether it be a homer, a foul or even a strikeout, the fans find something to talk about when Babe appears with his bludgeon." On the verge of the fifth anniversary of his major league debut, the 24-year-old superstar had captured the fancy of the baseball public in a way that the great Ty Cobb never could.

On their second day in St. Louis, it was yet another doubleheader, though Babe sat out the first game. It was back out to leftfield for game two, and he led off the sixth inning by depositing his tenth home run of the season into the rightfield bleachers. He also added a single, but it was for naught, due in part to a defensive miscue in which he was involved. Ruth and centerfielder Bill Lamar got mixed up on a popfly in the ninth which allowed two runs to score, giving the Browns a 4-3 win.

After a day of rain, Boston opened up a four-game series in Chicago on July 12. In the third frame with two on, one out, and one Boston run already in, starter Dickie Kerr was relieved by Dave Danforth. Ruth, the first batter he faced, took his first pitch to the opposite field, deep into the left-field bleachers for his first ever homer in Chicago. He almost added another with a long drive in the ninth that was caught by Shano Collins at the very edge of the rightfield bleachers, but he had now homered in every A.L. park at least once during his career. He doubled and singled as well in the game, and Boston never looked back for a 12-4 win.

The Red Sox began a five-game skid the next day, coming up on the short end of a 14-9 slugfest. Ruth's contributions were a triple in the sixth, a single in the seventh with the bases full that scored two, and two runs scored himself. The next day's 9-3 loss saw Babe hammer two doubles in his four at-bats, but circumstances were unfolding that were pointing to a return to the mound for him. Joe Bush was suffering from arm trouble, and Carl Mays had left the team amid conflicting reports. One said that he was called home due to an illness to his wife; another indicated that he was completely frustrated over a lack of support in several tough losses. Also, he had recently been involved in an incident where he had thrown a ball at a fan in the stands and was fined $100, which he refused to pay, believing the team should cover it.

A pitcher's duel between Bill James and Eddie Cicotte resulted in a 3-1 loss to close out the Chicago series. The only Boston run came on Ruth's sacrifice fly in the first, and then Cicotte shut the door. In the ninth, Babe drove a long foul out of the park, then struck out for the second time in the game. The Red Sox were utterly floundering in fifth place, with a record that now stood at 31-40. The pitching staff was hurting, the offense was struggling, and Barrow was being heavily criticized for the sorry state of the World Champions.

The sinking ship sailed on to Cleveland for a four-game engagement commencing July 16. Ruth, in left, went 0 for 2, though he walked and was robbed of a hit by shortstop Ray Chapman. Babe did a little robbing of his own, making a superb one-handed catch in the fifth off Bill Wambsganns, but again Boston lost 3-1.

With the pitching in need of reinforcements, Ruth made his first appearance on the mound in 22 days with his start against the Indians on July 17. Cleveland didn't hit him particularly hard, but bunched hits with walks, scoring one in the second, two in the fourth, and one in the fifth. Ruth went the distance, but Guy Morton was a bit better, shutting Boston down 4-0.

	IP	H	SO	BB
7/17/19 at				
Cleveland	8	9	0	5

At bat: 1 for 4

As of this date, Ruth was listed as tenth in the A.L. in batting at .330.

The Red Sox finally snapped their five-game skid the next day, with Ruth's bat being a major factor. He came up in the fourth with a runner on, and according to the *Post*, he "sent the sphere flying over the rooftops on Lexington Avenue". By the ninth inning, the Indians had taken a 7-4 lead, but Boston had the bases full via bases on balls. With Ruth coming up, Cleveland manager Lee Fohl went to his bullpen and brought in lefty Fritz Coumbe, who hadn't pitched since May. Fohl ordered Coumbe to keep the ball down low, but when he failed, Babe hammered it even farther than his first homer for an 8-7 win. Fohl was heavily criticized, and Coumbe reportedly broke down and cried. Babe, in the meantime, was given a royal reception by the Cleveland fans when he appeared on the field after the game.

Before the final Cleveland game on Saturday, July 19, embattled manager Fohl announced his resignation in the wake of his team's heartrending loss at the hands of Babe Ruth the day before. Tris Speaker was named as his successor, and led by example in his debut, going 3 for 3 in Cleveland's 7-4 win. Ruth, again in leftfield, doubled off the wall in the fifth, and had been intentionally walked in the third.

Detroit was the fourth stop on the tour, and in the opener on the 20th, the Sox' bats came alive. In Herb Pennock's five-hit, 8-0 shutout, Boston recorded 15 hits, and although Babe had five at-bats, not one of the hits was his. The only damage Ruth did this day was to teammate Oscar Vitt, with whom he collided in a desperate attempt to catch a fly. Vitt was forced to leave the game, though luckily for him no bones were broken.

Many Sox players were furious with Carl Mays, who was still away from the team, with rumors swirling that he may be traded to the Yankees. They felt that he should be dealt with severely, and that his desire to be traded not be granted. Ruth was again forced to take a turn in the rotation in Detroit on July 21. He pitched well for four innings, but then seemed to let down a bit. In the third he had walked Bobby Veach on a questionable call by Umpire Dineen, and Ruth and Veach then exchanged words, nearly coming to blows. Babe regained his composure though, and struck out the dangerous Harry Heilmann, but two costly errors by Schang would hurt. Down 6-1 in the ninth, Ruth slugged a solo home run over the rightfield wall and on to Trumbull Ave., which of course was the longest ever at Navin Field.

At this time, conflicting reports were surrounding the team and the presence of dissension in the ranks, as well as Barrow's status as manager. Some were calling for his firing, and Jack Barry was said to be half-expecting to be called back to manage. The players issued a statement signed by every member of the team declaring that there was no dissension and that Barrow was not to blame for the troubles.

On the 22nd, Dutch Leonard topped the Sox 2-1, and Ruth in left went hitless with two strikeouts. In Sam Jones' five-hit 8-1 win in the final Tiger game, Ruth's bat was again rather quiet as he singled in five trips.

The Red Sox then returned from their two-week road trip to a 20-day homestand, beginning against the Yankees. Babe's late-inning heroics gave Herb Pennock a 4-3 complete game win and sent the Fenway fans home happy. In the eighth inning, he came up with Bobby Roth on base and New York holding a slim 3-2 lead. Ruth fouled off Bob Shawkey's first offering, then swung and missed the second. Shortstop Roger Peckinpaugh, among the league's leading hitters at the time hollered in, "You've got his number, burn the ball over and get him easy". With a count of 1 and 2, Ruth knocked the next pitch into the rightfield bleachers, and the score stood at 4-3.

It was Babe's 15th homer of the season, and it seemed a foregone conclusion that not only would he break the A.L. record of 16 set by Chicago's Socks Seybold in 1902, but that Buck Freeman's N.L. record of 25 set in 1899 was in reach.

It was back out to the mound in game two of the Yankees series on July 25 as Ruth was continuing his dual role. Though the going was not smooth, he went the full nine and hung on for the 8-6 win. Ruth struggled, giving up 13 hits and striking out none, and of his teammates, the *Post* wrote " . . . every man behind him [was] anxious to see the good-natured batter hang up a win." In the third inning, he was involved in yet another collision in which the other man wound up on the losing end, this time, Yankees pitcher Allan Russell, who was on third as New York attempted a double steal.

> "Babe covered the plate, gave Russell a bump from his broad shoulder and mussed the New York twirler up so rudely that hard words were the result." *Boston Post 7/26/19*

That day's *Post* also included an article entitled, "Can't Locate Ruth's Alley", which spoke of how pitchers were frustrated by the fact that Ruth hit everything and didn't appear to possess a weakness at the plate. Noted New York writer Sid Mercer was quoted as saying, "'Tis better to give Ruth four bad balls and one base than one good ball and four bases."

Boston suffered a disappointing loss to New York on Saturday the 26th as Sam Jones gave up four runs in the ninth in an 8-5 loss. Ruth, in left, singled in his four at-bats. After the customary Sunday off, the Sox concluded their series with New York on Monday, handing them a 5-1 loss to take three out of four. Babe singled and walked in a game that was viewed from the box seats by Ty Cobb and Tiger manager Hugh Jennings, who had just arrived in town to begin a four-game series.

The Red Sox' 10-8 loss in the first game on Tuesday was overshadowed by Ruth's record-tying 16th home run. He had already slugged two doubles when he came to the plate with two out in the bottom of the ninth. Dutch Leonard had walked Bobby Roth, and tried to sneak the first pitch past Babe, which was promptly deposited in the centerfield bleachers.

The Tigers and Sox engaged in a doubleheader on Wednesday, the 30th of July, and Ruth saw action at all three of his positions that afternoon. Game one was rather uneventful for him as he went 0 for 2 with an intentional walk in the 3-1 loss. Game two saw Ruth start the game on first base, play seven innings there, then was brought in to relieve Bill James at the beginning of the eighth. The Red Sox came back to score two runs in the ninth for a 3-2 win, as Ruth came through with a fine relief stint. In his two innings, Babe struck out three, and the only hit he allowed was a double to Cobb. In his own four at-bats he was held hitless.

It was announced this day that Carl Mays had gotten his wish to be traded, going to the Yankees in exchange for pitchers Allan Russell and Bob McGraw, along with $20,000. Sox players were displeased that he was rewarded for his desertion of the team by being sent to a contender, and though Barrow and Frazee would have preferred to suspend him for the season, they were desperate for pitching help. One interesting piece of information that surfaced was that many Sox players believed that Mays was extremely jealous of Ruth's salary, and that this was a factor in walking out on the team.

The Red Sox closed out the month of July with a 12-inning 2-1 win over Detroit. Ruth, seeing time at both left-field and first base had a strong offensive day with two singles, two doubles, and an RBI in six at-bats. Recently acquired 19-year-old Waite Hoyt, making his first Red Sox appearance pitched the entire 12 innings. He had been picked up from the Baltimore shipyards, having hurled for the Dry-Docks, the team Ruth had nearly jumped to in 1918.

Boston continued to flounder in July, having gone 15-17 for the month, with their overall record now standing at 39-48. With two months remaining, the team stood little chance of rebounding, and all that was left to cheer about was Ruth's slugging and pursuit of the home run record. Not only was he hitting the ball out of the park, he was hitting well all-around, as his .321 average as of this date ranked eighth in the league.

Charles Comiskey's Chicago White Sox came to town to open the month of August with a three-game series, but a rainout on the 1st necessitated a doubleheader on Saturday. New Boston pitcher Allan Russell, who had been involved in the home plate collision with Ruth just a week before started, and pitched seven good innings in the Red Sox 5-3 win in game one. Ruth in leftfield went 0 for 4 against Eddie Cicotte, who took the complete-game loss. Ruth also went 0 for 4 in game two as Herb Pennock pitched a perfect game for six innings, then totally blew up for a 10-1 loss.

After the Sunday off, the two Sox teams went back at it on Monday to close out the series. In Sam Jones' complete-game 2-1 win, Ruth got on base five times without the benefit of a hit. He was walked four times, and was also hit by a pitch, and Arthur Duffey commented in the next day's column: "Poor old Babe was getting out of wind on being passed to first". Also appearing in his column that day:

> "'I can always feel it in my bones when I am going to crack out a four sacker,' claims old friend Babe. But Babe hasn't felt that way for these many a day."

Cleveland came in to replace Chicago as the Sox' Fenway opponent on August 5, and Babe was the center of attention a few times during the 7-5 Boston win. In the second inning he was given a great ovation as he came to bat, and slugged a tremendous drive that Tris Speaker caught up against the flagpole in center. In the fifth, he swung so hard he sent a pop fly to such unbelievable heights, third baseman Larry Gardner grew dizzy waiting for it to come down. A sudden gust of wind blew it out of his reach, and Ruth ended up on second with a double. Ruth also made a stellar defensive play in leftfield, leaping into the air to spear a long linedrive, robbing catcher Steve O'Neil of a double and saving a run in the process. In addition to Babe's double in three at-bats he also scored two of the Boston runs.

The next day's game was washed out, but the Red Sox squeaked out an 8-7 win over Cleveland on Thursday the 7th. In his two official at-bats, Ruth doubled and scored two runs. In *The Sporting News* issue of this date, the editorial page ran an item entitled "Here's to the Home Run Hero" that congratulated Ruth and wished him success in his ambition to become the all-time single season home run champ.

Among the bouquets tossed his way:

> " ...the Babe is just as ready to lay down a bunt under orders as he is to put the ball out of the lot when told to go up there and smash it ...(He) may have faults, but they are chiefly the faults of thoughtless youth ...Babe may rampage now and then, but taking him by and large he's all to the good—a big boy, not long out of his teens, deserving of all the hero worship that has been bestowed upon him .... "

Going into the final Cleveland game on August 8, Ruth was still seeking the record-breaking 17th homer, not having connected in nine days. Indian ace Stan Coveleski held him not only homerless, but hitless as well, as Cleveland scored one in the ninth to win, 5-4.

In the final series of the long homestand, St. Louis came in, starting off with a twin-bill on the 9th. Out of the pitching rotation for the time being, Babe spent both games on the afternoon in leftfield as the teams split the pair. He singled in the first game, which Boston lost, 5-3, and tripled in game two—a thrilling 11-inning, 4-3 win.

With the following day an off-day, Babe drove his automobile down to Bridgeport, Connecticut to appear in a benefit game to raise funds for Tuberculosis sufferers. In the exhibition, he pitched three innings apiece for each team, and hit a few homers that greatly pleased the crowd.

In reporting of Babe's charitable actions, *The Sporting News* referred to him as a "Big-hearted Boy". On the way to Connecticut, Ruth was pulled over by the police for reaching the excessive speed of 45 miles per hour. After explaining his mission to the officer and telling him that he may be late, he was allowed to go on his way.

❧

Boston's off-day was followed by a 1-0 pitcher's duel that Ruth helped to decide in a somewhat unusual manner. In the bottom of the seventh of the scoreless ballgame, Ruth came up with the bases filled. In a show of tremendous respect, Browns pitcher Alan

Sothoron walked Babe, figuring it was better to give the Sox one run than four. He had no way of knowing that the run he walked in would be the only run of the game.

The Browns evened the series at two in the final game as Urban Shocker got the complete game win in the 10-3 shellacking. Ruth singled in the first, but was thrown out at second attempting to stretch it, and also singled later. Among his four putouts in left-field was a noteworthy catch in which he ran to the top of the grassy incline in front of the wall and reached up and caught Joe Gedeon's fly ball with his bare left hand.

Wednesday the 13th was a travel day as the Red Sox were set to begin their two-week midwestern tour in Chicago. Boston opened the series by pounding the first-place White Sox, 15-6, with the main feature of the game being Ruth's record-setting 17th home run. Coming in the seventh inning off Erskine Mayer with one on, the fans marveled at the blast as it cleared the rightfield wall and landed in a soccer field.

8/14/19 at Chicago: At bat: 3 for 4, Hr, 2 singles 2 runs, 2 RBI, 2 walks

The next day the White Sox gave owner Charles Comiskey a 60th birthday present in the form of a 6-5 11-inning victory. Ruth stroked a double, and was robbed of what would likely have been a triple in the first by outfielder Oscar "Happy" Felsch. The 16th of August brought another one-run loss for Boston, 7-6, as the White Sox beat Sam Jones on a squeeze play in the ninth. Ruth added to his new A.L. home run record by putting another one over the rightfield wall—this one being the longest ever at Comiskey.

"Babe took his full swing, which has any swing beaten since the famous Casey fanned, but big Babe didn't fan. He hit the ball a way up and a way out". *Boston Post* 8/17/19

He also added a single in this game, which concluded the series. *Sporting News* White Sox Correspondent George S. Robbins wrote that the series was one of the most interesting ever seen at Comiskey, due in large part to Ruth's status as a big drawing card.

A doubleheader with the Browns awaited the Red Sox upon their arrival in St. Louis on the 17th. Babe drew the starting assignment in game one, his first pitching appearance in 18 days. His presence in St. Louis, where he was extremely popular, no doubt contributed to the largest crowd in the history of Sportsman's Park at around 27,000. Ruth would not disappoint his admirers as he delivered a fine all-around performance. He pitched great in a few tight spots and scored a complete game 2-1 win in the opener. In game two, manning leftfield, he came up in the first and slugged a two-run homer. The two runs were all Boston would need, though they tacked on four more for a 6-1 win and a sweep of the double-header.

	IP	H	SO	BB	WP
8/17/19 at					
St. Louis: 1st game	9	9	3	1	1

1st game: At bat: 0 for 4
2nd game: At bat: 2 for 4, HR, double, 2 RBI

The Red Sox were edged 4-3 by the Browns the next day. With one single in two official at-bats, Babe also reached via walk, and when hit by a pitch, he promptly stole second. Both Boston and Ruth went out meekly in the series finale on the 19th, with the Sox being shut out 5-0 on a one-hitter by Lefty Leifield as Babe produced no hits in three trips. In the *Boston Post* of this day, Arthur Duffey made a couple of noteworthy comments about the slugger:

> "Bigger ballparks make it more difficult for Ruth to reach Buck Freeman's old record. Like groceries, coal, and all the other commodities these days, home runs are hard to get."

and . . .

> "All around the circuit Ruth is a bigger attraction than Ty Cobb. So far on the western trip Babe has delivered at each stand the Red Sox have played."

Next on the agenda for the Red Sox was a three-game set versus Cleveland commencing on Wednesday the 20th. In Boston's 5-2 loss in the first matchup, Babe was 0 for 1, but the respect he had earned as a hitter was evident in the three intentional walks he was issued. Thursday's game was interesting in that Boston's of-fense had a quick burst early, and then completely shut down. Ruth's only hit of the game, a triple in the first drove in two runs, and he then scored one of the two other Sox runs that inning. Boston failed to get another hit the rest of the game, but the four scored in the first were enough as they hung on to beat Speaker's squad, 4-3.

The rubber game of the Cleveland series very nearly saw Ruth repeat his dubious actions of two years before against his old nemesis, Umpire Brick Owens. Babe had been intentionally walked in his first at-bat, and when he came up in the fourth inning, the count would be worked to three and two. With two out and a runner on first, only one run was needed to tie the score, but on the next delivery, Owens signaled a called third strike. Ruth angrily threw his bat toward the Boston dugout, and as the *Post* reported " . . . never said more in a minute in his life nor said it more vehemently." During Ruth's verbal tirade, Owens pretended not to hear, and then Babe finally started to walk toward his outfield position.

He then turned back at Owens, hurled a few more epithets, and took a few steps toward him with clenched fists. As Ruth came near, Owens took a firmer grip on his face mask with thoughts of self-defense in mind, but Indians catcher Chet Thomas stepped between the two as he had done two years before, and this time prevented a physical confrontation. Owens then ejected Ruth without further incident, and the Sox went on to lose, 10-7.

The traveling road show moved on to Detroit, where Ruth really did put on quite a show. The August 23 opener featured one unusual happening as Cobb, Heilmann, and Chick Shorten pulled off a triple steal with Ty scoring on the front end. The real fireworks that got spectators buzzing was Babe's grand slam off Hooks Dauss in the third, which not surprisingly was the longest ever hit at Navin Field. His only hit of the game, the slam would account for all the Boston runs as the Tigers prevailed, 8-4.

Ruth continued his assault on Detroit pitching the next day, beginning with his first at-bat. With one on he struck a towering blow, and came back in the sixth inning with a solo shot. As much as Babe had done to help his team win, he would need to do just a little more as the game went into extra innings. In the 11th he lashed a single to drive in Harry Hooper with the deciding run in the 8-7 game.

8/24/19 at Detroit (left-field)
At bat: 3 for 5, 2 HR, 4 RBI, 3 runs

On the final day in Detroit, Ruth hit yet another homer—his fourth in three days, which now brought his total up to 23 on the campaign. He added a single that day in the Sox 5-4 win, as Boston was set to return home having gone six and six on the western tour. On their return to town, Arthur Duffey commented in his column:

> "No wonder Harry Frazee's wearing that smile that won't come off in signing Babe Ruth to a three-year contract. Guess any other big-league magnate would feel the same way about it if they had such a star delivering as the Babe has been this season."

The Sox were set to kick off their first day back in Boston with a doubleheader against Connie Mack's Athletics, but rain would prevent all but six innings of the first game from being played. Young Waite Hoyt was hit hard, and the umps pulled the plug at the beginning of the seventh, with Philly leading 6-4. Ruth had scored one of the runs on his only hit, a triple of which Paul Shannon wrote: "(He) hoisted out one three-bagger that for altitude had anything ever seen at Fenway Park beaten by a city block."

The next day, Thursday, the two teams were able to complete a doubleheader, splitting the pair. Boston went down 8-3 in the opener with Ruth singling, walking, and scoring two in three official trips. Herb Pennock twirled a three-hit, 2-0 shutout in game two, nosing out the A's Jing Johnson, who pitched a four-hitter. Of the seven combined hits, all were singles, and Ruth's lone hit, which came in the fifth was the Sox first hit.

In the final game with Philadelphia, the Red Sox evened the series at two on the strength of a 7-1 win. Though Ruth walked and scored a run, he was officially 0 for 3, striking out twice against old scuffling partner Walt Kinney.

The team took the train down to D.C. following the game to play the Senators on Saturday, the 30th, but rain put the teams on hold until Sunday. Ruth was appearing in his 14th straight game in leftfield, and of the game Paul Shannon wrote: "Despite the savage whaling of the ball by Babe Ruth . . . ", the Sox still lost 6-2. After singling in the fourth, he scored on Scott's single, and in the ninth he came up with two outs to face Walter Johnson. The fireballer had relieved starter Tom Zachary in the eighth, and Ruth reached him for a double, but was stranded and the game ended.

Having gone just 14-13 for the month of August, it was painfully clear the Red Sox were going nowhere. The fans' main focus now was not where the team would finish in the standings, but rather how many home runs Babe would hit. He was performing as a full-time outfielder this month, as out of the 27 games the Sox had played in August, he was in left-field for 26 of them. Ruth's only pitching appearance had been his 2-1 victory in St. Louis on the 17th.

The arrival of September, however, saw Ruth make his return to the mound, starting the first game of a doubleheader back in Boston against Washington on the 1st. The Labor Day crowd jammed into Fenway Park, and cheered wildly each time Ruth came in from the mound.

> "Hats off to Big Babe Ruth, Boston battering ram and the uncrowned King of Fenway Park. If ever a monarch received the adoring adulation of his subjects…then Boston's mighty swatter, the champion slugger of all time gave such an exhibition yesterday and nearly 30,000 fans… lured by the reputation of Boston's home run king, paid tribute to our Babe last night."

Included in his crowd-pleasing performance that day was a complete-game 2-1 win, and though he gave up ten hits he was never in real trouble. At bat he was involved in both Sox runs— tripling in the third to drive in Roth, and scoring on a subsequent single. He came back playing left in the second game and again had just one hit, but he made it count. With one out in the seventh and the score tied at one, Babe showed his flair for the dramatic by slugging his 24th homer into the rightfield seats, receiving a grand ovation as the Sox went on to win, 4-1. After the game, he was hoisted onto the shoulders of enthusiastic fans and carried to the dugout.

Ruth was one home run away from tying Buck Freeman's mark, however, further research uncovered that Ned Williamson of the N.L.'s Chicago White Stockings had hit 27 back in 1884. Most seemed reluctant to accept the mark due to the exceedingly small park in Chicago in which Williamson played his home games.

The Yankees came into Boston to begin a series on Tuesday, September 2, but rain wiped out the entire set. It was that Wednesday that Arthur Duffey commented in the *Post,* "They're arguing now as to who has the greater wallop—Jack Dempsey or Babe Ruth". He also reported rumors that Ruth might be offered a movie role for the upcoming off-season.

Not having played since Monday, the Sox opened a week-end series at Philadelphia's Shibe Park on Friday the 5th. The Red Sox bats, including Ruth's, exploded in the 15-7 win as the contest featured a few noteworthy happenings. Boston pulled off a triple play in the second inning, and by the seventh they had built up a 15-1 lead on their way to setting a major-league record with 25 hits in the game. The biggest noise came in the third off Babe's bat, as his prodigious blast left the park and landed on 21st St. On the fifth anniversary of his first professional home run, he had now tied Freeman with his 25th of the season. He almost hit another in his next at-bat as his double off the wall was six inches shy of a home run.

9/5/19 at Philadelphia: At bat: 5 for 6, Hr, double, 3 runs

Boston closed out the Philly series the following day by sweeping both ends of a doubleheader, 11-3 and 5-3. Ruth played left in both, and in the first game, though officially 0 for 2, he also walked three times and was hit by a pitch. In game two he had just a single in four trips. That day, Arthur Duffey indicated that Ruth had signed a deal for $10,000 to appear in a movie, and commented "Probably it is a good thing that Harry Frazee signed up Babe to a three-year contract. Ten thousand for each film certainly is softer picking than playing a whole season's baseball."

With a day off on the 7th, the Sox shot over to Baltimore to play an exhibition against a team in the shipyard league. Fans got what they wanted to see, as Ruth hit two homers, and Frazee was predicting that the slugger would top Freeman's mark tomorrow in New York.

Fifteen thousand New York fans turned out at the Polo Grounds for the Monday doubleheader with big expectations. In the third inning of game one, in his desire to rip the cover off the ball, Ruth struck out on a vicious swing. In the bottom of that inning he crashed into the wall in left-field chasing a foul ball and hurt his elbow, but was able to stay in. Hitless so far, he came to the plate facing lefty Hank Thormahlen and gave the crowd what they wanted to see—a drive deep into the rightfield pavilion.

"When Babe had crossed the plate his face was wreathed with a big broad smile and he was compelled to doff his lid several times on the way to the bench." *Boston Post* 9/9/19

The clout had helped Boston defeat New York, 3-1, in game one, and in game two Ruth doubled and scored two runs in Waite Hoyt's impressive three-hit shutout for a sweep.

The *Post* ran a story at this time which contained an interview with Buck Freeman, who was now umpiring in the American Association. He said of Ruth:"I must congratulate him on his great work. Look at his wrists and you will find that they are tremendous. A man that hits as hard as he does must have abnormal development of the wrist and forearm." The *Post* also ran an article on Babe that contained the sub-title "Clouting Hercules Is One of Celebrities of Country".

The games of September 9 and 10 were rained out, and Ruth spent one of these evenings at Boston's Colonial Theater. He had gone to see Raymond Hitchcock, who performed a musical comedy revue, and when the audience realized Babe was among them, there was such a stir that he had to call him up to the stage and introduce him. His popularity had grown so enormous that fans were constantly asking for one of his home run bats, and admiring females were sending such a volume of mail that the entire team had to help him read it.

The Red Sox took a seven-game winning streak into their September 11 doubleheader with St. Louis at Fenway. Ruth's double, single, and run scored contributed to Herb Pennock's 4-0 shutout in the opener, but he went hitless in Allan Russell's 6-0 shutout in game two. Cleveland was Boston's next guest, in to start a series on Friday the 12th, and like the first game of the day before, Ruth doubled, singled, and scored once. Starter Sam Jones gave up three in the ninth though, and the Indians came from behind to win 4-3, stopping the Sox streak.

Cleveland prevailed by the same 4-3 score the next day as well, and though Ruth was 0 for 2, he did drive in a run with a sacrifice fly. The crowd, not happy to see the bat taken out of his hands, howled their disapproval when Elmer Myers walked him in the third to get to Wally Schang. In the next day's *Post*, Arthur Duffey expressed the belief that Babe's home run record will give other sluggers something to challenge for many years to come, and he also revealed Ruth's desire to establish a new golf driving record.

With the two teams off on Sunday, the Sox trekked down to New Haven, Connecticut for the day and squared off against a local squad in front of 4,500 fans at Lighthouse Point. The team, which featured Babe's future close friend Joe Dugan of the Athletics was beaten by Boston, 6-3. Ruth played first base that day, and in a pre-game ceremony was presented a $100 diamond pin by the New Haven Knights of Columbus.

Back in Boston, the final Cleveland game on the 15th was washed out as was the start of the Tiger series the next day. This set the stage for a doubleheader with Ty Cobb and company on September 17. Ruth's contribution in the opener was a double and a run scored, and the Sox went down, 7-6. One feature of the contest was Cobb, who struck out twice, getting ejected along with manager Hugh Jennings by Umpire Moriarty. The second game saw Tiger lefty Dutch Leonard lose a 2-1, three-hit heartbreaker, with Ruth going hitless. The teams wrapped up their brief series the next day, and Babe's only safety was a double in Boston's 8-2 loss.

The Chicago White Sox, on the verge of officially clinching the A.L. pennant, arrived in town for three games. On a dubious historical note, it is believed that the plot to intentionally lose the upcoming World Series was hatched during these days the White Sox were spending in Boston. Covert meetings were taking place at the Buckminster Hotel in Kenmore Square, in the shadows of Fenway Park.

September 19, 12 days before the fateful Fall Classic was to begin, Boston faced future conspirator Eddie Cicotte. Babe drove in the Red Sox first run on a groundout in the first, then sent across the second run with his double in the third, which tied the game. That was the extent of Ruth's offensive production, and that of the Red Sox as well, as Chicago nipped them 3-2.

The teams staged a doubleheader the next day, Saturday the 20th, and this was to be among the most special days to date in the baseball career of the 24-year-old slugging hero. It was officially declared "Babe Ruth Day," as he was to be honored between games of the twin-bill by the Knights of Columbus' Pere Marquette Council of South Boston, of which Babe himself was a member.

The outpouring of love and affection for him was evident as an overflow crowd of 31,000 jammed the Back Bay ballyard. Grandstand seats normally selling for 85 cents were being sold at the box office for $1.10, and 5,000 fans bought standing-room tickets, some standing behind ropes deep in the outfield.

Given the opportunity by Barrow to showcase all of his skills for his adoring fans, Babe took the mound to start game one. In the sixth inning with one out, having given up three runs on nine hits, Allan Russell was brought in to relieve Ruth. With Oscar

"Happy" Felsch having doubled, Ruth had now thrown his last official pitch as a member of the Red Sox.

In order to keep his potent bat in the lineup, Barrow sent him to leftfield to replace Bill Lamar for the duration of the game. Russell held Chicago hitless the rest of the way, and the teams went into the bottom of the ninth tied at three. With one out, Ruth, hitless so far, reached down and golfed an outside pitch from Lefty Williams over the leftfield wall to win the game as the crowd went wild. Williams, unable to hide his disgust, threw his glove out into leftfield.

Between games, the ceremony began, as Babe and Mrs. Ruth walked out to home plate and proceeded to accept many tokens of appreciation from the Knights. Among the gifts were $600 worth of U.S. Treasury certificates, cuff links, a fountain pen, and new spiked shoes in his size 11. Helen was presented with a traveling bag, and even Babe's teammates were each given a box of cigars. In all, it was considered the greatest day ever given to an athlete in Boston sports history.

Babe continued to make an impact on the field in game two, again serving in left. In the fifth inning he hit a terrific wallop that many claimed bounced into the bleachers for a homer, but was ruled a double by Umpire Billy Evans. He subsequently scored in Boston's 5-4 win, now having scored the winning run in both games on the day.

This game would close out the season at Fenway for the Red Sox as they were now heading out on the road for their final five games of the season. Boston baseball fans would have scores of opportunities to watch Babe Ruth play in person over the next decade and a half, but never again would it be while wearing the home white uniform of the Boston Red Sox.

ॐ

After a day off on Sunday the 21st, the Sox journeyed up to Portland, Maine for an exhibition on Monday. A rainout in New York on Tuesday forced a doubleheader versus the Yankees the following afternoon. The teams split the pair, the Sox shutting out New York in the opener 4-0, with Ruth going 0 for 3 and scoring a run. The Yanks then topped Boston 2-1 with Babe's 28th home run, now rendering him unequivocally the all-time single season record holder over old Ned Williamson. The homer, a patented Ruth blast over the rightfield grandstand came off Bob Shawkey in the ninth, tying the game until New York scored the game winner in the 13th.

On the way down to D.C. for the final series of 1919, the Red Sox stopped in Lancaster, Pennsylvania, to tangle with the Klein Chocolate Company team. A surprisingly close match, the Sox topped the men in brown, 3-1.

The next day, Saturday, Boston played its 22nd and final doubleheader of the season, as they were hosted by the Senators. The Red Sox erupted for five runs in game one's third inning, but that would be the extent of their scoring in the 7-5 loss. The two-run homer Ruth launched during the rally off Rip Jordan, which cleared the 45-foot wall in rightfield with 20 feet to spare accomplished three main things: it added further to his new home run record; it fulfilled his goal of hitting a homer in every A.L. park this season; and as had happened in each of these parks, it became the longest home run anyone had ever seen at Griffith Stadium.

The home run would also turn out to be Ruth's final official hit in a Boston Red Sox uniform, as he was replaced in leftfield by Roth in game two after one hitless at-bat. Babe had agreed to appear in an exhibition game in nearby Baltimore on Sunday, the 29th, and Barrow reportedly allowed him to skip the season finale in Washington that day. Many Washington baseball fans were said to be greatly disappointed at missing the chance to see him swing, and Ruth himself missed the chance at his 30th homer, which was believed to be a goal of his. One might speculate however, that as the star attraction at the Baltimore exhibition, Ruth was compensated rather handsomely.

With the Red Sox having been swept in their season-ending series with Washington, the record would show that the defending World Champions' 66 wins and 71 losses would land them in sixth place for 1919. The team had simply never gotten in gear, and since dropping below the .500 mark on May 22, they never again would rise above it.

❧

There was little doubt now that Ruth was regarded as primarily an outfielder, having spent 81 percent of the team's games there (111 of 137 games) as well as four others at first. With the utterly dominating offensive year he had posted, it would have been difficult to imagine him ever making a full-time return to the mound.

Several facts regarding his home run output alone are staggering: of the 33 homers hit by the Red Sox, only four were not hit by Ruth; ten of the other 15 major league teams hit less homers as a team than Ruth did individually; and the major leaguer who finished second to Ruth in homers for the '19 season was Gavvy Cravath with a mere 12.

Aside from Babe's major league lead in home runs, he also topped the majors in RBI, runs, slugging percentage, home run percentage, and total bases, and was second in walks.

His batting statistics for 1919 looked like this:

Games	AB	H	2B	3B	HR	HR%	R	RBI	BB	SO	SB
130	432	139	34	12	29	6.7	103	114	101	58	7

His pitching had become sporadic by '19, making just 17 appearances for the season, and going to the mound only three times in August and September.

Babe's pitching statistics for 1919 were as follows:

W	L	Pct.	ERA	G	GS	CG	IP	H	BB	SO	ShO	Sv
9	5	.643	2.97	17	15	12	133.1	148	58	30	0	1

Excepting his brief stint with the Red Sox in 1914, Ruth had just completed his fifth full season with the team. Still just 24 years old, he was without question the mightiest slugger the game had ever known, who also possessed a lifetime batting average of .308. He was, because of his bat, the biggest drawing card in the sport, yet he could also be counted on to pitch any given day and provide his team with a good chance to win. And arguably, he was the most valuable baseball player in the country at this juncture. As in 1918, if an MVP-type award had existed at this time, he would very likely have been its recipient. It is difficult to place a dollar value on this extraordinary type of talent, yet in a few short months, the attempt would be made.

ès

Babe re-joined his teammates after the Baltimore exhibition on September 28 and traveled up to Portland, Maine for an engagement versus a team of Maine All-Stars on the 30th. Typically, Ruth pleased the crowd at Bayside Park as he slugged a home run to help the Red Sox win 8-6. It had also been reported in the *Boston American* of September 29 that Babe was to make a guest appearance as an umpire of an Army-Navy baseball game in nearby Malden, Massachusetts to be played in honor of returning servicemen.

While the Chicago White Sox were in the process of authoring one of baseball's sorriest chapters, Babe was continuing his barnstorming with a game in the northern Boston suburb of Lynn. Playing on October 3 with a team called the Cornets, Babe toiled at first base and went 4 for 5, including a double and a two-run homer. It was not good enough, however, as the Cornets fell to the Red Sox, 9-8.

On that same day, a report came out of Chicago that stated that Babe had "torn up" his three-year contract. Naming a source that was "close to Ruth", the *Boston Herald* reported that he "based this astonishing action on the belief that he is doing himself an injustice not to better himself in any way possible." Babe apparently based this action on the way that Carl Mays had "put across" his transfer to the Yankees during the season resulting in a considerable raise for the cantankerous submarine pitcher. The report concluded "any such action would be condemned among baseball men as a flagrant injustice to the Frazee ownership and a breach of faith, as well as contract on Ruth's part." It would prove to be the straw that broke the back of Harry Frazee and set into motion a chain of events that would continue to reverberate throughout the baseball world many decades later.

The next day, October 4, Babe ventured to Attleboro, Massachusetts for yet another game. This small city near the Rhode Island border, about 35 miles southwest of Boston was the scene of what would come to be known to many as the "Little World Series". Attleboro and its neighbor, North Attleboro, were intense rivals, and had for several years played a post-season series for local bragging rights. This particular year's series took on special meaning as the towns decided that money would not be spared in fielding the best possible teams. They set out at once to sign up every available major leaguer to fill their rosters, and the participants in some of the games included Walter Johnson, Zack Wheat, and Sam Rice to name a few.

Ruth was brought into the game, and was believed to have been paid about 500 dollars to play the fifth and final game for North Attleboro. He arrived by auto that morning, accompanied by Helen and a personal secretary. The red carpet was rolled out as he was immediately taken to the Elk's Club for a reception, then given a tour of many local businesses, and shook hands with scores of youngsters.

Eight thousand people gathered at Attleboro's Brady Field to witness Ruth take the field for the North team, outfitted in his Red Sox road uniform. The North Attleboro Knights of Columbus honored him in a pre-game ceremony, presenting him with yet another diamond ring. He played leftfield, and in his four at-bats, his only hit was a single to rightfield in the fifth inning. His teammate Bobby Roth was the star that day as his pinch hit three-run homer in the eighth inning led North Attleboro to a 6-3 win. As the crowd watched Babe patrol leftfield, they had no way of knowing that his days of playing in a Red Sox uniform were down to a precious few.

On October 14, a banquet was held for Ruth by the members of the Greater Boston Councils of the Knights of Columbus at the city's Quincy House. Babe was presented with still another diamond ring, and Helen was the recipient of a large bouquet of flowers. He was continuing to play with a local K. of C. team and also continuing to wallop home runs, and reports began to circulate that Babe was headed to California to both make movies and play in west coast exhibitions during the winter. Amid what had now become the annual off-season rumor that the Red Sox would be sold, the *Boston Herald* stated that Babe wanted $20,000 from the Red Sox to play in 1920 or he would insist on being traded.

On October 25, Babe went to Fenway Park to turn in his two Red Sox uniforms from the 1919 season. He did not meet with Frazee, as he had left town for New York the night before. Leaving Fenway Park on that Fall afternoon, Babe had no idea of the significance of returning his uniforms, and in hindsight, it could be considered a "turning in of his Red Sox career". As he strolled out the door on to Jersey Street and walked past the seven-year-old ballpark, he didn't know that the next time he visited Fenway Park he would be a member of the New York Yankees.

Seven

The Transaction:
Sale of the Century

As Babe and Helen prepared to head for Los Angeles, an account in the *Boston Herald* declared Babe the world record holder for earnings in baseball for one year. Bob Dunbar chronicled how Babe had earned $2,500 to play in two exhibition games on the 18th and 19th of October. He was scheduled to make $10,000 for his stint in the Pacific Coast League, and then of course his salary with the Red Sox. "Babe's receipts from the Red Sox this last year were $15,000, not $9,000 or $10,000, as reported at various times. He was handed a $5,000 present, bonus, or what ever you call it by Owner Frazee a few days after that wonderful 'Ruth Day at the Fens.'"

Dunbar projected from April 1, 1919 to April 1, 1920, Babe would earn $27,500, surpassing Cobb, Speaker and Johnson as the highest paid player in baseball.

On November 2, 1919, a *Boston Post* front-page story accompanied with a photo of Babe and Helen arriving in Los Angeles, corroborated the Dunbar story. "Babe's income for 1919 will soar to a lofty figure. He has already received $10,000 for his services to the Red Sox team during the regular season. It is said that he also received a bonus from President Frazee at the close of the season for his excellent work during the 1919 campaign."

Babe made an instant impact on the Pacific Coast League. Traveling as a member of Buck Weaver's all-star team, he picked up where he had left off during the season. Smashing home runs at a prodigious rate and in that high-arcing manner that had become his trademark, he instantly had some writers wondering if he would not hit as many as 100 home runs were he to play a full season in the California league.

He was making an impact off the field as well. Demanding a payment of $10,000 before he would even set foot on a movie set, did not endear him to the hearts of the Hollywood magnates. It virtually ended his stint at a movie career before it even began. He would have to wait several more years before making his debut as a celluloid hero. This, coupled with the fact that one of his first comments about Los Angeles was that he didn't particularly care for the weather, left fans leery of this young brash ballplayer from the East.

By the time he arrived in Oakland around the 10th of November, he had already been booed by fans at a game in Los Angeles, because he had only doubled in four at bats and struck out twice. It did not take long for Babe to figure out that California was not Boston. In Oakland, rumors began to circulate again that Babe was on the verge of leaving baseball for a career in the boxing ring. This time, there were whispers of a possible title fight with reigning heavyweight champ Jack Dempsey.

The California press had turned out to interview Babe upon his arrival in the Bay city. For most of them, this was their first encounter with the Colossus who had taken baseball by storm. Briefed on his background and home run accomplishments, they waited for their chance to experience Babe first hand. He stunned them when he opened by telling them of his intention to "lick Ty Cobb on sight."

He was furious at quotes attributed to Cobb, which labeled him a "contract violator". Responding to Cobb's allegations, Ruth was quoted in *The Sporting News* of November 13, 1919: "A player is worth just as much as he can get, and Cobb has been paid all that he is worth, believe me, for quite a few years. I wouldn't say anything against Cobb if he held out for $100,000, why should he say anything about me? He ought to be tickled to see any player get as much as he can. I'll settle the question when I meet Cobb". Babe made no bones about the fact that he might substitute his fists for words when he next encountered the Georgia Peach.

At the end of November, the rumors intensified. *The Sporting News* reported that Babe's holdout was "more serious . . . than is generally believed in the East." A world tour was also mentioned, with reports that he would take his show on the road to such far away places as Honolulu and even Australia. Some saw this as just another negotiation ploy, and some were concerned that Babe was genuinely pursuing financial alternatives to playing for the Red Sox. *The Sporting News* viewed the situation in light of Carl Mays' departure from the Red Sox during the 1919 season when they wrote this of Babe's holdout. ". . . He has been analyzing the celebrated Mays case, and has arrived at the conclusion that a contract is not binding on a baseball star who chooses to disregard it and elects to shift to some other club. Some . . . even hint Babe has picked his club, a la Mays, that he too would join the Yankees."

December opened with a resurgence of talk that Babe would enter the ring. This time, however there was a new twist. A report out of Los Angeles said that Kid McCoy, a former boxer turned movie actor, would train him for 30 days and then evaluate Ruth as a boxer. If things were favorable, McCoy would then arrange a bout with Jack Dempsey for the world heavyweight championship. Upon hearing of this, Boston sportswriter Neal O'Hara wrote, "If Babe Ruth ever tackles Dempsey, he'll learn he hits a right-hander the same as a southpaw." The same release reported that Babe had officially abandoned his attempt to become a movie actor.

The Boston press did not see this threat to enter the fight game as anything but a ruse in which to gain an edge on Frazee. With his movie career temporarily interrupted and Babe not playing baseball every day, this left plenty of time for golf. Playing 54 holes a day, Babe was honing his game. He often would play with Buck Weaver of the 1919 Chicago White Sox. It was Weaver who had put together the team on which Babe was playing as they barnstormed the coast of California.

In October, Weaver was one of the eight members of the Chicago White Sox who were in on "throwing" the series to the Cincinnati Reds. It is interesting to speculate on what Babe and Buck may have talked about during their time together on the links and while traveling playing baseball. There is no evidence to suggest that Ruth was aware or became aware of the inner machinations of the 1919 White Sox World Series, however there was a vague reference to an incident that occurred toward the end of the year in a card game in Los Angeles and was reported in the *Boston Post.*

Ironically it was Babe who was portrayed as the villain in this particular circumstance. "There is a little story going around over a little scene that Ruth created over a card game with Buck Weaver of the White Sox as his particular target, which has not added to his [Babe's] popularity in sporting circles as Buck is very well thought of here not only as a ball player but as a Man." There was no mention of the specifics of the incident nor its precipitant, but it is now clear that the careers of Ruth and Weaver were at a crossroads headed in two distinctly opposite directions.

Throughout the month of December, Boston sportswriters speculated on how the Red Sox could improve over their dismal 1919 showing. Their weakness was pitching and would continue to be so, as Babe was now certain to be an every day player. To replace him as a premier left-handed pitcher would be no easy task. Frazee satisfied many when he acquired Harry Harper from the Washington Senators. A 25-year-old left-hander who had showed great promise in his early career, Harper had a terrible year in '19 going 6-21. He had always, however, been very effective against the Red Sox. Paul Shannon of the *Post* wrote "it could mean the 1920 pennant."

While Babe played golf in California and lobbied for his $20,000 annual salary, Frazee, shuffling back and forth between New York and Boston, had made up his mind and hints of his intentions began to appear. On December 21, the following headline appeared on page one of the sports section of the *Boston Sunday Post:* "BABE RUTH IN MARKET FOR A TRADE."

Two accompanying sub headings read: "Frazee states he will sell or trade any Red Sox player but Harry Hooper" and "Figure Ruth is disturbing element and make club a one-man team." Calling Ruth's contract position "untenable" Paul Shannon stated that neither Frazee or Barrow would consent to an interview to discuss the matter but offered his view on the possibilities of Babe moving on. "Red Sox fans need not be greatly astonished if the burly batter is allowed to pass on through some deal . . . popular as Ruth is with his mates, as good hearted, generous and open handed as all know . . . the Red Sox have of late become a one-man team and this fact has hurt morale considerably."

New York was mentioned as the potential club involved and Shannon stated that a trade rather than a flat-out sale might better be accepted by the Boston sporting public. He even went so far as to suggest that if the Yankees would give up; "an infielder, an outfielder and first string twirler . . . the fans would endorse the move." Shannon concluded by summarizing where Babe now stood in the eyes of the city; his "attitude, while putting a big dent in his popularity in the Hub, has irritated the Red Sox management, who are beginning to look upon the burly batter as a second Frankenstein."

The Red Sox fans were on notice— "Tarzan","Hercules","Cave Man","The Colossus","The Mauler","The Clouter","The Burly Batter",The Babe, was on the block.

As 1919 drew to a close, many speculated about the value of Ruth.When the St. Louis Cardinals were offered $70,000 plus four players for 23-year-old Rogers Hornsby,the question on everyone's mind was:What is Babe worth?Arthur Duffey of the *Post* answered the question by stating what he felt Ruth was not worth in salary terms,"If Eddie Collins andTy Cobb are worth $15,000 to theWhite Sox and theTigers,is not Babe Ruth worth $30,000 to the Red Sox? He is NOT!!"   The idea of a baseball player making that kind of money was thought absurd by most and obscene by many.

Two days before Christmas, the Red Sox sold Del Gainer to Toronto of the International League. Dick Hoblitzell had signed on to manage a minor league team in Akron, Ohio and had signed Jim Thorpe to a contract. Grover Cleveland Alexander declined an offer to become the pitching coach of the University of Illinois baseball team and teach a University course on the science of pitching. On the 30th of December,the aforementioned deal for Harry Harper was struck. The Sox got Harper, infielder Eddie Foster and outfielder Mike Menosky for Bobby Roth and Maurice Shannon.

On the last day of the year, Harold G. Reynolds, the Sporting Editor of the *Boston Post,* wrote a piece from LosAngeles on Babe's current contract situation. Under a headline which read "BABE WILL PLAY WITH RED SOX", Reynolds outlined why Babe would be back in Boston.Calling his talk of retirement,becoming an actor, and a boxer a "bluff", Reynolds wrote the following:"You couldn't keep Babe out of the national game unless you sentenced him to jail, and then probably he would organize a prison league. Ruth is not given credit for possessing any too much gray matter when it comes to business matters,but he is wise enough to know that he is lost unless he is with organized baseball."Within the story there was however a foreboding sentence which read in part;"unless Harry Frazee, the owner of the Boston Americans decides to dispose of the slugging star before the season opens." The announcement of the transaction was less than a week away.

Ruth's acquisition by the New York Yankees was front-page news in both Boston and NewYork.The smallest of newspapers, in hundreds of communities across the country, did not escape without, at least, a tiny blip about the sale. To crystallize the events surrounding the sale of Babe Ruth can best be done by examining and exploring four different and equally important aspects of the deal. They are: Red Sox owner Harry Frazee; the reaction of the media and fans; Babe Ruth himself; and last but certainly not least the gloom that has seemingly hung over the Boston franchise since Ruth's sale which somehow seems to mystically perpetuate as an heirloom to Red Sox fans even today.

ﺀﺎ

Harry H. Frazee: the best that could be said of him is that he was much maligned in Boston. The worst, and closest to accurate, is that he was reviled. Looked upon with scorn and disdain, he may have been the only man that youngsters in Boston learned to hate before they even knew his name. To many he was simply the "Guy who sold Babe Ruth."

Purchasing the Red Sox in November 1916 from Joseph Lannin for, what was reported to be, somewhere between $675,000 and $750,000, Frazee had Ruth in his employ for exactly three baseball seasons. In those three years, the Red Sox finished in second place in 1917, nine games behind the White Sox. First in '18, capturing the World Series and sixth in '19, 20 1/2 games out.

Taking the reigns from Lannin, Frazee, at 36 years old, was the youngest owner in baseball. Initially looked upon warily by Boston writers and fans, he endeared himself to both when by the end of 1916 he offered Clark Griffith of Washington $60,000 for Walter Johnson. Leaving the '16 team pretty much intact—and why wouldn't he—Frazee became very active when the call to arms in 1917 decimated the Red Sox. It was the addition of Strunk, McInnis, Schang, and Bullet Joe Bush that was critical to the Red Sox' success in 1918. By the end of the '18 season, Frazee had established himself as a hands on owner willing to do whatever was necessary to procure a winning franchise.

When Ban Johnson and the rest of the National Commission received the work or fight order of 1918, it was Frazee who spearheaded the drive to postpone it from July 1 to September to get in close to a normal season. Frazee was a driving force behind the many ceremonies held throughout the American League, during the 1918 season, in which the proceeds were donated to the Red

Cross. It was Harry H. himself who attempted, more than once, during the '18 campaign to set up a World Series to take to Europe and play before the boys at the front in France. Continually rebuked, or ignored, his idea never got off the ground.

Looking at the game as it was in 1918, Frazee had the vision to see the need for a "one-man commission" to sit at the head of Major League Baseball. Acting unilaterally at one point, Frazee offered the job to former President and Supreme Court Justice William Howard Taft. Astute a politician as he was, Taft gracefully declined his offer as not to become entrenched in the inner wars of baseball. Frazee's vision proved accurate, and one need to simply review the state of the game in the 1990s to see how sorely missed was that "one-man commission".

It has been written and chronicled throughout the years that Frazee was in desperate financial straits at the time that Ruth was sold. One story line goes that Frazee sold Ruth so he would have the money to finance a play entitled "No, No Nanette". Many a Red Sox fan is raised to understand that this is why Babe Ruth became a Yankee. For some inexplicable reason, this play and the sale of Babe Ruth have for years been linked. The reality is that H.H. Frazee's production of "No, No, Nanette" did not debut until 1924 at a Frazee-owned theater in Chicago and did not reach Broadway until September 16, 1925, two years after he had sold the team to Bob Quinn.

The Boston newspapers from the years of Ruth's tenure with the Red Sox, reveal nothing of financial difficulties on the part of Frazee. The 1918 attendance had dropped off by 138,343 but this was the result of the abbreviated war schedule. Besides, the 1919 attendance had rebounded to 417,291, an increase of nearly 168,000 and was the team's best attendance in the seven years of Frazee's ownership. In short, the notion that Frazee was looking for cash to finance his theatrical ambitions, and he saw Babe as the vehicle to procure that cash, appears inaccurate. It may be a more accurate appraisal of the subsequent sale of the many more who followed Babe to New York and the ultimate sale of the entire team in 1923. Harry's financial squeeze of late 1919 was more of a more immediate nature and would remain veiled until February of 1920.

On February 9, 1920 attorneys for Joseph Lannin, former owner of the Red Sox, and Harry Frazee were in a Boston courtroom. Frazee had given Lannin a note for $262,000 when he had purchased the team in 1916. Lannin asserted that Frazee owed him $125,000 (interesting figure) which was due on November 1, 1919 and had not been paid. An injunction by Lannin was sought and gained, preventing Frazee from "disposing of any of the stock or assets of the club and even from drawing any money out of the club", and an auction date was set for March 3. Frazee's contention was that he only owed $60,000, which he was ready to pay "anytime Lannin is willing to concede to Frazee the amount that is due." Frazee claimed that he had paid roughly $65,000 in debts that were the responsibility of Lannin.

The courts agreed with Lannin, and set March 3 as the date on which Fenway Park would go up for auction. That date would eventually be moved to March 10 and then cancelled as Frazee and Lannin settled their differences out of court and away from the public eye. It was at this time that the public became aware that Frazee's purchase price for the team in 1916 was $1 million.

The idea that Frazee was a tightwad and a skinflint is simply inaccurate. This especially applies in the case of Ruth. Frazee gave into his contract demands when he signed him in 1919 to a three-year deal. He repeatedly allowed him to play, and receive pay, on barnstorming teams, even though under the conditions of his contract he could have denied him the opportunity to do so. There were even times, during the season, when Babe was allowed to leave the team to participate in an exhibition game in which he would make an extra $500.

Much has been made of the fact, and Babe himself so stated, that on Babe Ruth Day at Fenway Park near the close of the 1919 season, Harry presented Babe with a nickel cigar. Frazee himself claimed that when Babe came to him during the 1919 season and lamented the fact that he could not achieve his pitching bonuses because he was playing the outfield, Frazee paid him anyway. Two reports in the Boston papers tell of Babe receiving a bonus from Frazee. One of them even went so far as to print that Frazee presented Ruth with the aforementioned $5,000 bonus for his record-breaking year of 1919. In light of this, does it become difficult to understand that when Babe mailed back his unsigned contract for the 1920 season and demanded, through the newspapers from 3,000 miles away, a doubling of his salary, that Frazee had simply had enough?

Despite Harry's suspected financial woes, there is no reason not to think that when he decided to move Ruth, he still would have preferred players over cash. Evidence to suggest this comes in the fact that Frazee offered Ruth, straight up, to the White Sox for Shoeless Joe Jackson and was refused by Charles Comiskey. This plus the fact that when Frazee went to Barrow for input on players to get from the Yankees it was Barrow who, not believing that any exchange of players would be worthwhile, suggested that he keep it a cash deal.

It is damning indeed that on November 1 Lannin claimed Frazee owed him the exact amount that Ruth was later sold for, however in fairness to Frazee, there is plenty of evidence to show that he did not sell Babe to satisfy his debt to Lannin. To begin with, Frazee had been making payments to the long-defunct Federal League as a result of a settlement to their suit in 1916 (see Chapter Three).

Frazee believed that these should have been Lannin's responsibility as he (Lannin) was the owner at that time the suit was settled. The fact that the courts did not see it that way is no reflection on Frazee's good faith intentions. Secondly, and perhaps most important, Frazee had just completed his most successful year (financially) as owner of the Red Sox.

Frazee was not a stooge and had to be aware that the only reason people came out to Fenway Park to watch his sixth-place team was because of Ruth. He therefore was fully aware that either a Red Sox team with Babe Ruth, or a pennant-contending team without him could well be the best answer to his financial problems. There was no reason not to think, at this time, that Frazee's objective was to build a winning baseball team through the acquisition of players. So when he vowed to take the money and use it to procure players that would again make the Red Sox a contender, no one had cause to doubt him, for he had done it before.

Upon Ruth's sale, Frazee issued what was roughly a 1,500-word statement explaining to the fans his reasons for disposing of Ruth. The *Boston Post* of January 6 printed it in its entirety. "Twice within the past two seasons, Babe has jumped the club and revolted. He refused to obey the orders of the manager and he finally became so arrogant that discipline in his case was ruined .... He had no regard for the feelings of anyone but himself. He was a bad influence upon other and still younger players."

Frazee continued his scathing attack on Ruth and revealed perhaps how hurt personally he was by Babe's behavior. "Out there on the West Coast, I could have prevented him from playing a single game as his contract signed by him gives me that right. But I allowed him to play unmolested. Then he sends me back his contract in an envelope without a scrap of writing for explanation. This is just a sample of how Ruth respects his written word and his obligations."

Babe's conditioning did not escape Frazee as he made a point to reveal that "…Ruth is taking on weight tremendously. He doesn't keep himself in shape …. He has a floating cartilage in his knee… that may make him a cripple at any time and put him out of baseball." This was as a result of his knee injury that occurred in the fall of 1918, and which had bothered Babe off and on during the '19 season.

The owner concluded his statement by informing the fans of his unsuccessful attempt to procure players for Babe. "Ruth's great value did not appeal to all the other owners. I could not get Joe Jackson for him and I know of at least two other stars that Ruth could not have been traded for …. Ruth could not remain on the Boston team under existing conditions."

From the time he had purchased the team in November of 1916 to the time of Ruth's sale, Frazee was an active innovator who was willing to take on the power structure of the game. He had spent money freely to secure players to help the Red Sox win. There was no hint, nor was their any mention of financial problems on the part of Frazee and the Red Sox. Those would surface five weeks later. There was the annual fall rumor of the team's potential sale; but that was generated as much by Ban Johnson as anyone. It must not be forgotten that it was Johnson who had secretly come into Boston in late 1918 in an attempt to find local investors to buy the team.

One accusation made of Frazee throughout the years is that he was an owner whose only concern was to "make a quick buck." It would be ludicrous to suggest that he did not want to make money. What businessman wants to lose it? However, the accusation that it was all he was in it for, appears unfounded. One needs only to look at the fact that he refused to sell the team during the winter of 1918 for $1.2 million. Examine the numbers and decide. In November of 1916, Frazee bought the team for $1 million. Roughly two years later he was offered $1.2 million. Would any businessman who wanted to make a quick buck turn down an opportunity to make $200,000 in a little less than two years?

He had formed a coalition with Jake Ruppert and Charles Comiskey and took on Ban Johnson and the National Commission in an attempt to infuse their vision on the future of baseball. This did not endear him to the hearts of Johnson, the National Commission or certain other American League owners. However, the fact that he had spent freely and had always worked toward strengthening the team on the field created a broad base of support in Boston. At this point in his tenure as owner and President of the Boston Red Sox, Frazee was widely respected and highly thought of by fans and the Boston press. All of that was about to change, for eternity.

                                        ❧

There were 11 newspapers in the city of Boston in 1920. The first radio station was still five years away and the idea of sending waves through the air that would turn into pictures on a screen in the living room was considered science fiction by most. The newspaper was the undisputed king of communication.

Obviously, all the newspapers printed this important story, however four newspapers "covered" the story. They were the *Boston Post*, the *Boston Herald,* the *Evening American,* and the *Boston Globe.* The *Post, Herald* and *American* ran stories about the sale for eight consecutive days. It was through these stories that the reaction of the media, the fans, and Babe himself can be felt. The sale of Ruth to the Yankees received far more support than anyone nearly 80 years removed could ever imagine.

The headlines of Tuesday, January 6, 1920 screamed the news that Babe was now a Yankee! Throughout the years, varying dates have been given as the announcement date. All of the newspapers of the sixth refer to late afternoon on Monday, January 5 as the time Frazee announced the transaction. The reported amount of the sale varied, ranging from $100,000 to $150,000. Only the *Boston Post* and the *New York Times* reported the correct figure of $125,000. None of them at the time mentioned the loan of $300,000 that Ruppert gave Frazee, using Fenway Park as collateral. It simply was not known.

The focus of all the stories was the price. Whichever paper reported whichever price, it was clear that it was more than twice as much as anyone had paid for a baseball player. Getting past that sensational aspect of the story, the reactions began .

More than 75 years has passed since Ruth's sale to the Yankees. It is easy to look at the transaction with the hindsight of all those years and ask the obvious question: "How could anyone sell

Babe Ruth?" Indeed that was the reaction of many of the time. In the Suffolk Athletic Club just north of the city, men "groaned, hissed and booed" when news of the deal reached them. Shocked was probably the word most often used to describe the initial reaction of the fans.

An editorial in the *Boston Post* on January 6 summed up the feelings of many fans: "The average home patron cannot view with great equanimity the transfer of a star of the first magnitude, the greatest drawing card in the game. Boston fans, therefore, are bound to be disgruntled." Citing that the money secured for Ruth would alone not be enough to lure other owners to transfer players to the Red Sox and adding in the fact that they no longer possessed many players who could be traded for established stars, the editorial proved prophetic when it stated that "the immediate prospects for a winning combination in Boston are not exactly brilliant."

Continuing its prophecy, the editorial concluded: "Cy Young and Tris Speaker went their ways, much to the disgust of the faithful, but the club did not suffer materially. But Ruth is different. He is of a class of ballplayers who flash across the firmament once in a great while . . . . During the past 20 years there have been three such superstars—Wagner, Cobb and Ruth. Wagner stayed with Pittsburgh (sic)... Cobb will never play except for Detroit. Money could never buy these two men. But Boston with Ruth is another story."

On the same page as this editorial, *Post* sportswriter Paul Shannon wrote the following:

> "Ruth . . . the biggest box office attraction in the game and the most spectacular player . . . would never have been allowed to leave Fenway Park had it been possible for the Boston club to handle him. Ruth's failure to respect the clubs training rules, his unwillingness to submit to any form of discipline, and the bad example he set for the other men formed a combination that President Frazee could no longer endure."

Acknowledging Ruth's greatness as a player, a gate attraction and "the most spectacular player to wear a Boston uniform since . . . Mike "King" Kelley." Shannon continued, "the regret at his sale will be considerably tempered by the knowledge he was posing as a holdout. And the dear public, wearied year after year by the lack of good faith and unwarranted demands of players who had small consideration for word or contract had rapidly begun to lose patience with the temperamental star. With Ruth gone from the Boston lineup, harmony is sure to be restored."

Concluding, he wrote: "It is believed that practically every man on the Boston team will be pleased at Ruth's sale to New York. Popular as Ruth was, on account of his big-heartedness, the men nevertheless realize that his faults overshadow his good qualities." Paul Shannon had been covering Babe Ruth since he joined the Red Sox in 1914, and his sentiments about Babe being a holdout were echoed in virtually every newspaper in the city.

Referring to Ruth as "Boston's beloved slugger," Ed Cunningham wrote on the front page of the *Boston Herald*, "Mutterings of the storm that will break loose today about the heads of the Boston management were heard last night and fans, almost to a man stoutly oppose the deal." Analyzing he continued, "Baseball fans know little of the internal affairs of a baseball club. They know the players as they act on the playing field and evidently care little of what happens off the field. The fans have their favorites and Ruth captured their hearts by his wonderful batting."

Acknowledging that Babe would probably "smash to bits" his new home run record playing 77 games at the Polo Grounds, Cunningham went on record as being against Ruth's demands from Frazee for a new $20,000 contract. "If that contract was out last season, in all fairness he could ask for an increase to $20,000 and undoubtedly would receive it, but he was not in a position to cast the signed contract aside merely as a scrap of paper." Ironically, Frazee stated that he would have been willing to give Babe a raise "if he had come and requested it in a different attitude then the one taken."

Herald columnist Bob Dunbar talked of Boston fans being "staggered" and "astonished" at the news of the deal. However he did add that "there are two sides to every issue" and that "management is seldom given consideration and generally is censured." Dunbar went on to say that "Frazee believes that he has not been squarely dealt with", then hit the nail right on the head when he concluded, "The departing of Ruth ... is regretted by all."

It was the *Boston Herald* cartoonist Franklin Collier who penned the famous cartoon portraying for sale signs on the Boston Public Library, the Boston Common and Paul Revere's statue. However Dunbar shed a little light on that as well when he wrote in his column of January 8, "My good friend Franklin Collier is very much upset over the going from here of Ruth. You see Franklin dearly loved to build a cartoon around that delightful 'phiz' of the Colossus...instead of having him around every day at Fenway Park Collier will have him but 11 times in the season." Is it possible that Collier's "vision" of the sale was somewhat tainted through the view of a self serving eye ?

James O'Leary, writing for the morning edition of the January 6 *Boston Globe* stated that it would be for "sentimental reasons" that the fans would view the deal with "disfavor". He further stated that if they would reserve judgment "the chances are that they will agree with President Frazee and others that the sale of Babe will eventually redound (sic) to the welfare of the Boston club." O'Leary clearly came down on the side of the Red Sox owner when he stated,"...it is hard to see how Frazee could have turned down New York's offer for the star, and it looks as if he had made a good bargain."

O'Leary even wrote an article that appeared on the front page of the January 15 edition of *The Sporting News*. Under a headline which read "FRAZEE FINDS DEFENDER IN HIS RELEASE OF BABE RUTH", O'Leary detailed what he termed Frazee's "many convincing points" and then summarized with, "When it began to look as if Ruth regarded himself as bigger than the Boston club, bigger than the game itself, Frazee made up his mind that there would have to be a change, in order to avoid more serious trouble in the future."

Concluding, O'Leary wrote, "The Boston fans are sorry that he goes, there is no mistake about that, but they will have to reconcile themselves to his absence, as they did in the cases of Cy Young, Tris Speaker and others ... The old game will go on just the same."

In the evening edition of the *Globe*, John J. Hallahan came out "strongly against the action," yet in his article he stated, "There is no getting behind the fact that Ruth is after the money." Despite not supporting the trade, Hallahan could not come out in support of Ruth's contract maneuvers.

The *Boston Evening Transcript* went so far as to print in their front page story of January 6 that there was "Remarkable unanimity of opinion that the Red Sox made a good deal in disposing of the home run hitter. Nearly everyone agrees that Ruth is too big to stay in Boston." It further stated that the "Red Sox players doubtless will be pleased with the disposal of the incorrigible slugger and team play should be in more evidence." Needless to say, they too were not speaking very favorably of the fact that Babe was demanding a new contract.

The *Boston Evening American* was the most critical of the Red Sox for selling Babe. American sportswriter Nick Flatley stated that they had "lost the greatest drawing card the game has ever known, and the esteem of many of thousands of supporters . . . ." Calling Babe "the greatest star ever known to this city where heroes (sic) and pennants . . . have become chronic", Flatley decried what he termed the exploitation of star athletes at the expense of the clubs chances of "glory."

He came to Ruth's defense regarding Frazee's contention that Babe was the cause of disturbance on the team. Stating that the only disturbance Babe caused was with his bat, he related that his teammates were as happy as Babe when the home run record fell during the '19 season.

Flatley went so far as to point the finger directly at Barrow as the cause of any dissension on the team. He cited the Carl Mays incident and the fact that "games were lost because pitchers who were getting pounded were left on the hill." He questioned whether Barrow had the "control or experience" to pilot a championship team and suggested that he (Barrow) had blundered in his handling of Ruth. "Ruth is young and his head, doubtless, has been turned a bit by the wonderful adulation his hitting aroused. But . . . he could have been handled in a manner that would have kept him a fixture in Boston."

Flatley continued his diatribe with a reference to Bill Carrigan and his dealings with Babe:

> "... he rode him to death and made him play baseball. That system, followed up, would have kept the ideas of movies and prize rings out of the heros (sic) skull. But Ruth got a little out of hand and rather than treat him psychologically, as they say, and bring him back, the Sox have traded him."

Recognizing how unique was Babe as a player, "a bird like Ruth hops into the picture once in a lifetime". Flatley accurately predicted the immediate future of the Red Sox, Babe and the Yankees. "Without Ruth . . . a second division club will not develop into a great money winner here in Boston. Babe will get $20,000 and probably more . . . He's likely, too, to hammer the Yanks into a pennant promptly."

The next day the *Post* reported that Babe had signed a two-year deal worth $45,000; the Yankees won their first pennant in

1921; and the Red Sox did not see another first division finish until 1934.

Among those who saw Ruth's departure as a positive event was Hugh Duffy, who had starred with Boston in the National League from 1892 to 1900 and would manage the Red Sox in 1921. Thinking Frazee had made the right move, Duffy said, "No matter how great a star is, he hurts a team if he does not fit with his fellow players."

Fred Tenney, former first baseman and manager of the Braves echoed Duffy's sentiments, "A player that fits an organization is of more value than any star not working in harmony with his club."

Babe had baseball men of equal stature come to his defense in the persons of two former managers, Bill Carrigan and Jack Barry. Barry referred to him as "the most willing member on my team" and said his problem with him was that he wanted to pitch "too much". Stating that the absence of Ruth would leave the Red Sox attack "lamentably deficient" Barry offered that he never "called on Ruth and found him lacking".

Carrigan was equally supportive, stating that he did not regard Ruth as "anywhere near the hard proposition to handle that he was made out to be." Carrigan neglected to mention that on the road he had Babe room right next to him, and Heinie Wagner was his designated chaperone. Charley Lavis a former owner of the same Providence club that Babe played on in the minors in 1914 said, "I figure the Red Sox club is now practically ruined."

The initial reaction of the fans could best be categorized as outrage. It was Babe and his quest for the home run record that had kept them coming to the park in 1919. In a year where the team finished in a dismal sixth place, it was Babe who gave them something to cheer for.

The more prominent members of Boston fandom were also consulted to solicit their opinions. Francis Hurney of the South Boston K. of C., and one of the organizers of the Babe Ruth Day held in September, said, "The management of the Red Sox will have to travel some to get a player . . . like Ruth and I'm sure the gate receipts this year will show a decided decrease now that the true sportsmanship in the game is banished." The Red Sox attendance fell off by less than 15,000 in 1920.

M.T. "Nuf-Ced" McGreevey, the founder of the Royal Rooters and one of the oldest long-standing Red Sox fans stated that it was the Yankees who were the "gainer[s]" in the deal. Calling Babe "a very big asset," McGreevey stated, "I think every real Boston fan will regret his departing." Johnny Keenan, McGreevey's 1920 counterpart was in concurrence with "Nuf-Ced's" evaluation: "It will be impossible to replace the strength Ruth gave the Sox. The Batterer is a wonderful player and the fact that he loves the game and plays with his all to win makes him a tremendous asset. . . . "

The *Boston Evening American*, for several days after the sale, solicited the fans to write letters declaring their opinions on the sale. All the letters they printed came with a byline attached. The bylines said such things as "Did WISE THING", "BIG MISTAKE MADE", "DISCORD STORY BUNK", "BABE WORKING FOR RUTH", "ANOTHER RAW DEAL" and "FRAZEE HARMED SELF". The newspaper concluded after reviewing all the letters received that: "The Babe Ruth controversy is still about fifty-fifty." They summed up the fans' feelings thusly, "The fans think that Ruth is some ball player . . . who can help out any team . . . when he is so inclined . . . they do not all believe Ruth was working for the best interests of the Boston Red Sox last summer."

It is interesting to note that nowhere in any newspaper over the eight-day period in which this story dominated the sports pages, was there one comment printed attributed to a teammate of Babe's. There could be a simple explanation for this, however it does seem a bit peculiar. Jack Barry made it a point to voice his comments to his local paper in Worcester, Massachusetts. Bill Carrigan made contact with the media from his home in Lewiston, Maine. Yet not one of Babe's mates had any comment that made its way into any Boston newspaper at the time of the sale.

ॐ

The initial reactions emanating from Ruth himself were two. The first came in the form of a telegram to his business manager Johnny Igoe dated January 5. It read simply, "Will not play anywhere but Boston, leaving for the East Monday." The second was a small article written by Gene Doyle and printed in the *Boston Post* of January 6 in which Doyle claims, "Ruth knew nothing of the deal until he was told by me." Stating that "the news surprises me a bit." Babe went on to say, "I think it's a dirty trick of Frazee to sell me to the New York team. If it is true . . . I will still hold out for a salary of $20,000 and I may demand part of the purchase price."

Babe's first in-depth reaction to the trade came in the *Boston Evening American* of January 7. Holding back nothing, he blasted Harry Frazee. Saying he was "not good enough to own any ball club, especially one in Boston," Ruth accused Frazee of doing "more to hurt baseball in Boston than anyone who was ever connected to the game in that city. The Boston people are too good for him, and it will be a blessing when he steps out or is ousted".

Continuing his salvo, Ruth hit at Frazee in regard to his contract. "Because I demanded a big increase in salary, which I felt I was entitled to, he brands me as an ingrate and a troublemaker ... Any fair-minded fan knows that my efforts on the Boston club last season warranted a larger salary and I asked for it. I have always hustled as hard as any man on the diamond ... doing everything I could to make the club win."

In closing, Babe commented that as much as he liked Boston and its fans, he was glad to be rid of him. For were it not for Frazee, Babe would have been content to play with the Red Sox to "the end of my baseball days".

Lost on Babe was the fact that back in Boston he received little, if any, support on his attempt to double his salary. His staunchest supporters—and there were throngs of them—felt he should honor the three-year deal he had signed at the beginning of the '19 season. No one doubted nor disputed the fact that he was the best player in the game. A large contingent recognized him already as the greatest slugger in the history of the game. Many even felt he was worth the $20,000 he was requesting. However, in the matter of his holdout, the vast majority of writers and fans sided with Frazee.

This was due, in large measure, to the fact that Babe had demanded a new contract while under an existing agreement. Fifty or so years removed, this action would be called "renegotiation," and would become fairly common practice among professional athletes. However, in 1920 it was totally unacceptable to even Babe's most ardent admirers. Even in New York where they were welcoming him with open arms, W.J. Macbeth wrote for the *New York Tribune*, "Ruth's attempt to flaunt the Red Sox in the face despite an unexpired contract called for a showdown as a matter of discipline."

Walking the Municipal Golf Links on Wednesday, the 7th, with Bill James of the White Sox and Gene Doyle of the *Post*, Babe continued his offensive against Frazee. Reacting to a comment attributed to Frazee which said that as a star Babe "would be an obstacle to the club winning pennants" Ruth responded, "I have been with the Red Sox six years . . . and we won three pennants, not so bad . . . I am not or never have been a disturbing element . . . I have always played for the interest of the public and the players."

Claiming that Frazee cared "nothing about the Boston people" and predicting that he expected Frazee to sell the team very soon, Babe again stated his intention to get a piece of the purchase price, and the following day sent a telegram to Frazee requesting $5,000 from the proceeds of the sale. He even went so far as to say that he would not report to New York without it. Frazee, making good on his earlier intent to not give Babe "so much as an old straw hat", gave him nothing.

On January 9, Babe took a more organized approach to his offensive against Frazee. Visiting the telegraph office in Los Angeles, he dispatched four telegrams to Boston. One each to the sports editors of the *Boston Herald,* the *Boston Post*, the *Boston Globe* and the *Boston American*. Each was printed in its entirety in each of the newspapers (see appendix). Of differing lengths with varying details, they were all of the same flavor. Babe hit back hard at Frazee.

Calling Frazee's statements "absolute falsehoods . . . meant to poison the minds of the Boston people against me." Babe challenged the Red Sox owner to find one player on his team who felt Babe was a disturbing element and stated he would give Frazee $100 for every player found. Accusing him of "putting me on the pan as a means of covering himself for my sale to New York" Babe stated, "This propaganda has been sent out to try and pacify Boston people over the sale. It is a rank injustice to both them and me, for there is not any of it true."

This was an underlying theme in all of them. It seems that Babe could tolerate just about anything but being fingered as a source of discontentment with his teammates. He was deeply hurt by the sale, and his hurt turned to anger at the contention that he was the source of trouble on the team. Denouncing again and again the truth of Frazee's statements, Babe threatened to "file suit for damages . . . . He is trying to injure me with the Boston fans and I will not stand for this. The people know me and I am just as strong for the fans of Boston as they are for me."

He gave tribute to the fans of Boston saying they have "no superiors". He credited them for their loyalty to the home team combined with fairness to give "due credit to visiting players". Calling his six years playing in a Boston uniform "pleasant ones", Babe said good-bye to Boston. "I regret having to leave Boston . . . . When I come back … in a New York uniform it will be like coming home."

In Boston, people waited for the "other shoe to drop" in the form of a major Red Sox acquisition or as some suspected, the actual sale of the team. Frazee failed in an attempt to get Happy Felsch from the White Sox, and the reality that it was easier to sell a big star than to buy one began to set in. Interestingly, Felsch along with Joe Jackson, Buck Weaver and others would play their last years in 1920, then be banned for life for their involvement in the 1919 World Series "scam".

With the initial furor dying down, the fans of Boston were willing to give Frazee time to make good on his promise to obtain more players. As much as they revered Ruth, and as great a player as everyone knew that he was, the fans sympathized with and supported Frazee's contention that Ruth was wrong for not living up to the three-year contract he had signed prior to the 1919 season. Besides, they had seen star players come and go before yet the success of the team on the field had continued. They knew that teams could survive the loss of major stars and re-emerge as contenders. They had seen it before; Cy Young left and they still won. Speaker left in 1916, and the pennant still flew at Fenway. Frazee had stated he had talked with Detroit, Chicago and St. Louis and expected to make a deal soon. The fans were willing to wait, the Red Sox new star could not be far away.

ào

As the outcry diminished, the posturing in the newspapers ceased. Babe never returned from the West Coast until the middle of February. On the same day that the attorneys for Lannin and Frazee were arguing before a Boston judge, Babe announced his intention to seek $15,000 of his purchase price from Frazee. He also stated he would "exceed" his home run record of 1919. Although he never got a dime or even "an old straw hat" from the $125,000 Frazee received for him, he did make good on his home run prediction.

Scattered reports had him signing for various amounts of money. He actually played for the $20,000 he sought in 1920. He would get $30,000 in 1921 and by 1922 he was earning an ungodly sum of $52,000 a year, or as Babe liked to think of it, $1,000 a week.

Both teams gathered up and headed South for spring training. Babe went to Jacksonville, Florida, where he would make his first headlines by going after a heckling fan in the stands. The Red Sox returned to Hot Springs, Arkansas, and when they left, the fans were still waiting for the arrival of the new players Frazee had promised.

The questions of the Red Sox fans regarding who Frazee would acquire were answered on March 27 when an announcement came out of New York stating that Frazee had purchased the Harris Theater on Broadway. No price was given, however it was reported that it had been built at a cost of $500,000, and only weeks before, a theater on the same block had sold for $650,000. So much for the money from Ruth going to purchase new players.

The Red Sox opened the 1920 season with four wins in a row, including a doubleheader sweep of the Yankees on Patriots Day, April 19. Over 35,000 people showed up to welcome home the Babe, and they broke down the fence in rightfield in their eagerness to get to the ball park. Playing centerfield and batting fourth for Miller Huggins, Babe went 3-8 in the doubleheader with a double and two singles. Cheered and given a "hearty hand", Babe's appearance at Fenway in enemy garb, to many, signified the official passing. Babe was gone.

Babe pulverized the record books in 1920, setting new major league records in runs scored, RBI, walks, slugging percentage, and as he predicted, home runs. His 54 home runs were more than every other TEAM in the league. He also led the Yankees in stolen bases with 14 as New York finished in third place, three games behind Cleveland.

Boston finished in fifth place, 25 1/2 games behind the leaders. The outfield, which had been anchored by Hooper and Ruth, was now made up of Hooper, Menosky and Hendryx. Hooper, having his usual solid year, led the team with seven homers.

Frazee took over the Harris theater in July, redecorated, renovated, and called it the "Frazee". The ultimate indignity came in late November when a report out of Chicago cited a transcript from the Suffolk County courthouse in Boston, Massachusetts which stated that on May 25, 1920, "there was executed by the organization controlling the Boston American League Baseball Club a mortgage for $300,000 in favor of Jacob Ruppert et al." Not only did Ruppert have Ruth, he basically owned Fenway Park as well. The book on Babe Ruth and the Red Sox was closed.

As the year drew to a close, Babe's golfing buddy from the previous winter, Buck Weaver, was making plans to take a one-man play to vaudeville houses designed to "prove his innocence of complicity in the alleged conspiracy to 'throw' the 1919 World Series." Harry Frazee's dream of a "one-man commission" came closer to reality as Ban Johnson appointed a committee of three to meet with a National league committee and Judge Kenesaw Mountain Landis.

Rumors in Boston had the team being sold to a group that included Boston College football coach Frank Cavanaugh and again, a young Boston banker named Joseph P. Kennedy. A cloud hung over Frazee as questions of the propriety of one owner carrying a mortgage on the other's ballpark were being looked into by Ban Johnson and the American league. The cloud would only grow darker—so dark that nearly 70 years after his death, it still hovered.

As for Babe, he stood on the threshold of immortality, poised to do what he'd always done—take the game of baseball to a level it had never known before.

━━━ ▪ Eight ▪ ━━━

Continued Fallout and What Might Have Been

The record is there to be examined, analyzed, and dissected, but the question that fans and historians alike are left to consider is, "What if Babe Ruth had not been sold, and spent his entire career with the Red Sox?"

While Babe Ruth played with the Red Sox from 1914 through the 1919 season, they compiled a record of 514 wins and 359 losses. In that same time frame, New York was a mediocre 430-445. Boston won the World Series in 1915, '16 and '18. They finished second in 1917 and slipped to sixth in 1919. New York, on the other hand, had finished in sixth place twice, fifth once and fourth once before rallying to a third-place finish in 1919.

In 1920, the Yankees finished with a record of 95-59, completing the most successful year in their history. In 1921 they won their first American League pennant and repeated the effort in '22 and '23, becoming only the second American league team to win three consecutive pennants.

The year 1923 brought New York its first World Series championship and Babe's first one since 1918. Three times in Babe's tenure as a Yankee from 1920 through 1934, they won over 100 games. Twice they won more than 105; in 1927 when they were 110-44, and in 1932 when they finished at 107-47. When New York won the 1932 pennant, it marked their seventh American league championship, supplanting Boston as the American league franchise with the most pennants. In Babe's 15 seasons as a Yankee, they captured seven American League pennants, and four times they won the World Series. From 1920 through 1934, they won 1,405 and lost 895 for a winning percentage of .611.

Babe slugged 189 home runs from 1920 through 1923, and registered slugging percentages of .847, .846, .672, and .764. No other man has had a slugging percentage in the .800s. His back-to-back 50 home run seasons (54 in '20 and 59 in '21) has never been duplicated except by him in 1927 (60) and 1928 (54). When he knocked in 170 runs in 1921, he shattered his own record of 137 set just the year before. The arrival of Babe Ruth in New York began an era of unprecedented and heretofore unmatched dominance in professional sports.

From 1920 through 1964, the Yankees won 28 American League pennants, and 20 of those 28 times they were crowned champions of the world. From 1936 through 1953, they were World Champs 12 times, including four in a row from '36 to '39 and a record five in a row under Casey Stengel (the leading hitter of the 1916 World Series) from 1949 to 1953. When the Yankees won the 1996 pennant, it marked their 33rd American League title. Since Babe Ruth became a Yankee, they have been American League champions an astounding 44% of the time. Their World Series victory in 1996 was the 23rd time they have worn the title of World Champs, or just under one-third of the time. No team anywhere in any professional sport can boast of such numbers.

The Red Sox of 1920 won 72 and lost 81, not an appreciable difference from the year before. In 1921, they hung on for a 75-79 mark. It would be 13 more years before they would win even 70 games in a season as they began a streak of woefulness that was unprecedented in baseball history.

A 61-93 record in 1922 earned them a place in the American league cellar. It was a place that they would grow accustomed to as they would finish there in '23, '25, '26, '27, '28, '29, and '30. Escaping in 1924 by finishing 1/2 game ahead of the Chicago White Sox, it would take until 1931 for them to rise to sixth place before again plummeting to new depths.

In 1932, they won 43 games while losing 111 to finish 64 games behind Babe and the Yankees. As baseball and the Red Sox stand on the verge of the 21st century, that season remains, by far, their worst. Beginning in '22 and stretching through 1933, the most wins they had in one season was 67 in 1924. From the time Ruth was sold to New York in 1920 until his last season there in 1934, the Red Sox were the antithesis of the Yankees, as their record was almost identical in reverse, 891 wins and 1,403 losses for a pitiful winning percentage of .388. In that timeframe, Boston lost 62% of its games, while the Yankees won 61% of theirs.

It would take 28 years before the Red Sox would play in another World Series. They finished in second place four times in those 28 years, each time behind the Yankees. After losing the 1946 World Series, they finished third in '47, lost a playoff game to Cleveland which decided the 1948 pennant, and finished second to the Yankees in 1949. Going into Yankee Stadium on the last weekend of the season needing to win one of two, they lost both and the Yankees began their streak of five straight World Series titles.

Twelve years of mostly third and fourth place finishes followed, as they were never really in a race. The '60s and expansion arrived, Ted Williams departed, and the Red Sox were back in the abyss. They finished no higher than sixth until their miracle year of 1967. Coming from ninth place the year before (1/2 game ahead of the Yankees), they won the pennant on the last day of the season and were finally going back to the World Series. Forty-eight years had passed since Babe Ruth had left Boston, and the Red Sox were making only their second appearance in the Fall Classic since Babe had last donned his red stockings.

Twice more since then Boston has played in the World Series. Three times (1988, '90, and '95) they won their division title and did not advance. In 1978 they played their second one-game playoff to determine an American League or divisional champion. That one they lost as well, to the Yankees. From the year that Babe left Boston to the onset of divisional play in 1969, the Red Sox finished in the second division a total of 26 times. They finished in second place six times, five times behind the Yankees. Four times they have played in a World Series since Babe became a Yankee, and in each one they lost four games to three. St. Louis beat them twice in 1946 and 1967, Cincinnati beat them in 1975, and the New York Mets (who played their first three seasons in Babe's favorite park to hit in, the Polo Grounds) bested them in 1986.

The fortunes of both of these organizations turned when Harry Frazee peddled Babe Ruth to Jake Ruppert. The fact that many of Babe's Boston teammates followed him to New York in the early twenties (including the entire pitching staff) had as much to do with the teams' immediate reversal of fortunes as anything else. However, nearly 80 years later, the sale of Babe Ruth still casts a shadow that hangs, at times, like gloom over the Red Sox and their fans. *Boston Globe* sportswriter and Massachusetts native Dan Shaughnessy wrote lightheartedly of this gloom in his 1990 book *The Curse of The Bambino*. Before the book, in the early 1980s, tee-shirts were sold outside of Fenway Park which read "Boston Red Sox: 1918 World Champs". Part of the vendor's sales pitch was that the Red Sox were indeed under a curse and it would last until the year 2018, a 100-year sentence to frustration and heartbreak for selling the "Colossus". Witches were called to Fenway in the 1970s to caste out demons and put an end to curses.

Virtually every Red Sox team that has won and proceeded to post-season play has had to deal with an onslaught of media asking them about "the curse" and the Red Sox propensity to lose big games in bizarre, unimaginable ways. With most of them not from Boston and lacking the first hand knowledge of Red Sox history, players would often become perplexed, which at times gave way to irritation and then to anger.

Although in Babe's last year in Boston the team finished in sixth place with a record of 66-71, it seems highly unlikely that they would have fallen to the depths they reached in the 1920s if he had remained in the fold. This was their first losing season since 1908. They were a proud franchise with a tradition of winning, having captured five of the first 15 World Series', three since Babe joined them in 1914.

If Babe had remained, one might assume that Barrow would have remained as well. Therefore, the aforementioned sale of Babe's teammates may not have transpired either. There is no reason to think that Boston's dominance would not have re-emerged and continued into the 1920s. Perhaps additional success would not have placed Frazee in the financial state where he felt it necessary to sell his players, and there may have been no sale to Bob Quinn in 1923.

Quinn owned the team from 1923 until 1933. In that dismal decade, the Red Sox won 671 games while losing 1,075, for a winning percentage of .384. Their best season came in 1931 when they won 63, lost 91 and finished in sixth place, 45 games behind Philadelphia. Without that decade of desolation, there may have been no sale in 1933 to Thomas A. Yawkey. Thirty-three at the time he bought the Red Sox, Yawkey may have purchased some other franchise in the American League, or perhaps even a National League team. Maybe he would have even chosen a team in the emerging National Football League instead of a baseball team.

With no sale of Ruth, there may have been no Quinn. With no Quinn, there may have been no Yawkey. The benevolent Yawkey was known for being very good to his players—some said too good. He established such a relationship with Ted Williams that it was Ted who spoke on his behalf when he was posthumously inducted into the Hall of Fame in 1980. Carl Yastrzemski states flatly that Thomas Yawkey was the reason he signed with Boston instead of Philadelphia. No sale of Ruth, no Quinn, no Quinn, no Yawkey, no Yawkey, no Yaz, and maybe no Williams. Ted's tempestuous ways may have been treated differently by another owner, and perhaps he would have been traded or worse yet, sold. Without Tom Yawkey owning the Red Sox, would Joe Cronin have ever been bought from Washington in 1934 for $250,000? Would Jimmie Foxx ever have made it to Fenway Park where he slugged 35 of his 50 homers in 1938? Would Lefty Grove have won his 300th game in some other uniform than Boston's? Maybe the Red Sox ticket office would today be located at 4 Frazee St. instead of 4 Yawkey Way.

By the mid-1920s, the Red Sox pitching corps that had once sported the names of Ruth, Leonard, Mays, Shore, Foster, Pennock, Bush and Jones had been replaced by such stalwarts as Collins, Ehmke, Wingfield, Wiltse, Harris, Weltzer, and Zahniser. It is debatable if even Babe could have lifted them from their forlorn fate. However, it seems doubtful that such a fate would have befallen them had he remained. Frazee had, up to the point where he sold Ruth, spent his money to acquire quality ballplayers. There is no reason not to think that if he had it, he would have continued to do so.

That the landscape of baseball history would have been radically altered had Babe remained with Boston is obviously indisputable. Indeed, an entire book could be written on the ripple effect it would have had on the way baseball is perceived worldwide. What is interesting to speculate about, however, is how Babe's own career may have changed had he continued to play for the Red Sox. Would his home run numbers have been quite so prolific? Yankee Stadium was tailor-made, or one could say custom-designed for his long, high rightfield drives. Would he have had as much success in Fenway with its relatively spacious rightfield? In 1918 when he led the A.L. in home runs with 11, all of them were hit on the road. In

1919, when he again led in homers with 29, 20 of them were hit on the road.

The greatest impact Babe had on the game was that he hit the ball higher, harder, and farther than it had ever been hit before. The baseball public marveled at how high his infield popups went. They would often be delighted if they happened to be present when Babe hit a long flyout during the course of an 0 for 4 afternoon. There is no way of knowing how many of Babe's Yankee Stadium home runs would have been outs at Fenway Park. With the way that Babe hit the ball, it does not seem as if there would have been many. Regarding the "House that Ruth built", might it not have even been built in 1923 with no Ruth, and the success he had helped to bring?

Throughout the history of Fenway Park, there have been many left-handed hitters who have had greater success due to its leftfield wall, with Fred Lynn and Wade Boggs as two more recent examples. With Babe's adroitness with the bat, it seems likely that he would have adapted well to its presence. There was the time in July of 1918, when he spent the morning with Barrow working on hitting the ball to left, then proceeded to bang three hits that afternoon to leftfield. It could be expected that Babe would have honed his off-field hitting skills, and before long would have been hitting opposite field home runs with startling frequency.

In all probability, Babe would have hit about the same amount of home runs. His talent and skills as a power hitter were unprecedented in the history of the game, and it seems implausible that they would have been contained by the dimensions of the park in which he played.

There are several other points to ponder regarding Ruth's imagined continuation in a Red Sox uniform. In 1929, numbers on the back of uniforms came into fashion, with Babe's number "3" signifying his third position in the Yankee order, the method most, if not all teams used to number their players. Having been firmly entrenched in the cleanup spot in the Red Sox order by 1919, it is logical to assume that Ruth may have worn number "4" on a Boston uniform. Today, in Fenway Park's rightfield corner, the numbers 9 - 4 - 1 - 8 are displayed to honor four retired greats from the team's history. Had Ruth spent his entire career in Boston, might the number "4" be displayed in honor of him rather than Joe Cronin?

As Ruth's career was winding down, it was well-known that he coveted a major league managerial position. In finishing his career with the Red Sox, would it have been a natural transition for him to have taken over as skipper of the team? If so, would he have taken a protege such as Ted Williams or some other young slugger under his wing?

Our final, lasting image of Babe Ruth alive, is an aged and shriveled figure standing in a baggy uniform at home plate for one final time two months before his death in 1948. Had he spent his career with the Red Sox, that heart-rending, poignant scene would likely have taken place at Fenway Park.

Despite his relatively brief tenure, Babe's mark remains in Boston and New England. In May of 1968, there was a street and park named after him in South Boston, where his first wife Helen lived, and where he was a member of the Knights of Columbus. Red Sox fans of New England in 1983 voted him the starting left-handed pitcher on their all-time Red Sox team. In 1995, he was one of the original inductees into the Boston Red Sox Hall of Fame, and around that same time a local baseball fan and historian spearheaded a drive that led to a plaque being dedicated on the spot where Babe played with the Providence Grays in 1914, commemorating his final minor league stop.

Yet somehow Boston remains almost apologetic about Babe's time spent with the Red Sox. Shocked that he left, saddened and disgusted by what transpired in the decade that followed his departure, and broken hearted over three generations of some of the most noteworthy failures in the history of the game, Red Sox fans have incorporated into their psyche an expectation of failure that becomes increasingly difficult to shake with the passage of each baseball season.

Even though he was one of the original inductees into their Hall of Fame, the Red Sox organization itself appears somewhat reluctant to call attention to the fact that Babe played for them at all. In this current age of the Internet and cyberspace, anyone with a computer can communicate with the Boston Red Sox. Greeted with an attractive home page, fans can peruse a myriad of areas of interests. Among them is a section labeled "Legends". Listed in this section are the following names in order of their appearance: Cy Young, Tris Speaker, Smoky Joe Wood, Tom Yawkey, Joe Cronin, Jimmy Foxx, Johnny Pesky, Ted Williams, Bobby Doerr, Carl Yastrzemski, Rico Petrocelli, Carlton Fisk, Luis Tiant, Fred Lynn, Jim Rice and Dwight Evans. Conspicuous by its absence is the name

George H. "Babe" Ruth. It is almost as if they would rather pretend that he was never there than acknowledge that they sold him.

The past cannot be altered, and only through acceptance can it be resolved. The time has come for the Boston Red Sox and their fans to embrace the time that he spent in Boston, to step out from the shadow of his sale and celebrate the time that he was among them. For before he became a Yankee and made his rendezvous with destiny, he had redefined the game of baseball as The Babe in Red Stockings.

▪Appendices▪

The following telegrams were sent by Babe Ruth to four Boston newspapers on January 9, 1920. They appear exactly as they appeared in their respective newspapers on January 10, 1920.

BOSTON AMERICAN

The following dispatch from Babe Ruth givs (sic) that great sluggers viewpoint on the stories that have been spread concerning him- as well as the trick can be done over 3000 miles of wire.

Nick Flatley, *Boston American*:

I have read in the Los Angeles papers about Frazee putting me on the pan as a means of covering himself for my sale to New York. I have read where he said I was a disturbing element on the club. I want you to deny this for me. I will give $100 for every player on the Boston Club and in the American League that he can show I am not friendly with. The trouble is I have always stuck up for the players and he knows it.

Back in 1918, in Cleveland, just before the season closed, the boys delegated me to find out what date our salaries would run to. I saw Barrow and he said there would be no trouble about that, as we would be paid until September 15. This statement he made in front of all the players. We played on and clinched the pennant.

The latter part of August we asked him again, and at that time he came out and said we were only going to be paid until September 2. As he had previously stated that we would be paid until the fifteenth, I told the fellows to make him stick to his original agreement and not to take the field until he made good that promise. He finaly (sic) came through.

This is the only reason Frazee has for saying I was a troublemaker. I acted for all the boys at their request and Barrow made his statement before all the fellows.

Statements that have appeared in the papers, credited to Frazee, about me so far have not been true, and I am very seriously considering filing suit for damages if he makes any more. He is trying to injure me with the Boston fans and I will not stand for this. The people know me, and I'm just as strong for the fans of Boston as they are for me.

I fully appreciate the stand the people made to stop this sale, and while it's true I have been sold, I regret having to leave Boston. I have been with the Red Sox for six seasons and during that time we have won three pennants. Those six years have been pleasant ones for me and I have enjoyed playing before the Boston public.

I have appeared in all the American League cities, and I can truthfully say Boston fans have no superiors. They are fair and stick by the home team, but always give due credit to visiting players. When I come back to Boston in a New York uniform, it will be like coming home.

You understand the conditions about as well as anybody and as I am 3,500 miles from Boston, I have very little means of defending myself from the attacks of Frazee. If I were in Boston I could do a better job. I will fully appreciate it if you will see that I get a fair shake and that is all I ask.

Babe Ruth

It is interesting to note that Babe was indignant about the salary situation of 1918 described herein. Upset with what amounted to a breaking of a promise by Barrow, he urged his teammates to stand firm and not take the field until the management were made to stick to their "original agreement". Strange he did not apply that same logic to his original agreement regarding the three-year contract he had signed in 1919.

BOSTON POST

Howard G. Reynolds, sporting editor of the *Post*, received the following telegram from Los Angeles last night, signed by Babe Ruth:

The statements which have appeared up to date and credited to Harry Frazee are absolute falsehoods and meant to poison the minds of the Boston people against me. If the owner of the Boston club has any more assertions like the ones just made to make he had better be very careful, as I will take the matter to court and give him a chance to prove that they are lies.

Let the *Post* make a canvass of the members of the Red Sox and find out whether or not I am a disturbing element on the ballclub. I will pay the expenses. I want the public to know who is in the right in this matter. It is true that I regret having to leave Boston and that is why I have expressed myself as I have. It is bad enough at having been sold, without Frazee coming out with untrue statements. When he found out the fans were against the deal he started a propaganda to put me in bad. I take exceptions to this and if there is any doubt in the minds of the people about my popularity with the players of not only the Boston club but in the American League I am willing to go to the expense of proving it.

Anything you want to know I will be pleased to give you the information, thanking you for all past favors, I remain,

Babe Ruth
1008 West 11th street,
Los Angeles

BOSTON HERALD

LOS ANGELES Cal. Jan 9.

Burt Whitman
Sporting Editor
Boston Herald

Wish you would print the following message to the Boston fans for me:

All of the interviews credited to Frazee which have been printed in the Los Angeles papers, and I suppose they were the same as printed in Boston, are untrue and meant only to put me in bad with the Boston fans. I was as much surprised on hearing of the deal that transferred me to New York as were the Boston public.

I never have been a disturbing element on the Red Sox. This can be proven readily by asking any of the boys who are on the club. I am friendly with all of the fellows and I firmly believe that they all would go the limit for me and regret my leaving the club as much as I do going.

If there is any doubt about my being on friendly terms with the fellows I will pay willingly any expense that the fans and press might incur to take the trouble to find out. This propaganda has been sent out to try to pacify Boston people over the sale. It is a rank injustice to both them and me, for there is not any of it true.

I am thinking very seriously of taking the matter to court to prove these statements untrue and show Boston fans that they are being tricked by the so-called sportsman Frazee.

The Boston club is my favorite, and naturally I wanted to remain there, but as the deal is completed I suppose I will have to go to New York. I hadn't the slightest idea that the deal was on and I think that Frazee surely showed himself up in his true colors when he tries to belittle me to cover up his blunder.

I appreciate the stand taken by the Boston people and very shortly hope to be in Boston to thank them in person for their support.

Thanking you for past favors and wishing you success, I remain your friend,

Babe Ruth

BOSTON GLOBE

The following telegram to the *Globe* was received from "Babe" Ruth last night, and is self-explanatory:

Los Angeles, Calif, Jan. 9- Have read some of the statements given to the press and made public by Pres Frazee of the Red Sox. None of them is very complimentary to me. This was to be expected. I would appreciate it very much if you would give me a little space to deny these accusations.

Since I have been a member of the Boston club I have made good with the Boston public.

If there is any doubt in the minds of the Boston people about my standing with the other members of the Red So, let anybody make a canvass. This will readily prove whether or not I am a disturbing element in the club.

From all reports, the sale has proved a serious blow to the club and I am being made the goat. I am going to return to Boston in the near future and at that time the fireworks will start.

I have enjoyed playing on the Boston club since the first day I put on a uniform. I have given the club at all times the best I had, and the owners as well as the players know it.

I appreciate the support I have received from the fans and will always remember my Boston friends. With best wishes and kindest regards, I remain,

"Babe" Ruth

Bibliography

Allen, Lee. (1966). *Babe Ruth: His Story in Baseball.* Putnam.

Asinof, Eliot. (1963). *Eight Men Out.* Henry Holt & Co.

Clark, Elery Jr. (1979). *Red Sox Fever.* Exposition Press.

Clark, Elery Jr. (1975). *Boston Red Sox—75th Anniversary.* Exposition, Banner.

Creamer, Robert. (1974). *Babe: The Legend Comes to Life.* Simon & Shuster.

Curran, William. (1990). *Big Sticks.* Harper Perennial.

Gallagher, Mark. (1996). *The Yankee Encyclopedia.* Champaign, IL: Sagamore Publishing.

Golebeck, Peter. (1992). *Fenway: An Unexpurgated History o the Boston Red Sox.* P. Putnam's Sons.

Halberstam, David. (1989) *Summer of '49.* William Morrow an Company.

Honig, Donald. (1990). *The Boston Red Sox: An Illustrated History.* Prentice-Hall.

Kenmisch, Al. (1975). The Babe Ruth Beginning. *S.A.B.R. Research Journal.*

Lowry, Philip J. (1992). *Green Cathedrals.* Addison-Wesley.

McGarigle, Bob. (1972). *Baseball's Great Tragedy: The Story of Carl Mays.* Exposition-Banner.

Meany, Tom. (1947). *Babe Ruth.* Grosset & Dunlop.

Neft, David, & Cohen, Richard. (1990). *The World Series, Complete Play by Play of Every Game 1903-1989.* St. Martins Press.

Neft, David; Johnson, Roland; Cohen, Richard, and Deutsch, Jordan. (1974). *The Sports Encylopedia: Baseball.* Grosset & Dunlap.

Pirone, Dorothy Ruth, & Martens, Chris. (1988). *My Dad The Babe.* Quinlan Press.

Ruth, Babe, & Considien, Bob. (1948). *The Babe Ruth Story.* Dutton.

Shaughnessey, Dan. (1990). *The Curse of the Bambino.* Dutton.

Smelser, Marshall. (1975). *The Life that Ruth Built.* Quadrangle/The New York Times Book Co.

Sobol, Ken. (1974). *Babe Ruth and the American Dream.* Ballantine Books.

Stein, Irving. M. (1992). *The Ginger Kid—The Buck Weaver Story.* Elysian Fields Press.

Thorn, John & Palmer, Pete. (1989). *Total Baseball.* Warner Books.

Wagenheim, Kal. (1974). *Babe Ruth, His Life and Legend.* Praeger Publishers.

Walton Ed. (1978). *This Date in Boston Red Sox History.* A Scarborough Stein & Day.

Zingg, Paul. (1993). *The Baseball Encyclopedia.* MacMillan.

Newspapers

Boston Globe	*Christian Science Monitor*	*Baltimore Sun*
Boston Herald	*Worcester Telegram*	*Quincy Patriot Ledger*
Boston American	*New York Times*	*Lebanon Daily News*
Boston Post	*New York Herald Tribune*	*Meredith News*
Taunton Daily Gazette	*Lowell Sun*	*Sporting News*
	Providence Journal	*The Sporting Life*

(* Denotes Complete Game, ND denotes no decision, S denotes save.)

BABE'S 1914 PITCHING RECORD

DATE	W/L	OPP.	SCORE	IP	H/A	COMMENT
7/11	W	Cleveland	4-3	7	H	First career start
7/16	L	Detroit	2-5	3	H	Left in 4th, 1st career loss
10/2	W	NY	11-5	9*	H	1st complete game
10/7	ND	Washington	11-4	3	H	1st Relief appearance

BABE'S 1915 PITCHING RECORD

DATE	W/L	OPP.	SCORE	IP	H/A	COMMENT
4/16	ND	Philadelphia	6-6	4	A	Called/Darkness
4/24	L	Philadelphia	3-6	3 1/3	H	Allowed no hits
4/26	W	Philadelphia	9-2	7*	H	Called/Rain
5/6	L	New York	3-4	13*	A	Hit 1st career HR
5/11	L	Detroit	1-5	5 2/3	A	Abysmal Outing
5/19	ND	Cleveland	2-5	3 1/3	A	Allowed 1 H in relief
5/22	L	Chicago	3-11	1	A	Shortest start to date
5/29	L	Philadelphia	1-2	8 2/3*	A	Lost in 9th
6/2	W	New York	7-1	9*	A	HR broke 1-1 tie
6/17	W	St. Louis	11-10	7 1/3	H	1st game after broken toe
6/21	W	Washington	8-3	9*	A	7 K's
6/25	W	New York	9-5	9*	H	2 for 3, 3rd career HR
6/29	W	New York	4-3	10*	H	Speaker went 5 for 5
7/5	W	Washington	6-0	9*	H	1st career shutout / sixth win in a row.
7/9	L	Detroit	4-15	1/3	A	Pulled after allowing 2H, 2BB
7/13	W	Cleveland	7-3	9*	A	Put sox in 1st place
7/21	W	St. Louis	4-2	8 1/3	A	Hit home run
7/25	ND	St. Louis	8-9	2 1/3	A	4 unearned runs
8/10	W	St. Louis	10-3	9*	H	1st appearance in 2 weeks
8/14	W	Washington	4-3	9*	H	Beats Walter Johnson
8/19	ND	Chicago	1-2	2	A	Relief
8/21	W	St. Louis	4-1	9*	A	6 K's, 1 BB
8/25	ND	Detroit	2-1	8 2/3	A	Sox won in 13th
8/28	W	Cleveland	5-3	6 1/3	A	Mays saves game for Babe
9/2	W	Philadelphia	8-3	9*	A	5 K's, 1 BB
9/6	L	New York	2-5	7 1/3	A	Took no-hitter into 8th
9/10	W	Philadelphia	7-2	9*	H	15th win -5 hitter
9/14	W	Chicago	2-1	9*	H	Threw 2 hitter
9/20	W	Detroit	3-2	8 2/3	H	Relieved by Foster
9/24	L	St. Louis	4-8	2	H	Pulled with no outs in 3rd

BABE'S 1915 PITCHING RECORD cont.

DATE	W/L	OPP.	SCORE	IP	H/A	COMMENT
10/2	ND	Washington	1-3	2	A	Relief
10/6	W	New York	4-2	9*	A	5 Hitter, 6 K's

Babe beat both St. Louis (4-1) and New York (4-2) the most times. Neither Washington (3-0) nor Cleveland (2-0) defeated him. He was 3-2 versus Philadelphia, 1-1 against Chicago and the Tigers (1-2) were the only team who beat him more than he beat them. Babe was 10-2 at Fenway and 8-6 on the road. A monthly breakdown shows Babe had trouble early as he went 1-1 in April and 0-4 in May. Once he righted himself, he was virtually unbeatable going 5-0 in June, 3-1 in July and 4-0 in August. He finished strong with a 4-2 September and a 1-0 October. From June 1 until the end of the season, he was 17-3.

BABE'S 1916 PITCHING RECORD

DATE	W/L	OPP.	SCORE	IP	H/A	COMMENT
4/12	W	Philadelphia	2-1	8	H	Opening Day win
4/17	W	Washington	5-1	9*	H	Beats Walter
4/20	W	Philadelphia	7-1	9*	A	Dominating 5 hitter
4/25	W	New York	4-3	10*	A	2BB, 2ER
5/1	L	Washington	3-5	7 1/3	A	First loss of year
5/5	ND	New York	4-8	8+	A	6 BB
5/10	L	Cleveland	2-6	9*	H	First home loss
5/20	W	St. Louis	3-1	5 2/3	H	Left throwing no-hitter
5/24	W	Detroit	4-0	9*	H	1st shutout of yr
5/27	L	New York	2-4	9*	A	Had 2 of Sox 3 H
6/1	W	Washington	1-0	9*	H	Beats Walter Johnson
6/5	W	Cleveland	5-0	9*	A	2nd straight shutout
6/9	ND	Detroit	5-6	8	A	Was 3 for 3, HR
6/13	W	St. Louis	5-3	5 1/3	A	Homered, Shore got save
6/17	L	Chicago	0-5	8*	A	Erratic - allowed 12 Hits
6/22	W	New York	1-0	9*	H	4th shutout of yr
6/27	W	Philadelphia	7-2	9*	H	10 K's
7/1	L	Washington	2-4	3 1/3	A	Fell apart in 4th
7/7	ND	Cleveland	2-1	7	H	Walked in tying run
7/11	ND	Chicago	5-3	1/3	H	Started game while Foster warmed up
7/11	W	Chicago	3-1	9*	H	5 K's, 1 BB, 1 ER
7/15	W	St. Louis	17-4	6	H	Left leading 13-2
7/18	W	St. Louis	4-3	9*	H	Tripled, scored twice
7/20	L	Detroit	2-3	5	H	Lost in relief (13th inn.)
7/25	L	Cleveland	4-5	7+	A	Walked 4 (2 scored)
7/29	L	Detroit	8-10	1/3	A	Shelled in 1st (3rd consec loss)

BABE'S 1916 PITCHING RECORD cont.

DATE	W/L	OPP.	SCORE	IP	H/A	COMMENT
7/31	W	Detroit	6-0	9*	A	Throws 2 hitter
8/4	L	St. Louis	1-6	5	A	Allowed 9 H
8/12	ND	Washington	2-1	7	A	Allows only 2 H
8/15	W	Washington	1-0	13*	A	Beats Walter Johnson
8/19	ND	Cleveland	2-1	6	H	Left with dizzy spells
8/23	S	Cleveland	7-3	2	H	Year's only save
8/24	W	Detroit	3-0	9*	H	Throws 3 hitter
8/29	L	St. Louis	3-5	5	H	Allowed 1 H in relief
8/31	L	St. Louis	1-2	9*	H	Pitched well, no support
9/4	W	New York	7-1	9*	A	In command, 1 BB
9/5	ND	Philadelphia	2-5	4	A	Relief, CG day before
9/9	W	Washington	2-1	9*	A	Beats Walter Johnson
9/12	ND	Washington	3-4	8 2/3	A	Johnson gets win
9/17	W	Chicago	6-2	9*	A	20th win of yr
9/21	W	Detroit	10-2	9*	A	Hit triple & single
9/25	W	Cleveland	2-0	9*	H	8th shutout of yr
9/29	W	New York	3-0	9*	H	Back to back shutouts
10/3	L	Philadelphia	3-5	5	H	Pennant already won

No team beat Babe more than he beat them. Cleveland was the only team to play .500 against him as Babe was 2-2 versus them. It was against Cleveland that he registered his only save of the year. He was 4-1 vs. New York, 4-2 vs. Washington and Detroit, 4-3 vs. St. Louis, 3-1 vs. Philadelphia and 2-1 vs. Chicago. He was much better at home, where he won 13 and lost only 5 as opposed to 10-7 on the road. His best month of the year was September when he was 6-0. He was also undefeated in April, going 4-0. He was 2-3 in May, 5-1 in June, 4-4 in July, 2-3 in August and 0-1 in October. Of his league leading nine shutouts; three came against the Tigers and two each came at the expense of, New York, Cleveland and Washington. His two against Washington were opposed by Walter Johnson and they both were 1-0 games. One of them 13 innings.

BABE'S 1917 PITCHING RECORD

DATE	W/L	OPP.	SCORE	IP	H/A	COMMENTS
4/11	W	New York	10-2	9*	A	2nd opening day win in a row.
4/16	W	Philadelphia	6-1	9*	A	7 K's, A's run unearned
4/21	W	New York	6-4	9*	H	had triple and 2 doubles
4/25	W	Washington	5-4	9*	H	7 BB
4/30	W	Philadelphia	6-3	9*	H	So cold fingers & arm went numb.
5/7	W	Washington	1-0	9*	A	3rd 1-0 win over Johnson

BABE'S 1917 PITCHING RECORD cont.

DATE	W/L	OPP.	SCORE	IP	H/A	COMMENTS
5/11	W	Detroit	2-1	9*	A	5 hitter
5/15	W	Cleveland	6-5	5 2/3	A	8th straight win
5/18	L	Chicago	2-8	2 1/3	A	Year's 1st loss
5/24	W	St. Louis	4-2	9*	A	Tripled, 5K's, 1 BB
5/29	W	Washington	9-0	9*	A	2nd shutout of yr
6/1	L	Cleveland	0-3	9*	H	Took 1 hitter to 9th
6/6	L	Detroit	0-3	9*	H	Gave up 3 in 1st inning
6/13	W	St. Louis	2-0	9*	H	2 run double, 3 hitter
6/16	L	Chicago	2-7	9*	H	Joe Jackson 3 for 5
6/20	W	New York	3-1	9*	H	6 K's, 0 BB
6/23	ND	Washington	4-0	0	H	Shore's perfect game
7/3	L	Philadelphia	0-3	9*	H	Returned from suspension
7/6	L	Cleveland	1-3	9*	A	Pitched well, no support
7/11	W	Detroit	1-0	9*	A	Gave up 1 hit, in 8th
7/15	W	St. Louis	4-2	10*	A	Virtually unhittable
7/19	W	Chicago	3-2	9*	A	Hit hard in 8th & 9th
7/21	ND	Chicago	5-5	5	A	Allowed only 5 H
7/26	W	St Louis	11-2	9*	H	2 for 3, 5 fielding assists
7/30	W	Chicago	3-1	9*	H	4 hitter
8/3	L	Cleveland	1-2	9*	H	Walked only one, no support
8/10	W	Detroit	5-4	9*	H	Babe's homer wins game
8/14	L	Philadelphia	1-3	8*	A	Little offensive support
8/18	W	Cleveland	9-1	9*	A	5 hitter
8/20	S	Chicago	3-1	2/3	A	First save of yr
8/21	L	Chicago	0-2	9*	A	Lost pitchers duel
8/25	S	St. Louis	3-2	1	A	2nd save in 5 days
8/27	L	Detroit	1-5	9*	A	Ty Cobb 3 for 4
8/31	W	Philadelphia	5-3	9*	H	20th win
9/4	W	New York	4-2	9*	H	Beat NY in 1HR 20 Min
9/10	L	Washington	1-2	9*	A	Allowed 6 H
9/15	W	New York	8-3	9*	A	Took shutout into 9th
9/20	L	Detroit	0-1	9*	H	5th time he was shutout
9/24	W	Chicago	3-0	9*	H	5th shutout of yr
9/29	W	St. Louis	11-0	9*	H	3 for 3, 3R
10/2	L	Washington	0-6	9*	H	Walter Johnson beats him

Babe dominated New York and St. Louis in 1917 going 5-0 against them both. He was 3-2 versus Philadelphia and Washington and 3-3 against Detroit and Chicago. He was 2-3 against Cleveland. He was almost identical at home (12-7) as on the road (12-6). In 9 of his 13 losses he surrendered three runs or less and in five of those the Red Sox were shutout. He began the year brilliantly, going 5-0 in April and 5-1 in May. He faltered a bit in June at 2-3 and rallied back for a 5-2 July. In August he was 3-4 with three of those losses being 2-1, 3-1 and 2-0. In September he was 4-2, and in October he was 0-1 as he lost a meaningless game to Walter Johnson, 6-0. It was the only time Johnson beat him in head-to-head competition.

BABE'S 1918 PITCHING RECORD cont.

DATE	W/L	OPP.	SCORE	IP	H/A	COMMENT
4/15	W	Philadelphia	7-1	9*	H	3rd opening win in a row
4/19	W	New York	9-5	9*	H	Gave up 13 hits
4/24	L	Philadelphia	0-3	9*	A	Scoreless until 8th
4/29	W	Washington	8-1	9*	H	5 hitter
5/4	L	New York	4-5	9*	A	Hit first "Called Shot"
5/9	L	Washington	3-4	9 2/3*	A	5 for 5 vs. Walter Johnson
5/15	W	Detroit	5-4	9*	H	Dramatic 9th inn. win
6/2	L	Detroit	3-4	9*	A	Returns after hospital stay
6/7	L	Cleveland	7-14	0	A	Walked both batters faced in relief
7/5	W	Philadelphia	4-3	10*	A	First start in over a month
7/17	W	St. Louis	4-0	5*	H	Last career shutout with Red Sox, rain shortened.
7/29	W	St. Louis	3-2	9*	A	Back in rotation
8/1	W	St. Louis	2-1	9*	A	2nd win in 3 days
8/4	W	Cleveland	2-1	12*	A	4 hitter
8/7	W	Detroit	4-1	9*	A	Allowed 7H in 10th win
8/12	L	New York	1-2	9*	H	NY had 4 hits, Sox only 3
8/17	W	Cleveland	4-2	9*	H	5 Hitter
8/20	L	Cleveland	4-8	7	H	Only start not completed all yr
8/24	W	St. Louis	3-1	9*	H	stole home
8/31	W	Philadelphia	6-1	9*	H	Clinches pennant

Babe enjoyed the most success versus the St. Louis Browns, going 4-0 against them. He was 3-1 against Philadelphia, 2-1 against Detroit, 2-2 versus Cleveland, 1-1 against the Senators and 1-2 versus New York. He did not make a pitching appearance against the White Sox. He was 8-2 at Fenway Park and 5-5 on the road. Once again, his best months of the year were the first and last, as he went 3-1 in April and 6-2 in August. He was 1-2 in May, 0-2 in June and 3-0 in July. From the time he was reinserted to take a regular turn in the rotation on July 29, until the end of the year, he was 8-2. He completed 18 of his 19 starts.

BABE'S 1919 PITCHING RECORD

DATE	W/L	OPP.	SCORE	IP	H/A	COMMENTS
5/3	W	New York	3-2	9*	H	Double, run scored, RBI
5/15	W	Chicago	6-5	11	A	Allowed 13 H, 8 BB in relief
5/20	W	St. Louis	6-4	9*	A	Hit grand slam homer
5/26	ND	Cleveland	7-12	2	A	Wild; relieved after 2nd inning
5/30	W	Philadelphia	10-6	9*	A	Double, 2 singles, run, RBI

BABE'S 1919 PITCHING RECORD cont.

DATE	W/L	OPP.	SCORE	IP	H/A	COMMENTS
6/5	ND	Detroit	2-1	3	H	Removed for pinch runner - wrenched his knee
6/10	L	Chicago	3-5	9*	H	4 Sox errors, 3 unearned runs
6/14	L	Cleveland	2-3	13*	H	13 inning pitchers duel
6/20	W	St.Louis	2-1	9*	H	Tripled and scored both
6/25	L	Washington	3-8	9*	H	Issues Barrow ultimatum/pitch or play.
7/17	L	Cleveland	0-4	8*	A	1st game pitched in 22 days
7/21	L	Detroit	2-6	9*	A	Hit longest HR ever at Navin Field
7/25	W	New York	8-6	9*	H	13 H, 0 SO!
7/30	W	Detroit	3-2	2	H	Only hit to Cobb
8/17	W	St. Louis	2-1	9*	A	3 hitter
9/1	W	Washington	2-1	9*	H	Last win in a Red Sox uniform.
9/20	ND	Chicago	4-3	5 1/3	H	HR in 9th wins it

In his 14 decisions of 1919, Babe was 3-0 versus St. Louis and 2-0 against New York. He had one win against; Philadelphia (1-0), Washington (1-1), Detroit (1-1), and Chicago (1-1). He was 0-2 versus Cleveland. He was 5-3 at Fenway and 4-2 on the road. He was 4-0 in May, 1-3 in June, 2-2 in July and 1-0 in August and September.

BABE'S MONTHLY BREAKDOWN

MONTH	RECORD	WINNING PCT.
APRIL	13-2	.867
MAY	12-10	.546
JUNE	13-9	.591
JULY	18-10	.643
AUGUST	16-9	.640
SEPTEMBER	15-4	.790
OCTOBER	2-2	.500
TOTAL	89-46	.659

As is obviously indicated by this chart, Babe started and finished strong. He was virtually unaffected by the "Dog Days" as he was a collective 33-15 (.688) during the closing months of the season. In the three seasons in which the Red Sox were in a pennant race, ('15, '16, and '18) Babe was 26-8 (.765) during the stretch months. This takes into account that the '18 season ended on September 3 and includes the month of July of that year. The other two years, August, September and October are counted. One of those losses was the last game of the year in '16 when, with the pennant clinched, Carrigan ordered Babe to "give the outfielders a workout". Babe literally took one for the club that day.

BABE'S BREAKDOWN BY TEAM

TEAM	RECORD	WINNING PCT.	HOME	W.P.	AWAY	W.P.
St. Louis	20-4	.833	11-3	.786	9-1	.900
New York	17-5	.773	11-1	.917	6-4	.600
Philadelphia	13-6	.684	8-3	.727	5-3	.625
Washington	12-6	.667	7-2	.777	5-4	.555
Chicago	7-6	.538	4-2	.667	3-4	.429
Detroit	11-10	.524	6-4	.000	5-6	.455
Cleveland	9-9	.500	3-5	.375	6-4	.600
TOTALS	89-46	.659	50-20	.714	39-26	.600

Numerologists could feast on the fact that Babe's winning percentage at Fenway Park throughout his tenure as a pitcher was .714 !!! He clearly enjoyed the confines of home more than the mounds of the road. The only exception was Sportsman's Park in St. Louis. He had the most trouble with Cleveland at home, due in no small degree to the fact that Tris Speaker and Smoky Joe Wood rose to the occasion on their return to the place they once called home. His total dominance of the Yankees at home slipped to a mere .600 percentage at the Polo Grounds. It seems that Babe's focus on "swinging the willow" in those friendly confines distracted him from his mound duties. He could have gone without road trips to Navin Field in Detroit and Comiskey Park in Chicago. His outstanding performance at Sportsman's Park can't help but fuel the speculative fires of what might have been if he were a St. Louis Brown.

It is interesting to note that no team bested the Babe. Cleveland played him even but no club got the better of him. There are but a handful of pitchers in the history of the game who can make that claim.

BABE IN THE WORLD SERIES

DATE	PLACE	OPP.	IP	H	BB	SO	R	ER	ERA	W/L
10/2/16	Braves Field	Brooklyn	14	6	3	4	1	1	0.64	W
9/5/18	Comiskey Park	Chicago	9	6	1	4	0	0	0.00	W
9/9/18	Fenway Park	Chicago	8+	7	6	0	2	2	2.25	W
TOTALS			31	20	10	8	3	3	0.87	3-0

NOTES: The Red Sox played their home games for the 1916 World Series in the new state-of-the-art Braves Field. The Cubs chose the venue of Comiskey Park in 1918. There were reports at the time that this was done to neutralize Babe's big bat, however it seems more logical to assume it was for a larger seating capacity with the more distant outfield fences an added benefit.

Babe surrendered a home run to Hy Myers in the first inning of the first game and was not scored upon again until the 8th inning of his third game. He threw 29 2/3 consecutive scoreless innings, a record he held until 1961. It was this achievement of which Babe was the most proud. His ERA of 0.87 is second on the all-time World Series list among pitchers who have pitched 30 or more World Series innings. Of the 20 hits Babe surrendered, only two were for extra bases, and his World Series opponents hit but .177 against him.

His 14-inning complete game victory in the 1916 World Series remains, to this day, the longest complete game win in the history of the World Series. Unless the use of pitchers takes a drastic u-turn, this record will never be broken.

BABE'S RECORDS WITH THE BOSTON RED SOX

Babe still holds the following Red Sox records for left-handed pitchers:
GAMES STARTED - 41 in 1916
COMPLETE GAMES- 35 in 1917
INNINGS PITCHED- 326 1/3 in 1917
SHUTOUTS- 9 in 1916 (Babe still shares this American League record with Ron Guidry who threw 9 shutouts in 1978)
BEST LIFETIME WINNING PCT. (100 decisions) - 1914-1919 .659
THE ONLY RED SOX LEFTY WITH BACK TO BACK 20 WIN SEASONS- 1916 (23) and 1917 (24).

NOTES: At the time of his death in 1948, he still held the record for most wins in a season by a lefty with 24 in 1917. Mel Parnell won 25 games for Boston in 1949 becoming the first Red Sox lefty since Ruth to win 20. He won 21 games in 1953 and since then, no Red Sox lefty has cracked the 20-win barrier. Babe still owns the Red Sox record for the most grand slam home runs in a season, 4 in 1919.

The Perfect Yankee ($22.95)
by Don Larsen with Mark Shaw

By all accounts, the no-hit, perfect game pitched by New York Yankee right-hander Don Larsen in the 1956 World Series qualifies as a true miracle. No one knows why it happened, or why an unlikely baseball player like Don Larsen was chosen to perform it. In *The Perfect Yankee,* Larsen and co-author Mark Shaw describe for the first time the facts surrounding one of the most famous games in baseball history.

Autographed copies (Larsen) are available by calling Sagamore Publishing at 1-800-327-5557. **Bonded leatherbound limited edition available.** The leatherbound edition of *The Perfect Yankee* is limited to 500 and is autographed by **Don Larsen and Yogi Berra.**

Lou Boudreau: Covering All the Bases ($24.95)
by Lou Boudreau with Russell Schneider

The personal story of one of the most extraordinary men in baseball history. While leading the Cleveland Indians to a World Series victory in 1948, he invented the "Ted Williams shift", and became the only player/manager ever to win the American League Most Valuable Player award. Boudreau tells about winning the 1944 American League Batting Championship with a hit in his final at-bat of the season, and how he became the youngest manager in baseball history at the age of 24. His illustrious playing career culminated in 1970, when he was voted into the Baseball Hall of Fame.

Chicago Cubs Seasons At The Summit:
The 50 Greatest Individual Seasons ($19.95)
by William Hageman and Warren Wilbert

The Chicago White Stockings, later to become Wrigleyville's lovable Cubbies, were charter members of the National League, and the only franchise that has operated continuously in the same city between the first game played on April 22, 1876 and today. During that time, over 1,750 ballplayers have pulled on Cubs uniforms, and out of that number, coauthors William Hageman and Warren Wilbert have chosen the players who have put together individual seasons of such magnificence that they have merited a top-50 billing.

Available at your local bookstore
or by calling Sagamore Publishing
at 1-800-327-5557.